European Union Enlargement

European Union Enlargement provides a comparative analysis of the post-war European policies of those states that joined the European Union between 1973 and 1995.

The volume draws upon new empirical research in order to investigate the policies that these 'newcomer' states followed towards European integration since 1945, with a perspective on their experience of membership and its possible Europeanising effects. A final comparative chapter draws the national European policies of the 'newcomers' together.

This book includes in-depth studies focusing on the European policies of the UK, Denmark, Ireland, Greece, Portugal, Spain, Austria, Finland and Sweden. It will interest students and researchers of the European Union as well as those concerned with European politics and contemporary history in general.

Wolfram Kaiser is Professor of European Studies at the University of Portsmouth and Visiting Professor at the College of Europe in Bruges.

Jürgen Elvert is Professor of Modern History at the University of Cologne and Senior Fellow of the Center for European Integration Studies at the University of Bonn.

Routledge Advances in European Politics

European Union Enlargement

A Comparative History

Edited by Wolfram Kaiser and Jürgen Elvert

Routledge
Taylor & Francis Group

LONDON AND NEW YORK

First published 2004 by Routledge
2 Park Square, Milton Park, Abingdon, Oxfordshire, OX14 4RN

Simultaneously published in the USA and Canada
by Routledge

270 Madison Avenue New York, NY 10016
Routledge is an imprint of the Taylor & Francis Group

Transferred to Digital Printing 2005

© 2004 Wolfram Kaiser and Jürgen Elvert for selection and editorial
matter; individual contributors their contributions

Typeset in Baskerville by Taylor & Francis Books Ltd

British Library Cataloguing in Publication Data
A catalogue record for this book is available from the British Library

Library of Congress Cataloging in Publication Data

ISBN 0–415–33137–4

Contents

Contributors

Jürgen Elvert is Professor of Modern History at the University of Cologne and Senior Fellow of the Center for European Integration Studies at the University of Bonn.

Michael Gehler is Professor of Contemporary History at the University of Innsbruck and Senior Fellow of the Center for European Integration Studies at the University of Bonn.

Maria Gussarsson is Lecturer in Contemporary History at the University of Stockholm.

Kostas Ifantis is Associate Professor of International Relations at the University of Athens and Visiting Fellow at the Hellenic Foundation for European and Foreign Policy, Athens.

Wolfram Kaiser is Professor of European Studies at the University of Portsmouth and Visiting Professor at the College of Europe in Bruges.

Johnny Laursen is Professor of Contemporary European History at the University of Aarhus.

Ricardo Martín de la Guardia is Reader in Contemporary History in the Department of Modern and Contemporary History and the European Studies Institute, University of Valladolid.

Edward Moxon-Browne is Jean Monnet Professor of European Integration at the University of Limerick.

Hanna Ojanen is Senior Researcher at the Finnish Institute of International Affairs in Helsinki.

António Costa Pinto is Professor of Modern European History and Politics in the Institute of Social Science at the University of Lisbon.

Nuno Severiano Teixeira is Professor of International Relations at the New University of Lisbon.

Preface

We are indebted to a number of institutions and colleagues who have helped us to bring this project to fruition. In particular, we would like to thank the Fritz Thyssen Foundation for funding a workshop at the Center of European Integration Studies (CEIS) of the University of Bonn, which allowed us to discuss the draft chapters to increase the cohesion of the book, and for their financial assistance towards the preparation of the manuscript; Marcus Höreth from CEIS and Jürgen Sikora from the University of Cologne for the efficient organization of the workshop; and Sally Eberhardt for her valuable assistance in preparing the manuscript for publication.

The book is the result of a long-term European collaborative project on EU enlargements and Europeanization in historical perspective, entitled 'Constituting the European Union: Integration Dynamics and Magnetic Effects'. We are especially grateful to Ludger Kühnhardt, the director of CEIS, for supporting our network in its early stages.

Finally, we would like to acknowledge our wives' and our children's total lack of interest in our peculiar academic preoccupations. We are grateful to them for not allowing us more time to pursue them even more at their expense.

List of abbreviations

AIFTA	Anglo-Irish Free Trade Area
AIP	Associação Industrial Portuguesa
AMAE	Archivo del Ministerio de Asuntos Exteriores
AP	Alianza Popular (Spain)
BDI	Bundesverband der Deutschen Industrie (Germany)
BNG	Bloque Nacionalista Galego (Spain)
CAP	Common Agricultural Policy
CC.OO.	Comisiones Obreras (Spain)
CDC	Convergència Democràtica de Catalunya (Spain)
CDS	Centro Democrático Social (Portugal)
CDU	Christian Democratic Union (Germany)
CEOE	Confederación Española de Organizaciones Empresariales
CFSP	Common Foreign and Security Policy
CICE	Inter-ministerial Commission for the Study of the European Economic and Atomic Communities (Spain)
CIP	Confederação da Industria Portuguesa
CIS	Centro de Investigaciones Sociológicas (Spain)
CiU	Convergència i Unió (Spain)
CMEA	Council for Mutual Economic Assistance
COMECON	Council for Mutual Economic Assistance
CSCE	Conference for Security and Cooperation in Europe
CSU	Christian Social Union (Germany)
EC	European Communities/Community
ECSC	European Coal and Steel Community
ECU	European Currency Unit
EDC	European Defence Community
EDU	European Democratic Union
EEA	European Economic Area
EEC	European Economic Community
EFTA	European Free Trade Association
EMA	European Monetary Agreement
EMS	Economic and Monetary System

EMU	European Monetary Union
EPC	European Political Community (1953)
EPC	European Political Cooperation
EPP	European People's Party
EPU	European Payments Union
ERP	European Recovery Programme
ETA	Euskadi Ta Askatasuna (Spain)
EU	European Union
EUCD	European Union of Christian Democrats
FBI	Federation of British Industries
FCMA	Treaty on Friendship, Cooperation and Mutual Assistance (Soviet Union - Finland)
FET de las JONS	Falange Española Tradicionalista de las Juntas de Ofensiva Nacional Sindicalista (Spain)
FINEFTA	Finland-EFTA Association
FPÖ	Freedom Party (Austria)
FRAP	Frente Revolucionario Antifascista y Patriótico
GATT	General Agreement on Tariffs and Trade
GDP	gross domestic product
HB	Herri Batasuna (Spain)
IBRD	International Bank for Reconstruction and Development
IDU	International Democratic Union
IMF	International Monetary Fund
KKE	Communist Party of Greece
LO	Landsorganisationen (Sweden)
MBFR	Mutual Balanced Forces Reduction
MFA	Movimento das Forças Armadas/Armed Forces Movement (Portugal)
MFN	Most Favoured Nation
MTK	Finnish Central Union of Agricultural Producers
NATO	North Atlantic Treaty Organization
NEI	Nouvelles Equipes Internationales
NFU	National Farmers Union (Britain)
NORDEK	Nordic Economic Union
OECD	Organization for Economic Cooperation and Development
OEEC	Organization for European Economic Cooperation
ÖVP	Austrian People's Party
PASOK	Pan-Hellenic Socialist Movement
PCE	Partido Comunista de España
PCP	Partido Comunista Português
PNV	Partido Nacionalista Vasco
PP	Partido Popular (Spain)
PS	Partido Socialista (Portugal)

PSD	Partido Social Democrata (Portugal)
PSOE	Partido Socialista Obrero Español
SAP	Social Democratic Workers' Party (Sweden)
SEA	Single European Act
SFIO	French Socialist Party
SI	Socialist International
SPÖ	Austrian Socialist Party
TCO	Tjänstemännens Centralorganisation (Sweden)
TUC	Trades Union Congress (Britain)
UCD	Unión de Centro Democrático (Spain)
UDC	Unió Democràtica de Catalunya (Spain)
UGT	União Geral de Trabalhadores (Portugal)
	General Workers' Union
UGT	Unión General de Trabajadores (Spain)
UNRRA	United Nations Relief and Rehabilitation
	Administration
VAT	Value Added Tax
VÖI	Association of Austrian Industrialists
WEU	Western European Union

Introduction

Wolfram Kaiser and Jürgen Elvert

At the European Council in Copenhagen in December 2002, the European Union (EU) decided to include ten more states in 2004 in its Eastern and Southern expansion and at least a further two – Bulgaria and Romania – by 2007–8. The historical experiences, economic interests and political priorities of most of the new member-states differ substantially from those of the fifteen older member-states. However, enlargement should prove advantageous both for the EU and the new member-states. For the EU, for example, it will increase its export opportunities, give firms easier access to a skilled workforce to keep ageing Western European societies competitive, and enhance its security on the future border with the successor states of the former Soviet Union, facilitating the better control of illegal migration, drug-trafficking and other new security threats in post-Cold War Europe. For the new member-states, it will facilitate their continued economic transformation, provide better market access in agriculture and other sectors and help to further stabilize their, in some cases, still fragile democracies.

At the same time, however, the cultural, economic and political variations between the EU and most of the new member-states have also raised numerous fears about the future of European integration. These have concerned, for example, the tight limits to fiscal transfers to Eastern Europe which could be large enough to further undermine the stability of ailing Western European economies and state budgets, such as in Germany and France, but too small to have a significant stimulating effect on the economies of the new member-states which would be comparable to Ireland or Spain in the 1980s and 1990s. Other fears are related to the proper institutional balance between larger and smaller member-states, as the enlargement includes only Poland as a larger member-state on a par with Spain, or possible adverse effects of nationalist anti-EU movements, in countries like Poland and Slovakia, on the future domestic political stability of the EU. In the increasingly heated political debate about the possible future membership of Turkey, moreover, the fears about ineffective fiscal transfers, the possible dilution of the current level of integration and the import of political instability into the EU have been massively aggravated by widespread concerns about the cultural compatibility of Turkey and 'Europe'. As the strong opposition of the former Liberal French President Valéry Giscard d'Estaing and the former Social Democratic West German Chancellor Helmut Schmidt to Turkish membership has demonstrated, these concerns are not limited to Christian Democrats in the European People's Party who may want to protect 'their' Christian occidental 'core Europe' against a predominantly Islamic country which lies geographically mostly outside Europe. Some of these various fears associated with the EU's enlargement have acquired almost apocalyptic dimensions. They have frequently been exploited for their own purposes by populist political leaders and parties in the EU and the future member-states.

Cohesive as the EU of the fifteen may seem compared to some of the new member-states, however, similar fears about the possible effects of enlargement on the existing institutional structure, economic vitality and political cohesion were associated with all three previous enlargements of the original 'core Europe' of the six founding member-states of the European Coal and Steel Community (ECSC) created in 1951–52 and the European Economic Community (EEC) created in 1957–58: France, Italy, West Germany, the Netherlands, Belgium and Luxembourg. Many in the old 'core Europe' feared that the first enlargement of 1973 to include Britain, Denmark and the Republic of Ireland would undermine the *finalité politique* of the EC and prevent its further deepening. More concrete fears related, for example, to the relegation of the previously predominant Christian Democrats to second place in EC politics and in the European Parliament, as they did not have any partners in Britain or Denmark. Against the background of the structural economic crisis of the 1970s and the internal dispute about the structure of the budget and a possible British rebate, the EC states were already very concerned when Greece joined in 1981 – and Spain and Portugal followed in 1986 – about the effects of fiscal transfers to the economically under-developed South that could end up as a large *Mezzogiorno* of the Community. When Austria, Finland and Sweden joined the EU in the third round of enlargement in 1995, these member-states with highly developed economies became net contributors to the budget. In this case, the dominant concerns related to the political, not the economic, effects of their membership. Would the inclusion of Austria not, for example, lead to the formation of a 'Germanic' bloc inside the EU, as many French politicians feared in the early 1990s? Would the neutrality of Austria and Sweden and the slow reorientation of Finnish security policy after the collapse of the Soviet Union not undermine EU plans for strengthening its Common Foreign and Security Policy and, possibly, developing a common defence capacity and policy?

With increasingly different historical experiences, economic structures and political priorities in the EU, all enlargements have led to a search for new unity in diversity and a greater deepening of integration. The prospect of Northern enlargement after the end of the Cold War, for example, strengthened the determination of Jacques Delors, then President of the European Commission, and other leading federalists such as the German Chancellor Helmut Kohl, at the beginning of the 1990s, first to sign and ratify the Maastricht Treaty to secure a higher level of integration before negotiations could be further complicated by the inclusion of new members. Once inside the EU, moreover, new member-states were exposed to the various pressures of common policy-making, the inclusion in dense transnational networks and cross-border socialization. These pressures have contributed to their progressive 'Europeanization' and, in some cases, to their inclusion in a new 'core Europe' within the enlarged EU, as in the case of Finland and participation in the Euro, for example. Although EU research has recently begun to look at the resulting process of economic, political and broader societal convergence, the enlarged EU of the fifteen or twenty-five member-states is nevertheless less homogeneous in many ways than the old 'core Europe' of the six founding member-states. In order to better understand the EU and its policy-making, therefore, it is crucial to analyse these variations, their historical origins and social, economic, political and cultural determinants.

This book aims to contribute to the research agenda of the widening and deepening of the EU by discussing in a systematic fashion the national European policies of the nine member-states that joined the EU between 1973 and 1995, including a comparative chapter which draws the different experiences together. All country chapters are structured in the same way. After a short introduction to the socio-economic and political conditions of European policy-making after the Second World War, they proceed to discuss the evolution of European policy during the period of non-involvement in the 'core Europe' integration process in the ECSC/EEC – whether as a result of different political priorities as, for example, in the case of Britain and Sweden which joined the European Free Trade Association (EFTA) in 1959; of economic under-development, as in the case of Greece, which became associated with the EEC in 1961; or because of the prevailing political conditions, as in the case of Spain at the time of Franco's dictatorship. As appropriate, the chapters assess whether the creation of the ECSC/EEC, its external consequences and the relevant country's possible membership in or relationship with these institutions were openly debated by economic and political elites or even in parliament, the media and by public opinion. They discuss the early pressures for membership, if any, and why they were not politically influential enough; whether the reasons were of a domestic nature, such as specific economic interests, a hegemonic political culture miti-gating against membership or negative perceptions of 'core Europe', or related to the international context for policy-making. They also explain the motives for opting for alternative structures such as EFTA, as in the case of Britain, Sweden, Denmark, Austria and Portugal, as well as Finland which became associated with EFTA in 1961, assessing in what respects this option was more compatible with the preferences of particular political elites or social groups and their interest group organizations; to what extent, finally, these preferences depended on the international legal and political status of the country concerned and its foreign policy, especially neutrality, and motives and norms possibly associated with it.[1]

The second main section of each chapter goes on to discuss the origins of the application for membership in the EEC, and the motives and expectations linked to it. When the country in question applied for membership, what were the main political, economic and social groups driving the process of rapprochement with the EU? Were they political parties, economic interest groups, parts of the media, and what role, if any, did public opinion play? Where applicable, the chapters discuss the domestic and external reasons for major political and economic groups changing their stance from initial opposition to support for EC/EU membership, such as in the case of the Danish, Swedish, Austrian and Greek Social Democrats. They also consider the role of changes in the international context for European integration, especially the end of the Cold War. It also appears important to know how the perceptions of 'core Europe' have changed over time, and how this possibly has influenced attitudes to EC/EU membership. If, for example, the EC/EU was seen in some quarters on the political Left in Britain and Scandinavia as too Catholic and conservative, dominated by the Christian Democrats during the first two decades after the Second World War, did this perception change, and if so, due to which factors? Finally, the chapters also assess (in as much as the rudimentary state of research in this area allows) the possible role of transnational influences such as institutionalized and more informal networks and European socialization in facilitating a rapprochement with the EC/EU. What, for example, was the significance of party links in the Socialist International in bringing about a more positive attitude to the EC/EU among many Social Democratic parties? And how did the work of political foundations and think-tanks contribute to the pre-accession Europeanization of Greece, Portugal and Spain?

In discussing these fundamental questions of national European policy-making leading up to EC/EU membership, with a perspective on the experience of membership, the individual chapters and the book as a whole aim to contribute to the debate about the EU and the integration process in three main ways. To begin with, the book advances the comparative study of the national European policies of the 'newcomers' to the enlarged EC/EU. Much of the research on the contemporary history and politics of the EU is still focused on the old 'core Europe', especially the Franco-German relationship. While such a 'core Europe' perspective (although neglecting alternative scenarios for cooperation and integration such as the Organization for European Economic Cooperation and the European Free Trade Association) may be justified to some extent for the early post-war period, it fails to capture the more complex institutional dynamics and policy-making of the enlarged EU. For a long time, the 'core Europe' perspective was also strengthened by the neglect of European integration as a research topic in 'newcomer' states, while others, such as development policy in the case of Scandinavia, were regarded as politically more important and were often better funded.

More recently, however, research on national European policy and the EU has expanded significantly in many of the new EU states, as is also reflected in the annotated bibliography at the end of this book which gives an introduction to the most important publications on the subsequent enlargements, as well as on the European policies of the 'newcomers'. British policy towards 'Europe', in particular, has been extensively researched. However, much of the literature is very specialized on a short time-span or a particular policy area. In the case of countries like Finland, Greece and Portugal, moreover, very little has been published in English. For the first time, the chapters in this book analyse the European policies of the 'newcomers' over a long period, systematically discussing major research questions in a comparable way, based on the most recent literature and, wherever possible and appropriate, primary sources that are now available for the earlier period. The comparative perspective should also help to overcome the nationally introspective character of much of the research on the European policies of different EU states by demonstrating, for example, the similarities and differences in the reasons why both Britain and Denmark have often been regarded as 'awkward partners'.

This book also creates for the first time a suitable basis for the comparative study of the Europeanization effects of EU membership on the 'newcomers', as well as of their own influence on the integration process and, more generally, the transformative character of the successive enlargements on the larger EU. To analyse Europeanization effects, it is obviously necessary to develop a comparative framework for the pre-accession period. However, much of the nascent research on Europeanization appears to take an a-historical approach which may be able to develop a methodology to assess short-term change, but fails to capture the long-term social, economic, political and cultural transformation as a result of membership.[2] At the same time, most research in International Relations and comparative politics on the integration process and day-to-day EU politics has traditionally shown little interest in the contemporary history of European integration. As a result, this research often lacks a more sophisticated understanding of *longue durée* change in the EU.

More recently, against the backdrop of widespread doubts about the explanatory and especially the predictive value of theoretically driven approaches to understanding political processes, some scholars appear to have taken a greater interest in the historical evolution of the EU in the search for empirical evidence for their theories. In a striking example of this new trend, Andrew Moravcsik has analysed European integration from the 1960s to the present, including Franco-British relations over possible British accession.[3] Yet his study is based on a selective reading of the expanding literature and no primary sources, with some evidence presented – as historians have shown[4] – with the theory-driven purpose of defending his liberal inter-governmentalist interpretation of the integration process. While the chapters in this book are important in their own right for the comparative study of the contemporary history of national European policies of the 'newcomers', they should also inform future research in the social sciences about the complexity of long-term change in the enlarged EU, in order to support a more sophisticated use of integration history in theoretical debates.

Finally, this book also aims to contribute to the theoretical debate about integration itself – not by adding another 'theory' which often does little more than slightly modify existing theoretical approaches.[5] Instead, the chapters provide substantial empirical evidence on the country cases in recognition of the main assumptions of the major competing theories, to overcome the disjuncture that often exists between theorizing integration and empirical research on national European policies or, indeed, particular institutions or policy sectors in the EU.

As Sieglinde Gstöhl has pointed out in her recent study of the European policies of Norway, Sweden and Switzerland, there is really no sophisticated integration policy theory.[6] The classical theories have tended to concentrate on the deepening of integration, especially the major leaps in the integration process, although Moravcsik implicitly extends his theory through the discussion of the European policy of Britain as an outsider in the early 1960s.[7] At the same time, neo-functionalists have always suggested that integration can provoke policy changes among adversely affected outsiders, leading to geographical 'spill-over', but they have never pursued this line further or sought empirical evidence for it.[8]

It is clear enough, however, that in order to explain integration preferences, a domestic perspective is important. Simon Bulmer has rightly argued that different economic structures, political institutions and traditions result in different policies on 'Europe' or – inside the EU – on major issues of further integration.[9] Different theories emphasize different factors. Elite theories, for example, locate the major sources of (European) policy innovation in changes in the belief systems and political interests of national decision-makers. Such a perspective might be particularly suitable for countries with a highly deferential political culture such as the Britain of the 1960s, where the majority of the population will usually be prepared to follow the lead of the government of the day on external policy issues.[10] In contrast, institutional theories put greater emphasis on differences in the set-up of national institutions in influencing policy outcomes. Finally, pluralist theories, as in the case of liberal inter-governmentalism, see the primary sources of influence on (European) policy-making in well-organized domestic pressure groups that have coherent and politically important sectoral economic interests. All these approaches, however, share rationalist assumptions about actors who have clearly defined agendas and interests as well as about rational inter-state bargaining of preferences determining policy outcomes in organizations like the EU.[11]

Constructivist approaches, on the other hand, emphasize non-material conceptions of state power and influence.[12] As a result, they study the role of 'soft' factors such as collective memory, historical orientations, identity and ideology and their impact on interest formation and national preferences, showing that decision-making processes are culturally embedded and that the resulting policy choices are path-dependent. Constructivism first developed in the analysis of foreign policy and international relations more generally and has only recently begun to be applied more widely to national European policies, the EU and the integration process, in particular with a view to analysing the relationship between identity change and European preferences[13] and the forms and effects of cross-border processes of communication and socialization.[14] As 'soft' factors are clearly more difficult to assess, and certainly cannot be measured quantitively, constructivists tend to be quite modest in their theoretical claims about EU politics and the integration process, compared to rational choice-based theories, as becomes clear, for example, in the recent debate between Jeffrey T. Checkel and Andrew Moravcsik about the explanatory value of constructivist approaches.[15]

Rationalist theories are clearly useful for elucidating economic interests and their possible impact on decision-making processes. As Gstöhl has convincingly argued in relation to the 'laggards' Norway, Sweden and Switzerland, however, they fail to explain why states that should have a clear economic interest in participating in integration may nonetheless abstain from it.[16] After all, economic theory suggests that small, highly industrialized and trade-dependent countries like Sweden and Switzerland (or for that matter, Belgium and the Netherlands) are more likely to integrate than larger or less advanced countries. These states should have feared trade diversion, the resulting welfare losses, and long-term competitive disadvantages as a result of their possible self-exclusion, and they should therefore have joined the EC/EU at an early stage. The fact that they did not can only be explained by considering ideational as well as material factors, for example, negative perceptions of 'core Europe' and Social Democratic ideological dominance in the case of Scandinavia, and small state nationalism and a strong tradition of decentralized governance and direct democracy in the case of Switzerland, where a small majority of the population even refused to join the European Economic Area (EEA) in a referendum in December 1992. Equally, the Greek Socialists should have displayed an enthusiasm for EC membership comparable to their sister parties in Spain and Portugal, as the economic structures and expectations of the material benefits of membership were similar in all three countries in the second half of the 1970s and in the 1980s. Nevertheless, they initially opposed and were then highly ambivalent about EC membership for a long time, making Greece in the 1980s another candidate for the 'awkward partner' label first used by Stephen George in relation to Britain.[17] It seems, therefore, that their policy towards 'Europe' can only be explained by particular historical experiences, going back to the civil war, a highly polarized domestic political culture and a tradition of charismatic leadership, in this case of the party's long-time leader, Andreas Papandreou.

The contemporary history of international relations and, more particularly, of national European policies and the origins and evolution of the current EU has always chosen a more inclusive explanatory approach combining material and ideational factors, or rational choice and constructivist elements. In this more empirical tradition, this book has no rigid theoretical framework into which all chapters have to fit. Instead, it recognizes that conflicting evidence exists in the case of individual countries and concerning the cross-country comparison which, for different cases and time-spans, can be taken to support interpretations that emphasize the importance of more material or ideational factors. Thus, this book emphatically demonstrates that any theoretical approach that claims exclusive competence to explain national European policies, the integration process and EU politics collapses in the face of the more complex empirical evidence. Integration theories are useful for conceptualizing the integration process and EU politics, but there are also narrow limits to their explanatory and, even more so, their predictive value.

Notes

1 For a comparative study of neutrality and European policy, see the contributions to Michel Gehler and Rolf Steininger (eds), *The Neutrals and European Integration 1945–1995*, Vienna: Böhlau, 2000.
2 As an introduction to recent research on Europeanization, see Kevin Featherstone and Claudio M. Radaelli (eds), *The Politics of Europeanization*, Oxford: Oxford University Press, 2003.
3 Andrew Moravcsik, *The Choice for Europe: Social Purpose and State Power from Messina to Maastricht*, London: UCL Press, 1999.
4 See especially the contributions by Jeffrey Vanke (pp. 87–100), Marc Trachtenberg (pp. 101–16) and even Alan S. Milward (pp. 77–80) (who otherwise sympathizes with some of the basic assumptions of liberal inter-governmentalism about the predominance of the nation–states and the inter-state bargaining of interests derived from domestic interest group pressures) in the *Journal of Cold War Studies*, 2001, vol. 2, no. 3.
5 For an excellent introduction to the competing theories of the EU and the integration process, see Ben Rosamond, *Theories of European Integration*, London: Macmillan, 2000.
6 Sieglinde Gstöhl, *Reluctant Europeans: Norway, Sweden, and Switzerland in the Process of Integration*, London: Lynne Rienner Publishers, 2002, p. 4
7 Moravcsik, *The Choice for Europe*, pp. 164–76.
8 Ernst B. Haas, *The Uniting of Europe: Political, Social and Economic Forces 1950–1957*, London: Stevens, 1958, pp. 313–17; Philippe C. Schmitter, 'Three neo-functional hypotheses about international integration', *International Organization*, 1969, vol. 23, no. 1, pp. 161–6, here p. 165.
9 Simon Bulmer, 'Domestic politics and European Community policy-making', *Journal of Common Market Studies*, 1983, vol. 21, no. 4, pp. 349–63.
10 As first suggested by Gabriel Almond and Sidney Verba, *The Civic Culture: Political Attitudes and Democracy in Five Nations*, Princeton, NJ: Princeton University Press, 1963.
11 See also Mark Pollack, 'International relations theory and European integration', *Journal of Common Market Studies*, 2001, vol. 9, no. 2, pp. 221–44.
12 See, for example, in relation to constitutional policy inside the EU, Wolfgang Wagner, 'Interessen und Ideen in der europäischen Verfassungspolitik: Rationalistische und konstruktivistische Erklärungen mitgliedstaatlicher Präferenzen', *Politische Vierteljahresschrift*, 1999, vol. 40, no. 3, pp. 415–41, and, in respect to the European policies of the Nordic countries, C. Ingebritsen and S. Larson, 'Interest and identity: Finland, Norway and European Union', *Cooperation and Conflict*, 1997, vol. 32, no. 2, pp. 207–22.
13 For conceptual suggestions in a comparative contemporary historical perspective, see Wolfram Kaiser, 'Culturally embedded and path-dependent: peripheral alternatives to ECSC/EEC "core Europe" since 1945', *Journal of European Integration History*, 2001, vol. 7, no. 2, pp. 11–36. See also the useful contributions to Mikael af Malmborg and Bo Stråth (eds), *The Meaning of Europe: Variety and Contention Within and Among Nations*, Oxford: Berg, 2002.
14 See, for example, Jeffrey T. Checkel, 'Why comply? Social learning and European identity change', *International Organization*, 2001, vol. 55, no. 3, pp. 553–88.
15 Jeffrey T. Checkel and Andrew Moravcsik, 'A constructivist research program in EU Studies?', *European Union Politics*, 2001, vol. 2, no. 2, pp. 219–49.
16 Gstöhl, *Reluctant Europeans*, p. 3.
17 Stephen George, *An Awkward Partner: Britain and the European Community*, Oxford: Clarendon Press, 1992.

1 'What alternative is open to us?'

Britain

Wolfram Kaiser

'We are with Europe, but not of it. We are linked, but not compromised. We are interested and associated, but not absorbed ... We belong to no single Continent, but to all.' This is how Winston Churchill, then a Conservative back-bencher in the House of Commons, famously characterized Britain's semi-detached relationship with continental Europe in 1930.[1] By the end of the Second World War, this relationship had become even more distant. The collapse of the continental European economy as well as the demise as great powers of France, defeated by Germany in 1940, and of Germany, defeated by the Allies in 1945, seemed to suggest that Britain's economic and political interests, more than ever, lay elsewhere.

Economically, Britain's infrastructure had suffered serious destruction during the war. Its war effort, which in many ways had been more 'total' than that of the German Reich,[2] had necessitated a complete reorientation towards war production, severely limiting Britain's ability after 1945 to produce and export consumer goods. Moreover, Britain was highly indebted as a result of the war and in a very precarious financial position when the United States threatened to stop lend-lease and to demand market rates for loans in 1945. Britain's new economic dependency on the United States was underlined by the no-new-preference rule of the General Agreement on Tariffs and Trade (GATT), which was effectively directed against the Commonwealth preference system. It also showed in Britain's reluctant promise to make sterling convertible once its exports had reached 75 per cent of the pre-war rate, a promise the government made to facilitate the resolution of the question of US loans.

In other words, the British economic situation was serious after 1945, but it also differed in several important respects from that of most continental European countries. First, British infrastructure was less thoroughly destroyed. In particular, its comparatively healthy coal and steel production made it somewhat less dependent on European cross-border cooperation for its economic reconstruction. Second, Britain's recovering foreign trade became even more redirected towards the sterling area (as well as the United States) than after the initial introduction of Commonwealth preferences at Ottawa in 1932. This was largely due to the need to earn US dollars and other convertible currency to fight the balance of payments problems. It also resulted from the inability of most European countries to absorb British exports and to pay for them in hard currency. Even in 1955, ten years after the end of the war, 47 per cent of British exports still went to the sterling area and only 28 per cent to the whole of Western Europe.[3] Moreover, Britain still held 25.5 per cent of world exports five years after the war, in 1950.[4] Third, the continuing global role of sterling as a reserve currency alongside the US dollar also seemed to demand a strengthening of the economic ties with the Commonwealth. Taken together, these factors overshadowed the secular trend away from trade between industrialized and agricultural export countries towards more trade between industrialized countries, mitigating against a closer economic engagement with Western Europe after 1945.

Politically, the United Kingdom came out of the war victorious, with the unquestioned assumption of a continued world power role in the post-war period. British leadership of the Commonwealth, which was socially embedded in British emigration and continued family ties, seemed more cohesive than ever after the common experience of fighting Germany and Japan in the Second World War. Moreover, the lend-lease crisis in 1945 and the unilateral ending of nuclear collaboration by the United States in 1946 did not substantially undermine the idea of Anglo-American unity and solidarity, and the bilateral relationship became crucial for maintaining Western unity in the evolving Cold War.[5] As Winston Churchill had already told Charles de Gaulle, the leader of the Free French government, in Marrakech in January 1944, 'How do you expect that the British should take a position separate from that of the U.S.? … Each time we must choose between Europe and the open sea, we shall always choose the open sea.'[6] Britain eventually exploded its own nuclear bomb in 1952, underlining the special British position alongside the two new super-powers, the United States and the Soviet Union. As Joseph Frankel has rightly emphasized, Britain's nuclear armament 'formed an integral part of her conception of her world role' in the 1950s.[7] In contrast, the Western European link contributed little after 1945 to enhancing this role.

The continued British claim to world power status was rationalized by Churchill in his 'three circles' speech in October 1948.[8] To him, British foreign policy had to concentrate on maintaining the British world role by effectively managing the three circles which made up the Western world after 1945: the Commonwealth, the Anglo-American relationship and Western Europe. At the time, Churchill was leader of the Opposition. However, his strong preference for maximizing Britain's global influence through the three circles was entirely shared by the political elite. In British politics after 1945 no one was initially prepared to strengthen what clearly appeared to be the weakest link, Western Europe, *at the expense of* the two others, while Britain was still enjoying, according to Christopher Bartlett, 'the Indian summer of her career as a world power'.[9]

Thus, functional economic and political pressures limited the options of British governments over Europe. They tended to favour a semi-detached attitude and a policy of strictly inter-governmental cooperation, which was easily compatible with Britain's two other, more important circles. This preference is reflected in British policy towards the creation and subsequent operation of the Organization of European Economic Cooperation (OEEC) in 1947–48 and of the Council of Europe in 1949–50.[10] At important junctures, however, British policy-makers did have a choice and exercised it, especially over the Schuman Plan in 1950, in the Spaak Committee in 1955, over the creation of the European Free Trade Association (EFTA) in 1959–60 and in the case of the two British applications of 1961 and 1967 to join the European Economic Community (EEC), which finally led to British EC accession in 1973. Indeed, many political scientists and contemporary historians have argued that British post-war governments actually had an 'unusually free hand to experiment in the external field'[11] because British foreign policy was characterized by a well-established permissive consensus which largely left foreign policy-making to those who ran the Empire, with little interference from economic interest groups, the media or public opinion.[12]

In the British case, the way in which the integration efforts in continental Europe were perceived and how they impacted upon policy-making was much more determined by cultural influences on the elite in politics and Whitehall, such as dominant historical orientations, cultural prejudices and ideological preferences. Elite assumptions about the Second World War as a triumph of 'the British way of life' and its political institutions[13] and about an almost moral right to a continued world power role combined with widespread popular feelings of contempt for continental European political and cultural traditions to strengthen the imagined 'otherness' of 'the Europeans' and the idea of British singularity, over and above the real differences in the economic situation and political commitments.[14] To the majority of the political elite and, even more so, the population at large, Western Europe appeared somewhat like Czechoslovakia to Prime Minister Joseph Chamberlain in 1938: a far-away country (or region) of which the British knew little and cared about only insofar as it mattered in the Cold War.

After 1945 British European policy-makers operated under particular circumstances. These included Britain's dependency on extra-European trade, its Commonwealth link and preference system, its global political role and its close relationship with the United States. These factors influenced the rationale behind the EEC applications and the expectations of membership. Yet, Britain was not *per se* a special case. British European policy-makers shared important perceptions and preferences with others in Western Europe, especially outside the EEC/EC. The British case is peculiar, but not in every respect unique.[15]

British attitudes to early 'core Europe' integration and EFTA

The French government proposed the Schuman Plan, the first 'core Europe' project, in May 1950 to deal with the imminent American and British demand to lift restrictions on German production of coal and steel. It would guarantee French access to German resources of coke and coal and allow the regulation of steel markets. It would also serve as a suitable starting point for Franco-German cooperation and reconciliation.[16] None of these motives had any direct relevance for Britain. Such limited sectoral integration did not generate any functional economic pressures on Britain to integrate its own comparatively healthy coal and steel industries with those of continental Europe, nor did it threaten to undermine British political leadership of the inter governmental Western Europe in the wider OEEC. It also appears that Ernest Bevin, the Socialist Foreign Minister, and others in the government believed that the plan would fail anyway. In any case, the French – and especially the Christian Democrats – did not actually wish British participation. Their insistence on advance agreement on the supranational principle, which Schuman eventually put in the ultimatum of 1 June 1950, partly reflected the French aim to break the inter-governmental deadlock over Europe in the OEEC and the newly created Council of Europe. The British had various objections to supranationality ranging from the Labour Party's nationalist economic ideology to the constitutional principle of parliamentary sovereignty as incompatible with a supranational pooling of resources.[17]

Later in the same year, the Attlee government supported the Pleven Plan for a European Defence Community. It did so only reluctantly, however, because it saw it – not the alternative NATO option – as the only politically feasible solution to the urgent question of West German rearmament. The British had grave doubts about the military efficiency of such a supranational army. They were also adamant that Britain, with its world-wide military role, could not participate in such an army. When the Conservatives regained office in 1951, this policy remained fundamentally unchanged.[18] On 28 November 1951, Foreign Secretary Anthony Eden stressed publicly that Britain could never join a European army. There is now a consensus among historians of British European policy that there was never in fact any chance that a Conservative government would reverse the initial decision against British participation.[19] The Churchill government was divided. Yet this only concerned the issue how best to safeguard British leadership of Western Europe. Eden benevolently supported the European Defence Community (EDC) because the United States advocated it. In May 1952, he agreed to sign a fifty-year mutual security treaty with the EDC to ease the ratification process. Churchill and Harold Macmillan, among others, appeared more 'pro-European' in their public statements. In fact, they hoped that the EDC would fail, allowing Britain to put forward an alternative solution. They were primarily concerned about the possible domination of European institutions by the Germans.

Essentially, these early strategic decisions in relation to 'core Europe' were not politically controversial in the United Kingdom. The same was still true for the British decision of 1955 against participation in a Western European customs union. The Eden government has often been accused of having 'missed the bus' which apparently took the Six directly from the conference in Messina in early June 1955 to the Italian capital for the signing of the Rome Treaties in March 1957.[20] However, it was not at all clear in 1955 that the bus, which the European

Coal and Steel Community (ECSC) governments boarded at Messina, was actually roadworthy, or that the driver and passengers would be able to avoid a major diplomatic accident on the way. The success of the initiative was not guaranteed. The analogy is also misleading because no British minister seriously considered buying a ticket. At that time, British membership in a European customs union, by over-emphasizing the European 'circle' in Britain's external relations, still appeared to be politically incompatible with its world role. Economically, British participation would have put an end to the Commonwealth preferences through the imposition of a common external tariff in a customs union. After the failure of the EDC in the previous year, moreover, government ministers and the Foreign Office were utterly convinced that the ECSC states would be unable to achieve any meaningful results, especially in view of the continuing domestic resistance in France to trade liberalization in a customs union.[21]

The Economic Section of the Treasury and the Board of Trade warned, however, that more British trade could become redirected towards Europe, with a further decline in the importance of the already reduced Commonwealth preferences, so that Britain's long-term interests could possibly lie in closer economic integration in Western Europe.[22] Russell Bretherton, the British representative in the Spaak Committee which met during the second half of 1955, warned early on that the ECSC governments were determined and might actually succeed without Britain, with adverse economic and political effects on British leadership in the OEEC.[23] Such mildly dissenting voices in the administration were suppressed in a conservative intellectual climate dominated by the established 'three circles' doctrine, however, and never reached the political level where Macmillan, who was now Foreign Secretary, remained mainly concerned about the possible domination of any new organization by West Germany. Yet his fears only translated in the futile attempt in late 1955 to discredit the Messina initiative in Washington and Bonn, which upset Spaak and others in the ECSC governments and, if anything, increased their determination to proceed.[24]

While no significant functional economic or political pressures mitigated in favour of a pro-active British policy to contribute to the formation of a Western European customs union, Britain's (self-)exclusion in case such a customs union was set up anyway was widely seen as very dangerous. It was this fear of exclusion from such a customs union – the fear of possible serious competitive disadvantages for British companies in the customs union and in third markets – which led the Treasury and the Board of Trade to devise the so-called Plan G for a Western European free trade area in 1956.[25] Such a free trade area would have given British companies tariff-free access to the continental European market without jeopardizing the Commonwealth preferences. In trade terms, it would have given Britain the best of all worlds. The structural imbalance in the British proposal, which included no meaningful incentives for France to cooperate in setting up such a free trade area after it ratified the Rome Treaties in 1957, was the main reason for its ultimate failure when French President Charles de Gaulle vetoed the proposal in late 1958.[26] After de Gaulle's veto, the British government decided to set up the EFTA of the so-called 'outer Seven' together with Norway, Sweden, Denmark, Austria, Switzerland and Portugal. Much ground had been covered in the talks in the OEEC, so that overall, the negotiations went smoothly, with the Stockholm Convention initialled in November 1959. EFTA was a free trade area with a largely inter governmental structure, a small secretariat in Geneva and only bilateral concessions in agriculture which were not formally part of the Convention. As such, it was very much in line with the original British proposal.[27]

By agreeing to the small EFTA, the British, in the words of David Eccles, President of the Board of Trade, decided to marry 'the engineer's daughter when the general-manager's had said no'.[28] As in the case of Plan G three years earlier, negative reasons were decisive. The Conservative government did not support the creation of EFTA for its own sake, on its merits. They believed that they had no other choice. To do nothing after de Gaulle's veto appeared out of the question, if only because it could be seen by other OEEC states as a sign of weakness, leading to a further decline in British influence and prestige in Western Europe.[29] Moreover, only if Britain led an institutionalized counter-alliance did it seem possible to preserve a more or less united front in relation to the EEC. The government feared that several OEEC states like Denmark would otherwise conclude bilateral treaties with the EEC. If one stone in the row fell, however, others would follow suit. Macmillan, who had been Prime Minister since January 1957, feared that 'if we cannot successfully organize the opposition group ... then we shall undoubtedly be eaten up, one by one, by the Six'.[30] The British primarily hoped that the creation of EFTA would put counter-pressure on the EEC countries, especially West Germany, thus inducing a policy change to allow the resolution of the trade conflict in Western Europe. The new organization was conceived as a bridge to the EEC to facilitate a later arrangement between the two blocs. The British government never regarded EFTA as an aim in itself.

From laggard to leader of an enlarged 'core Europe'?

When the EFTA Convention took effect on 3 May 1960, the British government had already begun to reconceptualize its relationship with the EEC. On 27 May 1960, the Lee Committee of officials submitted a report which advocated 'near-identification', a form of far-reaching association with the EEC while avoiding its supranational implications.[31] When consultations with German and French officials in the winter of 1960–61 showed that such a solution was neither feasible nor, indeed, desirable, as Britain would be excluded from core decision-making processes, the Macmillan government concluded in the spring of 1961 to submit a conditional application for EEC membership, subject to satisfactory solutions for British agriculture, the Commonwealth and EFTA.[32] De Gaulle eventually vetoed the ongoing accession negotiations with the United Kingdom in January 1963.[33] The Labour government under Harold Wilson, first elected in 1964, decided in May 1967 to submit another application.[34] When de Gaulle refused to countenance any negotiations, Wilson left the application on the table.

Accession negotiations finally took place after de Gaulle's retirement from French politics and the EC Council at The Hague in 1969. They were successfully concluded in 1972, leading to British EC membership as of 1 January 1973.[35]

The analysis of the governmental decision-making processes in 1960–61 and 1966–67 shows a strong continuity with regard to the long-term structural economic arguments for EEC membership. First came the need to secure equal access to the EEC market for British industrial exports. The Europeanization of British trade patterns had accelerated. By 1961–62, Britain for the first time exported more to Western Europe than to the Commonwealth.[36] Within Western Europe, moreover, the EEC market was greater in volume and seen as much more important in the long term than the EFTA market, with competitive disadvantages for British exporters potentially resulting from the implementation of the EEC's customs union programme. Second, Britain had significantly lower increases in productivity and growth than the EEC countries and experienced recurring sterling crises.[37] Structural problems and politically manipulated stop-and-go cycles were increasingly seen as hampering Britain's economic development. EEC membership would impose more competition on British exporters who still preferred 'soft' Commonwealth markets. It would thus provide a solution to what was increasingly regarded as Britain's economic disease. As the Conservative MP Nigel Birch phrased it in the House of Commons in 1961, 'What we want here is a good shake-up.'[38] EEC membership was also seen as a strong political framework for stabilizing sterling and safeguarding its continuing role as a reserve currency.[39]

When the Labour government contemplated a new approach to the EEC in 1966, another Whitehall report essentially reiterated the same arguments. Officials predicted that:

> [our] involvement [in the EEC] would act as a catalyst in speeding up the economic expansion of Britain, in bringing progressive advantages of scale to important industries, and opportunities for specialization … Our involvement would … provide a spur to efficiency and rationalization generally of a unique and urgent character, bringing results that we should not achieve without it.[40]

As the pressure on sterling continued, Labour advocates of EEC membership felt the need for a European framework for economic and monetary policy more strongly, just as the Conservative government had done in 1961.[41] According to Richard Crossman, the failure of Labour's initial, nationalist economic policy led not only George Brown and Michael Stewart, but also Harold Wilson and James Callaghan to conclude that 'the attempt to have a socialist national plan for the British Isles' had to be abandoned.[42] EEC/EC membership, now combined with Wilson's hobby-horse of a technological and scientific revolution including European collaborative projects like Concorde, was once more seen as the best means to revitalize the British economy.[43]

As in the case of Austria and Sweden in the early 1990s, the economic ratio-nale for joining the EEC was very general and the predicted benefits contingent on a number of assumptions which were difficult to prove. As the 1960s progressed, it became clear that the discriminating effects of the EEC's industrial tariffs were actually limited due to their progressive substantial reduction, not least as a result of the Dillon and Kennedy rounds of the GATT. In fact, struc-tural problems in British industry and non-tariff barriers were greater obstacles than tariffs. Despite relatively rising tariff barriers, Britain's exports to the EEC actually grew at an annual average rate of 9 per cent during the 1960s and thus slightly faster than its exports to the other EFTA states where British producers enjoyed significant tariff advantages.[44] The British EEC applications did not, in other words, reflect any overriding strategic economic objective, such as the need to safeguard agricultural exports, as in the case of the Irish and Danish applica-tions in the 1960s. As such, the economic rationale could easily be disputed. It could only be made to seem much more convincing to a reluctant electorate by exaggerating the supposedly automatic benefits at a time of a deepening economic crisis in the late 1960s and early 1970s.

Was, then, the economic rationale thrust upon the governments by domestic pressure groups determining British European policy, as liberal inter-governmentalist interpretations would suggest?[45] Nothing could be further from the truth. Unlike as in the case of the British free trade area proposal of 1956, the Macmillan government did not even consult with repre-sentatives of the Federation of British Industries (FBI) or the Trades Union Congress (TUC) in any systematic way before it decided to go ahead with the EEC application. Edward Heath, who was responsible for European questions, only enquired about the likely FBI reaction to the envisaged application for the first time at the end of June 1961.[46] The FBI was in fact split over the issue.[47] Large export-oriented international companies tended to favour membership, while many small and medium-sized businesses were very apprehensive about the effects of greater competition in the home market. The FBI leadership was preoccupied with internal interest mediation. It left the strategic decision to the government and was more concerned with the details of the accession negotiations. The leadership of the National Farmers Union (NFU), which was an important electoral constituency of the Conservatives, was actually strongly opposed to EEC member-ship and the necessary change in the British subsidy system of deficiency payments, although views of individual farmers were more mixed.[48]

In 1967, the Wilson government opted for another EEC application despite growing scepticism among the trade unions. Having in their majority supported membership in 1961, they were becoming more and more influenced by the Labour Left which was hostile to the EEC. The EEC applications were naturally facilitated by the large majority of some 70 per cent of 'informed opinion' and even more among the foreign policy elite in favour of EEC membership.[49] However, they were in no way induced by domestic economic interest groups which did not in fact attempt to steer the policy-making process in any particular direction. In the British case, moreover, the economic arguments were of a long-term structural nature. As such, they can hardly explain why the Macmillan and Wilson governments launched their applications in 1961 and 1967, and not in 1959 or 1965, for example.

In fact, foreign policy considerations were much more important in the decision-making process, especially before the first EEC application. By 1961, not only Macmillan, but also Lord Home, the Foreign Secretary, and practically the entire Foreign Office were convinced that Britain could only safeguard its close relationship with the United States and thus its world power status from within the EEC.[50] With few exceptions like Peter Thorneycroft, however, most leading Conservatives continued to formulate European policy within the established 'three circles' doctrine, trying to adjust it to rapidly changing external circumstances. By the early 1960s, the Commonwealth link had become less important not only for British trade, but also politically. Decolonization made the Commonwealth extremely difficult to manage. The controversy about the possible exclusion of South Africa for its Apartheid regime in 1960–61 demonstrated that even the old 'white' Commonwealth countries were no longer prepared to follow British leadership for the sake of it.[51] The argument in favour of a greater British role in Western Europe was also strengthened considerably when the EEC foreign ministers began to hold regular talks in the autumn of 1959 and when the EEC governments started their Fouchet negotiations on foreign policy cooperation in the spring of 1961.[52] Macmillan and the Foreign Office feared that such a much more cohesive political entity would be so much stronger economically and politically that it would become the principal ally of the United States in world politics. As Pierson Dixon, the British ambassador to France, concluded in a letter to Rab Butler, the new Foreign Secretary, in 1964, after the failure of the entry negotiations:

> We shall not have enough strength to prevent the world being organized in a way which eventually may reduce us to the status of Portugal, though not, one may hope, to the extinction of the Venetian Republic, unless we join and lead some larger land mass. We might join the United States but could not hope to lead it. We could hope to lead Europe, and must try to join it.[53]

Against this background, the Conservative government hoped that EEC membership would fulfil three distinctive foreign policy functions. The first of these was to hand Britain the political leadership of the EEC and of a possible political and defence community, which would in future legitimize Britain's claim to a special international role alongside the two superpowers. In John F. Kennedy's 'Grand Design' for the future of transatlantic relations, Britain would essentially form the European pillar, on the foundation of the EEC. The widespread assumption – also in the Foreign Office – was that once Britain was inside the EEC, it would take the lead. As Otto Clarke, a senior official in the Treasury, told an unconvinced Tony Benn later, in 1966, 'we [have] run an Empire from Whitehall, and so when we [go] into Europe, our civil services [will] run rings around the Europeans'.[54] Aside from the experience of running an Empire, this expectation was also rooted in the British political elite's belief in a historically grown right to leadership deriving from Britain's role in the Second World War and its superior democratic institutions. The British also hoped that France and West Germany would again require British mediation due to the intra-EEC frictions caused by de Gaulle's institutional preferences and international policies.

The second function of the EEC application was to appease the US administration and thus to stabilize what most Conservative leaders still regarded as a 'special relationship'. The new Kennedy administration elected in November 1960 clearly wanted Britain to join the EEC in order to exercise through them greater influence over its future development, especially in foreign and defence policy. The Americans made their strategic objective quite clear in talks with the British government on several occasions during the spring of 1961, especially during a visit to London by George Ball, Under-Secretary of State for Economic Affairs, in March and during the summit between Macmillan and Kennedy one week later, in early April.[55] For Macmillan, in particular, the EEC application was in the first instance a transatlantic policy initiative.[56] As such, it also reflected growing British concerns that the Kennedy administration, with its anti-proliferation policy, could decide to again stop nuclear collaboration with Britain which had only been resumed in 1958. By 1961, however, the British were totally dependent on the United States for the future provision of long-range missiles to replace the ageing and vulnerable bomber fleet.[57] In this sense, the British EEC application was also – thirdly – designed to keep the Americans generally happy and to induce them to continue their support for a formally independent British nuclear deterrent.

The key political argument in favour of membership remained virtually unchanged throughout the 1960s. In an inter-ministerial report, officials argued in 1966 that only EEC membership could in the long run guarantee 'the maintenance of maximum influence with the United States'.[58] Like Macmillan in 1961, George Brown, when he became Foreign Secretary in 1966, was utterly convinced that once inside the EEC, Britain would quickly assume its leadership. He wrote in his memoirs published before British accession in 1971 that Britain was 'destined to become *the* leader of Europe' [his italics], of a 'new European bloc which would have the same power and influence in the world as the old British Commonwealth had in days gone by'.[59] It was this broad political argument about British leadership of an enlarged EEC, constantly impressed upon British governments by the Foreign Office in the 1960s,[60] which Brown and Stewart, his predecessor as Foreign Secretary, put forward in support of membership at the ministerial meeting at Chequers on 22 October 1966 which decided in favour of a tour of the EEC capitals by Wilson and Brown in early 1967 to prepare the application.[61] Just as in 1961, the transatlantic argument was strengthened by continued US support for British EEC membership which President Lyndon B. Johnson reiterated in a letter to Wilson in November 1966.[62] To appease the Labour Left, Wilson at times emphasized Anglo-American differences in foreign policy, particularly over Vietnam. Yet he was keen in principle to continue the British role as junior partner of the United States within NATO.

The foreign policy rationale for joining the EEC was thus general and the predicted political benefits were contingent on a number of assumptions that later proved to have been as unrealistic as the anticipated economic advantages. The general nature of the British accession motives has to do with the historical legacy and the wider economic and political commitments of a great power that had once ruled half the world. London was not Dublin or Copenhagen. It had been the centre of a global empire which still exercised a strong influence on the intellectual context in which the political elite, which was still socially very cohesive, discussed foreign policy and took its decisions. However, the lack of more clearly focused and realistic strategic aims in relation to 'core Europe' integration also derived from the fact that, with few individual exceptions like Heath, who eventually took the United Kingdom into the EC as Prime Minister in 1972–73, most Conservative and Labour politicians advocating EEC/EC membership saw and experienced it as an option of last resort after all other strategies had failed to guarantee economic prosperity and global influence. The supporters of the 'core Europe' concept, mostly on the Left of the Conservative Party and on the Right of Labour, were a small minority.

When the Conservative government first discussed its plan for a wider Western European free trade area in 1956, even Prime Minister Anthony Eden, who (according to Robert Rothschild) had told the Belgian Foreign Minister Paul-Henri Spaak that 'I can feel in my bones that we are not Europeans',[63] admitted that an alternative trade policy based on the Commonwealth was no longer feasible. The creation of EFTA also resulted from a lack of alternatives and then proved to be useless for Britain's wider political objectives. Subsequently, it became obvious that the desired economic association between EFTA and the EEC was unrealistic. France was opposed to it and the United States was hostile because it would have involved economic discrimination against it without political benefits. Thus, by the spring of 1961, the choice for the Macmillan government was between doing nothing and applying for EEC membership.

The choice of the Wilson government was reduced in a similar way after 1964. The Labour Party had fought the general election on the basis of a foreign and trade policy centred on the Commonwealth.[64] It quickly became clear, however, that the continued Europeanization of British trade patterns and the ever increasing diversity of the political as well as trade interests of the other Commonwealth countries made such a policy unrealistic. Moreover, just as the Macmillan government had come to realize the political limits of EFTA in 1960, the Wilson government too became disillusioned with it during the surcharge crisis of 1964–65.[65] Instead of submitting to the blatant British breach of the Convention, the Swiss and the Scandinavians in particular attacked the British vociferously over the extension of their import surcharge of 15 per cent to EFTA members.[66] Unlike quotas, which Douglas Jay, the President of the Board of Trade, had recommended to reduce imports and thus to stabilize sterling, the import surcharge was illegal.[67] Subsequently, the Wilson government re-examined the option of some form of loose economic association with the EEC and also found it wanting. In March 1965, a Foreign Office memorandum concluded that EEC association

> would probably require acceptance of most of the obligations of full membership without a corresponding degree of control. We should appear as second-class citizens and the effect could even be to frustrate rather than promote the achievement of the type of European policies we want.[68]

The Labour government even contemplated a transatlantic economic commu-nity with the United States and Canada as advocated by Senator Jacob Javits in 1962 only to find that this too was unrealistic as the American administration had no serious interest in it.[69] Burke Trend, the Cabinet Secretary, phrased his conclusions in the rhetorical question, 'What alternative is open to us?'[70]

The peculiar combination of a great reluctance on the part of the majority of the political elite (except for the small Liberal Party) and the population at large with high-flying, totally exaggerated hopes about what EEC membership could nonetheless deliver economically and politically, also reflected how little most decision-makers and the average British citizen were socially networked in Europe. The Conservatives had only rudimentary links with some centre-right parties in Europe such as the German Christian Democratic/Christian Social Union (CDU/CSU), but were excluded from the quite cohesive policy commu-nity of continental European Christian Democrats, which had been a driving force behind 'core Europe' integration after 1945. When Heath, realizing the disadvantages of non-participation in such transnational cooperation mecha-nisms, very abruptly tried to take the Conservatives into the European Union of Christian Democrats in 1965–66, he was rebuffed by the centre-left Belgian, Dutch and Italian parties that wanted nothing to do with English, Protestant Conservatism.[71] The Labour Party was, of course, linked with other Social Democrats in the Socialist International. However, it had long since regarded the more doctrinaire continental European Socialist parties and their Marxist tradi-tion with suspicion. Where they were included in transnational networks, most Labour politicians felt much more drawn towards the reformist Scandinavian Social Democrats who were shaping what appeared to be very progressive welfare state policies. Denis Healey, for example, has explained his initial opposi-tion to EEC membership and his enthusiasm for EFTA with his 'admiration for Scandinavian socialism'.[72]

Business organizations and the trade unions were also not well integrated in networks involving EEC countries. The FBI had concentrated on its links with the Scandinavian and Swiss industry organizations, working for the EFTA option in 1958–59. Their contacts in the EEC were mostly with the German *Bundesverband der Deutschen Industrie* (BDI) whose leadership was moderately pro-British and in favour of EEC enlargement.[73] The BDI leadership was not, however, representative of business organizations in the EEC as a whole so that the FBI was never well informed about EEC politics. Most British citizens also had only limited personal experiences of continental Europe, including the EFTA states. Worker migration from Southern Europe and British tourism on the continent began to facilitate the cultural (re-)discovery of 'Europe', but only had very long-term and sometimes perhaps even adverse effects on the dominant British perceptions of 'core Europe'. Not all the British were 'little Englanders', though. Many continued to have more world-wide family ties and other personal links in the old Commonwealth states and the United States and also felt greater sympathy for them.

Thus, the EEC applications by Britain were not socially and culturally well embedded. The low intensity of transnational European networking meant that few in British politics or in the population at large felt any real empathy with the 'core Europe' project.[74] It could of course be argued that much of EEC politics was also quite pragmatic and interest-driven in the 1960s. Early integration in the 1950s, however, had created emotional bonds through elite networks, more regular government contacts, institutionalization of cooperation and societal links, with common memories and a shared, quite elaborate symbolic political culture from the celebration of the Christian Democrat 'founding fathers' Robert Schuman, Alicide de Gasperi and Konrad Adenauer to the Karls Prize and the holding of hands by de Gaulle and Adenauer during a service in the cathedral at Reims. These bonds gave added stability to the 'core Europe' project and made it easier for the EEC governments to overcome even very severe friction such as during the 'empty chair' crisis of 1965–66. In a somewhat more rudimentary form, such emotional bonding started in EFTA after its creation in 1959–60,[75] but it was not really desired by most British politicians who regarded the organization as a temporary arrangement and a tool for sorting out Britain's bilateral relationship with the EEC.

The under-developed transnational networking as well as the lack of knowledge of the EEC countries and of empathy for their integration project allowed cultural prejudices to influence British diplomacy in Europe to a greater extent than in the case of smaller applicant countries such as Denmark or Austria. This is especially true of the very pronounced and widespread anti-German sentiments, for example, in the case of Macmillan who feared that the EEC would be dominated either by a 'Fourth Reich' after Adenauer or, alternatively, by de Gaulle whom he alternately compared with Napoleon and Hitler. In 1959 the Prime Minister told ministers that 'the position in Europe today is the same as after the battle of Austerlitz in 1805'.[76] After the French veto he concluded that de Gaulle was the Hitler of the 1960s and Adenauer 'the Pétain of Germany'.[77] These prejudices translated into aggressive personal diplomacy. De Gaulle, who also did not come out of the Second World War as a Germanophile, praised the Germans as 'a great people' during his tour of the country in 1962 to cement the bilateral relationship.[78] In contrast, Macmillan, believing that 'Germans … never yield to the force of argument, but only to the argument of force',[79] threatened to withdraw the British Army on the Rhine, if the government in Bonn did not comply with British demands over Europe.[80] Needless to say, the

German Chancellor, who regarded these threats as 'simply embarrassing',[81] was only further encouraged to oppose EEC enlargement.[82]

Equally influential for British attitudes towards 'core Europe' was the idea that the EEC had been invented and was still run by Catholic, culturally backward Conservatives. British Conservatives and Socialists had very little understanding of political Catholicism and Christian Democracy. For the Tories, who had traditionally seen themselves as the first defenders of Protestant (Anglican) England against 'Rome' and its vassals, especially in France and Ireland, it was the overall dominance of Catholicism in 'core Europe' that was most repelling. British Socialists, on the other hand, had traditionally represented immigrant working-class Catholics from Ireland. For them, just as for many on the political Left in Scandinavia and Austria, it was the supposedly backward cultural values, for example, of family life and subsidiarity, and the allegedly conservative economic and social policies which made an unconditional engagement with 'core Europe' not very desirable.[83] These images were of a *longue durée*. British politics was slow to grasp the progressive secularization and the resulting declining influence of the Catholic Church on politics and social life in the EEC, the often strong Christian Democratic support for an extension of the welfare state and the ascendancy of reformed Social Democrats from Willy Brandt in West Germany to François Mitterrand in France.

The persisting cultural perceptions and prejudices also significantly reduced the moral threshold for political leaders for dragging 'Europe' from the sphere of foreign policy characterized by a broad consensus from Conservative Imperialists to left-of-centre Socialists in favour of the Atlantic Alliance and against unilateral disarmament, into domestic party politics. This process was started by Churchill when he attacked the Attlee government for allegedly not being sufficiently concerned about and engaged in Western Europe at the time of the emerging Cold War. Macmillan is the main culprit, however. He hoped that combined with other policy innovations, such as indicative economic planning and regional policy, his new European policy would help the Conservatives in the long term to acquire a modern party image and that it would split the Labour Party where a significantly greater proportion than among the Tories was violently opposed to the EEC.[84] Wilson, an equally shrewd tactician, also had domestic political interests in making an EEC application in 1967. Opinion polls fluctuated wildly in Britain in the 1960s. Yet they showed increasing support for EEC membership since 1964, culminating in a Gallup poll which showed 68 per cent in favour and only 14 per cent opposed in October 1966.[85] In these circumstances, Wilson believed that his new European policy would deny Heath, the Tory leader, the one important policy platform on which to attack the Labour government.[86] More significantly, the application could help to appease Brown, who was very pro-EEC, and his supporters within the government and the party.[87] Wilson knew that there was no short-term danger of a serious internal Labour Party split over 'boring our way into Europe', as Barbara Castle described it at a Cabinet meeting in April 1967.[88] De Gaulle would veto British membership – and Wilson thought only until the next general election.

These mostly short-term advantages in managing intra-party conflict over Europe and annoying the political opposition were compatible with pursuing strategic interests in the application as such, but not actual membership. Macmillan correctly anticipated that this posture would secure American good-will and help Britain to retain its formally independent nuclear deterrent. Equally, Wilson predicted that it would further isolate de Gaulle among the Six.[89] As a result, both British EEC applications were launched despite the fact that the first was likely to fail and the second was certain to be vetoed by de Gaulle. Macmillan knew that the chances were slim after he decided against offering to cut the Anglo-American tie in favour of collaboration with France to build a bilateral nuclear force.[90] Wilson was fully aware – and this was corroborated by his continental European interlocutors during 1966–67 – that de Gaulle's views had not changed one iota and that Britain would never join the EEC before his retirement from French politics.[91] Macmillan and Wilson preferred these short-term party political and foreign policy advantages to the alternative of a broader inter-party consensus on the basic desirability of membership in the EEC, with catastrophic consequences in continental Europe and at home for the stability and credibility of British European policy-making, lasting beyond accession until the present.

Expectations, disappointments and structural ambivalence

British European policy-making between 1945 and British accession to the EC in 1973 was largely government-driven. This has to do with the strength of a Prime Ministerial executive in a constitutional system with majority voting and single party governments with – in most cases – a clear majority of seats. It also resulted from the traditional permissive consensus in foreign policy with an electorate generally prepared to follow the lead of the government of the day. This only changed slowly when the Macmillan and Wilson governments deliberately party-politicized the European issue, thus turning it into one of a domestic rather than foreign policy nature. In this respect at least, the British example conforms to inter-governmentalist assumptions about European policies driven and negotiated by states and governments. When it comes to the formation of national preferences, however, the liberal inter-governmentalist emphasis on electorally relevant domestic economic interests could not be further from the truth, at least until British EEC accession. The relevant interest groups – FBI and NFU for the Conservatives and TUC for Labour – were in no way driving forces. They did not attempt to influence the major strategic decisions of 1950 and 1955 against participation in the ECSC and the EEC, of 1959 in favour of setting up EFTA, or of 1961 and 1967 for the two EEC applications. The FBI was split and mainly concerned with the conditions of membership. The leadership of the NFU, still an important domestic constituency of the Conservatives, even opposed EEC membership in 1961. At the same time, the Labour Party effectively came out against joining the EEC at its Party Congress in 1962 in spite of the markedly more positive attitude of most unions, which had a bloc vote in the party and crucially helped organize its core electoral support.

British governments in the 1960s experienced certain functional economic pressures which mitigated in favour of a rapprochement of sorts with the EEC. Up to a point, policy integration in the EEC had the potential to spill over into EFTA as a competing economic bloc, where Denmark demanded a common agricultural policy and Portugal structural economic aid based on the EEC example.[92] These pressures undermined EFTA as a possible intergovernmental alternative to the EEC limited to trade liberalization. Moreover, EEC integration appeared to have contributed significantly to the stabilization of the French economy, to the more rapid economic development of Italy and, more generally, economic progress among the six EEC states. It seemed to have done so not only through liberalized trade, which the British had in EFTA, but also through greater competition forcing structural transformations upon previously pampered national industries, as well as supranational welfare state policies to facilitate adjustments in agriculture and regional development. Whether any of these policies actually contributed to the economic growth in the EEC/EC in the late 1950s and the 1960s, or perhaps even hampered it, is not relevant. They anchored the image of the EEC as a modern and efficient framework for economic development in the British domestic economic discourse.

It remains true, however, that after de Gaulle's exit from French politics, the United Kingdom could have secured its core economic interest of safeguarding equal access to the EEC market for British producers through other means than membership, as Switzerland and Sweden did in 1972–73. In the British case, crucially, it was the perception of functional *political* pressures which induced the first EEC application and remained important for the second: the fear of the EEC as an increasingly stronger political as well as economic entity becoming the primary partner of the United States not only in world trade, as was already happening in the 1960s, but also in world politics, replacing the United Kingdom. This is essentially why, in the eyes of most British decision-makers in the 1960s, Britain had to join the EEC and to lead it. Thirty years after British accession, the British world role has further diminished. At the same time, the EU – despite some recent progress – has not yet developed into a cohesive actor in foreign and defence policy. This is perhaps why some EU critics on the nationalist right of the Conservative Party have begun to advocate a British withdrawal from the EU into a position comparable to that of Norway, that is, economic association with the internal market through the European Economic Area without acceptance of the *finalité politique* of the integration process. At the time of the British EEC applications, however, the United Kingdom was still a world power in decline, and its political leaders did not want it to become another Norway.

The UK governments' motives for EEC membership and their domestic and diplomatic strategies in the 1960s and early 1970s created massive long-term structural problems for Britain in the EU. The first of these was the huge gap between the expectations of benefits and the reality of the integration experience. EC membership did not provide an automatic cure for Britain's economic problems. These problems were of a structural nature and had to be tackled domestically. It also did not hand Britain the political leadership of 'Europe' on a plate. The Franco-German relationship had developed over twenty years and was of much greater structural importance for the stability and internal dynamic of the EU, at least well into the 1990s. The erratic European policies of British governments – especially during 1974–79 – marginalized Britain even more. As the former West German Chancellor Willy Brandt put it in his memoirs, the leadership expectation was based on a 'misunderstanding' on the part of the British political elite.[93] To make matters worse, the reality of membership was experienced as an even greater disillusionment by the political elite as well as the population at large because it coincided with the oil crisis and the subsequent economic stagnation in the 1970s. At that time, most EC policies were long since in place. In particular, the structure of the EC budget guaranteed that Britain became the only net contributor apart from West Germany despite the fact that it actually fell back in GDP terms behind even Italy in the 1970s, a problem that was only *de facto* (although not structurally) rectified at the Fontainebleau Summit of 1984.

The advocates of EC membership also burdened British membership in the long term by playing down its domestic effects on Britain, for example, on its traditional constitutional structure and the doctrine of parliamentary sovereignty. By selling membership in terms of how it was actually seen by most politicians – a pragmatic policy choice delivering economic and political benefits without irreversible long-term commitments – they may have facilitated the two-thirds majority in the 1975 referendum that was called by the new Labour government elected in 1974. However, they also allowed the formation and political use of the myth of a still largely autonomous great (if not world) power constantly threatened by illegitimate intrusion from 'Brussels' which has become part of the political (folk) culture of British EU membership and its reporting in the tabloid press. However, British politicians from Macmillan to Wilson probably created the greatest long-term structural problems for the continuity and reliability of British policy inside the EC by dragging 'Europe' into domestic politics and regularly using it for short-term tactical advantages within their own parties and against the opposition.[94] The adversarial political system provided institutional incentives for such political behaviour. However, it has also reflected the limited emotional attachment of British leaders to membership and the low priority they have given to enhancing British influence in the EU in the long term. British leaders from Margaret Thatcher to Tony Blair have prided themselves on their leadership in times of war. In times of peace, they have not often shown such leadership – at least not over 'Europe'.

Notes

1   Quoted in David Dimbleby and David Reynolds, *An Ocean Apart: The Relationship between Britain and America in the Twentieth Century*, London: BBC, 1988, p. 207.

2 See, in a comparative perspective, the contributions to Mark Harrison (ed.), *The Economics of World War II: Six Great Powers in International Comparison*, Cambridge: Cambridge University Press, 2000.

3 Donald Maclean, *British Foreign Policy since Suez 1956–1968*, London: Hodder & Stoughton, 1970, p. 81.

4 B.W.E. Alford, *British Economic Performance 1945–1975*, London: Macmillan, 1988, p. 15.

5 For an excellent introduction, see David Reynolds, 'A "special relationship"?: America, Britain and the international order since the Second World War', *International Affairs*, 1985–6, vol. 62, no. 1, pp. 1–20.

6 Quoted in Robert J. Lieber, *British Politics and European Unity: Parties, Elites, and Pressure Groups*, Berkeley: University of California Press, 1970, p. 18.

7 Joseph Frankel, *British Foreign Policy 1945–1973*, Oxford: Oxford University Press, 1975, p. 307. Similarly Margaret Gowing, 'Nuclear weapons and the "Special Relationship"', in W.M. Roger Louis and Hedley Bull (eds), *The 'Special Relationship': Anglo-American Relations since 1945*, Oxford: Clarendon Press, 1986, pp.117-28, p. 125.

8 See also Klaus Larres, *Politik der Illusionen: Churchill, Eisenhower und die deutsche Frage 1945–1955*, Göttingen: Vandenhoeck & Ruprecht, 1995, p. 60.

9 Christopher John Bartlett, *A History of Post-War Britain 1945–1974*, London: Longman, 1977, p. 121.

10 Cf. John W. Young, *Britain, France and the Unity of Europe 1945–1951*, Leicester: Leicester University Press, 1984; Geoffrey Warner, 'The Labour governments and the unity of Western Europe, 1945–51', in Ritchie Ovendale (ed.), *The Foreign Policy of the British Labour Governments, 1945–1951*, Leicester: Leicester University Press, 1984, pp. 61–82.

11 Max Beloff, *New Dimensions in Foreign Policy: A Study in British Administrative Experience 1947–59*, London: Allen & Unwin, 1961, p. 15.

12 Similarly Frankel, *British Foreign Policy*, p. 237; William Wallace, *The Foreign Policy Process in Britain*, London: Royal Institute of International Affairs, 1975; Christopher Hill, 'Public opinion and British foreign policy since 1945: research in progress?', *Millennium: Journal of International Studies*, 1981, vol. 10, no. 1, pp. 53–62.

13 Alfred F. Havinghurst, *Britain in Transition: The Twentieth Century*, Chicago: Chicago University Press, 1979, p. 449.

14 For some perceptive (if provocative) insights in cultural influences on British European policy, see also Christopher Coker, 'Dünkirchen und andere britische Mythen', *Europäische Rundschau*, 1991, vol. 19, no. 2, pp. 107–18.

15 The best overview of British European policy in the entire post-war period is John W. Young, *Britain and European Unity 1945–1999*, Basingstoke: Palgrave, 2000. As an introduction to recent historical and International Relations/political science literature to Britain and Europe, see Wolfram Kaiser, 'A never-ending story: Britain in Europe', *British Journal of Politics and International Relations*, 2002, vol. 4, no. 1, pp. 152–65.

16 For the pre-history of the ECSC, see also Dirk Spierenburg and Raymond Poidevin, *The History of the High Authority of the European Coal and Steel Community: Supranationality in Operation*, London: Weidenfeld & Nicolson, 1994, and the contributions to Klaus Schwabe (ed.), *Die Anfänge des Schuman-Plans, 1950–51*, Baden-Baden: Nomos, 1986.

17 On Britain and the Schuman Plan, see, in greater detail, Edmund Dell, *The Schuman Plan and the British Abdication of Leadership in Europe*, Oxford: Oxford University Press, 1995; Christopher Lord, *Absent at the Creation: Britain and the Formation of the European Community, 1950-2*, Aldershot: Dartmouth, 1996. British association with the ECSC negotiated in 1954 is discussed in John W. Young, 'The Schuman Plan and British association', in J.W. Young (ed.), *The Foreign Policy of Churchill's Peacetime Administration 1951–1955*, Leicester: Leicester University Press, 1988, pp. 109–34.

18 The degree of continuity in British European policy from 1950 to 1952 is also stressed in John W. Young, 'Churchill's "no" to Europe: the "rejection" of European

union by Churchill's post-war government, 1951–2', *Historical Journal*, 1985, vol. 28, no. 4, pp. 923–37.

19 See also Saki Dockrill, *Britain's Policy for West German Rearmament, 1950–1955*, Cambridge: Cambridge University Press, 1991, pp. 80–8.

20 See, in essence, Anne Deighton, 'Missing the boat: Britain and Europe 1945–1961', *Contemporary Record*, 1990, vol. 3, no. 3, pp. 15–17. The talks in the Spaak Committee are also interpreted as 'a vital opportunity [that] was missed' in John W. Young, '"The parting of the ways"? Britain, the Messina Conference and the Spaak Committee, June–December 1955', in J.W. Young and Michael Dockrill (eds), *British Foreign Policy, 1945–56*, London: Macmillan, 1989, pp. 197–224, here p. 217.

21 See, for example, PRO CAB 134/889/8th, 1 November 1955.

22 Cf. Wolfram Kaiser, *Using Europe, Abusing the Europeans: Britain and European Integration, 1945–63*, London: Macmillan, 1999, pp. 39–41.

23 PRO CAB 134/1026/26th, 11 July 1955.

24 See, in greater detail, Kaiser, *Using Europe*, pp. 48–9.

25 For the origins of the free trade area proposal, see, in greater detail, Kaiser, *Using Europe*, Chap. 3; James Ellison, *Threatening Europe: Britain and the Creation of the European Community, 1955–58*, Basingstoke: Macmillan, 2000, Part I.

26 On the negotiations see also, from a British perspective, Ellison, *Threatening Europe*, Parts II and III; Karl Kaiser, *EWG und Freihandelszone: England und der Kontinent in der europäischen Integration*, Leiden: Sythoff, 1963.

27 On the creation of EFTA, see Mikael af Malmborg and Johnny Laursen, 'The creation of EFTA', in T.B. Olesen (ed.), *Interdependence versus Integration: Denmark, Scandinavia and Western Europe, 1945–1960*, Odense: Odense University Press, 1995, pp. 197–212; Wolfram Kaiser, 'Challenge to the Community: the creation, crisis and consolidation of the European Free Trade Association, 1958–72', *Journal of European Integration History*, 1997, vol. 3, no. 1, pp. 7–33.

28 Eccles to Macmillan: PRO PREM 11/2531, 14 July 1958.

29 PRO CAB 130/123/GEN 580/4th, 5 March 1959.

30 Harold Macmillan diaries, 7 July 1959, Bodleian Library, Oxford.

31 PRO CAB 134/1819/27, 27 May 1960.

32 On the first British EEC application, see, in greater detail, Wolfram Kaiser, *Using Europe*, Chap. 5.

33 The accession negotiations are analysed from a multilateral perspective in Piers N. Ludlow, *Dealing with Britain: The Six and the First UK Application to the EEC*, Cambridge: Cambridge University Press, 1997.

34 For the second British application, see the contributions to Oliver J. Daddow (ed.), *Harold Wilson and European Integration: Britain's Second Application to Join the EEC*, London: Frank Cass, 2003.

35 On the accession negotiations and British EEC entry, see (although not archive-based), Christopher Lord, *British Entry to the European Community under the Heath Government of 1970–74*, Aldershot: Dartmouth, 1993.

36 Maclean, *British Foreign Policy*, p. 81.

37 Statistics on productivity and GNP growth can be found in L.A. Monk, *Britain 1945–1970*, London: Bell, 1976, p. 127; Alec Cairncross, *The British Economy since 1945*, Oxford: Blackwell, 1992, p. 376.

38 House of Commons Debate, vol. 643, col. 546, 28 June 1961.

39 See also Michael Pinto-Duschinsky, 'From Macmillan to Home, 1959–64', in Peter Hennessy and Anthony Seldon (eds), *Ruling Performance: British Governments from Attlee to Thatcher*, Oxford: Blackwell, 1987, pp.150-85, p. 151.

40 'Future Relations with Europe, Report by a Group of Officials', 5 April 1966, PRO PREM 13/905.

28 *Wolfram Kaiser*

On the link between the failure of Labour's economic policies during 1964–66 and the second EEC application, see also Uwe Kitzinger, *The Second Try: Labour and the EEC*, Oxford: Pergamon Press, 1968, p. 12.
42 Richard Crossman diaries, 30 April 1967, quoted in Richard Crossman, *The Diaries of a Cabinet Minister*, vol. II: *Lord President of the Council and Leader of the House of Commons 1966–68*, London: Hamish Hamilton and Jonathan Cape, 1976, p. 355.
43 See also Lynton J. Robins, *The Reluctant Party: Labour and the EEC, 1961–1975*, Ormskirk: G.W. & A. Hesketh, 1979, p. 57.
44 'Zehn Jahre EFTA-Handel', *EFTA Bulletin*, 1970, vol. 11, no. 4, p. 24.
45 As essentially argued by Andrew Moravcsik, *The Choice for Europe: Social Purpose and State Power from Messina to Maastricht*, London: UCL Press, 1999, pp. 164–76.
46 Robinson to Heath, 28 June 1961, PRO FO 371/158274/186.
47 Cf. the instructive study by Stephen Blank, *Industry and Government in Britain: The Federation of British Industries in Politics, 1945–65*, Farnborough: Saxon House, 1973. On the attitudes of pressure groups, see also Lieber, *British Politics*.
48 Cf. Kaiser, *Using Europe*, pp. 169–73. See also the relevant chapters in Herbert Schneider, *Großbritanniens Weg nach Europa: Eine Untersuchung über das Verhalten und die Rolle der britischen Handels- und Industrieverbände, Gewerkschaften und Farmerorganisationen zwischen 1955/56 (Spaak-Komitee) und 1961 (EWG-Beitrittsverhandlungen)*, Freiburg: Verlag Rombach, 1968.
49 William Wallace, *Foreign Policy and Political Process*, London: Macmillan, 1971, p. 100.
50 Similarly Sean Greenwood, *Britain and European Cooperation since 1945*, Oxford: Blackwell, 1992, p. 80.
51 Cf. William Norton Medlicott, *Contemporary England 1914–64*, London: Longman, 1967, p. 570 ff. As an introduction to the process of British decolonization, see John Darwin, *Britain and Decolonization: The Retreat from Empire in the Post-War World*, London: Macmillan, 1988.
52 On the Fouchet negotiations, see also Georges-Henri Soutou, 'Le Général de Gaulle et le Plan Fouchet d'union politique européenne: un project stratégique', in Anne Deighton and Alan S. Milward (eds), *Widening, Deepening and Acceleration: The European Economic Community 1957–1963*, Baden-Baden: Nomos, 1999, pp. 55–71.
53 Dixon to Foreign Office, 21 July 1964, PRO PREM 11/4810.
54 Tony Benn diaries, 24 October 1966, in Tony Benn, *Out of the Wilderness: Diaries 1963–1967*, London: Arrow, 1988, p. 480.
55 30 March 1961, PRO FO 371/158162/45; 6 April 1961, PRO PREM 11/3311.
56 This argument is developed in greater detail in Kaiser, *Using Europe*, Chap. 5.
57 Cf. Lawrence Freedman, *Britain and Nuclear Weapons*, London: Macmillan, 1980, p. 7 and, archive-based and in greater detail, Ian Clark, *Nuclear Diplomacy and the Special Relationship: Britain's Deterrent and America, 1957–1962*, Oxford: Clarendon Press, 1994.
58 'Future Relations with Europe, Report by a Group of Officials', 5 April 1966, PRO PREM 13/905.
59 George Brown, *In My Way: The Political Memoirs of Lord George-Brown*, London: Victor Gollancz, 1971, pp. 209–11.
60 For the influence of Foreign Office thinking on the conversion of Labour politicians to EEC membership, see, for example, Michael Stewart, *Life and Labour: An Autobiography*, London: Sedgwick & Jackson, 1980, p. 146. For a personal testimony of Foreign Office support for EEC membership 'bordering almost on the fanatical', see also Joe Haines, *The Politics of Power*, London: Jonathan Cape, 1971, p. 71.
61 For a summary of this meeting, see Trend to Wilson, 28 October 1966, PRO PREM 13/909. See also Richard Crossman diaries, 22 October 1966, quoted in Crossman, *The Diaries*, vol. II , p. 82.
62 Johnson to Wilson, 16 November 1966, PRO PREM 13/910, in reply to Wilson to Johnson, 11 November 1966, ibid.

63 Quoted in Michael Charlton, 'How (and why) Britain lost the leadership of Europe: "Messina! Messina!" or, the parting of the ways', *Encounter*, 1981, vol. 57, no. 3, pp. 9–22, here p. 16.

64 For a brief introduction to Labour's foreign policy during 1964–70, see Chris Wrigley, 'Now you see it, now you don't: Harold Wilson and Labour's foreign policy 1964–70', in R. Coopey, Stephen Fielding and Nick Tiratsoo (eds), *The Wilson Governments 1964–1970*, London: Pinter, 1993, pp. 123–35.

65 Cf. Wolfram Kaiser, 'Successes and limits of market integration: the European Free Trade Association 1963–1969', in Wilfried Loth (ed.), *Crises and Compromises: The European Project 1963–1969*, Baden-Baden: Nomos, 2001, pp. 371–90.

66 Joint Council, Sixth Meeting, at Ministerial level, Geneva, 22 February 1965, EFTA Archives, FINEFTA/JC.SR 6/65. On the surcharge crisis, see also T.C. Archer, 'Britain and Scandinavia: their relations within EFTA, 1960–1968', *Cooperation and Conflict*, 1976, vol. XI, no. 1, pp. 1–23, here pp. 6–10.

67 Cf. Douglas Jay, *Change and Fortune: A Political Record*, London: Hutchinson, 1980, pp. 298–309. See also James Callaghan, *Time and Change*, London: Collins, 1987, pp. 169–72.

68 EFTA–EEC Links – Memorandum by the Foreign Secretary, 18 March 1965, PRO PREM 13/306.

69 Dean (Washington) to Foreign Office, 29 October 1966, PRO PREM 13/909.

70 Trend to Wilson, 28 October 1966, PRO PREM 13/909.

71 Charles R. Dechert, 'The Christian Democratic "International"', *Orbis: A Quarterly Journal of World Affairs*, 1967, vol. XI, no. 1, pp. 106–27, here p. 118, although not archive-based. The relationship between continental European Christian Democrats and British and Scandinavian Conservatives in the 1960s is also discussed in Wolfram Kaiser, 'A policy community in retreat: the Christian Democrat network in the EC', in Antonio Varsori (ed.), *Actors and Policies in European Integration from the Rome Treaties to the Creation of the 'Snake' 1958–1972*, Baden-Baden: Nomos, forthcoming.

72 Denis Healey, *The Time of My Life*, London: Michael Joseph, 1989, p. 210.

73 Wolfram Kaiser, 'Quo vadis, Europa? Die deutsche Wirtschaft und der Gemeinsame Markt 1958–1963', in Rudolf Hrbek and Volker Schwarz (eds), *40 Jahre Römische Verträge: Der deutsche Beitrag*, Baden-Baden: Nomos, 1998, pp. 195–213.

74 For some cultural aspects of British distance to 'core Europe', see also Piers Ludlow, 'Us or them? The meaning of Europe in British political discourse', in Mikael af Malmborg and Bo Ström (eds), *The Meaning of Europe: Variety and Contention within and among Nations*, Oxford: Berg, 2002, pp. 101–24.

75 On the nascent EFTA identity, see, in greater detail, Wolfram Kaiser, 'A better Europe? EFTA, the EFTA Secretariat, and the European identities of the "Outer Seven"', in Marie-Thérèse Bitsch, Wilfried Loth and Raymond Poidevin (eds), *Institutions européennes et identités européennes*, Brussels: Bruylant, 1998, pp. 165–83.

76 29 November 1959, PRO PREM 11/2679.

77 Harold Macmillan diaries, 28 January 1963, Bodleian Library, Oxford.

78 Hans-Peter Schwarz, *Adenauer: Der Staatsmann 1952–1967*, Stuttgart: DVA, 1991, p. 765. On de Gaulle and Germany, see also Jean Lacouture, *De Gaulle, The Ruler 1945–1970*, London: Harvill, 1991. De Gaulle's oratory reminded Adenauer, who did not have a strong belief in the collective good sense of his own people, of 'the Führer'. See Adelbert Schröder, *Mein Bruder Gerhard Schröder*, private print, 1991, p. 125, quoted in Schwarz, *Adenauer*, p. 765.

79 29 December 1960–3 January 1961, PRO PREM 11/3325. See also Gustav Schmidt, 'Vom Anglo-Amerikanischen Doppel zum Trilateralismus: Großbritannien – USA – Bundesrepublik 1955–1967', *Amerikastudien*, 1994, vol. 39, no. 1, pp. 73–109.

80 See, in greater detail, Wolfram Kaiser, 'Against Napoleon and Hitler: background influences on British diplomacy', in Wolfram Kaiser and Gillian Staerck (eds), *British Foreign Policy 1955–64: Contracting Options*, Basingstoke: Macmillan, 2000, pp. 110–31,

here pp. 121–4; Alistair Horne, *Macmillan 1957–1986*, vol. II of the official biography, London: Macmillan, 1989, pp. 135, 258. On the background to the stationing of British troops in West Germany, see Olaf Mager, *Die Stationierung der britischen Rheinarmee – Großbritanniens EVG-Alternative*, Baden-Baden: Nomos, 1990. On the controversial issue of stationing costs for the British troops, see Hubert Zimmermann, *Money and Security: Troops, Monetary Policy, and West Germany's Relations with the United States and Britain, 1950–1971*, Cambridge: Cambridge University Press, 2002.

81 Adenauer to Heuss, 20 April 1960, quoted in Daniel Koerfer, *Kampf ums Kanzleramt: Erhard und Adenauer*, Stuttgart: DVA, 1987, p. 399.

82 Adenauer had a long-standing preference for 'core Europe' integration and did not suddenly shift from being an 'Atlanticist' to being a 'Gaullist'. For this misleading view, see Anne Deighton, 'British–West German relations, 1945–1972', in Klaus Larres (ed.), *Uneasy Allies: British–German Relations and European Integration since 1945*, Oxford: Oxford University Press, 2000, pp. 27–44, here p. 28.

83 See, for example, Jay, *Change*, p. 302.

84 On Macmillan's domestic political rationale, see also Kaiser, *Using Europe*, pp. 146–9, corroborated by D.E. Butler and Anthony King, *The British General Election 1964*, London: Macmillan, 1965, p. 79; Nigel Ashford, 'The Conservative Party and European Integration 1945–1975', PhD thesis, University of Warwick, 1983, pp. 137–44.

85 'Six's leading people want Britain to join', *Daily Telegraph*, 24 October 1966. Opinion poll data is collated and analysed in Peter Spang Goodrich, 'British Attitudes toward Joining Europe: 1950–1972', MA thesis, University of Maryland, Baltimore, 1972.

86 This is also emphasized by Young, *Britain and European Unity*, p. 89. See also Lieber, *British Politics*, p. 263.

87 For this view, see also Ben Pimlott, *Harold Wilson*, London: HarperCollins, 1992, p. 397. On Labour Party politics over the EEC application, see also Uwe Kitzinger, *Diplomacy and Persuasion: How Britain Joined the Common Market*, London: Thames and Hudson, 1973, p. 281; Brian Lapping, *The Labour Government 1964–1970*, Harmondsworth: Penguin, 1970.

88 Barbara Castle diaries, 13 April 1967, quoted in Barbara Castle, *The Castle Diaries 1964–70*, London: Weidenfeld & Nicolson, 1984, p. 242.

89 See, for example, Palliser to Wright, 21 October 1966, PRO PREM 13/897.

90 This linkage between European and nuclear issues is discussed in greater detail in Wolfram Kaiser, 'La question française dans la politique européenne et nucléaire britannique 1957–1963', *Revue d'histoire diplomatique*, 1998, vol. 112, no. 2, pp. 173–204.

91 For several examples, see Wolfram Kaiser, 'Party games: the British EEC applications of 1961 and 1967', in Roger Broad and Virginia Preston (eds), *Moored to the Continent? Britain and European Integration*, London: IHR/University of London Press, 2001, pp. 55–78, here pp. 68–70.

92 Cf. Kaiser, 'Successes and limits'.

93 Willy Brandt, *Erinnerungen*, Zurich: Propyläen, 1989, p. 453.

94 This is also emphasized, albeit only in relation to the Conservative Party, in Jim Bulpitt, 'Conservative leaders and the "Euro-ratchet": five doses of scepticism', *Political Quarterly*, 1992, vol. 63, no. 3, pp. 258–75, here p. 266.

2 A kingdom divided

Denmark

Johnny Laursen

Introduction

The kingdom of Denmark was, at the time of its entry into the European Communities (EC) in 1972–73, deeply divided between those in favour of EC membership and those opposed. While some Danes saw EC membership as a pragmatic adaptation to economic and political necessities, there existed among others an alarming feeling that something – sovereignty and independence – had been given away and that the nation was facing dramatic challenges.

A historical perspective is required in order to appreciate the impact of the imminent EC membership on the political imagination of the Danes. The sheer time span of the kingdom's existence as an independent power is a particularly important factor. By 1972, Denmark had been an independent kingdom for more than a thousand years. Most notions of Danish nationhood and of national identity were, however, far younger. Denmark was for many years part of the multinational double monarchy Denmark–Norway combined with the Duchies of Schleswig-Holstein. It was the loss of, first, Norway in 1814 and then, in 1864, of the Duchies that established Denmark as an ethnically homogenous nation–state.[1] The military defeat by Prussia in 1864 left a definite mark on the modern Danish memory, not only in the form of memorial days and monuments, but also in an acute sense of small state vulnerability and a keen sense of external pressures on nation, culture and language.[2] This process took place not only in wars with German states in 1848–50 and 1864, but was also interwoven with the introduction of the first democratic constitution in 1849. Hence, the perception of Danish democracy and conceptions of national identity are closely linked to each other.[3]

The experience of the inter-war years and the Second World War added other peculiarities to the self-perception of many Danes. With a democracy practically immune to fascism, a broad, stable consensus government prevailing in the 1930s and an emerging welfare state with an early corporatist cooperation between strong labour unions and employers, the Danes tend to see their past as a combination of external weakness and inner cohesion. These experiences have left a particular and pronounced small state nationalism in Denmark, especially among many on the Left and many liberals.[4]

Denmark followed a strategy of neutrality and defence of sovereignty in an attempt to balance the two powers that controlled the Baltic Sea – Germany and Great Britain. This intrinsic balancing act was primarily conducted by the Foreign Ministry and by a small elite of diplomats and politicians. Up until 1945, a certain German orientation competed with a close alignment with Great Britain. Extra caution was employed in Denmark's relationship to Germany in 1920 when Denmark, as part of the peace settlement, regained sovereignty over Northern Schleswig and with it a small German-speaking minority. A mix of adaptation, *realpolitik* and balancing was henceforth combined with a striving to mould the world as the Danes would like to see it in more idealist terms within the framework of the League of Nations. Denmark's foreign policy tradition, as it developed already before the First World War, thus combined a striving for peaceful arbitration on the basis of international law with formal neutrality.[5] With the coming of the League of Nations, Denmark joined forces with the other – neutral – Scandinavian states in an attempt to further the rule of international law on a basis of international cooperation. In the 1920s this development went hand in hand with the growing influence of the Social Democrat labour movement and with the pacifist Social Liberal Party, the *Radikale Venstre*.[6]

Pan-Scandinavianism originated in the mid-nineteenth century and in the national romanticism of many Scandinavian intellectuals. In the 1920s the intellectual impact of this elitist phenomenon began to broaden. *Norden* associations were founded in all Scandinavian countries, and during the Finno-Soviet Winter War and the Second World War, Scandinavian emotions caught a grip on the popular imagination, especially of the occupation-weary Danes. After the Second World War, pro-Nordic emotions were at a high tide in Denmark. Intellectuals and the populace alike shared a notion of 'Nordic democracy' as something separate from European democracy. Against the background of interwar and occupation experiences, it was widely believed that Nordic democracy was a value more deeply rooted in or more shared among Scandinavian democracies than it was on the European continent. There was also a growing notion of the existence of particular Scandinavian social values such as an emphasis on social equality, full employment and social legislation.[7] Here it is necessary to distinguish between such notions of international order and of Denmark's place in Europe that were held by the governing elite and by central civil servants, on the one hand, and by the mass organizations, intellectuals and the public as such, on the other. While elitist decision-making has tended to focus on adaptation to the international environment, the popular sentiment has tended to favour stronger identity- and value-based criteria. Although Danish foreign policy has been democratized since the Second World War, a certain tension has remained between elite and popular views up until 1972 and henceforth.

Thus, it can be said that the referendum campaign over Denmark's accession to the European Communities in 1972 was not only fought over the future of the country. It was in many senses fought also along historical and identity issues that had played a crucial role in the perceptions many Danes had of themselves, of their country and of its place in Europe historically. The entry into the Community was not only a political challenge, it was also a challenge in terms of identity, perceptions and prejudices.

After 1945 Denmark set out to establish a foreign policy along these traditional lines. In the immediate post-war years, the country was completely dependent on Great Britain in terms of security and trade. The export of food products (bacon and butter) across the North Sea was crucial for the economic heartbeat of the country and for the earnings of the farmers. This traditional dependency was consolidated with Denmark's participation in the UK-initiated so-called Uniscan cooperation: a – mostly – consultative Anglo-Scandinavian cooperation within the Organization for European Economic Cooperation (OEEC) framework.[8] The towering role of Great Britain was, however, soon checked by the re-emergence of the German economy as another centre of gravitation for the Danish economy. At the same time the United Nations and Nordic cooperation emerged as important pillars in Danish foreign policy. At the outbreak of the Cold War scare in 1948, the Social Democrat leader Hans Hedtoft attempted to rally Denmark, Norway and Sweden behind a Nordic defence pact, but failed.[9] Thus, the aim of relying on the international world organization and on a Nordic defence pact crumbled in 1948–49, when Denmark, together with Norway, joined the Atlantic Alliance. Here, the gap between widely held perceptions of Denmark's role in world affairs and Danish *realpolitik* once again began to open. If Denmark's accession to the EC in 1973 marked a head-to-toe split between the elite and the populace, then the momentous change in security policy in 1949 was the first important crack along this line of division. Danish entry into NATO as a founding member-state in 1949 had left many left-wing Social Democrats and neutralists disgruntled, and they were more suspicious when it came to joining the integration process in the late 1950s and early 1960s. Examining the traumas and tensions within Denmark's security policy helps to explain why the Danish left-wing, in contrast to the Left in the six founding member-states of the European Economic Community (with the initial exception of the German Social Democrats), viewed the integration process with apprehension.

The domestic set-up showed great continuity in the years between the 1920s and the early 1970s. For a large part of the period between 1945 and 1972 Denmark was ruled by Social Democrat minority governments or by coalition governments led by the Social Democrats. The Social Democrats were in power from 1947 to 1950 during the first negotiations on the Marshall Plan, the OEEC, Uniscan and the first Nordic consultations. They resumed power once again in 1953 and remained in office until 1968. From 1968 until 1971, a centre-right tripartite government of Social Liberals, Agrarians and Conservatives initiated negotiations on the terms for Danish entry into the EEC. In 1971, the Social Democrats returned to power and finalized these negotiations.

The Danish political system has been dominated by the four 'old parties': Social Democrats, Social Liberals, Agrarians (Venstre) and Conservatives. The Communist Party has traditionally been insignificant. The split among Danish

Communists after the Soviet invasion of Hungary in 1956 gave rise to the – virulently anti-EEC – Socialist People's Party during the 1960s.[10] Due to the tradition of minority governments, alliances could be found across the political spectrum on a number of important foreign policy issues. This was particularly important with regard to Denmark's much contested choice to join the Atlantic Alliance in 1949. This decision took place amidst the backdrop of the Nordic disappointments that particularly burdened the Social Democrat Party. The 'Atlantic' majority of the Social Democrats and the Agrarian and Conservative Parties constituted a traditional centre-pillar of the security policy for decades after 1949, but constituted also a need – especially for the Social Democrats – to emphasize their continuing adherence to the principles of the UN and to Nordic consultations. This held good for NATO policies and on a number of accounts also for European issues (in Danish political lingo known as 'market policies').

One constitutional peculiarity is also important for understanding the background to Danish foreign and European policy. Until 1953 Denmark had a bicameral parliament. The bicameral system was abandoned with the new constitution of 1953 and replaced by a unicameral parliament, the *Folketing*. The new constitution included the now well-known Article 20 which ruled that sovereignty could only be ceded to international organizations or to supranational institutions by force of a popular referendum or if carried by a majority of five to one in parliament.[11]

Denmark and 'Europe' after 1945

The first Danish reaction to the federalist or pro-European schemes was one of great reluctance. Only a few representatives from the resistance movement and from the main parties kept abreast with the efforts in Europe to intensify European cooperation. At the Congress of The Hague in May 1948, the Danish representatives maintained a reserved position, and at the establishment of the Council of Europe in 1949 they supported the Anglo-Scandinavian 'functionalist' approach.[12]

The foreign policy outlook of many Danes and many Danish politicians continued to be characterized by an emotionally and politically motivated Nordism. In the wake of the frustrated hopes for committed Nordic cooperation in 1948–49, new attempts were directed towards building an intra-Nordic parliamentary assembly. In 1952 the so-called Nordic Council met for its first session. The Council is an intra-Nordic parliamentary assembly, alternating between the Nordic capitals with annual sessions of about one week. The Council is strictly consultative, but important insofar as cabinet ministers and (usually) prime ministers take part in the sessions.[13] At the start of the Marshall Plan, the Scandinavians started to investigate the possibility of building a Scandinavian customs union along the lines of the Benelux customs union. These studies were several times thwarted because of incompatible economic interests, protectionism and sectoral lobby groups.[14] However, in 1954 a new and more authoritative round of negotiations – the so-called Harpsund negotiations – took place with the aim of creating a Nordic customs union – although without fish and agricultural products. These negotiations ran until 1958–59 when they failed under the impact of the Western European market schism between the six founding member-states of the EEC and the United Kingdom.[15] However, at the same time intra-parliamentary consultations in the Nordic Council saw several successes. Thus, in 1952, a Nordic passport union was established followed by the creation of a Nordic labour market in 1954.[16]

The Danish economy of the 1950s was characterized by a number of serious structural problems and by a powerful and costly economic modernization process from a primarily agrarian economy to a modern industrial economy. Agricultural exports were of great importance in order to finance the imports of fuel, raw materials and capital goods and in order to bridge the painful balance of payments problems in the 1950s (quite apart from the considerable political leverage of farmers and small holders). In the 1950s these problems worsened as Danish farmers faced increasing trade barriers on their main markets in West Germany and Great Britain.[17] The Liberal-Conservative government ruling between 1950 and 1953 paid scant attention to the sectoral integration plans of the Six in the early 1950s. The primacy of the trade relationship with Great Britain, formal concerns for sovereignty and scepticism with regard to economic regulation put the Danish government and the farmers in an aloof position. Danish farmers pinned their hopes on a utopia of international free trade of agricultural products and on the possibility of exploiting their superior competitiveness.[18] At this point – as noted by Alan Milward[19] – a strategic choice was confronting Danish farmers. In their competition with the other great exporter of agricultural products – the Dutch – over the growing and important West German market for food products, should the Danes rely on a liberal regime for international trade or should they – like the Dutch – seek to join a regional market group?[20]

In addition, the Schuman Plan could have given the Danes an early warning of the coming of the European integration process. For a while it seemed that Denmark could have joined the European Coal and Steel Community (ECSC) at quite an early stage. Jean Monnet and other Europeanists tried to tempt the Danish government to join the ECSC in 1952 at a time when steel and fuel supplies were scarce.[21] However, there was little enthusiasm among Danish decision-makers for this *demarche* and also little opposition to the supranational principles. Views in Copenhagen were characterized by the desire for economic expediency. In the end, the government declined the invitation, primarily owing to uncertainty with regard to Britain's position.[22] The correspondence between the Danish ambassador in Paris, Eyvind Bartels, and the Permanent Under-Secretary in the Foreign Ministry, Erling Kristiansen, on the expediency of Danish membership in the ECSC underlines the fact that the European issue also entailed thoughts about the relationship to the Southern neighbour. The latter wrote:

> Does it not still hold true that he who commands the Ruhr, commands Europe, *a fortiori* Western Europe? It lies close at hand that a development as the one presumed here would mark a short cut to a 'Viertes Reich' by a Western German-led 'Western European Greater Space'.[23]

In reply, the ambassador, somewhat under the spell of Jean Monnet, stated that joining the ECSC could actually be seen as the strategy to counter such a development, arguing that German power would remain whether Denmark joined or not:

> Even though the main purpose of the Schuman Plan is of economic character, it is clear that the idea of the French always has been that they with the Schuman organization could get a better hold on the dynamic Germans than if such an organization did not exist.[24]

In 1955 a new attempt was made to invite Denmark to associate with the ECSC, but at this point the Danish government gave priority to the Nordic customs union discussions with Sweden and Norway in which the steel market was central. Once again, the Danish government seems to have had few qualms about the supranational nature of the cooperation.[25]

In 1957, Denmark was faced with several difficult dilemmas in her European policies. While the Nordic customs union negotiations slowly began to assume the form of a concrete plan, the country was faced with the double challenge from the OEEC free trade area plan first proposed by Britain in 1956 and the Treaty of Rome. The creation of the EEC led to powerful domestic pressure from the Liberal, Conservatives and agricultural pressure groups for immediate EEC membership.[26] They feared that Dutch farmers would squeeze Danish farmers out of the affluent Continental (particularly the German) food markets owing to the EEC preference. The Minister for Economic Affairs, Jens Otto Krag, confided in his diary: 'We will probably end up amongst the Six. What a revolution. The most radical steps seem in certain cases to be the more easier to take.'[27] The government stalled and informally sounded out the Interim Committee (functioning as a caretaker 'Commission' for the Six until the establishment of the European Commission in 1 January 1958) in April 1957 about the possible conditions of full membership. Krag attempted to launch a bridging strategy, in which Denmark would join parts of the Treaty of Rome, while remaining tied to Scandinavia.[28]

At the same time, domestic pressure from trade unions and industry directed attention to the impact of EEC membership on the developing industrial sector, on the welfare and labour regimes and on the full employment policy. A public debate focused on the predominance of France and Germany, on the issue of national independence and, to a certain extent, on the cultural factors – especially with regard to the Schleswig border areas. After long, painful and tactical manoeuvres (with a crumbling of the Nordic market plans in 1959), the Social Democrats, the Social Liberals and the Conservatives opted for membership of the European Free Trade Association (EFTA), backed by a domestic coalition of trade unionists, industrial entrepreneurs and smallholders anxious about losing the British market.

In this process, however, the government had built a close relationship with the West German and French governments as well as with the European Commission. In the second half of the 1950s and the first half of the 1960s, German–Danish relations were becoming increasingly close. In 1955, mutual declarations on minority questions took the tension out of the border question, trade was intensifying with regard to industrial as well as to agricultural products and, in 1961, a mutual military command structure was agreed upon for the German–Danish forces in the Baltic, Denmark and Northern Germany.[29] Actually, Danish entry into EFTA took place amidst a background of close consultations with the German government and after the establishment of a German–Danish trade agreement that secured an important share of Danish food exports to West Germany. Krag liaised with the federal government during the EFTA negotiations in mid-1959 and also felt that the Germans saw Danish EFTA membership as a bridge between the blocs.[30] In Krag's words:

> The confidential results from London and the almost incredible friendliness in Bonn with an unchanged commercial treatment even though we join the Seven and with the intention that Denmark – and in particular myself – should be suitable as brokers between the European groups have made an impression.[31]

Thus, in a sense, Denmark's loyalties and interests were split between the Six and the Seven EFTA states. It would probably be more precise to say that Denmark – although a full member of EFTA – to a large degree was sitting on the fence between the Six and the Seven.[32] At this time the most central figure in the making of Denmark's European policy was the Social Democrat Krag, who was Minister for Economic Affairs and Foreign Trade between 1953 and 1958 and Foreign Minister from 1958 until 1962.[33]

Against this background, Denmark's position was very clear when the British government in 1961 moved to apply for EEC membership. The British move promised a unification of Denmark's main trading partners and a solution to the old problem with regard to securing export markets for agricultural exports. The government was already anxious about the effects of the emerging Common Agricultural Policy (CAP) and about the rapidly stagnating food exports to the EEC.[34] Price support regimes had been established for Danish farmers, and these constituted a serious burden for the Treasury. Consequently, the Danish application quickly followed the British one and was sweeping in its acceptance of the Treaty of Rome and the *acquis communitaire*.[35] Many of the economic problems with entering the EEC had vanished since 1957. In the years 1957–61, Denmark had experienced a rapid industrial modernization process with booming industrial exports to the EEC and to the Scandinavian markets. Certain not insubstantial problems did remain, however. The Danes were intent on not being confronted with a *fait accompli* with regard to their bacon and butter exports to the British market. They were also concerned that the CAP and EEC levies should not hurt Danish farming interests before full membership could take effect. During the negotiations, the Danish government forwarded requests for certain temporary regimes for the capital market and for a remaining part of the industrial sector that was lagging behind in adaptation. Investigations were pursued with regard to the compatibility between the social and labour regulations of the Six and Danish welfare and labour regimes. Opt-outs were sought for the Faeroe Islands and for Greenland along the lines of some of the French overseas territories.

The application in 1961 was backed by the four old parties, but met with opposition from the small Communist Party and from the rising Socialist People's Party. The main problem on the domestic front was the difficulty of containing the EEC-critical faction in the Social Democrat Party, in the trade unions and in the Social Liberal Party. At the same time cross-party committees were established in opposition to EEC membership which was either seen by such groups as a capitalist-conservative danger or as a threat to Danish nationhood and culture.[36] Pride, prejudice and a strong small state nationalism could be heard through the clamour of many of the warnings against EEC membership. Already in 1957, Jørgen S. Dich, an economist and neutralist, had proclaimed that:

> The European idea is created as a political instrument where the economy only is the means. It cannot be our aim to be led down the German–French garden path inspired by the Catholic Church who, helped by the European idea, aims at influence in the Nordic countries.[37]

Krag (who in 1962 became Prime Minister) pursued a consensus policy in European affairs with a platform that established a nexus between the British and the Danish applications. Solidarity declarations with regard to the EFTA states and Sweden helped to diffuse domestic opposition, in the same way as the Norwegian application in 1962 was used as a political painkiller for many Social Democrats.[38] The voice of Knud Heinesen, a young Social Democrat academic, is characteristic of the concerns Krag was fighting:

> I am not against ceding sovereignty as such, but I would have many misgivings about ceding sovereignty to the Rome-Union ... [Its] aim is to create a large private-capitalist Western Europe ... where the economic policies are used the same way as in Western Germany and France ... It should be clear that there is a considerable risk that such a rightist majority in the bodies of the Common Market will conduct a policy that crosses the intentions of a Social Democrat government and creates a bad climate for these.[39]

At the same time, trust-building cross-party consultations were established in the parliamentary Committee for Market Affairs established to monitor the negotiations. As in the late 1950s, a clear schism between the public political debate with its distance to things supranational and the real, diplomatic and very close contacts between Denmark and the Six can be discerned in the early 1960s. In 1962, the government was, however, forced to declare its intention to support the political integration process when it was rumoured that supporters of a 'core Europe' concept played with the idea of only letting Great Britain into the EEC and only allowing the smaller EFTA states to follow suit after a certain socialization of the British attitudes to European integration.[40]

In substance, Denmark had very close relations with the Six all through the Brussels Conference (1961–63). Relations with Charles de Gaulle's Fifth Republic (where Denmark was seen as the most continental of the Scandinavians) were intensifying and those with West Germany growing to the point of being a political alliance. Hence, it was not surprising that de Gaulle in early 1963 – after his veto against British EEC membership – informed Krag that Denmark could join the EEC on her own with farmers, food surplus and all.[41] Negotiations picked up from this point in 1967 at the second round of what was, at this time, more soundings than negotiations about the enlargement of what was now the EC after the institutional merger of the three Communities. At this point a clear understanding and cooperation existed between Krag's government in Denmark and Willy Brandt's foreign policy.[42]

When these soundings failed, however, Krag attempted what was later branded a Nordic 'tiger leap'.[43] At the Nordic Council session in 1968, the Danes proposed the creation of a Nordic Economic Union (NORDEK). With the rapid expansion of intra-Nordic industrial trade within EFTA, the emergence of new cooperation areas and a good long wait before an enlargement of the EC could be expected, the NORDEK plan did have something in its favour. The centre-right government that now assumed governmental responsibility and pursued these negotiations through 1968–70 was, however, deeply split over the issue. The agrarians and many Conservatives remained in favour of full EC membership, while the Social Liberals remained advocates of a stronger Nordic orientation. To make things more difficult, Krag's and the Social Democratic Party's shadow hovered over the project – partly owing to their contacts with the Norwegian and Swedish Social Democrats. A structural incompatibility seemed to burden the project. The Danes were keen to keep the option of EC membership open, and the Finns were concerned that a Western drift would arouse Soviet suspicion. Could a member of NORDEK join the EC? Should NORDEK agree to an association with the EC? The NORDEK venture failed in early 1970. Before then, the Six had extended an invitation to the new potential EC members at the Council meeting at The Hague in 1969 and the road was once again open for a new Danish EC application. The NORDEK *intermezzo* was, in the end, very important in order to demonstrate to many Danish voters and politicians that the Nordic alternative to the EC did not exist.[44]

From the application to accession

The negotiations between the EC and Denmark on Denmark's entry into the Community were smooth and had few problems. The motives for membership were clear: an enlarged European Community would embrace the all-dominant markets for Danish food exports and the swelling industrial exports. Public support for agriculture had become a burden on state finances and Denmark was, in the early 1970s, saddled by a balance of payments problem which to no small degree was rooted in the agricultural problems of the country. While the trade unions and industrial interest organizations in the late 1950s and early 1960s had been reluctant with regard to the competition from EEC companies, there was, in the early 1970s, little concern on that account. Denmark had developed a modern, competitive industrial export economy. The main industrial concern regarding EC membership was that there should not be a tariff wall between Denmark and her Scandinavian neighbours who provided important markets for Danish industrial products.

The Danish strategy in the negotiations was to seek the full effects of membership as soon as Denmark entered the Community. The CAP and its financing system, as it had developed, were well suited to Danish interests. The Danish negotiators therefore sought full membership as soon as possible. British losses on agricultural issues became Danish gains, such as the EC's insistence on a short transition period. Furthermore, in 1971 the Danish government managed to persuade the Commission that food exports to Great Britain should receive price subsidies. It was estimated that the value of the most important food exports would have risen by some 25 per cent after the end of the transitional period.[45]

The negotiations were quite unproblematic as regards the industrial sector. Danish industry did clamour for a longer transition period, but without much impact. Industry further requested a number of tariff-free contingents. The Danish negotiators maintained a reserved position on these demands, until it appeared that the British negotiators had managed to gain certain concessions in this area. Only then did the Danish negotiators secure a number of similar tariff-free contingents. The most important question in the industrial sector was whether a solution was found on the industrial trade between EFTA and the EC. This was settled with bilateral free trade agreements between the EC and individual EFTA countries.[46]

If the negotiations were fairly painless, numerous political problems remained. The nexus between the Danish application and the British remained an important political point, just as the Norwegian application and the consideration of Swedish, Finnish and other EFTA states' basic interests. On a number of accounts, the adaptation of Danish legislation to the *acquis communitaire* also touched upon sensitive issues. Most of the welfare questions were dealt with on a technical level and technical solutions were sought for what could be politicized and sensitive adaptations to the EC. For certain labour regulations, such as equal pay, the Treaty of Rome and EC legislation assumed that these issues were liable to legislation or government regulation. In Denmark, however, important aspects of labour affairs were subject to corporatist regulation in connection with collective wage agreements between trade unions and employers. EC requirements were simply adopted by the employers and trade unions. The Danish social pensions system and the Nordic labour market posed similar compatibility problems. Technical, but not unproblematic, solutions were found on these issues. Similarly, the sensitive question about the rights of EC citizens to acquire Danish property caused concern for the national balance in the Schleswig border areas. It was feared that West German citizens in particular would be able to purchase Danish farms and summer cottages. Special (temporary) agreements were established in this area, and for commerce across the Danish–German border. A special status was granted to Greenland and the Faeroe Islands. The former joined the Community with Denmark (but opted out after a referendum in 1986), while the latter (which had home rule) was granted the option of joining the Community by decision of the local parliament. Faeroese politicians chose not to avail themselves of this opportunity.[47]

The main feature of the Danish negotiations and the decision to join the EC was the highly politicized nature of the decision. Many of the future possible developments in Community policies or in the institutional character of the community became contested issues in the debate. The most decisive feature in this respect was the approach of the Social Democratic labour movement to EC membership. The strategy of the Social Democratic leadership with regard to soothing the qualms of their rank-and-file regarding the socio-economic and political consequences of EC membership was not only to have a long-term impact on Danish EC policies after entry into the Community, but was probably also instrumental in ensuring the required majority in the referendum.[48] During the negotiations of the centre-right government on the terms of entry, the Social Democrats had held an outwardly reserved, but basically positive stance. The Hague Summit of the Six in December 1969 had opened the door for enlargement of the Community, but it had also opened the question about a deepening of involvement in fields such as political cooperation and economic and monetary union. These open-ended projects gave cause for concern among Danish Social Democrats. There remained some weariness with regard to the outcome of the Davignon and Werner Reports of 1970 on a future deepening of the cooperation in such fields. The Social Democrats took a reserved position at least on including security issues in the European Political Cooperation (EPC) plan that was on the drawing board, and likewise they reserved the possibility of maintaining a national employment and economic policy with regard to a future monetary and economic union. Krag himself was anxious that a military dimension in the EEC should not hamper *détente* and create problems within NATO. As he said to the West German Foreign Minister Walter Scheel in November 1971:

> I warned against pretending to be able to make the EC into a military organization. It could further American withdrawal and cause suspicion and uncertainty in the Soviet Union. In the security and defence policy we must hold on to NATO and on this basis seek to promote *détente*.[49]

The left-wing parties in Denmark were particularly anxious to bolster the national (high) tax policy and the high level of public consumption that were seen as central instruments in the extensive welfare provisions and in maintaining full employment. During this time the parliamentary Committee on Market Affairs came to play a central role in the forging of an informal coalition between the government and the opposition on the main questions on Danish entry into the EC. The government gave frequent reports to the committee, and largely consulted the opposition on the stance to be taken in the negotiations.[50]

The journey of the Social Democrats from 1970 to the referendum in October 1972 was slow and cautious. At a May rally in 1971, a Social Democrat spokesman declared that Danish entry into the EC would have to be decided by a referendum, and not by a parliamentary majority of five to one. Soon after the Social Democrats took the formal decision to claim a referendum in order to avoid an internal rift and suffer an election campaign over the issue.[51] The centre-right government acquiesced to this unilateral move and agreed to a referendum. It was also clear that although entry into the Community enjoyed a parliamentary majority of 132 against 12 in May 1971, the Social Liberals and Social Democrats faced increasing opposition against EC membership. Thus, in August 1971, the Social Democrats lifted party discipline on the issue. In the general election in September 1971, a group of young Social Democrat EC sceptics gained seats in parliament, and in December 1971 a committee for Social Democrat EC sceptics was established. When the Social Democrat leader Jens Otto Krag regained the premiership in September 1971, he constructed his new Social Democrat government in such a way that moderate EC sceptics were also represented in the cabinet. Most notable was the cabinet minister for European affairs, Ivar Nørgaard, who agreed to EC membership but was vehemently opposed to a supranational deepening of the cooperation. At his first meeting with the Six in November 1971, Nørgaard took the opportunity to tighten the Danish reserves on the national sovereignty over distributionary economic and employment policies in such a way that it caused a certain consternation among the negotiators of the Six.[52] Nørgaard simply reserved Denmark's participation in the EMU: 'Our participation in the planned Cooperation must not prevent the Danish parliament from deciding an economic policy including tax policy and a social policy which will ensure greater equality between the various groups of the population.'[53]

These beliefs were doubtless genuine concerns among many Danish left-wing politicians, but there remained tactical elements in the Social Democrat line also. The main obstacle for the Social Democrats was the position of the trade unions. During 1972, congresses of two of the major trade unions, the metal workers and the general workers, saw majorities against EC membership, but in May the national trade union congress saw a large majority in favour of entry. During 1972, the labour movement began to build a platform for a 'yes'. It emphasized strong economic arguments in favour of joining, while future political aspects of the cooperation were played down. Finally, as late as September – the pending referendum was set for 2 October 1972 – a special Social Democrat Party Congress recommended a 'yes' to entry.[54]

In the referendum campaign the established parties and most of the important interest organizations backed a 'yes' to Danish entry. The three major non-socialist parties and the Social Democrats launched a concerted campaign, while the trade unions, industrial and agricultural interest organizations backed this effort with campaigns of their own and with financial support for the pro-EC parties. Against this formidable array of established interests, against the united front of the four 'old parties' and against an overwhelming parliamentary majority (although no longer a majority of five to one), the EC opposition could mobilize much less economic and organizational muscle. The opposition was primarily based on a cluster of left-wing parties ranging from the Socialist People's Party and the Left Socialists to the Communists, with the latter providing the backbone of organizational and activist support. The non-socialist opposition was much less based on organizations. Two small parties on the right-wing fringe of Danish politics did join the opposition. The Independents, or *De Uafhængige*, and Danish Unity, or *Dansk Samling*, together with the more centrist Georgist Party, the *Retsforbundet*, and many Social Liberals did take part in the opposition against EC membership, but had few resources, few members and little political clout. After a number of more or less successful attempts to bridge the differences between these groups, the EC opposition did manage to build a cartel against EC membership by late 1971. By early 1972 this cross-party cartel was known as the People's Movement against the EC, or *Folkebevægelsen mod EF*.[55]

The People's Movement faced marked problems. First, there remained the problem of building an alliance with the Social Democrat EC opponents who were weary of being associated with what many saw as a Communist-run venture. Second, the fact that the movement was not a symmetrical cross-party movement was apparent. The left-wing organizations – first and foremost the Communists – played a dominant role in the organization, and agitation tended to spread from the EC issue to other core left-wing issues less palatable for moderate conservative voters. Although the referendum campaign did see closer cooperation across the political spectrum, it remained a problem to rally well-known non-socialist personalities to the cause. Moreover, the movement had financial difficulties as it did not enjoy the support of the large interest organizations. It was, however, able to draw on the activism and organizational experience from the politicized youth – not least the Communists – who demonstrated a great deal of zeal, creativity and no little populist ability in appealing to the scepticism among the voters. This was to become the special brand of the 'no' campaign. The 'no' movement depicted itself as a poor, disadvantaged spokesman of the sentiment of the people against a moneyed, privileged establishment. The truth was probably that the popular basis of the no-movement rested on a combination of intellectuals and politicians, on the one hand, and the political organizations of the left-wing parties and the small group of right-wing parties, on the other. There can be no doubt that the movement managed to rally large segments of the people – also many depoliticized Danes – behind the opposition to the EC, but it was largely backing in the form of voting 'no' on 2 October. The initiative, inspiration and backbone of the movement came from intellectuals, politicians and the politically active youth and much less from the political mobilization of the man on the street. The campaign strategy was to call on the popular scepticism against the political elite, against the nature – especially the political nature – of the Community and its member-states and to call for a national and/or Nordic stance.[56]

The pro-EC camp countered this with a coordinated, thoroughly financed campaign that focused on the economic necessity of EC membership. The political aspects were played down and the role of the veto-institution emphasized. The Prime Minister prepared two speeches for the opening of parliament the day after the referendum: the 'yes' speech and an alternative speech – or as Krag called it, 'the bleak speech' – and it was rumoured that the government was ready with an austere economic emergency plan in case of a negative outcome of the referendum.[57] Krag wrote in his diary on 24 August: 'If it is a no, we shall have to walk the Canossa walk to Brussels and ask for new negotiations in the same weak position as the one the Swedes have negotiated from.'[58]

The threat of devaluation hovered over the voters, but first and foremost the Social Democrats proceeded with a gradual attempt to defuse the political mines in the form of fears for the future political and politico-economic development of the Community. This was most likely the reason why the 'yes' camp eventually managed to win the doubters and sceptics for a 'yes', not least those among the Social Liberals and the Social Democrats. Thus, the referendum on 2 October 1972 resulted in a 'yes' vote of 63.3 per cent for membership versus 36.7 per cent against. The turnout was 90.1 per cent.[59]

Structural causes were important for the journey and outcome when Denmark's relationship to the European Community was decided in the early 1970s. Long-term identity patterns and perceptions of what were believed to be unique features of Danish society and of Danish politics *vis-à-vis* the founding members of the Community played an important role. More recent political and socio-economic changes also influenced the country's actual societal structures as well as the outlook of many Danes, however.

The particular character of Denmark's security and defence policy, with its cross-party consensus between liberal-conservative parties and the Social Democrats and its latent neutralism and longing for a stronger UN, was a drag on a more active Danish assent to a stronger commitment to the EPC plans in the early 1970s. Many Social Democrats and many of the predominantly neutralist and pacifist Social Liberals were suspicious that EC membership would be the first step towards a more hard-line foreign policy in the days of the Cold War. Conversely, many EC opponents and activists were motivated by an attempt to deal a blow to Denmark's Atlantic commitments through the defeat of the attempt to join the EC. The so-called Nordic alternative was – latently – a more neutralist option. Although almost no one on either side of the debate admitted it, the question of EC membership had potential consequences for the nation's security policy and for political cooperation in Western Europe. If EC accession were thwarted, it could potentially also weaken the Atlantic majority in Parliament and Denmark's links with its militarily stronger Western European allies. A successful accession would – on the other hand – imply closer political ties to the major European NATO partners.

Moreover, the socio-economic structures of Danish society were in important areas different from those of the Six founding members and from the assumptions of those who drafted the Treaty of Rome. The marked degree of corporatist regulation of the labour market and the powerful position of the trade unions posed obstacles. This was also true for the welfare structures. With its principle of a tax-financed universal entitlement of social rights, the Danish social security system already diverged from the prevalent forms of social legislation in the rest of continental Europe by the end of the nineteenth century. It added to the difficulties that this was also an area where Nordic cooperation had left successes in the form of a Nordic labour market and a measure of harmonized social legislation and transferability of social rights across borders in Scandinavia. As it turned out, most of these potential problems amounted to nothing after Danish membership of the EC.

All these factors contributed to the strength of the EC opposition, to the caution of the 'yes' camp and to the European foot-dragging of especially the Social Democrat labour movement. It is easy to underline such particular features in a single nation's experience. The question is, however, whether these forces would have gained the strength they had and left the legacy that they did, had it not been for the timing of this first successful enlargement process. Danish society was, as it happened, marked by two overall phenomena in the late 1960s and early 1970s. First, the country experienced a surge in political activity by the youth and by intellectuals who had found an expression for their left-wing fervour in the opposition against the Vietnam War. This generational phenomenon added large numbers of activists to the number of small left-wing parties that were sprouting in these years – most notably the resurgence of the Communist Party. This was not a unique Danish phenomenon. What was unique was that these left-wing groups came to embrace the Nordism and strong national sentiments that had earlier been the monopoly of more traditional right-wing and moderate groups in Danish politics. The Danish left became nationalized in its opposition to EC membership.

Second, Danish society had in the late 1960s seen the peak of a rapid modernization process that had changed the nation from a predominantly agricultural economy to an industrial, urbanized economy. In this process the traditional, rural society was challenged by modern culture. The expanding welfare state and public services gave rise to a very large public sector that also claimed high taxes and the introduction of Value Added Tax (VAT). These changes also affected traditional party loyalty. During the decade the traditional four-party newspaper system began to break up as tabloids and electronic media won the day. In a referendum in 1963 the Social Democrats had seen the first sign that their voters might not continue to follow the party line and adhere to the traditional party discipline. By 1972, a wave of reforms had swept over the country. In 1972, voters were not only tax weary, but also less loyal to their parties and more disgruntled with regard to the monumental changes in Danish culture and politics. A large part of the scepticism *vis-à-vis* EC membership must be seen in the context of the coming voter rebellion that created a landslide election in 1973, doubling the number of parties represented in parliament, causing a right-wing secession from the Social Democrat Party (giving birth to the Centre-Democrats) and making the newly created populist tax protest party, the Progress Party, one of the largest parties.

Finally, for all of its more or less unique character, the Danish EC scepticism should be studied against the backdrop of the constitutional provisions that were mobilized in 1972 in order to facilitate a ratification of Denmark's entry into the Community. Had it not been for the painstakingly precise and tough regulation in the constitution of the conditions under which sovereignty could be ceded to international organizations, the world might have known considerably less of the views of the ordinary Danes on the institution of the veto, on the CAP or on the Commission. To a certain degree, the difference between the views of a Dane and say, for example, a French citizen, is that the former – thanks to tougher ratification requirements – was asked to vote in a referendum in 1972, whereas France joined the EC in 1957 by parliamentary ratification. Two questions remain with regard to the Danish referendum institution. First, whether the referendum gave voice to the EC scepticism of the Danes, or whether to some degree it set the perfect conditions for populist campaigns, thus, also contributing to the scepticism. Second, whether the citizens of other EC member-states would have behaved much differently if subjected to similar polarized 'yes' and 'no' campaigns.

Conclusion

The Danish case provides a hard test of the existing theories of the European integration process. Denmark's European policies are characterized by a number of dichotomies. On the one hand, the policy has been, since 1945, marked by the lack of strong institutional doctrines with regard to supranationality, federalism and institutional questions. On the other, the actual track of Denmark's policy does follow the same path as the 'functionalist' Anglo-Scandinavian group, and institutional and sovereignty matters were of growing importance – at least politically and emotionally – throughout the period. Similarly, Denmark can in many ways be considered one of the core members of the Scandinavian or EFTA 'clients' of British European policies. However, Denmark maintained and expanded her relations with France, the Federal Republic and with Community institutions such as the European Commission. In particular the 'small alliance' between Denmark and the Bonn government made it possible (and necessary) for Denmark to move in a grey zone between the Six and the other Anglo-Scandinavians for a long time. Finally, Denmark's European outlook and policies are characterized by a schism between the elite positions and the positions marked in the public debate.

From an elite perspective, the Danish case supports some assumptions of neo-functionalism and Alan Milward's[60] nation–state perspective and related inter-governmentalist explanations[61] of the integration process in International Relations. The former provides answers to the growing awareness and orientation towards the European integration process in the Danish bureaucratic and political elite. Alan Milward's focus on the integration process as a problem-solving mechanism for the nation–states and the attention paid to the domestic policy processes formulating primary national interests is a central requirement in understanding the seemingly shifting strategies between European and Nordic alignments and between the rural and urban interests. Also Moravcsik's liberal inter-governmentalist interpretation of the integration process offers valuable tools to explain how influential domestic interests converged to promote EC membership. The Danish case is, however, a difficult one. How does one explain the case of a country that almost joined the Six, then did not? Instead, it waited for the right moment to join. And, for a while, other domestic forces brought the country very close to joining a Nordic community. Actually, answers to such questions require a study of the nature of the Nordic 'integration process' and would have to include Nordic integration theories.[62]

The key to explaining the transient nature of Danish European policy might be found in the economic modernization process of the country and in its changing foreign policy orientation towards – particularly – West Germany and Great Britain from 1945 to 1972. The contested and changing nature of what was seen as the national interest might be taken as one key focus to explain the bargains and compromises forming Denmark's European diplomacy (and lack thereof), but only with caution. Economics remained a crucial factor for the Danish European policy, but as we have seen in the case of the Danish Social Democrats, perceptions, tactics and foreign policy played an important and complicating role also. It is also important to explain the split between elite and population over Europe in the Danish case. Moreover, the appeal of Nordism and growing EEC scepticism require other theoretical tools also: the constructivist approach might be able to help explain the growth of the anti-EC coalitions and of the 'Nordic alternative' in the minds of many Danes. However, it would be too simplistic to attribute to the elite cool calculations and to the population looser concepts of Danish nationalism. The elite was split over European affairs, and a great deal of the anti-EC protests had their roots in hard politics as well as in lofty ideals or long-reigning perceptions. It is the exchanges between the layers of explanation that pose the real difficulty: the linkages between economic rationales, politics and perceptions of, for example, sovereignty and identity. The most illuminating part of the Danish case is undoubtedly how the Danes joined the integration process, and the long-term consequences of the choices made on entry into the Community.

The fact that Denmark joined the Community on the basis of a referendum seems to have set the precedent that the people must be asked at every new instance of changing the authority or the division of power within the European Union. This was not the only legacy from the Danish path to the EC. The Market Committee (today the Committee on European Affairs) has remained a central factor in the making of Danish European policies since 1972. The debated concrete issues were quickly resolved. It turned out that the economic gains surpassed what the yes campaigners thought to be wildly exaggerated promises, while the sombre warnings of the 'no' campaigners on the social and economic effects of EC membership appeared to be groundless. Nevertheless, several of the reservations remained – not least about the European role in security policies and about participating in the Economic and Monetary Union. However, first and foremost, the kingdom remained divided on the European question for many years after 1972 – not least the Social Democrat labour movement.[63]

The heritage of Denmark's path to EC membership is a backlog of EC scepticism and a powerful extra-parliamentarian anti-EC lobby. The internal struggles in the Social Democratic labour movement and in the Social Liberal Party have left a trail of factionalism on European questions that is present even in contemporary Danish politics. The emphasis on economic matters in Denmark's accession to the community and in the referendum campaign has left many voters and political activists inherently sceptical towards the institutional and political aspects of the European integration process. After the Single European Act and particularly after the end of the Cold War, the Social Democrat Party has made a slow, but decisive turn towards a stronger pro-European stance, but the history of the entry negotiations and of the formative years of Danish European policy seems to have taken its revenge. Although elite views are turning towards more pro-EU sentiments, there remain strong currents of popular hesitation and suspicion voiced through – among others – the political platform of the strongly national and anti-EU Danish People's Party. This can be seen in the string of conflictual referenda on each major amendment of the Treaties of Rome, first on the Single European Act in 1986, then in 1992 the 'no' in the first referendum on the Maastricht Treaty 1992.[64] The flurry of domestic and European negotiations led to four Danish opt-outs from the Maastricht Treaty agreed upon at the Edinburgh Summit, and then ratified by a new referendum in 1993. It is worth noting that the opt-outs on the Common Foreign and Security Policy and on the Economic and Monetary Union had their roots in the accession history of 1971–72, and that the two others, on Home and Justice Affairs and on EU citizenship, can be seen as areas heavy with sovereignty implications.[65] And history seems to go on taking its revenge. The referendum on joining the EMU in 2000 ended up with a 'no' despite positive opinion polls. Sovereignty is still an ongoing concern for the Danes.

Notes

1   Uffe Østergaard, 'Peasants and Danes: national identity and political culture in Denmark', *Comparative Studies in Society and History*, 1992, vol. 34, no. 1, pp. 3–27.
2   Uffe Østergaard, 'Danish identity: European, Nordic or peasant?', in Lise Lyck (ed.), *Denmark and EC Membership Evaluated*, London: Pinter, 1992, pp. 167–77; Lene Hansen, 'Historie, identitet og det danske Europadilemma', *Den Jyske Historiker*, 2001, no. 93, pp. 113–31.
3   Carsten Due-Nielsen and Claus Bjørn, *Fra Helstat til nationalstat 1814–1914, Dansk Udenrigspolitiks historie*, vol. 3, Copenhagen: Gyldendal, 2003, pp. 75–6, 103–8, 236 ff.,

269–70, 313–14; also Lorenz Rerup, 'Fra litterær til politisk nationalisme', in Ole Feldbæk (ed.), *Dansk identitetshistorie*, vol. 2, Copenhagen: C.A. Reitzel, 1991, pp. 368 ff.

4 Henrik S. Nissen, 'Folkelighed og frihed 1933', in Feldbæk, *Dansk identitetshistorie*, vol. 3, 1992, pp. 607–32.

5 Regarding Danish foreign policy in the inter-war period, see Ole Karup Pedersen, *Udenrigsminister P. Munchs opfattelse af Danmarks stilling i international politik*, Copenhagen: G.E.C. Gad, 1970; Viggo Sjøquist, *Danmarks udenrigspolitik 1933–1940*, Copenhagen: Gyldendal, 1966; and Viggo Sjøquist, *Peter Munch: Manden – politikeren – historikeren*, Copenhagen: Gyldendal, 1976.

6 Sherman S. Jones, *The Scandinavian States and the League of Nations*, Princeton, NJ: Princeton University Press, 1939; William A. Rappard, 'Small states in the League of Nations', *Political Science Quarterly*, 1943, vol. 49, pp. 544–75.

7 Thorsten B. Olesen and Johnny Laursen, 'A Nordic alternative to Europe? The interdependence of Denmark's Nordic and European policies, 1945–1998', *Contemporary European History*, 2000, vol. 9, no. 1, pp. 59–92.

8 Juhana Aunesluoma, 'An elusive partnership: Europe, economic cooperation and British policy towards Scandinavia 1949–51', *Journal of European Integration History*, 2002, vol. 8, no. 1, pp. 103–19.

9 Thorsten B. Olesen, 'Brødrefolk, men ikke våbenbrødre: diskussionerne om et skandinavisk forsvarsforbund 1948–49', *Den jyske Historiker*, 1994, no. 69–70, pp. 151–78; Thorsten B. Olesen and Karl Molin, 'Security policy and domestic politics in Scandinavia 1948–49', in Thorsten B. Olesen (ed.), *Interdependence versus Integration: Denmark, Scandinavia and Western Europe, 1945–1960*, Odense: Odense University Press, 1995, pp. 62–81; Nikolaj Petersen, 'Atlantpagten eller Norden? Den danske alliancebeslutning 1949', in Carsten Due-Nielsen, Johan P. Noack and Nikolaj Petersen (eds), *Danmark, Norden og NATO 1948–1962*, Copenhagen: Jurist- og Økonomforbundets Forlag, 1991, pp. 17–42.

10 Niels Christian Nielsen, 'Man har et standpunkt …: SF's EF-politik 1959–1993', *Den jyske Historiker*, 2001, no. 93, pp. 53–72.

11 Stanley V. Anderson, 'Article Twenty of Denmark's new Constitution', *American Journal of International Law*, 1956, vol. L, no. 3, pp. 654–9.

12 Finn Laursen, 'The discussion on European Union in Denmark', in Walter Lipgens and Wilfried Loth (eds), *Documents on the History of European Integration*, vol. 3, Berlin: de Gruyter, 1988, pp. 566–627; Frode Jacobsen, *Jeg vil være en fugl før jeg dør*, Copenhagen: Gyldendal, 1979, pp. 51–8; and Mette-Astrid Jessen, 'Den svære begyndelse: Socialdemokratiet og Europa 1945–1950', *Den jyske Historiker*, 2001, no. 93, pp. 12–31.

13 Stanley V. Anderson, *The Nordic Council: A Study of Scandinavian Regionalism*, Stockholm: Norstedts, 1967.

14 Niels Amstrup, 'Nordisk samarbejde – myte eller realitet? Planerne om økonomisk samarbejde fra 1945 til 1950', in Ole Karup Pedersen et al. (eds), *Nær og Fjern: Samspillet mellem indre og ydre politik*, Copenhagen: Politiske Studier, 1980, pp. 155–80.

15 Johnny Laursen, 'Fra nordisk fællesmarked til Helsingfors Konvention: Nordisk økonomisk integration, 1945–1962', *Den jyske Historiker*, 1994, no. 69–70, pp. 179–200.

16 Anderson, *The Nordic Council*, pp. 17–20.

17 Vibeke Sørensen, *Denmark's Social Democratic Government and the Marshall Plan 1947–1950*, Copenhagen: Museum Tusculanum Press, 2001, pp. 114 ff., 184 ff., 273–93.

18 Vibeke Sørensen, 'How to become member of a club without joining: Danish policy with respect to European sector integration schemes, 1950–1957', *Scandinavian Journal of History*, 1991, vol. 16, no. 2, pp. 105–24; Vibeke Sørensen, '"Free trade" versus regulated markets: Danish agricultural organizations and the Green Pool, 1950–1954', in Richard T. Griffiths and Brian Girvin (eds), *The Green Pool and the*

Origins of the Common Agricultural Policy, London: Lothian Foundation Press, 1995, pp. 202-22, pp. 213–15; and Anders Thornvig Sørensen, *Et spørgsmål om suverænitet: Danmark, landbruget og Europa, 1950–53*, Aarhus: Aarhus University Press, 1998, pp. 90–1, 94, 100, 135–40.

19 Alan S. Milward, *The Reconstruction of Western Europe 1945–51*, London: Methuen & Co., 1984, pp. 432–4.

20 Ibid., pp. 453–4.

21 National Archive, Copenhagen (NA), Foreign Ministry (UM) 74.C.13.f./II: Eyvind Bartels to Hialmar Collin, 2 October 1952.

22 UM 74.C.13.f./II: Notat vedrørende Danmarks stilling til det europæiske kul- og stålfællesskab, 1 December 1952.

23 UM 74.C.13.f./II: Erling Kristiansen to Eyvind Bartels, 11 October 1952.

24 UM 74.C.13.f./II: Eyvind Bartels to Erling Kristiansen, 1 December 1952.

25 Hans Branner, 'Danish European policy since 1945: the question of sovereignty', in Morten Kelstrup (ed.), *European Integration and Denmark's Participation*, Copenhagen: Political Studies Press, 1992, pp. 297–327; Hans Branner, 'På vagt eller på spring? Danmark og europæisk integration 1948–1953', in Birgit Nüchel Thomsen (ed.), *The Odd Man Out? Danmark og den europæiske integration 1948–1992*, Odense: Odense University Press, 1993, pp. 29–64; and Sørensen, 'How to become member', pp. 107, 110–11, 120 ff.

26 UM 73.B.66.a./V: Referat af møde i det udenrigspolitiske nævn og folketingets vareforsyningsudvalg den 28. februar 1957; see also Johnny Laursen, 'Mellem Fællesmarkedet og frihandelszonen. Dansk markedspolitik 1956–58', in Thomsen, *The Odd Man Out?*, pp. 65–72.

27 Labour History Archive, Copenhagen (ABA)/J.O. Krag's private archive (JOK PA), Krag's diary, G, 28 February 1957.

28 UM 73.B.66.c: Udkast til økonomi- og arbejdsministerens udtalelse ved mødet i Bruxelles den 16. april 1957 kl. 12, 15 April 1957.

29 Poul Villaume, *Allieret med forbehold: Danmark, NATO og den kolde krig, En Studie i dansk sikkerhedspolitik 1949–1961*, Copenhagen: Eirene, 1995, pp. 251 ff., 265–7.

30 Auswärtiges Amt, Berlin/Politisches Archiv des Auswärtigen Amtes, Referat 410/Bd. 173: Besprechung des Herrn dänischen Aussenministers mit Vertretern des Bundesregierung im Hause des Herrn Bundesministers von Brentano am 25.6. 1959, 26.6. 1959; UM 73.B.66.f./9/a/III: F. Hvass: Referat, 29 June 1959.

31 ABA/JOK PA, Krag's diary, I, 4 July 1959.

32 Johnny Laursen, 'Det danske tilfælde: En studie i dansk Europapolitiks begrebsdannelse, 1956–57', in Johnny Laursen et al. (eds), *I tradition og kaos (Festskrift til Henning Poulsen)*, Aarhus: Aarhus University Press, 2000, pp. 238–77; Laursen, 'Mellem Fællesmarkedet og frihandelszonen', pp. 73–82; Mikael af Malmborg and Johnny Laursen, 'The creation of EFTA', in Olesen (ed.), *Interdependence versus Integration*, pp. 197–212.

33 Bo Lidegaard, *Jens Otto Krag 1914–1961*, vol. I, Copenhagen: Gyldendal, 2001, pp. 541–7, 604–7.

34 NA/Social Liberal Party archive, cabinet meeting, 31 July 1961.

35 UM 108.B.2/Dan: Dansk erklæring, 31 July 1961; UM 108.B.2/Dan: J.O. Krag to Viggo Kampmann, 22 July 1961.

36 Søren Hein Rasmussen, *Sære Alliancer: Politiske bevægelser i efterkrigstidens Danmark*, Aarhus: Aarhus University Press, 1997, pp. 64–70.

37 'Europa-tanken er ikke nogen leg i sandkasse', *Berlingske Tidende*, 27 November 1957, p. 10.

38 See Krag's letter to the Euro-sceptics in the trade union leadership: ABA/Economic Council archive, no number, marked 'EF': Krag to Frederik Dahlgaard and Jørgen Paldam, 8 July 1961.

39 Knud Heinesen, 'Lad os blive udenfor', *Aktuelt*, 8 September 1961.

A kingdom divided 51

40 Johnny Laursen, 'The great challenge: the social and political foundations of Denmark's application for EEC membership, 1961–63', in Stuart Ward and Richard T. Griffiths (eds), *Courting the Common Market: The First Attempt to Enlarge the European Community, 1961–63*, London: Lothian Foundation Press, 1996, pp. 211–27.
41 UM 108.B.2/Dan: Telegramme, Paris Embassy to Danish Foreign Ministry: Krags notat vedrørende samtalen med de Gaulle, 28 January 1963; Laursen, 'The great challenge', pp. 221–4.
42 Johnny Laursen, 'Denmark, Scandinavia and the second attempt to enlarge the EEC, 1966–67', in Wilfried Loth (ed.), *Crises and Compromises: The European Project 1963–1969*, Baden-Baden: Nomos, 2001, pp. 407–36; Bo Lidegaard, *Jens Otto Krag 1962–78*, vol. II, Copenhagen: Gyldendal, 2002, pp. 345–8.
43 Jens Christensen, 'Danmark, Norden og EF 1963–1972', in Thomsen, *The Odd Man Out?*, pp. 137–9; Lidegaard, *Jens Otto Krag*, vol. II, pp. 349–50, 469–81.
44 Poul Nyboe Andersen, *Det umuliges kunst: Erindringer fra dansk politik 1968–77*, Odense: Odense University Press, 1989, pp. 24 ff.; Christensen, 'Danmark, Norden', pp. 138–45.
45 Morten Rasmussen, 'How Denmark made Britain pay the bills', in Jørgen Sevaldsen, Claus Bjørn and Bo Bjørke (eds), *Britain and Denmark: Political, Economic and Cultural Relations in the 19th and 20th Centuries*, Copenhagen: Museum Tusculanum Press, 2003, pp. 617–37.
46 Andersen, *Det umuliges kunst*, pp. 45–56; Christensen, 'Danmark, Norden', pp. 145–7; and Morten Rasmussen and Johnny Laursen, *Denmark's Road to the EEC, 1945–72: The State of the Art*, Aarhus: History Department, Aarhus University, 2002, pp. 21–8.
47 Folketingstidende, 1971–72, B, II, Betænkning, Markedsudvalget, 25 August 1972, clmns 2794–852.
48 Jens Engberg, *I minefeltet: Træk af arbejderbevægelsens historie siden 1936*, Copenhagen: Arbejderbevægelsens Erhvervsråd, 1986, pp. 111–17.
49 Jens Otto Krag, *Dagbog 1971–1972*, Copenhagen: Gyldendal, 1973, pp. 87–8.
50 Morten Rasmussen, 'Ivar Nørgaards mareridt: Socialdemokratiet og den Økonomiske og Monetære Union 1970–72', *Den jyske Historiker*, 2001, no. 93, pp. 73–95; Lidegaard, *Jens Otto Krag*, vol. II, pp. 536 ff.
51 ABA/JOK PA/Krag's diary, 7 May 1971.
52 Rasmussen, 'Ivar Nørgaards mareridt', pp. 86–9; Lidegaard, *Jens Otto Krag*, vol. II, pp. 511–13, 542–6, 562–3, 569–71.
53 UM 108.Dan.A.2: Brussels mission to the Danish Foreign Office, no. 968, 22 December 1971, EF-Danmark udvidelsesforhandlingerne.
54 Ibid.
55 Rasmussen, *Sære Alliancer*, pp. 74–6.
56 Rasmussen, *Sære Alliancer*, pp. 76–81; Hans Martens, *Danmarks ja, Norges nej: Folkeafstemningerne i 1972*, Copenhagen: Munksgaard, 1979, pp. 116–22.
57 Lidegaard, *Jens Otto Krag*, vol. II, pp. 601–13; Engberg, *I minefeltet*, pp. 110 ff.
58 Krag, *Dagbog*, p. 252.
59 Peter Hansen, Melvin Small and Karen Siune, 'The structure of the debate in the Danish EC campaign: a study of an opinion-policy relationship', *Journal of Common Market Studies*, 1973, vol. 15, no. 2, pp. 93–129.
60 Alan S. Milward, *The European Rescue of the Nation-State*, London: Routledge, 1992.
61 Andrew Moravcsik, *The Choice for Europe: Social Purpose and State Power from Messina to Maastricht*, London: UCL Press, 1999.
62 These theories are presented in Johnny Laursen, 'Det nordiske samarbejde som særvej? Kontinuitet og brud 1945–73', in Johan P. Olsen and Bjørn Otto Sverdrup (eds), *Europa i Norden: Europeisering av nordisk samarbid*, Oslo: Tano-Aschenhoug, 1998, pp. 34–63; see also Johnny Laursen, 'Nordic ideas and realities: dynamics and images in Nordic cooperation', in Knud Erik Jørgensen (ed.), *Reflective Approaches to European Governance*, London: Macmillan, 1997, pp. 146–63.

63 Jens Henrik Haahr, *Looking to Europe: The EC Policies of the British Labour Party and the Danish Social Democrats*, Aarhus: Aarhus University Press, 1993.

64 Karen Siune, Palle Svensson and Ole Tonsgaard, 'The European Union: the Danes said "no" in 1992, but "yes" in 1993: how and why?', *Electoral Studies*, 1994, vol. 13, no. 2, pp. 110 ff.

65 Nikolaj Petersen, 'Denmark and the European Community 1985–1993', in Carsten Due-Nielsen and Nikolaj Petersen (eds), *Adaptation and Activism: The Foreign Policy of Denmark 1967–1993*, Copenhagen: Jurist- og Økonomforlaget, 1995, pp. 189–222.

3 From isolation to involvement

Ireland

Edward Moxon-Browne

Introduction

The uniqueness of the Irish case among 'newcomers' rests largely on its intense but ambiguous relationship with Britain. On the one hand, in 1949, Ireland left the British Commonwealth[1] but, at the same time, maintained agreements with Britain regarding both trade and migration which ironically foreshadowed similar degrees of integration in continental Europe ten years later. In particular, the establishment of a passport-free zone,[2] not to mention the continuation of a monetary union,[3] between the two countries pre-dated Schengen and the introduction of the Euro, respectively, by at least twenty years. Ireland's case is also unique in that its eventual approach towards EEC/EC membership was mediated, and moderated, by its relationship with the United Kingdom. While, on the one hand, wishing to distance itself from its nearby neighbour and historic colonizer, it shared many of its sentiments regarding European integration and, more relevant for our purpose here, was constrained in its approach to European integration by its dependence upon British policy positions with which it had little in common. The experience of EU membership for Ireland provides the context within which, paradoxically perhaps, it has been able to exhibit the greatest freedom of manoeuvre *vis-à-vis* its neighbour: entering the European Monetary System (EMS) in 1979 and adopting the Euro in 2002, for example.[4]

The broader implications, however, of the Irish experience should not be forgotten.[5] Although the Irish case is intrinsically interesting, its evolution since the 1950s has several instructive implications for the broader development of the European integration process. First, its relatively backward economic position in 1973 and its subsequent *volte-face* as a 'Celtic Tiger'[6] in the 1990s have provided a test bed for the redistributive policies of the EU. Second, the country's avowed policy of military neutrality has provided a challenge to the evolution of a common defence identity within the EU. Third, the fact that Ireland has always been the second smallest member-state provides a measuring stick for the notion that 'size does not matter' and that within the EU institutions, solutions to problems are sought by consensus, and not on the basis that 'might is always right'. Ireland has always been an advocate of this 'community method': the question is only how often this community method prevails. Fourth, although Ireland's approach to European integration could formerly be interpreted as highly dependent upon British policies, more latterly the development of Irish positions separately from those of Britain is a reflection of the degree to which the process of integration, despite its purported and oft-lamented erosion of national sovereignty, allows a small state to diversify its external dependence and increase its range of foreign policy options. This final point is relevant not only to other small states but it applies equally to many of the states that joined the EU in the first decade of the twenty-first century.

There are a number of well-known theories of integration which attempt an explanation as to why nation–states, whose sovereignty is a badge of their identity, are willing to dilute, pool, share, or modify, that sovereignty in the face of external challenges that seem to require new assumptions both domestically and in the international arena. It seems useful not to attribute to any one theory or approach a monopoly of wisdom about the integration process. However, those writers who see the integration process as a means whereby the state is strengthened (or at least its weakness delayed or disguised) seem to be vindicated by the Irish experience. This view is in stark contrast to the more traditional federalist[7] and functionalist[8] paradigms that assume a diminution of national sovereignty as part of the integration process. As we shall see, the motivation lying behind Irish interest in the European Free Trade Association (EFTA),[9] and subsequent formation of the Anglo-Irish Free Trade Area (AIFTA),[10] was not a desire to surrender or even vitiate national sovereignty, but rather to optimize national opportunities against a background of rapidly changing European scenarios. The fulfilment of Irish expectations, realized only by full membership of the European Economic Community (EEC), expressed itself in a complex balancing act between costs (in terms of supranational decision-making) and benefits (in terms of wider trade prospects and lucrative financial assistance). Although Milward is often regarded as the standard bearer of the view that the integration process 'rescues' the nation–state, his work can also be seen as an anchor to which several distinct but congruent perspectives are linked.[11] Milward's argument is that nation–states in the post-war period were faced with the dilemma of an increasingly transnational economic environment (which tended to erode national autonomy) and increasing demands from electorates for security and welfare (which tended to make such autonomy all the more necessary). Integration became, therefore, a way in which this dilemma could be mitigated, if not entirely avoided. According to Milward, governments remain in control in the integration process and the motive is to preserve their own capacity to act. The emergence of apparently supranational elites in Brussels is, according to this view, merely a mechanism through which national governance is preserved, not an end in itself. Other theoretical approaches can be seen to reinforce and refine what Milward is arguing. Taylor, for example, has portrayed the elites of EC member-states as being in a consociational relationship with each other. In other words, they make bargains among themselves to maintain their power bases in national settings.[12] Allied to this view is the concept of 'nested games', or two-level games through which national elites negotiate at different levels simultaneously – domestic interest groups and supranational policy-makers, often playing one off against the other.[13] The way in which convergent interests in different national settings can provide the impetus for further integration was conspicuous in, for example, the lobbying activity that preceded the 1992 project.[14] These approaches characterize, and are illustrated well in, the gradual absorption of Ireland into the mainstream of European integration. This is seen in attempts by the Irish government to bargain its way into transnational organizations; it is seen in its handling of domestic lobby groups; and it is seen in the evolution of public opinion which consistently views European integration as not only compatible with, but supportive of, national independence. The 'Celtic Tiger' syndrome constitutes perhaps the defining moment of this outlook: the success story was perceived as a distinctly national achievement, and yet no one doubted that it resulted from, and was an integral part of, Irish participation in the European Union.

Ireland and 'Europe' after 1945

Unlike virtually every other country in Western Europe, Ireland emerged from the Second World War having abstained from participation in it, and also having been relatively unscathed by it. The origins of Irish neutrality lay in what was seen as the British 'occupation' of the six counties in Ulster.[15] This was to make Irish membership in NATO in 1949 unthinkable since it would be tantamount to recognition of the border between the Republic and Northern Ireland as a legitimate international boundary. Irish abstention in the Second World War had several consequences for Ireland's international position in the immediate post-war period. First, the United States had viewed the Irish position with some dismay since the USA had come to Europe to help win a war in which in this case a European country seemed unwilling to participate: this led in turn to economic difficulties in Ireland in the late 1940s when the generosity of the United States towards the rest of Europe was not matched in Ireland. Second, Irish neutrality left a sour taste in the mouth of the British government which saw the neighbouring island as a 'soft underbelly' that might have been prone to German attack.[16] Ironically, although Eamon de Valera earned in some quarters the bitter reputation of being a Nazi sympathizer, in fact, Irish neutrality had displayed considerable favour towards the Western Allies.[17] Third, Irish abstention from the Second World War played a significant psychological role in denying Irish public opinion the emotional involvement in the fate of Europe that was to lead in other countries to the genesis of an integration movement. The relative detachment of Ireland in the war served only to delay perceptions that the country's fate might lie in continental Europe; and it underlined the mental insularity that was itself the mirror of a geographical insularity that permitted the policy of abstentionism in the first place.[18]

Emigration has traditionally played a role that can be seen as psychological, economic and social. The post-war period in Ireland was characterized by high levels of emigration and this persisted right into the 1960s. Emigration had an ambivalent effect on the Irish political economy: on the one hand, it siphoned off discontent that might otherwise have exploded into a serious revolutionary challenge but, on the other, it deprived the economy of sections of society that Ireland could ill afford to lose: the young, the energetic, the educated and the enterprising. While emigration might have forged important economic and personal links with the European continent, the flow of migration was principally westwards to the United States, where language, family ties and greater economic rewards all combined to 'Atlanticize' the Irish psyche at the expense of potential ties with geographically more proximate destinations in Western Europe.

Geography itself played a role since the two preceding points can be explained in part by Ireland's geographical position. As a French historian had noted a century earlier, Ireland is 'an island behind an island'[19] and to this could be attributed its strategic peripherality that made neutrality possible (albeit as a 'free rider'), its lack of identification with the political parties of Western Europe whose right–left philosophical spectrum was at odds with the essentially nationalist[20] parties of Ireland, and the high degree of economic dependence on its neighbour with whom it conducted a lot of its trade, and was consequently under no compulsion to seek new markets elsewhere.

To peripherality we can add poverty. The Irish economy passed through dire straits in the 1950s: its industries were under-developed and uncompetitive; its agriculture highly dependent on a single but volatile market; and its trade partners too few to allow for real diversification. Poverty also meant a high degree of introspection on the part of successive governments. To many politicians 'Europe' was a remote and rather costly concept: Irish participation in international organizations, associations, or committees was sparse and this was the consequence of either a real lack of expertise within Ireland's elites, or real economic hardship which made attendance at meetings a luxury that could be ill afforded.[21]

The most important political issue which dominated the post-war period was the legacy of Ireland's partition in 1920. This affected relations with Britain, it legitimated neutrality, and it was the issue by which foreign relations were often judged. Ireland used its membership in international organizations to publicize the partition issue: this was, for example, seen as the principal benefit accruing from UN entry in 1955. The apparent obsession with partition in Ireland was not reflected in concern abroad. In European fora, delegations from other countries were bemused, if not irritated, by repeated allusions to this topic.[22]

There were, however, powerful economic forces that seemed to be 'pulling' Ireland towards greater involvement with countries on the European continent. By the end of the 1950s, Ireland's economic choices were beginning to be constrained by external events over which it had little control. Having joined the Organization for European Economic Cooperation (OEEC) comfortably as it was a loose inter-governmental organization that gave Irish politicians their first experience of post-war continental thinking, the parting of the ways between EFTA and the EEC in 1959 caught Ireland in a uniquely awkward position.

Having stood back from the EEC largely because Britain had done so, but also in the realization that its economy could not have withstood the competition in any event, Ireland was chagrined to see itself ignored when the alternative EFTA was established under British tutelage in the Stockholm Convention. Although Ireland made last-minute, but largely token, gestures to be associated with one or other of these organizations, it proved to be too little and too late. During the 1960s, although it was not always made explicit, Ireland's policy towards the EEC was to wait until Britain joined. The intervening decade gave the Irish economy time to 'catch up' so that by 1973 when it finally entered, its economy was able to adapt, albeit with some derogations. For example, Ireland's labour market was to be protected, for five years, from an influx of foreigners seeking jobs.

Irish external trade relations turned out to be both an incentive towards, and a reflection of, greater interdependence. Membership of the EEC became the logical outcome of a more outward-looking strategy adopted by Irish policy-makers from the early 1960s onwards. Prior to that, economic policy had been based largely on industrial protectionism and a reliance on domestic capital formation and home-grown entrepreneurship. From 1960 onwards, the emphasis was on lowering trade barriers, and the creation of conditions in Ireland that would be more conducive to inward investment. Thus trade became a greater proportion of GDP as Ireland moved towards, and into, full membership of the EEC/EC.[23] While exports constituted only 32 per cent of GDP in 1960, this had risen to 38 per cent by 1973 (the year of entry) and 65 per cent by 1988. Likewise, imports that were 37 per cent of GDP in 1960 had risen to 45 per cent at the time of EC entry. Membership of the EC for Ireland responded to, and encouraged further, a need to open up the economy to broader and more diverse markets. At the same time as trade was increasing as a share of GDP, the commodity composition of Irish trade was also changing. In 1955, food, drink and tobacco made up 68 per cent of Irish exports, but by 1972 (on the eve of Irish accession to the EC), this sector had fallen to 46 per cent. The shift towards manufactured goods (12 per cent of exports in 1955, 40 per cent of exports in 1972) was again a key factor in the push to find new markets, and to protect traditional ones, by participating in the tariff-free zone of the EEC. The pursuit of EEC/EC membership was also driven by the need for more geographically diverse markets. An excessive reliance on the British market carried with it the risks of being unduly affected by cyclical changes in one country's economy. The percentage of Irish exports going to the EC (other than the UK) actually doubled between 1960 and 1970, while exports destined for the UK fell nearly 10 per cent in the same period. Thus, EC entry consolidated a diversification that had already begun. However, Irish trade with countries *outside the EC* also expanded after EC entry; and this expansion, while beneficial for the Irish economy, puts Irish EC membership in some sort of perspective.

It was in agriculture more than in any other sector that the prospects of EEC membership were to be most obviously beneficial.[24] First, Ireland had a relatively high proportion of its population in farming (in 1970 the EC-12 had 14 per cent of its workforce in agriculture against 27 per cent for Ireland). Second, agricultural exports were, and remain, important to the Irish economy. In 1988, two-thirds of Irish farm production was being exported. The Common Agricultural Policy with its system of guaranteed prices, import levies and export subsidies constituted a virtual 'goldmine' for Ireland and provided a very favourable context for productivity increases and a greater orientation towards exports. A buoyant agricultural sector also contributed to a wider prosperity in Ireland by stimulating demand for consumer goods.

The relationship with Britain was to undergo change in the 1960s. There were economic and political aspects to this reorientation. Northern Ireland became a burning issue between the two governments at exactly the same time as both were concluding their entry negotiations with the EC. Towards the end of the decade, and despite a warming of relations between Dublin and Belfast that was epitomized by the personal discussions between the two Prime Ministers, Sean Lemass and Terence O'Neill, the onset of violence in Northern Ireland, the subsequent introduction of the British Army, and the imposition of Direct Rule following 'Bloody Sunday' in 1972 all combined to put the 'national question' at the forefront of the political agenda in the Republic. EC member-ship, in addition to the various economic benefits that might flow from it, was also expected to carry a political bonus: as part of the universal objective of minimizing the significance of national frontiers across the EC, the border between Northern Ireland and the Republic would be rendered less conspicuous and less contentious. Within the context of growing cooperation within the EC, relations between London and Dublin could proceed without arousing as much unease as highly visible bilateral encounters.[25]

On the economic front, the signing of the AIFTA agreement in 1965 was to provide Ireland with a valuable opportunity to demonstrate to the Six its preparedness for wider competition within the EEC; and it also compensated for Ireland's exclusion from EFTA five years earlier. Despite the AIFTA, exports to the EEC/EC increased more rapidly than to Britain in the late 1960s, under-lining Ireland's need to participate in a wider tariff-free regime.

From the application to accession

The Irish application to join the EEC was lodged on 31 July 1961 and although this application preceded the British one by about ten days, the inevitability of the latter event was confirmed before Dublin made its bid. Despite being the first of four countries to lodge its application, the Irish were the last to have their request accepted and it was not until October 1962 that negotiations with Ireland opened. The fact that Ireland had been negotiating for a shorter time than other applicants when the veto by de Gaulle was imposed in January 1963 probably proved to be a blessing in disguise. It meant that less effort had been wasted, and it also meant that the Irish government had more time to assemble its own arguments in favour of its request for negotiations to be accepted. Dublin soon discovered that Brussels viewed economic problems as far more important than political issues such as neutrality or Northern Ireland. The fact that the Irish application lapsed simultaneously with that of the British underlined the extent to which Ireland had come to realize that accession without Britain would have been an economic disaster, not least because of the overwhelming dependence of Irish agriculture on the British market. As the Irish Prime Minister Sean Lemass told a group of businessmen in Cork in November 1962, 'a failure of the British negotiations would require us to reconsider our position in the light of circumstances which may then prevail'.[26]

The shock of the breakdown in the accession negotiations was almost palpable in both Dublin and London. It was clear that neither government was really prepared for such a reverse and both were quick to confirm that EEC entry was their eventual objective. The Irish Prime Minister spoke of 'taking every step which will further this objective and avoiding any that might make it more difficult to attain'.[27] This set the tone for Irish government policy during the next few years: various alternatives were mooted but always within the parameters of eventual Community membership. First, the idea of a bilateral trade agreement with the EEC was floated but this seemed unlikely to be of much benefit in the context of the General Agreement on Tariffs and Trade (GATT) rules. Second, membership of EFTA would hold some attraction if it played a part in bridging the gap between the EEC and its potential new members but, unless the scope of EFTA was extended to include agriculture, the benefits for Ireland would be negligible or even non-existent. Third, membership of the GATT which had been explored tentatively in 1960 assumed a new relevance if EEC membership was to be delayed; and the prospect of tariff-cutting in the new Kennedy Round was, in any case, likely to create a more competitive international commercial environment. Fourth, and perhaps inevitably, the bilateral trade relationship with Britain remained of paramount importance. Although this bilateral relationship was unlikely to provide all the answers to the Irish predicament, it was inevitably part of almost any solution given the amount of trade between the two countries.

While Ireland's external trading environment remained fluid, the government was nonetheless determined to continue with a variety of measures designed to make the economy more competitive either in preparation for eventual EEC entry or simply to survive in an increasingly interdependent Europe. Between 1961 and 1963, a whole series of reports were commissioned into all the main sectors of the Irish economy.[28] The purpose was to restructure; to plan manpower needs; to provide training and retraining; and to assist exports in a more proactive way. The drive towards a more competitive economy was stimulated by a series of tariff cuts in the wake of the 50 per cent reductions achieved by both the EEC and EFTA. Ireland was the only democracy in Western Europe not to have begun tariff reductions and the 10 per cent annual cuts scheduled for 1963, 1964 and 1965, respectively, were a belated attempt to catch up.

Against a background of uncertainty over which the Irish government had little control, it was, perhaps, inevitable that the bilateral trading relationship with Britain should become a welcome port in the storm. London was, if

anything, slightly more pessimistic than Dublin about prospects for an early resolution of the impasse, facing enlargement, in Paris. Discussions between the two
countries centred on ways to exploit greater benefits from their existing trade
relationship. Essentially this meant making it easier for British manufactured
exports to penetrate the Irish market in return for Britain being more generous
towards Irish food exports, especially meat and dairy produce where Ireland was
in competition with agreements preferential to Commonwealth producers.[29] As
Ireland was already committed to some reductions in tariffs, it was pointed out to
the British that rising purchasing power in a more prosperous Ireland would be
good for British exports. On the other hand, the duties imposed by Britain on
Irish exports of man-made fibres had been a long-standing bone of contention
that the Irish now hoped would be resolved.[30]

The fact that Britain (and therefore Ireland) did not accede until 1973 was far
from being unwelcome for Ireland. It gave the government ten years to prepare
Irish public opinion, and especially Irish industry, for the rigours that membership would entail. It was clear that car assembly and textiles, for example, would
suffer once protection was removed. On the other hand, efficient enterprises and
especially those benefiting from foreign direct investment could do very well
indeed in an expanded market. In agriculture, there was a similarly double-
edged implication. The potential opportunities offered by the Common
Agricultural Policy were enormous in the context of exports from Ireland to the
rest of the EEC, but these opportunities could be exploited only if greater levels
of efficiency were achieved and, more importantly, the challenge of the British
market being opened to greater competition effectively met.[31] Paradoxically,
perhaps, the so-called Luxembourg Compromise of January 1966 had reassured
public opinion in Britain that the Community was not moving inexorably
towards the dissipation of national sovereignty where individual member-states
might lose their influence. The insistence by the French that unanimous voting
would continue to be the rule in the Council of Ministers helped to prepare
British opinion (and thereby the Irish government) for a second application.

The second application was lodged in 1967. Although there were no reservations expressed this time in Brussels with regard to the Irish application,
negotiations never really started, being thwarted once again by a French 'non'. It
seems clear that de Gaulle's motives for excluding Britain were now primarily
concerned with agriculture even though his suspicion that Britain might also act
as a Trojan horse for American foreign policy within the EEC was not insignificant. In his press conference held on 16 May, de Gaulle alluded to Britain's
propensity to import food cheaply from the Commonwealth with the result that,
if she submitted to the CAP, either her balance of payments would be crippled
by levies or she would be forced to raise consumer prices to continental
European levels, and consequently damage her competitiveness in exports.
Ironically, Ireland was not vulnerable to these accusations but, by 1967, the Irish
and British economies were so interdependent – especially in agriculture – that
an Irish membership bid without Britain would have been equally unacceptable
to France. Despite this second rebuff by de Gaulle, Ireland mirrored Britain's

determination to seek entry at the next available opportunity. Irish ministers continued to make regular visits to Brussels and the other capitals of the Six in an effort to keep alive the membership bid. In 1969 de Gaulle resigned and the prospects for British and Irish membership immediately looked brighter. Irish Foreign Minister Patrick Hillery met his French opposite number in New York shortly afterwards and was given to understand that a new move on EEC enlargement was imminent. However, it soon became apparent that the Elysee was planning to deal with the British application separately, and then proceed to the other three. This would have been disastrous for Ireland but, by meeting personally in London with Dutch Foreign Minister J.M. Luns, Patrick Hillery succeeded in convincing him (in his role as President of the Council) to link the Irish and British applications. At the ensuing Hague Summit, it was agreed to invite Britain, Ireland, Denmark and Norway to open negotiations. During a tour of the Six, Hillery emphasized to his hosts the need to avoid any disruption to Anglo-Irish trade. The role of the British negotiators proved crucial to the success of the Irish application. All three British chief negotiators in succession, George Thomson, Anthony Barber and Geoffrey Rippon, agreed to give informal but highly valued briefings to their Irish counterparts during the negotiations.[32]

The overall aim of Ireland in the accession negotiations was to enter the Community on the same day as the other applicants. What this implied, however, was that because Ireland was in some respects 'catching up' with the Six, it should be allowed to continue with some of its special measures designed to protect vulnerable sectors of the economy. The *acquis* had to be accepted, nonetheless, and was not itself open for negotiation. On animal and plant health, Ireland won the right to continue border controls to maintain the island's disease-free status. Industrial development aids and special arrangements for the motor assembly industry, which were important for employment, were negotiated successfully. Maintaining employment was also the rationale for a special five-year transitional period during which the Irish government could continue to operate its controls on the entry for employment of nationals of the member-states in the enlarged Community.[33] Fisheries proved to be the major sticking point because the principle of non-interference with the *acquis* was involved. During the negotiations, the Six had concluded an agreement whereby member-states would gain reciprocal access to each other's waters. This would have adversely affected the Irish fishing industry because the Irish fleet, not being a deep sea fleet, would not have benefited fully from the waters of other coastal states who, on the contrary, would have been allowed into Irish territorial waters on which Irish fishermen were heavily dependent. The compromise reached was that Ireland be allowed to maintain a 12-mile coastal zone (in contrast to a 6-mile zone for the Six) up to 1982 when the whole fisheries question would be revisited. On sugar beet, there was again a compromise. The Irish Farmers Association wanted a quota of 240,000 tonnes, but the Commission would offer only 140,000 (a figure raised to 150,000 tonnes after pressure, including protest marches in Ireland). Throughout the negotiations, the Irish team kept the principal lobbies back home informed. The concern was not simply that the

Oireachtas would eventually need to ratify the Treaty of Accession but also that a majority vote would need to be secured in a referendum: this was constantly in the mind of the chief Irish negotiator as he shuttled between Dublin and Brussels often losing a whole night's sleep in prolonged bargaining sessions.[34]

Following signature of the Treaty of Accession on 22 January 1972, and in the wake of a major expression of public support, Ireland finally entered the EC in January 1973. A referendum, required by the Constitution whenever it is to be amended (Article 46.2) was held in May 1972 and yielded 83 per cent in favour of accession. The Constitutional amendment, necessary to allow Community legislation to apply directly in Ireland, took the form of a simple insertion in Article 29 which effectively nullified clauses elsewhere in the Constitution that recognize the principle of national parliamentary sovereignty.[35] Following the conclusion of the entry negotiations, the government published a White Paper setting out the terms that had been agreed for entry, and explaining the rationale for, as well as the precise wording of, the forthcoming referendum.[36] In order to head off any opposition to entry in the referendum campaign, the White Paper made a powerful case for membership based on both the lack of alternatives available and the enhanced influence that Ireland might deploy in the enlarged Community. The section of the White Paper entitled 'Sovereignty' expressed with classic simplicity the justification for smaller nation–states embracing integration as a response to the forces of globalization more than twenty years before the term *globalization* became part of popular parlance.[37] Following the positive referendum result, the government turned its mind towards the secondary legislation necessary to enable membership to take place and consequently the European Communities Bill was enacted in the autumn of 1972. The ten-year delay in starting the entry negotiations had enabled the government to argue the case for entry thoroughly and persuasively. The inevitability of entry, once the British negotiations had succeeded, was probably the single most important factor in producing the decisive referendum result. The signing of the AIFTA agreement in 1965 had been significant in at least three respects: (1) it provided evidence to the governments of the Six that Ireland could compete on its own terms with Britain; (2) it demonstrated to the same governments that Ireland was aware of the realities of its trading position; and (3) it displayed a certain sophistication in the sense that it constituted a step backwards (towards dependence on Britain) in order to take two steps forward towards the EEC/EC.[38]

Conclusion

From a theoretical perspective, Ireland's gradual 'pull' towards European integration is marked most clearly by the *external* forces at work. First, the Rome Treaty (1957) had been signed with little consideration for Ireland.[39] Second, the EFTA was established without Ireland's participation not because of any antipathy towards Ireland but (what was worse) a feeling that Ireland was simply not a key player. Third, Ireland participated in the OEEC and the Council of

Europe but made very little impact on either and was affected by them only marginally. Nevertheless, participation in these organizations contributed to a valuable learning experience whereby neo-functionalist assumptions about *spill-over* can be seen to have some validity. On the one hand, a taste of international collaboration at the inter-governmental level made it easier for Irish policy-makers to contemplate participation in more sharply focused and supranational institutions. On the other hand, experience of collaboration in one sector whetted the appetite for collaboration in other sectors. There is evidence that growing (and diversifying) transnational trade flows led to expectations of greater political and economic cooperation. It is clear that new foci of loyalty emerged in Brussels and Strasbourg, and that these penetrated the hitherto insular (and Atlantically-oriented) Irish political psyche. Ireland was, therefore, increasingly affected by a 'process whereby political actors in several distinct national settings are persuaded to shift their loyalties, expectations and political activities towards a new centre'.[40]

A natural corollary of this process was that the social construction of 'Europe' itself underwent important change in the 1950s and 1960s in Ireland. From cultural and human rights dimensions, the concept of Europe became increasingly political and economic in content. More importantly, the metamorphosis of the self-perception of Irish people as spectators on the sidelines of Europe to being players within it, can be monitored in the 1960s when a range of social changes in Ireland (the advent of television, the liberalizing pronouncements emanating from Rome after Vatican II, and modest prosperity) nurtured and reflected a need for a more outward-looking economic policy and some adaptation to changes taking place (for other reasons) on the continent of Europe. Up until the 1960s, Europe had been perceived in public discourse as 'war-ravaged', 'divided' and 'a place of conflict'. Ireland, by contrast saw itself as 'peaceful', 'peace-loving', 'neutral' and 'immune' to ideologies such as fascism and communism that had torn Europe apart. As the pace of economic integration quickened, Europe was seen as demonstrably 'prosperous', 'strong', 'progressive' and 'united', while Ireland was relatively speaking 'poor', 'peripheral', 'dependent', 'divided', 'a place of conflict' and 'weakened by emigration'.

In fact, the so-called 'national question' haunted debates on European integration in Ireland in the 1970s.[41] Membership of the EC seemed to offer a prospect of resolving the conundrum of divergent national identities that lay at the heart of the Northern Ireland conflict. A common phenomenon in many EU countries is the propensity of citizens to be attached to dual, or even multiple, identities. Thus, Germans and Spaniards, for example, display strong attachments to regional identities in areas like Bavaria or Catalonia while simultaneously holding a national citizenship and a feeling of 'being a European'. Obviously, such multiple identities are exhibited with varying degrees of intensity in different parts of the EU, and it is also true that such identities are contextual in the sense of varying according to the individual's immediate environment. Thus, a Catalan will feel his regional identity most strongly outside Catalonia, and his national identity most strongly outside Spain. Germans and

Spaniards, for example, may be most keenly aware of their common European identity when visiting, say, Japan or the United States.

In the case of Ireland, a persistent ambiguity has existed whereby strongly nationalist traits in the political culture have co-existed alongside high levels of support for EU membership. Explanations for this ambiguity have centred around two separate but linked lines of argument. One line of argument suggests that Irish support for EU membership has been rather superficial, even if pragmatic. Thus, propositions in Eurobarometer surveys relating to support for fairly abstract concepts such as 'European unity' or 'more integration' command high levels of assent, while more specific questions about a 'common EU army' or 'paying more taxes to achieve European integration' yield less support. It is also true that the EU has been perceived as a primarily economic organization yielding distinct and measurable benefits in, for example, regional policy or agriculture, while its political implications such as greater coordination in foreign policy, a weakening of neutrality, or more majority voting, are viewed with only lukewarm enthusiasm. Another line of argument is that European integration, far from weakening the nation–state, actually serves to sustain it. Thus, for a small and peripheral state like Ireland, it is immensely important that the institutions provide a forum through which an Irish government can express its policy preferences on the same footing as the 'big players' like Germany or Britain. Ireland therefore supports the transnational role of the European Commission, and takes European Community law seriously. In some ways, the EU is viewed, like the United Nations, as an organization where the norms of international law protect the rights of the weak against the strong and provide a framework for the peaceful resolution of disputes according to procedures that are based on consensus rather than coercion. The relationship with Britain lies at the confluence of nationalist and Europeanist streams in Irish political consciousness. Ireland's European mission is largely grounded in the belief that the historic dependence upon, and even subservience to, Britain could best be overcome by membership of an organization where both countries are treated, nominally at least, as equals. '[T]he possibility that a small state might protect itself against large ones by means of the establishment of cross-national institutions ... seems to have been present in the Irish case.'[42] This transition from dependence to interdependence has intersecting economic and political dimensions. The geographical diversification of Irish trade, cemented by Ireland's adhesion to the EMS in 1979 and the Euro in 2002, has provided a much-needed stimulus to the country's tiny but highly globalized economy; and this has been reflected in a political 'diversification' in the sense that issues like Northern Ireland have been much more susceptible to solution in a transnational forum such as the EU, or in Ireland's bilateral relationship with the United States (which also reflects a vital economic component in terms of foreign direct investment).

At first sight, the paradox of nationalist and European sentiments co-existing may seem perplexing. For a small, newly independent state, the process of European integration provides a protective 'shell' within which distinct national interests can be stimulated and sustained. In terms of its welfare and security, the traditional twin objectives of any national interest, Ireland has benefited enormously from its membership of the EU, and so there is no paradox. The apparently negative reaction of the Irish electorate to the ratification of the Nice Treaty does not, on a closer inspection, contradict Ireland's attachment to the European integration project. On the contrary, because what was being offered was not clear, and in particular because it did not seem obviously to protect the interests of smaller countries like Ireland, there were healthy doubts about it, and who is to say how other EU electorates might have reacted, had they been given the opportunity of a referendum?

Despite the negative image of Irish support for the EU generated by the result of the first Nice referendum result (2001), it is worth emphasizing that Irish enthusiasm for EU membership remained consistently high throughout the 1990s at a time when support in many other EU countries was declining. Today, Ireland has the lowest percentage of people saying that they would be 'relieved' if the EU was abolished – only 3 per cent. In the rest of the EU the average is about 11 per cent. Even during the first Nice referendum, over 70 per cent of Irish people retained a favourable attitude towards the EU. Today, also, twice as many Irish people are satisfied with the way that decisions are made in the EU than are dissatisfied. In the context of this broad and consistently positive support in Ireland for the EU, the result of the first Nice Treaty referendum appears anomalous. It reinforces the argument that the reason for the low turnout, and the low yes vote was the absence of any campaign to explain the merits of the Nice Treaty. The fact that the second referendum yielded twice as many yes votes and a higher turnout must have been due to the intensive efforts made by the Irish government to 'sell' the Treaty, since the Treaty itself remained unchanged. In the second referendum many of those who had abstained came out to vote in favour of the Treaty. Opinion surveys show that at the end of the second referendum campaign, familiarity with the EU institutions and with the Nice Treaty was much greater than had been the case in the first referendum campaign. One-third more had become aware of associated developments: the Charter of Human Rights and the Convention on Europe. Most importantly, three times as many people claimed to understand what the Nice Treaty was about in October 2002 than had done so sixteen months earlier.[43] The first Nice Treaty referendum result in Ireland is sometimes depicted as reflecting Irish disillusionment with the process of European integration. Worse still, it has been seen as evidence that Ireland was selfishly denying to the countries of east and central Europe the benefits from which their own economy had so handsomely benefited. None of these arguments really holds water. What is more likely is that Irish voters were, in the absence of any attempt to explain it, genuinely puzzled by the implications of the Nice Treaty, and genuinely concerned about the remoteness of the EU and its institutions. The National Forum on Europe established by the Irish government in the wake of the first referendum débâcle, has gone a long way towards closing the gap between the public and the EU policy-making process both by giving anti-EU groups an arena within which they could air their concerns, and by 'bringing the Forum to the people' in various locations around the country. The success of the 'road show' approach was reflected in the numbers of people attending, the coverage in the local media and, if imitation is the sincerest form of flattery, by the instinctively introverted Joint Committee on European Affairs of the Irish parliament holding some meetings in regional venues.

What we have argued in this chapter is that the absorption of Ireland into the European integration process was not predicated on the assumption, most evident perhaps in the thinking of the governments of the Six, that the nation–state was, at best, obsolete economically and, at worst, politically dangerous, but rather that the nation–state needed to adapt itself to the new realities of a more transnational world. In this view, European integration for a 'newcomer' is perceived as a way of protecting its nationhood while, at the same time, maximizing opportunities offered by a more globalized world. The familiar 'contest' between globalization and European integration which became an intellectual fact of life in the 1990s, has had a peculiar resonance for Ireland. Exceptionally globalized in terms of the extent to which its political and economic fortunes are determined beyond its shores, Ireland derives from its membership of the European Union not so much a feeling that its nation–state has been 'rescued' *à la* Milward, except perhaps from its ex-colonial dependency on Britain, but more a release of innate possibilities in social, political and economic terms. If globalization makes life possible for the Irish economy, the EU makes that life better by building some sort of regional defence against a ruthless and unpredictable world trade regime. Regional integration is not, so this argument goes, simply a by-product of globalization, it is a conscious attempt to optimize national prospects within the relative safety of a regional and mutually interdependent set of policy-making procedures.[44] If this analysis is correct, the experience of Irish membership of the EU may be relevant for other member-states and, indeed, explains the preference of prosperous European states like Switzerland and Norway to eschew EU membership. In their case, the opportunities offered by globalization are greater than the potential dangers, and the need for 'regional protection' is proportionally less.

Notes

1   The *Republic of Ireland Act* in 1949 ended the ambiguity of de Valera's *External Relations Act* of 1936 which had enabled Ireland to conduct itself as a republic in domestic affairs while maintaining the King as a figurehead in external relations. The decision to leave the Commonwealth was not a necessary corollary of the new Act and in effect it had little impact in the sense that Britain continued to treat Irish immigrants as Commonwealth citizens. On the other hand, it exacerbated the division between North and South in Ireland by provoking reciprocal legislation at Westminster that copperfastened the position of Northern Ireland as part of the United Kingdom.

2   The common travel area between Ireland and the United Kingdom means that passports are not required for travel between the two countries.

3   Prior to Ireland's decision to join the European Monetary System (EMS) in 1979, there had existed parity between the two currencies since 1826.

4 In both cases, Irish policy deviated from Britain's: a measure of how far Ireland's economic self-confidence had developed since EEC entry in 1973 which was undertaken deliberately in tandem with British entry.

5 These implications are explored in David Coombes (ed.), *Ireland and the European Communities*, Dublin: Gill and Macmillan, 1983.

6 The term 'Celtic Tiger' is applied to Ireland's spectacular economic performance in the 1990s and is borrowed from the 'Asian' tiger economies of the 1970s. The 'Celtic Tiger' phenomenon is explored *inter alia* in Paul Sweeney, *The Celtic Tiger: Ireland's Continuing Economic Miracle*, Dublin: Oak Tree Press, 1999, and, more recently, Paedar Kirby, *The Celtic Tiger in Distress*, London: Palgrave, 2001, and Peter Clinch, *After the Celtic Tiger: Challenges Ahead*, Dublin: O'Brien Press, 2002.

7 See, for example, Michael Burgess (ed.), *Federalism and Federation in Western Europe*, London: Croom Helm, 1986.

8 See David Mitrany, *A Working Peace System*, Chicago: Quadrangle, 1966.

9 The European Free Trade Association (EFTA) was established by seven countries under British leadership and formalized in the Stockholm Convention. Its purpose was partly to provide a waiting room, and partly a more lasting alternative, for those countries that were either unwilling or unable to join the EEC at the outset.

10 The Anglo-Irish Free Trade Area (AIFTA) was established in 1965 as a means of promoting a smooth transition for Ireland from an era of high protection to conditions of free trade. AIFTA helped this transition to be effected with a minimum of disruption to the Irish economy and produced trade benefits that would themselves greatly assist the transition. The Agreement was essentially an interim measure to prepare the Irish economy for EEC membership – a goal that was achieved even before the transitional period prescribed in the Agreement had expired. See Denis Maher, *The Tortuous Path*, Dublin: IPA, 1986, p. 184.

11 See Alan Milward, *The European Rescue of the Nation-State*, London: Routledge, 1992.

12 Paul Taylor, 'The European Community and the State: assumptions, theories and propositions', *Review of International Studies*, 19??, vol. 17, no. 2, pp. 46–75.

13 Robert Putnam, 'Diplomacy and domestic politics', *International Organization*, 1988, vol. 42, pp. 427–60, and Andrew Moravcsik, 'Liberal intergovernmentalism and integration: a rejoinder', *Journal of Common Market Studies*, 1999, vol. 33, no. 4, pp. 267–306..

14 See, for example, William Sandholtz and John Zysman, '1992: recasting the European bargain', *World Politics*, 1989, vol. 27, no. 4, pp. 99–128.

15 An *aide-mémoire* from the Minister of External Affairs (S. MacBride) to the US Ambassador in January 1949 stated that any military alliance contemplated with

> ... the state that is responsible for the unnatural division of Ireland, which occupies a portion of our country with its armed forces, and which supports undemocratic institutions in the north-eastern corner of Ireland, would be entirely repugnant and unacceptable to the Irish people.
>
> (Quoted in Ronan Fanning, 'The United States and the Irish participation in NATO: the debate of 1950', *Irish Journal of International Studies*, 1982, vol. 1, no. 1, p. 38)

In the light of EEC membership, the Irish view has been considerably modified. Prime Minister Sean Lemass said in 1960 that a consequence of joining the EEC would be that 'we will be prepared to yield even the technical label of neutrality', *Dail Debates*, 1981, vol. 327, p. 1423. Foreign Affairs Minister Patrick Hillery said ten years later that 'we have never adopted a permanent policy of neutrality in the doctrinaire or ideological sense', *Irish Press*, 2 December 1970. In 1981, Prime Minister Charles

Haughey emphasized that neutrality is 'compatible with our membership of the European Community', *Dail Debates*, 1981, vol. 327, p. 1423.

16 Joseph J. Lee, *Ireland 1912–1985: Politics and Society*, Cambridge: Cambridge University Press, 1989, p. 245.

17 Ibid., p. 244.

18 Robert Fisk *In Time of War: Ireland, Ulster and the Price of Neutrality 1939–45*, London: Deutsch, 1983, *passim*.

19 Jules Blanchard, *Le Droit ecclésiastique d'Irlande*, Paris: Larousse, 1958, p. 11.

20 The exceptional characteristics of the Irish party system are outlined in John Coakley and Michael Gallagher (eds), *Politics in the Republic of Ireland*, 3rd edn, London: Routledge, 1999, where reference is made to the 'sheer difficulty of fitting the major Irish parties into the principal European families', p. 129.

21 See Miriam Hederman, *The Road to Europe*, Dublin: IPA, 1983, p. 22.

22 Tom Dwyer, *Irish Neutrality and the USA*, Dublin: Gill and Macmillan, 1977, notes American irritation with the Irish propensity to link neutrality to Irish unity in the Second World War while Miriam Hederman alludes to a 'lack of empathy' between the Irish and other delegations a few years later when Irish delegates used the Council of Europe to raise the issue of Irish unity. See Hederman, *The Road to Europe*, p. 35.

23 Rory O'Donnell, 'The internal market', in Patrick Keatinge (ed.), *Ireland and EC Membership Evaluated*, London: Pinter, 1991, pp. 7–41.

24 Patrick Cox and Brendan Kearney, 'The impact of the Common Agricultural Policy', in Coombes (ed.), *Ireland and the European Communities*, pp. 158–82.

25 On 30 January 1972, thirteen civilians were shot dead by British soldiers in Derry. The Irish ambassador to London was subsequently withdrawn and the British Embassy in Dublin was burned by an angry crowd following a protest march. 'Direct rule' over Northern Ireland was imposed on 25 March 1972. The political implications of EEC membership for Ireland (North and South) are discussed in Garret Fitzgerald, *Towards a New Ireland*, Dublin: Torc, 1973, where he argues in particular that Northern Ireland would benefit more from EEC regional policy within a united Ireland than it ever could within the United Kingdom.

26 Quoted in Maurice Fitzgerald, 'Ireland's relations with the EEC from the Rome Treaties to membership', *Journal of European Integration History*, 2001, vol. 7, no. 1, pp. 11–24, here p. 18.

27 Quoted in Maher, *The Tortuous Path*, p. 163.

28 Among topics covered were: export marketing; industrial grants; cotton and linen; leather footwear; paper and cardboard; motor assembly; and fertilizers.

29 Maher, *The Tortuous Path*, p. 173.

30 Duties were charged by the British on any article in which man-made fibre was used, on the full value of the article (irrespective of how little man-made fibre was involved) and even where the man-made fibre was of British origin. See Maher, *The Tortuous Path*, p. 174.

31 Fitzgerald, 'Ireland's relations with the EEC', p. 18.

32 Patrick Hillery 'Negotiating Ireland's entry', in James Dooge and Ruth Barrington (eds), *A Vital National Interest: Ireland in Europe 1973–1998*, Dublin: IPA, 1999, p. 21.

33 'We have been given a five-year transitional period ... during which we can continue to operate our present controls on the entry for employment of nationals of the member-states of the enlarged Community', *The Accession of Ireland to the European Communities*, Dublin: The Stationery Office, 1972, Para. 3.45.

34 Recalling those times, Patrick Hillery writes:

> All-night sessions meant sometimes leaving for the hotel and without going to bed, eating and flying to London. The memories of the night sessions are of poor sandwiches and disgusting coffee ... and pressures like a visit from President Malfatti of the Commission to try to convince me that I was holding

everything up. Perhaps my early training as a house doctor in the Mater Hospital in Dublin was good preparation for this.

(*How I Negotiated Irish Entry to the EEC*, Dublin: IPA, 1999, p. 24)

35 A new Article 29.4.3 read in part: 'No provision of this Constitution invalidates laws enacted, acts done or measures adopted by the Communities, or institutions thereof, from having the force of law in the State.' In Clause 4.8 of the White Paper the reasons for the amendment were explained thus: '[I]ncompatibilities exist between certain provisions of the Constitution and certain provisions in the laws of the Communities. For the purpose of our accession to the Communities it is necessary that the incompatibilities be removed.'
36 *The Accession of Ireland to the European Communities.*
37

The powers which, by becoming a member of the Communities, we would agree to share with the other member-states would in fact be enhanced rather than diminished by the cooperation involved. It is by this sharing of powers that the Communities ensure that they act in harmony for the benefit of all member-states and that the interests of all member-states are served in the formulation and pursuit of Community policies and actions.

(*The Accession of Ireland to the European Communities*, Para. 6.15)

38 Fitzgerald, 'Ireland's relations with the EEC', p. 20.
39 Except in relation to farming where the provisions of the Common Agricultural Policy suited Irish conditions.
40 Ernst Haas, *The Uniting of Europe*, Stanford, CA: Stanford University Press, 1968, p. 16.
41 In fact, the European Community was itself an object of sectarian division in Northern Ireland where it was perceived by unionists as being favourable to Irish unity and, by extension, to the Catholic viewpoint. See, for example, E. Moxon-Browne, *Nation, Class and Creed in Northern Ireland*, Aldershot: Gower, 1983, Chap. 9, pp. 154–66.
42 Coombes (ed.), *Ireland and the European Communities*, p. 63.
43 John O'Brennan, 'Ireland's return to "normal" voting patterns on EU issues: the 2002 Nice referendum', *European Political Science*, 2003, vol. 2, no. 2, 5–13.
44

Rather than be forced to choose between the national polity for developing policies and the relative anarchy of the globe, west Europeans invented a form of regional governance with polity-like features to extend the state and to broaden the boundary between themselves and the rest of the world.

(William Wallace and Helen Wallace (eds), *Policy-Making in the European Union*, Oxford: Oxford University Press, 1996, p. 16)

4 State interests, external dependency trajectories and 'Europe'

Greece

Kostas Ifantis

Introduction

Greece became the tenth member of the European Community (EC) in 1981. The country's drive for membership and its role and policies in the context of European integration have been the subject of notable political and academic interest over the years. For a long time, Greece was not regarded as a 'mainstream' member-state. However, since the early to mid-1990s, Greece has been seen as one of the most 'orthodox, pro-integrationist countries',[1] consistently advocating deeper, more rapid and comprehensive, pro-federalist policy initiatives. And this is something that enjoys widespread support both from the body politic as well as from the vast majority of the Greek people. It can be argued that Greece's sense of 'European-ness' forms an organic part of the modern national cultural discourse. An attempt to pin down the historical particularities of Greek national discourses, taken on their own, is beyond the scope of this discussion. However, a few words about the shifting (or non-shifting) perceptions and attitudes of Greeks towards post-war Europe and European integration and the extent to which these are embedded in dominant national cultural patterns will be useful. For Constantinos Tsoukalas, the image of Europe and more generally of the West in Greece, developed as a direct reflection of the image of Greece itself.[2] The most vivid illustration of this has been offered by Nobel Prize-winner George Sepheris who in the 1950s spoke of 'Greekness' as a transhistorical continuous process where European modernism and native primitivism would constantly enrich each other in a totally original symbiotic plenitude.[3] Through such discursive exhortations, Westernization and Europeanization appeared as prerequisites for social progress and economic development. This notion of 'belonging to Europe' was manifested in concrete political terms in the post-war international environment and especially after the emergence of the European institutional project. This was a turning point that transformed the cultural discourse into actual policy options and preferences. After having lived for more than a century as a typically Balkan country, Greece seemed able to actively place its present and project its future within the remarkable European integration process. As Tsoukalas has noted:

If the idea of Europe still functioned as the epitome of a universal civilization, Greece had, by now, no reason to feel permanently excluded in the long run. And consequently, for the first time since independence, the country seemed to be following the path that might lead towards the 'final solution' of its congenial discursive contradiction.[4]

The European prospect was further enhanced by very specific social and economic phenomena: Greek worker migration to Northern Europe, especially West Germany (and resulting re-migration, investment, etc.), shipping and tourism seemed to have been powerful sources not only of growth but also of cosmopolitanism and Europeanization. Although it is hard to sustain the argument in analytical terms, all three processes must have contributed to bridging the communication and societal values gap, depicting, as a result, Europe and the country's 'European destiny' in a concretely meaningful, positive and most attractive way.[5]

Therefore, in terms of the dominant element in the Greek political culture, commitment to Europe is central.[6] Moreover, viewed through the lens of Greek politics, the EU is seen as a vital framework for enhancing security – although lacking military capabilities – for a country which is located in a very dangerous region and perceives a serious external security threat, and is therefore very strongly security-conscious. European integration is a force for modernization, for the raising of living standards, for better public financing alongside fiscal discipline and for economic liberalization. It could be argued that the centrality of European integration in the Greek process of development and modernization represents the continuity of structural dependency of Greece on foreign power centres, albeit in a totally different form, in a totally different international framework, and with a totally different impact. As Loukas Tsoukalis has perceptively written:

> Greece combines some of the characteristics of Ireland and Portugal (the pursuit of economic development and modernization) with the feeling of external vulnerability found in a country like Finland. There is undoubtedly much more at stake in Greece with EU membership than in most other countries of the Union.[7]

Internal and external turbulence and extensive foreign interference combined to shape the country's systemic physiognomy. Throughout the twentieth century, Greece experienced considerable turbulence in its external and internal relations. Economically, it was classified in the category of a poor, agrarian, raw material-extracting, trade-dependent, and externally indebted nation; in short, under-developed. Politically, it was polarized, operating under personalistic and clientelistic political parties whose main purpose was to distribute the largesse controlled by an over-loaded state sector. At the same time, the history of the modern Greek state illustrates continuous trends of foreign intervention and interference by competing Great Powers. Greece had been under the constant influence and protection of the Great Powers throughout the nineteenth and twentieth centuries. There are three major themes – intimately connected and mutually reinforcing – of pre-1974 Greek politics: first, political polarization between the republicans and the royalists in the first half of the twentieth century, followed by a schism between communist and anti-communist forces in the post-war period. Second, continued interference by the Great Powers in Greek politics; and, third, frequent intervention by the military in politics. The role of the military, its dependence and independence with respect to the Greek political elites, is a recurring pattern in Greek politics from 1909 onwards. The impact of this on Greek political development has been quite adverse: between 1909 and 1974, Greece experienced five international wars, two civil wars (1917–18 and 1946–9), ten major military revolts, three periods of military/authoritarian rule, and two periods of foreign occupation during the First and Second World Wars.[8] In general, the term 'praetorian' can be used to describe Greece's internal political profile, while the term 'penetrated' fits its condition of near total dependency on the Great Powers.[9]

While foreign interference in Greek affairs had receded to relatively low levels during the inter-war period, the post-war years reversed this pattern drastically. Greece emerged from the Axis occupation as a thinly disguised protectorate of Great Britain and later of the United States. Four years of pre-war military rule followed by four more years of occupation had reduced Greece to a condition of political and institutional vacuum. The profound lack of political legitimacy coupled with a lethal internal struggle for power, and the strategic competitive arrangements among the Great Powers 'converged to produce a scenario allowing for maximum external interference in the affairs of Greece'.[10] In the context of the anti-communist state culture that dominated the post-civil war years, non-democratically accountable political structures such as the monarchy, the military, and institutionalized foreign influence and (in many cases overt) interference 'had been accorded *de facto* and *de jure* veto powers over crucial policy areas ("reserved domains") that systematically subverted the democratic process'.[11] The interventions, influences, and reactions affecting Greek polity during the 1950s and 1960s can only be understood if viewed within the scope of modern Greek historical experience, especially that of the immediate post-war era.

The Greek civil war began to take on large-scale proportions early in 1947.[12] This was happening at a time when Great Britain had notified Washington of its inability to support both militarily and economically the Athens government beyond 31 March 1947. In the framework of the Truman Doctrine, the USA stepped in to foot the bill and to replace London as the 'protector' of post-war Greece. The American aid which was poured into Greece was massive indeed. Between May 1947 and June 1956 this aid has been estimated to be in the region of $2,565 million – the highest per capita aid received by any under-developed country.[13] It is not necessary to illustrate in great detail the near complete dependency of the Athens government on external American support. The vital problem of the post-war and post-civil war Greek governments was political survival through the consolidation of the country's Western orientation. This led them to assume a posture of nearly total dependence on the USA. The issue of Greece's dependency on the USA and the American strategic interests in the Eastern Mediterranean, in which Greece occupied a special position as the sole non-communist Balkan state, is of paramount importance in the attempt to explain the country's European policy choices.

In this framework, the immediate post-civil war years were a period of unprecedented socio-economic change. Driven forward by a 6.6 per cent average growth, Greece was literally transformed from an under-developed country into a promising newly industrializing state. Manifestations of this rapid and in some cases impressive change were the rebuilding of an infrastructure destroyed almost completely by ten years of war, occupation and civil conflict; significant increases in literacy; fast urbanization processes; high rates of industrial production; and what Nikiforos Diamandouros has called, 'the gradual but unmistakable ascendancy in Greek society of cultural practices and values intimately linked with modernity'.[14]

In the mid-1950s with the outbreak of the Cyprus conflict, the political parties – especially those of the Left and Centre opposition – began to point out that Greek association with the USA and NATO 'called for national sacrifices because the United States was tilting in favour of more "important" NATO allies, such as Britain and later Turkey. Moreover, ... Greece was burdened with a disproportionate share of defence-related costs.'[15] Reactions to US tutelage emerged even stronger in the 1960s. The reduction in a perceived threat from the communist north coupled with a smouldering Cyprus crisis, resulted in even more frustration that had been gathering as a result of long years of US interference. A powerful movement sprang up – advocating more independence from US intervention and a move towards foreign policy strategies that could better defend and advance Greek national interests in Cyprus outside what was perceived to be a suffocating NATO (i.e., American) strategic interest framework.[16] The European policies of the Greek state that led to the 1961 Association Agreement with the EEC should be placed firmly in this external dependency context.

The imposition of the seven-year right-wing military dictatorship only temporarily contained the overt deterioration in Greek–American relations. Throughout the 1967–74 period, US foreign policy was supportive, by and large, of the military regime. Thus, in the mind of the vast majority of Greeks – both elites and the people – Washington was identified with the junta. Thus, the aftermath of the dictatorship found Greek political forces agreeing that Greece should attain the maximum feasible degree of independence from US interference and tutelage. The transition to democracy was accomplished with a minimum of disorder and violence, since in the minds of almost all Greeks, Turkey posed the greatest and most immediate threat to the country's territorial integrity.

Loukas Tsoukalis has identified three important background factors to the EEC accession debate and to the more general post-1974 Greek political discourse: one is the military dictatorship as the most explicit expression of US interference and tutelage; the second is the Cyprus crisis and the Greek–Turkish conflict; and the third is the charismatic personality of Constantine Karamanlis. The first two are more or less directly linked to foreign and security policy considerations.[17] Despite the ideological affinity between Greece and the member-states of the EEC/EC, analysis supports the view that Greek association with the European integration project had been primarily affected by structural factors, that is, considerations of national security interest, as well as geopolitical and dependency and anti-dependency strategic imperatives.

Greece and 'Europe' after 1945

Greece was the very first country to seek association with the EEC. For some, the European policies of Greece were born in the mid-1950s.[18] However, its backward economy, the still present impact of the Second World War and of the bloody civil war, as well as Greece's preoccupation with the Cyprus issue, meant that the country was by no means able to actively participate in the initial phases of the integration process that took place in the early 1950s. In the late 1940s, Greece was still tortured by the civil conflict, while by 1952 it had – without any public or even elite-level debate – become a member of NATO.

The issue of Greece's dependency on the USA is important here. In the 1950s, the politics of direct US *control* became the politics of heavy *influence*. Throughout this period, US diplomatic representatives interfered quite overtly in Greek politics. The US presence was multifunctional, often resulting in direct and parallel relationships between both Greek and US military functionaries and bureaucrats. Thus, Washington had a very heavy input, if not direct responsibility, on decisions dealing with the economy, the armed forces, the security apparatus and the like.[19] Other tangible forms of US influence would include threats to terminate or reduce American aid, economic dependency on the USA (especially for loans designed to correct balance-of-payments disequilibria), the promise and presence of direct investments in the investment-hungry Greek economy, and the like. But, at the same time, unlike the civil war period, political reaction to US interference was continuous and at times quite sharp.[20]

The 1961 Association Agreement with the EEC should be viewed in this context also. In the economic field, although American capital and investments had played a dominant role in the expansion of the Greek economy, at least in part because of the preferential terms accorded to them by the Greek state, the nature of US investment activity failed to significantly increase Greek export capabilities and to reduce the demand for imports. Thus, Greece's chronic balance-of-payments problem remained largely unresolved, while much of the country's industrial power and influence was concentrated in the hands of foreign investors with potentially dangerous consequences for the long-term prospects of the country's economic development.[21] Despite the achievement of high growth rates between the early 1960s and the early 1970s, this growth was not in practice export-led, and economic performance led to a balance of payments deficit, the formation of a gigantic but incapable public sector, sustained mainly through foreign public borrowing, and the recurring lag of government revenues behind the growth of expenditure.[22] In general, the political economy of post-war Greece has been marked by a series of patchy and fragmented economic policy frameworks, reflecting both the politicization of the economy and the powerful US presence in almost all aspects of Greek politics. Accession to the EEC was, thus, seen as a means to slowly but steadily reduce the traditional trade deficit of Greece and to help the country meet its financial needs, gradually limiting the continued American involvement in the Greek economy and American political and security interference.

The creation of the EEC and EFTA presented Athens – as well as other non-member-states – with the negative prospect of political and economic isolation. The state of the Greek economy was one of crisis, which combined a worsening of the balance of payments with stagnation in industrial investment and production.[23] Moreover, since the mid-1950s there had been a visible trend of growing dependency of Greek export trade from the Soviet bloc, which had the very serious potential to threaten the prospects of achieving some form of production quality and competitiveness. The Greek governments became very concerned with the scenario that the economy could tie itself to the under-developed socialist economies with profound political and security implications.

Monetary reform and a balanced programme for economic modernization allowed the right-wing Constantine Karamanlis government in July 1961 to sign the Athens Agreement, which, at that point, was the culmination of Karamanlis's effort to formulate and pursue a concrete European agenda. This agenda encapsulated his European vision, which by all accounts determined his European policies both before as well as after the dictatorship.[24] Pre-association negotiations followed a short period of ambivalence in Athens. Originally, Greece was more interested in EFTA, feeling that a partial association involving only the more developed countries 'would appear designed to further increase their wealth with complete disregard to the basic problems of the other peoples of the EEC'.[25] Instead there should be a broader union, strengthening Western unity by including all OEEC members, and guided by the need to promote growth in the less developed regions. Thus, right from the start, the Greek position was that integration must be accompanied by economic convergence. However, the negotiations for a broader union between the OEEC countries broke down at the end of 1958.

For Greece, the EEC choice was made for two basic reasons. One was the political aspects of the Rome Treaty which distinguished it clearly from the aim of establishing a simple free trade area. The EEC was seen as a strong institutional formation and an attractive financial support framework. Other political factors also played a role. Relations with the UK were under considerable strain as a result of the Cyprus issue. At the same time, Greek–German relations were rapidly improving.[26] The other was the inclusion of agriculture.[27] The British-sponsored EFTA which came into existence in May 1960 only covered industrial goods while Greece was mainly interested in agricultural products; tobacco and cotton alone provided 47 per cent of Greece's total exports in 1960. Greece's eventual decision was influenced by the particular content of the British proposal, which did not fit Greek economic and political interests at the time; the fate of that proposal; and the position of Germany, which – through a combination of political and economic reasons – eventually dropped the free trade area option. The EEC appeared the more attractive option[28] for a country desperately seeking support for its agricultural sector and the protection of its weak industrial base from rigorous European competition.

It should be made clear, however, that Greece's aim was association. Although, in the preamble of the Agreement we read that the Contracting Parties recognize 'that the support given by the European Economic Community to the efforts of the Greek people to improve their standard of living will facilitate the accession of Greece to the Community at a later date', during the unofficial talks in 1958, the objective seemed to be association, not full membership. Most of the arguments were in favour of an association status. The main reason was the realization that exposure to the EEC competitive environment would prove a very high hurdle to overcome. By all accounts, the Greek economy was too frail to be exposed to international competition and liberalization policies. There were conflicting views as well as differences between the positions of the two sides. Thus, full membership was not meant to follow automatically, the association being of unlimited duration.[29] It can be argued that the Association Agreement did not represent a major policy change. As Susannah Verney notes:

> Greece's relationship with its Western allies revolved more or less exclusively around the umbilical link to the United States. Initially, Greek participation in Western European organizations often seems to have been seen as a way to tighten transatlantic links, rather than as of intrinsic value on its own.[30]

In terms of national policy priorities, participation in the early stages of European integration was hardly central.

The Association Agreement was thoroughly and carefully negotiated for almost two years, and it was generally considered to be the most encompassing and complex agreement signed by the EEC with a third country for many years. The delay in the negotiation conclusion was the result of the EEC's realization that it was setting a very important precedent. At the same time, the delay can also be attributed to the difference of interests and views between the EEC and Greece as well as among member-states. On the economic side, the underlying principle was that there could and should be no balance between the commitments of Greece and the Community. The Greek government seemed to concentrate mainly on three areas: first, the provision of free access to Greek agricultural exports; second, the provision of financial support for the country's economic development; and third, the attraction of foreign investment. Hence the focus of the negotiations was on agriculture and financial aid. On agriculture, the agreement envisaged the eventual harmonization of agricultural policies. On financial aid, the agreement provided for the creation of a suitable framework and the setting up of common institutions, while Protocol 14 provided that the EEC would grant to Greece loans to a total of $125 million over a period of five years. The primary purpose of the assistance was to help the industrial restructuring of the Greek economy. A third issue was the elimination of trade restrictions and the gradual establishment of a full customs union. There the concern in Athens would centre around the impact on the prospects of Greece's industrialization as well as the implications for the country's balance of payments.[31] The agreement established a two-tier transitional period leading gradually to a customs union for industrial goods. No symmetry was required in the transitional arrangements of the two parties. Trade restrictions were to be abolished within a twelve-year period, and for some products manufactured in Greece at the time within twenty-two years, thus providing, a framework for protecting the emerging fragile Greek industrial sector.

The Association Agreement as well as overall European policies enjoyed only partial support among Greek political elites. Both the Right and the Centre aligned themselves behind this strategy. In the 1960s, these forces saw an association with the EEC as strengthening ties with the West – the EEC and NATO were seen as part and parcel of the same alliance – and consolidating the internal political status quo. Association with the EEC was seen by the government as a way to defuse the internal and external communist danger. The Left, on the other hand opposed it because they saw it as an attempt by foreign monopolies to overrun the country's economy. Industry would collapse while agriculture would be eliminated, leaving Greece as a cheap source of raw materials for the capitalist West. It should be borne in mind that the first application for association with the Six came from a country, a member of NATO, which had emerged in 1949 after a long and bloody civil war. In this context, it is easy to explain the reaction of the Greek Left. The EEC was denounced as a plot of allegedly revanchist Germany and the imperialists, while the signing of the Association Agreement was seen as putting an end to the last vestiges of national sovereignty and all hopes for economic development.[32] Only the Progressives, a small conservative party, advocated immediate full membership.

Overall, the debate was limited and primarily an 'intra-bourgeois' one. As such, its form, procedure and content reflected elite aspirations, anxieties and strains.[33] Participation was minimal, and consultation limited to elite level; no other groups and interests were encouraged to participate. In fact, evidence suggests that the prospect of integration inspired little enthusiasm in business circles. This is understandable given the structure of Greek exports and the low level of internationalization of the Greek economy. Moreover, the politically more weighty traditional sectors were better protected, albeit with inconsistencies, while modern, capital-intensive and technologically advanced industries were not granted protection. Under these conditions, it seems that Greek business interests regarded the association with scepticism, to say the least.

The absence of a broader societal debate has to be seen as a result of a weak civil society and a democratically under-developed state. Throughout the history of modern Greece, the state had occupied a hegemonic position in practically every aspect of Greek society. The gigantism of the state was exemplified in the over-employment in the public sector, the high amount of public expenditure as a share of GNP, and the extensive regulatory role performed by the state and the latter's overwhelming participation in economic activities.[34] The state's extensive regulatory role over the economy constituted a further strong expression of state gigantism with particular importance for the country's position in the integration process. It must be stressed, however, that the gigantic character of the Greek state did not mean a powerful or effective state. It was rightly described as 'a colossus with a feet of clay' in terms of its organizational and functional capabilities.[35] Gigantism resulted from a varied set of peculiar socio-economic conditions, the most important of which was the patron–client system operated by the political parties. Therefore, it would not be an exaggeration to suggest that the state was used by political parties as a means of distributing favours in order to maximize their electoral appeal.[36] The state's predominant position in the Greek socio-economic system also manifested itself in the over-centralization of powers, functions and competencies in the state apparatus located in Athens with very little regional powers and autonomy. Athens controlled practically everything at regional level. Greece was rightly considered as the most centralized unitary European state in the post-war capitalist West.[37] The role of the Greek state, therefore, suffers from a dual tradition of dependency. As a 'peripheral' nation, the Greek state has been dependent, both economically and militarily, on external powers (Britain and, after the Second World War, the United States), while at home, social institutions and voters have been dependent on state paternalism and the allocation of favours. Hence, this enormous and profound democratic deficit inhibited the emergence of autonomous interest representation. The government take-over of the trade union movement throughout the 1950s, the 1960s and to a much lesser extent in the 1970s was typical of the post-war policy preference to control social development and to stifle autonomous societal organization. In such an environment, organized interests failed to substitute for political parties as a source of societal input into the decision-making process.[38]

The physiognomy of the Greek state apparatus as well as the closed nature of the process affected the agenda and the outcome in terms of policy options, but at the same time, revealed the true nature of the decision to seek association status. In the context of the paramount security interests of the country and given its structural dependency status on the United States, Greece's association was seen as a link with Western Europe that would facilitate its western economic orientation without upsetting relations with Washington.

The military coup of 21 April 1967 inflicted a severe blow on the implementation of the Association Agreement. Responding to initiatives and pressure by the European Parliament, the Commission decided on 28 November 1974 to freeze the Agreement by limiting it to its 'current administration'. This decision brought prior arrangements of the association parties for the harmonization of agricultural policies to a standstill and the sum of $56 million still owed to

Greece under the Financial Protocol was frozen.[39] Tariff dismantlement, however, proceeded on schedule, and in 1973 the Commission entered negotiations with the military government to extend the tariff regime to the three new members.[40] In 1974, the deficit in agricultural trade with the EC meant that, from the Greek viewpoint, the association was not functioning satisfactorily. However, Loukas Tsoukalis concludes that its political and economic impact was considerable. On the economic side, the Association Agreement was part of the growing internationalization of the Greek economy, a process which aimed at opening the country up to a closer relationship with its Western European partners. It put an end to the anti-export bias of the tariff structure and gradually provided the framework for a higher degree of export-led growth. There was a big shift in the case of Greek exports to the EEC.[41] The manufacturing sector enjoyed notable growth rates while undergoing an important internal restructuring process. On a political level, there can be no full comprehension of the post-1974 Greek government reactions to the prospect of membership without taking into account the experience of the association.[42] Even at a tactical level, when Karamanlis pursued full membership, the Agreement was used as a strong basis for facilitating full engagement in the vigorous and effective campaign that followed.[43]

From application to accession

In 1974, Greece sought membership of the EC mainly for political reasons.[44] Membership was seen by the Conservative political elites as an opportunity to place the country in an institutional framework within which the development of an international political role and the shaping of a regional identity, free from US influence, patronage and intervention, would be facilitated. The application for accession was filed by the Prime Minister at the time, Constantine Karamanlis, who saw membership as the paramount factor in achieving political stability, consolidating democracy as well as securing the conditions (financial resources, large market) for the modernization of the Greek socio-economic system.[45] The collapse of the seven-year military dictatorship (1967–74) and the 1974 Cyprus crisis contributed immensely to reinforcing this policy direction. Because of the widely held view in Greece – and elsewhere in Europe – that American foreign policy was greatly responsible for the success and preservation of the Colonels' regime and the way in which US policies in Cyprus seemed to have consistently favoured Turkey to the detriment of Greece and the Greek Cypriot majority, successive Greek governments attempted to re-evaluate and redefine the relations with the United States. Application for membership, thus, should primarily be interpreted as a security policy decision. Membership was perceived as a means to balance US influence and power, while cementing Greece's Western orientation and commitment.

In general, the post-junta period was marked by the quest for an independent foreign policy. A quest which can be viewed as a belated expression of the independence trends that had been in evidence in Western Europe since de Gaulle first questioned US leadership. For Greece it meant an attempt to escape from the post-war situation where the norm had been the subordination of national interests to those of Greece's allies and 'protectors'. This quest was enhanced by the dominant perception of the Turkish threat in the Aegean and the American and NATO tolerance – if not support – of what Greeks perceived as Turkey's anti-status quo and expansionist aims. This perception contributed immensely to the emergence of a foreign policy consensus in Athens that cut across ideological and party lines. According to Van Coufoudakis, this consensus was based on the need for an independent foreign policy in view of the Turkish threat and the US attitudes and policies towards that threat; second, the assumption that an interest divergence existed between Greece and the USA; and, third, the rejection of American interference in Greek politics. Supported by this consensus, Karamanlis attempted to pursue a foreign policy agenda, which included a series of policy initiatives that would have been unthinkable before 1974.[46] Following the Turkish invasion of Cyprus in 1974 and the lack of any meaningful US (and NATO) response, Greece withdrew from NATO's integrated command structure. Karamanlis also started the first major renegotiation of the status of American military bases in Greece. The decision to return to NATO's military wing in October 1980 did not signify any serious normalization of Greek–American and Greek–NATO relations. Rather, it was a decision taken in the context of the pressing need to retain a credible diplomatic balancing strategy against Turkey.[47]

However, the most important decision was to immediately seek full EEC membership. By setting as a primary goal the accession of Greece to the EC, Karamanlis took a strategic foreign policy decision which had a most positive impact on the consolidation of Greece's newly established democratic institutions and on its formulation of long-term political, economic and security policies. For Karamanlis, membership would mark the end of a period of 'peripheralization', at best, and political isolation, at worst, while enhancing Greece's quest for more independence from Washington and thus balancing Turkey's perceived revisionist threat. This was reflected in the negotiations with the Commission.

The formal negotiations were concluded at deputy and ministerial levels at a conference between the Community and Greece, and they lasted from 27 July 1976 (opening ministerial meeting) until 23 May 1979 (concluding deputy meeting). However, it was by no means a smooth process. Adopted on 28 January 1976, the Commission's Opinion amounted to a qualified and lukewarm statement. The prospect of Greek accession was met with considerable scepticism. The Commission's key proposal was the establishment of a pre-accession stage, which was to precede any transitional period that might be agreed upon in the context of the accession negotiations.[48] Like Karamanlis, the Commission viewed the application as primarily political, designed to redress the balance of power between Athens and Ankara as well as enhance the prospects of a fragile democracy. Thus, the admission was a purely political decision, which carried 'a serious risk of embroiling the Community in the Greek–Turkish dispute, upsetting the balance the EC had formerly aimed to preserve in relations with its two Associates'.[49] The implication of the fact that the EEC placed itself at an equal distance from the two countries was that by accepting Greece as a full member, the Community would effectively become a party to the 'Aegean Cold War'.

The Commission's 'unenthusiastic' Opinion was met with great determination by Karamanlis, who in February 1976 successfully decoupled the Greek accession from a solution of the Greek–Turkish dispute. Although, it could have formed part of the EEC's debate on the wider political implications of Greece's accession bid, the timing was such – less than two years after the Turkish invasion – that the Commission's approach was raising questions of a strategic nature for Athens which it was not willing to discuss in the framework of its membership prospects.[50] Although Greece gave firm assurances that it would not block the development of EC–Turkish relations, it was unavoidable that the Greek–Turkish impasse would eventually become a Community problem. The Council of Ministers unanimously accepted without any qualifications the Greek application during the same month and, since then, the restoration of full symmetry between Athens and Ankara has remained an elusive and, in most instances, unattainable objective. It is worth noting that the Turkish factor did not emerge at all during the negotiations phase, while Greece pursued a conciliatory policy in the Aegean throughout the pre-accession period. This reflected the belief in Athens that both a crisis atmosphere and an explicit linkage of membership with Greece's diplomatic deterrence strategy had the serious potential of jeopardizing the negotiations process.[51] However, the security considerations were paramount, hence the serious political commitment behind the application for full membership and the subsequent emphasis on considerable flexibility and moderation as dominant elements of the Greek negotiating strategy with the EEC.

This was also reflected in the internal arrangements and the organizational structure of the Greek negotiating scheme, especially after the early phases of the negotiations. Responsibility was initially situated in the Ministry of Coordination. However, as the negotiations progressed, the Ministry of Foreign Affairs acquired a dominant role, a reflection of the highly politicized dimension of the negotiations. The team responsible for the finalization of the Greek positions, the actual conduct of the negotiations at deputy level, and the preparation for the negotiations at ministerial level, was the Central Committee of Negotiations headed initially by Nikolaos Kyriazidis, Deputy Governor of the Bank of Greece, under the auspices of the Ministry of Coordination. It could be argued that this choice reflected a specific negotiating preference and a focus on the economic dimension of the accession process. However, as soon as the negotiations started, it became evident that the issue of membership required a more political, pragmatic and flexible approach.

On the Greek side, the emphasis was on speed and conclusion of the negotiations at almost any cost. This meant that the assessment of the likely impact of membership entered very superficially, if at all, in the formulation of Greece's negotiation positions, and in any case, specific arguments rarely rose beyond a mere identification of those sectors of the economy that were considered 'sensitive' and general requests for protection. It is indicative of the Greek approach that defence of the association *acquis communautaire* was never considered as a bargaining line to adopt. Economic considerations were subordinated to political ones. This resulted in a clash between the government and Kyriazidis, as well as a rift within the negotiating team itself and led to the resignation of Kyriazidis in early January 1977, less than two months after the negotiations had begun. This event profoundly reflected the reality of the Greek government's political preferences. Membership acquired the status of an ultimate political and security objective, thus making the economic terms of entry an issue of an 'easy' sacrifice. Vyron Theodoropoulos, Secretary General of the Ministry of Foreign Affairs, was appointed by Karamanlis as the new head of the Committee.[52] At the same time, the Minister of Foreign Affairs took the lead, replacing the Minister of Coordination in the negotiations at ministerial level. The 'reshuffle' confirmed that, for Athens, the prospect of EEC entry was a foreign and security policy aim, 'grand strategic' in nature, indeed.[53]

It is impressive indeed, that the economic implications of accession were never considered seriously. For its accession to the EC, Greece accepted the *acquis communautaire* without raising any questions that might have delayed the negotiations. As Panayotis Ioakimidis has emphasized, the main aim of negotiations was not the modification of the *acquis communautaire* but some kind of formulation of transitional arrangements to allow Greece to adjust smoothly to Community conditions and to enable the Community to absorb the effects of the entry of a new member.[54] While in the 1973 enlargement, the transitional arrangements were exclusively for the benefits of the candidate-states, in the case of Greece, negotiations aimed at protecting the Community from the impact of the admission of a relatively under-developed country.[55] At the same time, the Greek government did its best to disentangle its own approach to membership from the very complex intra-EC debate about future transfers of resources, the size and distribution of EC funds and the implications of such funds for the coordination of economic policies within the EC. Athens repeatedly emphasized that Greece would not be seeking enormous economic support, its membership would not present the EC with any serious financial challenge, and that in any case, its impact upon the balance of budgetary advantages within the EC would be rather small.[56] William Wallace has pointed out that the Greek government was slow to appreciate the implications for the Greek economy, industry and agriculture or the rules of competition and taxation. In reality, the calculation of the economic costs to be suffered or the benefits to be gained never really topped the agenda.[57] For Greece, without reference to their historical context and to the wider Greek security imperatives, the terms of entry could never be considered satisfactory.

Moreover, the possibility, or indeed, the certainty of further membership applications from countries in a similar economic position to Greece clearly affected both Greece's and the Commission's attitude and approach. The unexpectedly rapid approach of Spain and Portugal towards the EC transformed the context of Greece's application. The prospect of membership applications by the other two countries posed a serious threat to the Greek membership timetable, 'for it created an environment in which "globalization" of negotiations and simultaneous entry seemed a comfortable choice to those who were viewing Greece's accession with increasing apprehension'.[58] Again, it was the determined personal intervention of Karamanlis that finally averted globalization, insulated Greek entry from the applications which followed it, and more or less secured the initial narrow context of the accession process.

The public debate throughout the negotiations was concerned primarily with the future path of Greece's political orientation. It elicited quite monolithic responses in favour of or against accession. This partly explains why the Karamanlis government pushed so hard to join the EC, as well as the decision to call early elections in November 1977. It was the desire to secure a renewed mandate on the issues of membership, the Greek–Turkish dispute, Greece's relations with the USA and NATO as well as the need to isolate the pre-accession process from electoral tensions.[59]

Although it is clear that it was systemic pressures that led to the decision to seek membership, this choice did not enjoy widespread support among the Greek political forces for the same reasons that the Greek government pushed for it: foreign and security policy considerations. Ultimately, it was linked to Cold War and strategic dependency on the US-dominated West. From the mid-1970s to the mid-1980s, the issue of Greek membership of the EC was a divisive one. The main pro-EC force was the conservative party of New Democracy. For the Greek Right, membership of the EC and the 'Europeanization' of foreign policy as well as domestic politics and economics appeared to serve as an alternative political ideology following the bankruptcy of the post-war anti-communism, which had been an almost exclusive political credo. Panayotis Ioakimidis has suggested that we can almost talk of an 'ideology of accession', which soon became a major attempt to finally fill the ideological vacuum that had emerged after the defeat and collapse of the expansionist vision of the *Megali Idea* (Great Idea) following the initial military successes against the decaying Ottoman Empire in the early 1920s.[60]

In the 1970s, the 'Eurosceptic' forces comprised the Pan-Hellenic Socialist Movement (PASOK), the rising force in Greek politics, and the Communist Party of Greece (KKE) – the orthodox/Stalinist party. Founded in 1974 by Andreas Papandreou, PASOK employed a radical language. Papandreou's tenure in Greek politics – after a distinguished academic career in the USA – had been flexible and cyclical, defying easy categorization.[61] His rhetoric fluctuated widely from period to period. In 1964–65, he expounded a brand of Keynesian liberalism but moved into Marxist (non-Leninist) anti-dependency discourse in 1968–74. Upon his return to Greece, he employed an anti-imperialist language similar to that often used in the Third World at that time and by 1977–81, he had moved towards a form of activist, anti-US socialism. In the 'Declaration of Principles' made public on 3 September 1974, Papandreou set as PASOK's fundamental goal 'the political and military independence of Greece and the creation of a state free from every foreign control or influence, a polity free of the control or the influence of the economic oligarchy'.[62] It was a strong anti-imperialist discourse with a heavy reliance on the 'dependency theory' developed on the basis of Latin American experience and as a criticism of neo-classical economic theories.

Minimizing US and Western patronage was seen as a prerequisite for improving national security, achieving national independence and eventually socialist change. The resulting rhetoric was the straightforward rejection of Greece's membership in the EC as pursued by New Democracy.[63] For the Socialists, Greece's accession could only take place on unequal terms, resulting in a distorted neo-colonial pattern of development. Andreas Papandreou saw EEC membership as a factor for further consolidation of the country's peripheral role as a satellite in the capitalist system.[64] Overall, the EEC structures would render national planning impossible, seriously threaten Greek industry, and finally lead to the extinction of the Greek agricultural sector.[65] It should be stressed, however, that in the period 1979–81, Papandreou and PASOK steadily softened their positions as indications increased that PASOK would win the elections.

KKE also regarded the EC as completely dependent and controlled by the USA. With Great Britain as a full member, it could be expected to adhere to the US policies favouring Turkey in the Aegean and in Cyprus. The prospect of membership was, thus, rejected along with the overall integration project as another even more powerful agent of monopoly capital and aggressive economic imperialism. The only left-wing force that was in favour of accession was KKE-Esoterikou, a rather small group which had split away from the KKE and had adopted a Euro-communist line, accepting the EC as the framework within which democratic socialism could be achieved and advocating the independence of the Community from the two Super Powers.[66] The lack of broad consensus for Greece's EC future until the mid-1980s impacted very negatively upon Greece's policy, objectives, and, above all, performance in the framework of the European integration process, especially during a time of revitalization and acceleration of the latter.

Conclusion: the quest for security and modernization

Greece's accession into the European Community in 1981 should be assessed as the most important development in the country's post-war history. Although the changing form of European integration creates problems for anyone attempting an academic analysis and the impact of membership on the policies and constraints of its constituent states (such as Greece) are not easily understood and evaluated, Greek membership has been and still is an event with 'far-reaching implications for both Greece's domestic politics and socio-economic structure as well as for its external orientation and international position'.[67]

To understand the Greek stance towards European integration, however, as well as Greece's process of Europeanization, it is imperative to take into consideration the salient features of the Greek international position. Throughout Greek modern history, the impact of foreign interference has been crucial. Greece was subject to manipulation and structural interference because of her strategic location and not because of her resources. On the other hand, the lack of resources made her vulnerable to interference once the Great Powers decided to act. Moreover, Greek fiscal insolvency, political instability, and, most importantly, ambitious foreign policies invited foreign interference. Greek reaction to foreign interference was rejection in principle and acceptance in practice. Interference in Greece, for the most part, depended upon the receptiveness of individuals and groups within the state to foreign overtures and upon the initiatives taken by individuals and groups, in and out of government, to solicit foreign involvement in their affairs. In either case, it was based usually on a perceived coincidence of one's own and foreign interests.[68]

Greek European policy-making throughout the post-war period has to be understood as part of the country's international security outlook and its structural dependency on the United States. Greek European preferences were largely shaped by the presence of US power and influence. Over-riding structural pressures – US influence and the Turkish threat – offered Greece specific policy choices. The Conservative Greek government chose instrumentally among (albeit very limited) policy options on the basis of which would be most likely to help her protect and promote very narrowly defined national interests. In the case of the Association Agreement as well as in the case of Greece's post-1974 membership drive, it was security considerations that shaped its European policies. It was always the realization that national security came to depend ultimately on the policies and preferences of others (the United States) that shaped what Susannah Verney calls 'a strategy of state'.[69] Greek dependency on the United States as the dominant structural force ultimately produced specific political outcomes in Greece's European policy both in 1961 and in 1974.

In the immediate post-war period, Greece's near total strategic and economic dependency on the United States left her as a bystander in the post-war quest for Western European unity.[70] In the late 1950s, the association process was not driven by domestic forces – for example, demands of powerful producer groups – but by the need to reduce Greek dependency on trade with the Soviet bloc, enhance Greek attractiveness for foreign (more European) direct investment, and improve the economy's capacity to generate employment which would more firmly anchor Greece in the Western capitalist world. The legacy of the Greek civil war meant that the 'communist danger' was always a paramount consideration. In the Greek case, the way in which the integration efforts in Europe were perceived and how they impacted upon policy-making were much more determined by international structural influences than by domestic pressures. Domestic considerations and policy preferences were certainly present but their impact only marginal. To the extent that an alternative foreign orientation was not an option, elite assumptions did not matter.

In the post-1974 period, EC membership operated as a means to change the nature of Greek–US relationship from tutelage to a more balanced one. Economic development, interdependence and geo-economics became very important variables to Greek strategy. Europe offered a powerful alternative to Greek foreign policy-makers and gradually led to the normalization of Greek–US relations through Greece's participation in the European integration process, especially in a period (the 1980s) when Western Europe as a whole had been actively addressing the issue of rebalancing its relationship with the United States.

Equally important has been the perception of the Turkish threat. Since the early 1960s, Turkey has been the main concern of Greece's security policy and the driving force behind most foreign policy initiatives. Actually, Turkey has dominated Greek security thinking and the formulation of its strategic needs and priorities. Most importantly, the 1974 Cyprus crisis was regarded as the major turning point in post-Second World War Greek security considerations. During the Cold War, Greece valued NATO more for its constraint of Turkey than for contributing to collective security against the Warsaw Pact. Consistent with this line of reasoning was the fact that it was Athens that attempted to engage the United States and NATO more actively in its defence and turn them into 'security-providing' hegemons. However, for most Greeks, the 1974 Cyprus crisis confirmed that the USA had never been an 'honest broker', and that NATO was not the institutional security safeguard they thought it was.

The Turkish invasion and subsequent occupation of the northern part of Cyprus were for Greece a highly traumatic experience, but also a basis for 'new thinking' in terms of security.[71] The 1974 crisis resulted in, among other things, the dual realization of, first, the limited value of NATO and US dependency as a security asset against the perceived Turkish 'revisionism', and, second, the limits of Greece's 'internal balancing' efforts, even with a dramatic increase in defence spending. Therefore, the quest for the adoption of a more sophisticated 'external balancing' strategy became, in the minds of the Greek policy-makers, the only way to enhance Greek deterrence. To this end, the European Community appeared as the most appropriate forum for Greece's 'external balancing' initiatives *vis-à-vis* Turkey.

At the same time, the modernizing effect of the actual membership has been profound. European membership since 1981 has shifted Greek dependency to a body whose common policies have become increasingly pervasive and penetrating in domestic society. Membership severely challenged the traditional relationship in Greece between the state and the economy, and even that of the state and society by reaching parts of the Greek economic and societal system US influence could not or did not seek to change. Until the mid-1980s, 'Europeanization' contributed to the consolidation of the newly established democratic institutions, generated pressures which set into motion administrative adjustments necessary for dealing with the 'burden' of membership, and balanced the Cold War foundations of the country's external orientation.[72]

Within the domestic party system, the endogenous movement for economic de-regulation in Greece was crucially strengthened by international, and specifically European, pressures.[73] For New Democracy in the mid-1980s, membership reinforced the shift away from state paternalism and ideological vagueness towards a more defined neo-liberal stance, along the lines of other centre-right parties in the EU. The New Democracy manifesto of 1985 and its 1989 programme expressed an ideological shift that was undoubtedly the result of a range of factors: it imported the predominant international centre-right philosophy, and it might even have occurred without European accession. Yet, the political environment created by EU membership – the cross-national networks and the new EU policy norms – also made a significant impact on how the party redefined itself in the opposition years of the 1980s. For New Democracy, modernization would come via less regulation, paralleling the philosophy of the single European market programme of 1985.

Structural constraints cannot be wished away, and the impact has probably been most profound in the case of PASOK, although its relevant ideological shift in domestic policy came somewhat later. Already in the late 1970s, Papandreou had mellowed his anti-Western rhetoric and his previous positions began to be strongly qualified. On the issue of the EEC, he dropped his outright opposition to accession as he prudently recognized that membership could affect the Greek–Turkish political and diplomatic balance in favour of Athens, thus offsetting – even to a limited extent – the perceived pro-Turkish stance of the United States and NATO.[74] As Kazakos notes, 'in the speeches of Andreas Papandreou, the ideology-producer of the party *par excellence*, a new realism in practical policy options was gradually and cautiously introduced'.[75] According to Kenneth Waltz, political structures encourage certain behaviours and penalize those who do not respond to the encouragement.[76] Although, faced with a still quite radical and unfavourable domestic audience dominated by leftist party activists, hegemonic communist discourse and aggravated by populist overtones, Papandreou's foreign policy could not but be the rational outcome of international systemic realities.

By the late 1980s, the trend towards foreign policy harmonization and integration with the EC and the West had moved into top gear. Within the Community, Papandreou emerged as a vocal supporter of European unity, pronouncing that conditions had changed drastically with Western Europe no longer dependent on the United States. At the end of the day, it can be argued that PASOK's foreign policy was not very different from that of its Conservative predecessors. In addition to defence policy,[77] it did not take Papandreou long to fundamentally alter a profoundly irrational European rhetoric and policy.[78]

In addition to systemic and power imperatives, several other factors also combined to bring about the mental reconciliation with Europe and the integration process, such as the realities of economic interdependence, best exemplified in the balance of payments crisis in 1985, and a learning process, not least the result of participation in the multilevel 'permanent' negotiation process in the Community institutions, etc. In the 1980s, PASOK's public sector strategy had fallen well short of its proclaimed socialist ideals. Its extension of state intervention lacked the coherence and consistency that some of its earlier statements had promised. Nevertheless, PASOK increased public spending and consumption, running up exceptionally high public deficits. However, its 1989 election manifesto recognized the need for a gradual liberalization of market mechanisms. Moreover, the flow of considerable financial transfers, which made Greece overly dependent on the EU, was certainly a powerful consideration, especially among some sectors of the social and production strata such as the farmers. The latter, particularly benefiting from these transfers, had become enthusiastic supporters of membership.[79] By the 1990s, the centre ground of economic policy debate had shifted significantly from that of the 1980s. The Greek Right continued to espouse free market economics and PASOK more fully committed itself to less statism. Echoing the policies put forward by the French socialists after 1984 or the British Labour Party after 1987, privatization became more and more compatible with socialist policies.

Throughout the membership years, European integration has posed a major challenge to the Greek state tradition and to those who have sought to uphold it. Especially in the 1990s, the Europeanization logic, with its new impetus reflected in the project of the Economic and Monetary Union (EMU), succeeded in cascading even further down the socio-economic system and beyond the narrow bureaucratic structures and (limited number of) elite level. As Featherstone has emphasized:

> A faltering endogenous momentum for economic liberalization was crucially helped and strengthened by the obligation to follow EU policies – notably the Single Market and EMU convergence – which upheld similar policy principles. Seen from the viewpoint of domestic Greek politics, therefore, EU membership and the Commission appear as both modernizing and liberalizing agents (as they do elsewhere in southern Europe).[80]

The EMU is a case in point: what seems to be a successful convergence strategy for joining the Euro zone, involved, without a doubt, important shifts of policy assumptions and practices that were bound up with the dynamics of the integration process itself and not just with predefined national policy objectives that integration was initially designed to serve.

It could be safely argued that for Greece, these are politics for modernizing/Europeanizing the state. Since the collapse of the military dictatorship, the country has managed to achieve admirable levels of affluence and political stability. EC/EU membership gave the Greek polity and economy a well-defined sense of direction and helped to transform the 'praetorian' Greek policy patterns. This process of transformation has led and keeps leading to a sizeable degree of European policy convergence, extending to policy goals and policy contents as well as to a convergence in policy instruments and policy patterns.

Notes

1 Panayotis C. Ioakimidis, 'Greece in the European Union: the new role and the new agenda', in Panayotis C. Ioakimidis (ed.), *Greece in the European Union: The New Role and the New Agenda*, Athens: MPMM, 2002, pp. 9-14.

2 Constantinos Tsoukalas, 'The irony of symbolic reciprocities: the Greek meaning of "Europe" as a historical inversion of the European meaning of "Greece"', in Ioakimidis, *Greece in the European Union*, pp. 75-89.

3 Quoted in ibid.

4 Ibid., p. 84.

5 Ibid.

6 Among others, see James Pettifer, 'Greek political culture and foreign policy', in Kevin Featherstone and Kostas Ifantis (eds), *Greece in a Changing Europe: Between European Integration and Balkan Disintegration?*, Manchester: Manchester University Press, 1996, pp. 17–23.

7 Loukas Tsoukalis, 'Greece in the European Union: political and economic aspects', in Ioakimidis, *Greece in the European Union*, pp. 37-45.

8 Theodore A. Couloumbis, 'Defining Greek foreign policy objectives', in Theodore A. Couloumbis and John O. Iatrides (eds), *Greek–American Relations: A Critical Review*, New York: Pella, 1980, pp. 21–47. On the role of the military in Greek politics, see Thanos Veremis, *The Military in Greek Politics: From Independence to Democracy*, London: Hurst, 1997.

9 Susannah Verney and Theodore Couloumbis, 'State–international systems interaction and the Greek transition to democracy in the mid-1970s', in Geoffrey Pridham (ed.), *Encouraging Democracy: The International Context of Regime Transition in Southern Europe*, Leicester: Leicester University Press, 1991, pp. 103-24.

10 See Theodore A. Couloumbis, John A. Petropoulos and Harry J. Psomiades, *Foreign Interference in Greek Politics: An Historical Perspective*, New York: Pella, 1976, p. 103.

11 Nikiforos Diamandouros, 'Greek politics and society in the 1990s', in Graham T. Allison and Kalypso Nicolaidis (eds), *The Greek Paradox: Promise vs Performance*, Cambridge, MA: MIT Press, 1997, pp. 23-37.

12 The Greek civil war lasted almost four years (1946–49) and it was bloody, costly, and damaging to the nation and its people. Estimates of battle casualties are staggering for a country of the size of Greece, which had just emerged devastated from the Second World War in which 550,000 people (9 per cent of the population) had perished. It has been estimated that between June 1945 and March 1949, the total cost in human lives to Greece was over 158,000 dead, of whom half were armed communist guerrillas and the rest were government troops, security forces, police, and civilians. Beyond these casualties, there were an estimated 700,000 refugees who were displaced from northern Greece, mostly to the Athens area. One should also consider the loss to Greece of 50,000 to 100,000 able-bodied men and women who fled at the end of the Greek civil war to the various countries of Eastern Europe and the Soviet Union. See, among others, Couloumbis *et al.*, *Foreign Interference in Greek Politics*, p. 117; Constantine Tsoukalas, *The Greek Tragedy*, Harmondsworth: Penguin, 1969; and Edgar O'Ballance, *The Greek Civil War*, New York: Praeger, 1966.

13 Theodore A. Couloumbis, *Greek Political Reaction to American and NATO Influences*, New Haven, CT: Yale University Press, 1966, p. 28.

14 Diamandouros, 'Greek politics and society in the 1990s', pp. 23–4.

15 Couloumbis, 'Defining Greek foreign policy objectives', p. 25.

16 Ibid.

17 'In Greece more than in probably any other Mediterranean country foreign policy issues have always occupied a central place in the domestic political debate.' See Loukas Tsoukalis, *The European Community and its Mediterranean Enlargement*, London: George Allen & Unwin, 1981, p. 107.

18 Konstantina Botsiou, 'Greece in the European Union: a historical account', in Ioakimidis, *Greece in the European Union*, pp. 17-36.
19 Alexis Papachelas, *O Viasmos tis Ellinikis Dimokratias: O Amerikanikos Paragontas, 1947–1967*, Athens: Estia, 1997.
20 This was especially the case after 1955 and the emergence of the Cyprus problem. See Couloumbis, *Greek Political Reaction to American and NATO Influences*.
21 See Stavros B. Thomadakis, 'Notes on Greek–American economic relations', in Couloumbis and Iatrides (eds), *Greek–American Relations*, pp. 75–90.
22 See Kostas A. Lavdas, *The Europeanization of Greece: Interest Politics and the Crises of Integration*, Basingstoke: Macmillan, 1997, pp. 57–66.
23 Tsoukalis, *The European Community and its Mediterranean Enlargement*, p. 28.
24 Botsiou, 'Greece in the European Union', p. 19.
25 White Book, 'Greece, the European Economic Community and a free trade area', Athens: Ministries of Coordination and Foreign Affairs, 1959, quoted in Susannah Verney, 'Greece and the European Community', in Kevin Featherstone and Dimitrios K. Katsoudas (eds), *Political Change in Greece: Before and After the Colonels*, London: Croom Helm, 1987, pp. 253-70.
26 'The new climate in Greek–German relations was indicated by the granting of a DM 200 million German state loan to Greece following Karamanlis' meeting with Adenauer in November 1958.' See Susannah Verney, 'The Greek association with the European Community: a strategy of state', in António Costa Pinto and Nuno Severiano Teixeira (eds), *Southern Europe and the Making of the European Union, 1945–1980s*, Boulder, CO: Social Science Monographs, 2002, pp. 109–56.
27 Tsoukalis, *The European Community and its Mediterranean Enlargement*, p. 28.
28 Verney, 'Greece and the European Community', p. 254.
29 Iacovos S. Tsalicoglou, *Negotiating for Entry: The Accession of Greece to the European Community*, Aldershot: Dartmouth, 1995, p. 10.
30 Verney, 'The Greek association with the European Community', p. 115.
31 Tsoukalis, *The European Community and its Mediterranean Enlargement*, p. 29.
32 Ibid.
33 Lavdas, *The Europeanization of Greece*, p. 105.
34 Constantine Tsoukalas, *Kratos, Koinonia kai Ergasia stin Metapolemiki Ellada*, Athens: Themelio, 1986.
35 Dimitri Sotiropoulos, 'A colossus with feet of clay: the state in post-authoritarian Greece', in Harry J. Psomiades and Stavros B. Thomadakis (eds), *Greece, the New Europe, and the Changing International Order*, New York: Pella, 1993, pp. 43-60.
36 On the Greek parties and traditions of clientelism in the 1960s, see Jean Meynaud, *Oi Politikes Dynameis stin Ellada*, Athens: Byron, 1974, and Elias Nikolakopoulos, *I Kahektiki Dimokratia: Kommata kai Ekloges, 1946–1967*, Athens: Patakis, 2001.
37 Panayotis C. Ioakimidis, 'The Europeanization of Greece: an overall assessment', in Kevin Featherstone and George Kazamias (eds), *Europeanization and the Southern Periphery*, London: Frank Cass, 2001, pp. 73-94.
38 Verney, 'The Greek association with the European Community', p. 118.
39 Verney, 'Greece and the European Community', p. 258.
40 The record of the association during the 1967–74 period reveals that the freeze was gradually compromised, since it proved almost impossible to decouple certain policy issues from tariff reductions. Thus, its effectiveness as an instrument of exerting political pressure against the regime was reduced considerably.
41 Tsoukalis, *The European Community and its Mediterranean Enlargement*, pp. 36–7.
42 Ibid., p. 33.
43 Botsiou, 'Greece in the European Union', p. 21.
44 Panayotis C. Ioakimidis, 'Greece: from military dictatorship to Socialism', in Alan Williams (ed.), *Southern Europe Transformed: Political and Economic Change in Greece, Italy, Portugal and Spain*, London: Harper & Row, 1984, pp. 33-60.

45 See Constantine Karamanlis, *The Ideal of a United Europe in Greece and the EEC: Political, Economic and Cultural Aspects*, Athens: Epopteia, 1979. Also, see Loukas Tsoukalis (ed.), *Greece and the European Community*, London: Saxon House, 1979.
46 Van Coufoudakis, 'Greek foreign policy, 1945–1985: seeking independence in an interdependent world – problems and prospects', in Featherstone and Katsoudas, *Political Change in Greece*, pp. 230–52.
47 Greece's reintegration followed protracted negotiations under the ever-present threat of a Turkish veto.
48 Tsalicoglou, *Negotiating for Entry*, p. 30.
49 Verney, 'Greece and the European Community', p. 261.
50 Tsalicoglou, *Negotiating for Entry*, p. 34.
51 Ibid., p. 35.
52 Vyron Theodoropoulos's professional career is indicative of the turn: he had served in Ankara, Istanbul, Cyprus, NATO and in Athens as Director of Turkish and Cypriot Affairs. He has published extensively on the Greek–Turkish relations and on the Cyprus question.
53 See William Wallace, 'Grand gestures and second thoughts: the response of member countries to Greece's application', in Tsoukalis, *Greece and the European Community*, pp. 21-38.
54 Ioakimidis, 'Greece: from military dictatorship to Socialism', p. 54.
55 Martin Blacksell, 'The European Community and the Mediterranean region: two steps forward, one step back', in Williams, *Southern Europe Transformed*, pp. 268–88.
56 Wallace, 'Grand gestures and second thoughts', p. 33.
57 Ibid., p. 24.
58 Tsalicoglou, *Negotiating for Entry*, p. 156.
59 Ibid., p. 44.
60 Ioakimidis, 'Greece: from military dictatorship to Socialism', pp. 55–6.
61 Theodore A. Couloumbis, 'Andreas Papandreou: the style and substance of leadership', in Theodore C. Kariotis (ed.), *The Greek Socialist Experiment: Papandreou's Greece 1981–1989*, New York: Pella, 1992, pp. 85–95.
62 PASOK, *Declaration of the Fundamental Principles and Aims*, Athens, 3 September 1974.
63 See Panos Kazakos, 'Socialist attitudes toward European integration in the eighties', in Kariotis, *The Greek Socialist Experiment*, pp. 257–78.
64 For an excellent treatment of PASOK's development and ideological profile, see Michalis Spourdalakis, *The Rise of the Greek Socialist Party*, London: Routledge, 1988.
65 Kazakos, 'Socialist attitudes toward European integration in the eighties', pp. 261–2. 'Dependency theory' as developed on the basis of Latin American experience and as a criticism of neoclassical economic assumptions was at the heart of PASOK's ideological identity. Extensive social and economic inequalities, marginalization on broad strata, and retarded growth through unfavourable specialization and profit extraction were all dependency products in a fundamentally peripheral state.
66 Verney, 'Greece and the European Community', p. 260.
67 Ibid.
68 See Couloumbis *et al.*, *Foreign Interference in Greek Politics*.
69 Verney, 'The Greek association with the European Community', p. 152.
70 Ibid.
71 See Yannis Valinakis, *Greece's Security in the Post-Cold War Era*, Ebenhausen: Stiftung Wissenschaft und Politik, S394, April 1994, p. 27.
72 Panayotis C. Ioakimidis, 'Contradictions between policy and performance', in Featherstone and Ifantis, *Greece in a Changing Europe*, pp. 33–52.
73 Kevin Featherstone, 'The challenge of liberalization: parties and the state in Greece after the 1993 elections', *Democratization*, 1994, vol. 1, no. 2, pp. 280–94.
74 At the same time, Papandreou reduced considerably the frequency and intensity of his anti-US and anti-NATO rhetoric, repeatedly declaring that a PASOK govern-

ment would avoid adventurist policies that might result in the compromise of Greek security interests. See Couloumbis, 'Andreas Papandreou: the style and substance of leadership', p. 90.
75 Kazakos, 'Socialist attitudes toward European integration in the eighties', p. 263.
76 Kenneth Waltz, *Theory of International Politics*, New York: Random House, 1979, p. 106.
77 Dependence on military equipment from the US remained strong and became crucial because of the Greek perception of a threat (Turkey). The highlight has been the decision to purchase an enormous amount of US military equipment, including F-16 fighter planes.
78 See Spourdalakis, *The Rise of the Greek Socialist Party*, p. 235. On the issue of ideological adjustment, see Kostas Ifantis, 'From factionalism to autocracy: PASOK's de-radicalization during the regime transition of the 1970s', *Democratization*, 1995, vol. 2, no. 1, pp. 77–89.
79 Ioakimidis, 'Contradictions between policy and performance', p. 39.
80 Kevin Featherstone, 'Introduction', in Featherstone and Ifantis, *Greece in a Changing Europe*, pp. 3-16.

5   In search of lost Europe

Spain

Ricardo Martín de la Guardia

On 18 July 1936 General Francisco Franco Bahamonde led a section of the Spanish Army in their uprising against the authorities of the Second Spanish Republic, which had been established in 1931. Throughout a civil war that lasted almost three years, he gradually overcame the resistance of the Republican forces. Before the end of the conflict, Franco had set himself to institutionalizing an authoritarian state: strongly centralist, it was characterized by the accumulation of power in his hands, as he became the Head of the State, the Commander-in-Chief of the armed forces, and the Leader of the Single Party, that is, the *Falange Española Tradicionalista de las Juntas de Ofensiva Nacional Sindicalista* (FET de las JONS). In this process, he received the support of large conservative sections of society, right-wing parties existing in the Republican years, and the Church, extremely influential on a population which was overwhelmingly Catholic. However, the regime's affinity with Fascism proved fatal when the Allied troops beat the Axis powers in the Second World War. In the new post-war order Spain, along with Portugal, became an exception in a continent whose Western half was on the way to democratization.

Consequently, in the aftermath of the Second World War, Spain was excluded from the emerging international order. At the Potsdam Conference, held from 17 July to 2 August 1945, the major allied powers, the United States, Britain and the Soviet Union, sentenced Franco's Spain to political ostracism on the grounds of her former collaboration with Nazi Germany and Fascist Italy; likewise, they ratified the decision taken at the San Francisco Conference two months before on the exclusion of Spain from the newly founded United Nations (UN).[1] Spain was, in fact, explicitly condemned by the UN on two occasions in 1946. It became isolated from the community of nations and could rely only on the support of Portugal, some Spanish-American countries – especially Argentina – and the Arab countries, apart from the Vatican. As Lorenzo Delgado Gómez-Escalonilla has argued, 'from the end of the World War onwards, the policy of Hispanidad, aimed at an understanding between Spain and Latin- or Spanish-American countries, was one of the essential elements in the Franco diplomacy'.[2]

Bleak as this outlook may have been, however, further developments made it impossible for such radical isolation of Spain to take place. The world bore witness to a process of confrontation between the two great powers, and the Cold War was unleashed. On 12 March 1947, in order to bring Soviet expansionism to a halt, US President Harry Truman presented his 'containment of Communism' doctrine in Congress as a guarantee for security, freedom and the preservation of the new world order. The conflict between the Soviet Union and the United States had a decisive influence on the future of Europe, and Spain was directly affected by this ideological division. For Europe, the new situation sparked off European integration; for Spain, the realignment of international relations led by the United States represented its eventual entry into the military, economic and political institutions of the Western allies.[3] In 1947 Spain had been denied the benefits of the Marshall Plan for the reconstruction of Western Europe, nor had it been invited to join the North Atlantic Treaty Organization (NATO) in 1949. In spite of these facts, on 4 November 1950, at a moment in the Cold War that was crucial in Europe and even more so in Asia, for Communism had succeeded in China and war had broken out in Korea, the UN changed their attitude towards Franco's regime by passing Resolution No. 386 (V), which declared that the 'Punishment' Resolutions of 1946 were ineffective. In the view of international public opinion, and according to a British diplomat's felicitous expression quoted in an article by Jean Creach which appeared in *Le Monde* on 10 November 1950, the Resolution was to be interpreted not as a 'victory won by Franco, but as a triumph of geography'.[4] In any event, from that moment on, Spain was in a position to normalize its foreign relations.[5]

Historiographical debates on the existence or non-existence of Franco's international policy as distinct from his conservative or traditional foreign policy seem at present inclined towards allowing that Franco did have a programme of his own.[6] During the years of rapport with the German and the Italian governments, the regime developed a conception of 'Europe' as inextricably linked with the 'sister nations' and therefore opposed to the supposedly decadent reality of the liberal democracies.[7] However, the outcome of the Second World War forced a radical turn in Spanish foreign policy and, of course, in the regime's idea of Europe. The loss of power of the *Falange* was felt in all state institutions, especially in the Foreign Ministry. The interdependence of the nation's economy and foreign policy, combined with her fitting into Cold War geographical strategy, now led Franco to leave it to his diplomats to normalize foreign relations: paradoxically, Europe's recognition was considered to safeguard Spain's domestic order. This motivation took precedence over Franco's ingrained mistrust of the outside world, where, in his limited view of foreign affairs, the three Internationals (Communist, Liberal, Masonic) ruled. For reasons which were exclusively pragmatic, then, 'Europeanism' soon beat autarchic *casticismo* in the shaping of Spain's international alignments. Bearing in mind that Franco's regime was a dictatorship, it is important to ascertain whether he was or not a key element in foreign policy decision-making. Both personal testimonies and historiography in general argue that he was rather prudent as to his involvement in foreign affairs. As long as the pillars of his regime were not called into question, Franco did not oppose the liberalization of relations with other countries.

Return to the international community

Spain's wishes finally came true between February and April 1951, when official relations were resumed with Greece, Belgium, the Netherlands, the USA, Luxembourg, Norway, Sweden, the United Kingdom and Denmark; the reconciliation with France and the Federal Republic of Germany took place respectively in December 1951 and November 1952. Despite such an advance, the Marshall Plan Administration persisted in refusing economic aid to Spain. Also, supranational organizations involved in European integration showed still considerable reluctance to regard Spain as a prospective member. In May 1951 the Council of Europe termed Spain a 'totalitarian regime' – like Yugoslavia – obviously implying that she could not sign their 1949 Charter. All in all, whether the political situation of Spain was acceptable or not, her relations and her entry into UN-dependent organizations were still problematic.

The following years also played an important part in the international recognition of Franco's Spain. On 27 August 1953 the Spanish government and the Vatican signed a new Concordat, which was to become the basic regulating framework for Church and State relations. Also relevant were the negotiations between Spain and the United States, culminating in three economic and military agreements which were signed on 26 September 1953 and which gave Franco financial aid in return for the establishment of US bases in Spain.[8]

In this way, once duly accredited, Spain finally succeeded in joining the UN on 14 December 1955, which implied not only the end of a ten-year period of ostracism, but also its partial integration into the existing international community: it could only become total when admitted in the European project that was being launched by the six founding members of the European Economic Community (EEC). In effect, the accession of Spain to United Europe lasted almost three decades as it necessarily demanded a complete transformation of the country which involved embarking on socio-economic modernization and establishing a constitutional and democratic government, analogous with those of the EEC members.[9]

In February 1957, in order to stimulate Spain's economic opening up and inevitable shift towards Europe, General Franco formed a new government.[10] According to Ambassador Raimundo Bassols, this 'technocratic' cabinet 'consisted of open-minded men, mostly Europeanists who, in their own true selves as well as in their actions, showed [themselves] to be prepared to put an end to [Spain's] humiliating isolation to the best of their abilities'.[11] As a matter of fact, one of the most fruitful periods for foreign affairs during Francoism (especially with reference to Europe) was due to Fernando María Castiella, Foreign Minister from that time until October 1969, when he was succeeded by Gregorio López Bravo. Certainly, one of his plans consisted of creating as many opportunities for dialogue as possible in relations with the EEC institutions. In a 'pro-European' and pro-NATO speech at Georgetown University, Washington, Castiella made himself clear: 'Conscious as we are of our European nature, we have tirelessly endeavoured to improve our relationships with the European countries.'[12] Nevertheless, it must not be forgotten that the reformist impetus of the new authorities could not extend beyond the existing constitutional framework: the lack of truly democratic political structures and the influence of Spanish political exiles on the Western European political parties and governments seriously restricted their chances of achieving this goal.

The Treaties of Rome had scarcely been signed when on 26 July 1957 the Spanish government appointed an 'Inter-ministerial Commission for the Study of the European Economic and Atomic Communities' (CICE), a branch of the Foreign Ministry. Its primary objective was to take whatever measures might be necessary to adapt the Spanish legislation and administration to the newly established framework, as well as to become a sort of preparatory school for Community expertise.[13] Whereas it must be admitted that CICE was hardly operative, it is no less true that on 21 July 1959, two years after it had been created, Spain joined the Organization of European Economic Cooperation (OEEC), an event which coincided with the implementation of the Economic Stabilization Plan.[14] Also a year earlier, in July 1958, Spain had joined the International Monetary Fund and the International Bank of Reconstruction and Development, the World Bank.[15]

In search of support for their intended approach towards the EEC, the Spanish diplomats, led by the Foreign Minister, spared no efforts to consolidate their relations with the Western democracies. Particularly significant were Castiella's visits to Great Britain and France in late August and early September 1959. At a Cabinet meeting on 6 September 1960, the assumption of diplomatic relations between Spain and the EEC was approved, a decision which endorsed the Foreign Minister's Europeanist policy and linked his success to that of the domestic economic Development Plan which had been launched by the government.[16] On 9 February 1962, Castiella presented an official application to the President of the EEC Council of Ministers to initiate negotiations between both sides. The text placed special emphasis on 'the European vocation of Spain, repeatedly restated throughout her history, [which] finds a new occasion to show now that the process of integration is shaping the ideal of European solidarity and making it come true'.[17] According to Castiella, the successful Spanish Stabilization Plan, conducted in collaboration with several international organizations, constituted an encouraging experience. Obviously, the Minister made no reference whatsoever to the political nature of the Spanish state.

The application had a great impact. In the media the aim of establishing links with Community Europe was regarded as one of the Spanish government's most important actions since the 1940s: in the eyes of the Spaniards, 'Europe' represented the possibility of rapid economic development and a brighter outlook. Personally, Franco saw the strengthening of the bonds with EEC institutions in purely economic terms, and avoided any political consideration.[18] On 30 December 1962, in a speech oozing carefully calculated ambiguity, he made his opinion clear:

About Europe, of which we are part, our feelings are clear and formally defined. As part of it, we have a definite European vocation, and as European, we defend relations on an equal footing which bind us in so far as they respect our personality.[19]

The Spanish proposal was, in fact, well received by the governments of some EEC countries: the French Gaullist government backed it up to a certain extent;[20] and the West German Economics Minister Ludwig Erhard even announced his support for the Spanish proposal.[21] The official EEC response was a cold silence, however. As a matter of fact, on 15 January 1962, in order to define criteria for examining future applications for membership, a report on 'the political and institutional aspects of accession or association with the Community' had been presented to the Parliamentary Assembly. In it, the following had been specified:

> Those states whose governments are not democratically legitimated and whose peoples do not partake in the political decision-making, whether it be directly or by means of freely elected representatives, cannot expect to be admitted to the society of peoples which form the European Communities.[22]

There was no way these norms could be avoided. If the only system of government that the EEC accepted was that of liberal parliamentary democracy, based upon the four fundamental freedoms, and if this was a prime requirement for membership, it was obvious that the Spanish regime did not fulfil it either in its origin or in its development. The Spanish question was current again at the European Movement Conference in Munich in June 1962, when members of the opposition to Franco both at home and in exile asked the European institutions to expel Spain until the regime was democratized – the so-called 'Munich Plot', in the eyes of the Spanish government and the official media.[23]

However, the Spanish government was not ready to throw in the towel in their aspirations to a negotiation process with the Six, as the Finance Minister, Mariano Navarro Rubio, reminded the Brussels authorities during his visit in November 1963. Soon Navarro's claim was seconded by the Development Plan Commissioner, as at the beginning of 1964 the following statements by Laureano López Rodó appeared in the French newspaper *Le Monde* and also in other European media: 'We have applied for association as a first step towards integration. I am convinced that France will back our entrance. As Erhard [now the Chancellor of West Germany] has assured me, "Europe is not complete without Spain."'[24] Not long afterwards, on 14 February 1964, the Spanish government formally submitted their second association request. The Community authorities replied four months later, on 6 June. The President of the Council of Ministers, Belgian Paul-Henri Spaak, informed the Madrid government that the European Commission had been granted permission to hold talks aimed at studying possible solutions to the economic problems that collaboration within the EEC framework would entail for both sides. Six months after the announcement, on 9 December 1964, two delegations, one from the EEC and the other from the Spanish government, finally met in Brussels, but negotiations proper did not start till one year later. Still, this limited rapprochement with Europe held out little hope for Castiella: 'They all want to round me up', he told his cabinet colleague Manuel Fraga.[25] Moreover, Castiella's fear was confirmed in June 1965, as Charles De Gaulle promised to veto any EEC enlargement unless the Common Agricultural Policy (CAP) were passed first.

It took four years, from 1966 to 1970, to define the relationship between Spain and the European Communities. During that time, the Prince of Spain, Juan Carlos, visited the seat of the European Commission, as well as France. The relevance of these state visits to the improvement of Spanish relations with EEC/EC countries playing a decisive role in Western politics would make him go to Paris once again in 1973 and also to Germany in 1972 and 1974.[26] Despite his efforts, the negotiations turned out to be particularly difficult due not only to the nature of the Spanish regime but also to the potential of Spanish agriculture, the economic sector that could be seen as a competitor by influential EEC/EC members such as France and Italy. The formula of 'association' would have led to rapid customs union, and was therefore dismissed. So was that of 'accession' for political reasons. As a result, in June 1970, the EC and Spain decided to conclude a purely commercial agreement in accordance with the then Article 113 of the Treaty of Rome.[27] As Article 1 stipulated an 'asymmetrical exchange of concessions', the Agreement was to be considerably more advantageous to Spain, which benefited from the most-favoured nation clause. The primary objectives of this two-way system of preferences were to consolidate and expand the existing economic and commercial relations between Spain and the EC and to create, in as short a period of time as possible, the appropriate conditions for trade between them to grow. The process was to go through two stages: the first would last a minimum of six years; the second stage would only be reached by common consent, as long as the necessary requirements were met. The Agreement was in force until Spain's EC accession.

One step forward: the long journey into the European Community

The implementation of the Preferential Commercial Agreement between Spain and the EC was altered by its northern enlargement to include Great Britain, Denmark and Ireland in 1973. The enlargement made it necessary to adapt the Preferential Commercial Agreement to the new reality of a Community of Nine – a first-rate commercial and industrial power with a population of some 260 million. In the autumn of 1972, at the request of the European Commission, an 'Additional Protocol' was negotiated so that the 1970 Agreement could be applied to the newcomers. The Spanish government was intent on deepening the relationship but domestic affairs were not favourable. The years 1973–75 marked an increase in Basque nationalist and extreme-Left terrorism, mainly from *Euskadi Ta Askatasuna* (ETA) and *Frente Revolucionario Antifascista y Patriótico* (FRAP); among their victims was the Prime Minister, Admiral Carrero Blanco, whom ETA assassinated in Madrid on 20 December 1973. A new cabinet under Carlos Arias Navarro made a last attempt to revive the regime: on 12 February 1974 a new plan of action was submitted to the *Cortes*, the Spanish Parliament, a plan that the media called 'The Spirit of 12 February'. Among other things, it specified Spain's position in Europe: 'In a European context where Spain inevitably belongs for reasons that are geographic, historical, and cultural, we once again reiterate our wish to take part in the integration process of Western Europe.'[28] Neither 'the Spirit of 12 February' nor Spain's participation in the Helsinki Conference helped to revive Spanish political life, however. In the twilight of the Franco era, the Head of State was taken ill and his regime was beset with serious problems both at home (terrorism, economic crisis, left-wing social upheaval, confrontation with certain sectors of the Church hierarchy) and abroad (the Sahara crisis). In September 1975, five out of a total of eleven death sentences for ETA and FRAP terrorists were confirmed in their court-martials. As a result, protest rallies were staged abroad. In view of these events, relations with the EC were affected to such an extent that on 7 October the European Council announced that 'under the present circumstances, negotiations between the EEC and Spain cannot be continued'.[29]

Three days after Franco's death on 20 November 1975 the monarchy was restored in the person of Juan Carlos I, whom Franco had designated as his successor in 1969. In December 1976 an Act for Political Reform was passed; its architect was the new Prime Minister Adolfo Suárez, appointed by the King on 7 July after the resignation of Arias Navarro. Only when the transition process towards democracy had been launched were relations with the EC resumed. This time, the Spaniards were determined to improve the old Preferential Commercial Agreement, still in force, by applying for membership. Many shared the view that the prospects would no longer be remote if political changes actually took place.[30] Some leading EC politicians made favourable statements. The German Foreign Minister, Hans Dietrich Genscher, said, for example: 'The democracies of Europe are expecting Spain as a partner ... That is why the Federal Government is keen on paving the way for Spain to become a full member of Europe.'[31]

In July 1976, shortly after Adolfo Suárez had designated Marcelino Oreja as Foreign Minister, the new cabinet issued a declaration of intent which highlighted Spanish integration into European and Community institutions as their primary objective. Unquestionably, despite noticeable differences between the political tendencies encompassed by his *Unión de Centro Democrático* (UCD), one of the most clearly defined priorities of Suárez's successive governments was this policy of Europeanism, a policy which, though nuanced, the main opposition parties and social forces more or less agreed with. It conveniently combined Spain's aspirations to resume her place in Western Europe with her eagerness to grant international legitimacy to the process of transition to democracy. In an interview published in *Ya* on 6 August 1976, Oreja left no room for doubts:

'There are no longer any political reasons for making it impossible to discuss Spanish integration into the EC, even though EC prerequisites for the eventual accession of new members still hold good.'[32] The goal of EC membership was to be attained with the support and involvement of the people and Parliament, for 'foreign policy-making, ... its benefits or disadvantages have a direct impact on the lives of all, hence it must be an essential ingredient in the activities of the representative institutions of the democratic system'.[33]

In effect, with regard to foreign policy-making during the transition to democracy, the principal political forces were unmistakably in favour of supporting rapid EC integration. Although the UCD was an ideological conglomeration of Liberals, Christian Democrats, Conservatives, Social Democrats and former Franco leaders, and consequently had a serious problem in defining a political programme, all its members were of one mind about Spain's quickly joining the EC.[34] The modernization of the *Partido Socialista Obrero Español* (PSOE) began in October 1974, when Felipe González was elected Secretary General at the Suresnes Party Congress in France. The support of northern and central European Social Democratic leaders such as Olof Palme, Willy Brandt and Bruno Kreisky had a decisive influence on his victory over the old Socialist exile leaders. The political and economic aid provided by the Friedrich Ebert Foundation, among others, served to consolidate González's position in the Spanish political scene after his arrival in Madrid in 1975. From then onwards, and at the successive Party Congresses, the moderate, reformist, deeply pro-European line prevailed not only because, as part of the PSOE tradition, it had been nourished by the European Socialist parties during the exile, but also because it was in accordance with the convictions of González and his team.[35]

Moreover, during the transition years, the moderate nationalist parties in Catalonia and the Basque Country declared their support for Spanish EEC membership. Both the then Christian Democratic *Partido Nacionalista Vasco* (PNV) and the electoral coalition *Convergència i Unió* (CiU), which has been dominant in Catalonia since 1979 and which is made up of the Christian Democratic *Convergència Democràtica de Catalunya* (CDC) and the Liberal *Unió Democràtica de Catalunya* (UDC), gave priority to establishing connections with their related European parties so as to make their claims known beyond the Spanish frontiers. The only political parties which criticized EC integration at the time were some far-Left separatists such as the Basque *Herri Batasuna* (HB) and the group which would eventually be known as *Bloque Nacionalista Galego* (BNG). In their eyes, the EEC was a superstructure which resulted from international capitalism and whose true aim was to keep the European peoples down in both national and social terms.

Trade unions and employers' organizations also played a significant part on the road to integration. The economic crisis that Spain experienced after 1975 and the weakness of democratic institutions led the Suárez government to promote a great social pact between political and trade union forces. Signed at the Moncloa Palace on 25 October 1977 by the UCD, the Conservative *Alianza*

Popular (AP – now called the *Partido Popular* – PP), the PSOE, the *Partido Comunista de España* (PCE), the PNV and the CiU, it was immediately endorsed by the two main trade unions, the Socialist *Unión General de Trabajadores* (UGT) and the Communist *Comisiones Obreras* (CC.OO.), as well as by the employers' organization, the *Confederación Española de Organizaciones Empresariales* (CEOE). By agreeing to wage restraint, left-wing parties and trade unions contributed to social peace; in return, the government committed themselves to effecting a complete fiscal reform and adopting a more extensive social policy so as to improve basic services such as health and education, among others. Consensus was thus the government's course of action;[36] it ensured them the implicit and explicit support of the social forces in their approach to the EEC, which was considered, after all, one more facet of the Spanish democratization process.[37]

The new regime was legitimized on 15 December 1978, when the Spanish people voted yes in a referendum on the Constitution. As Ecarnación Lemus has explained:

> seeing that neither the Monarchy nor the Reformist Coalition could build a democratic project on the past, the European integration provided them with a principle for the democratic legitimacy, with a guarantee for the democratic purity, of the reformist model.[38]

The transition to democracy continued with the general elections held on 15 June 1977, where Suárez's UCD was victorious, and culminated when the Constitution was sanctioned by referendum on 6 December 1978. During this process, on 27 April 1977, Spain ratified the International Covenant on Economic, Social and Cultural Rights and the International Covenant on Civil and Political Rights, both of which had been drawn up by the UN in 1966. Five months later, on 24 September 1977, she also joined the Council of Europe.[39] Likewise, on 4 October 1979, Spain also signed the European Convention for the Protection of Human Rights and Fundamental Freedoms.

In the last decades of the Franco regime Spanish society had undergone a radical transformation which played a crucial role after Franco's death. The developments of the 1960s and the 1970s had contributed to the growth of a middle class which, among other things, enjoyed the privileges of Western consumer standards, massive access to secondary and higher education and greater opportunities to travel abroad, that is, other than as migrant workers. It was this new society that made it possible for the political changes to be rapidly and peacefully effected. As a result of this process, the Constitution of 1978 defined Spain as a 'social and democratic state' where the rule of law was guaranteed; once the Constitution was in force, the state adapted all statutory regulations and all institutions, both political and socio-economic, to the Western European standard of democratic legality.

Perhaps for a change, Spain seemed not to be building castles in the air. While the President of the European Council, in the hands of the United Kingdom at the beginning of 1977, clearly stated that the enlargement of the EEC was an investment in Europe's democratic future, the Spanish authorities engaged on the political transition were ready to encourage Spanish accession. As the Interministerial Commission for Relations with the EEC had announced, one of the first foreign actions of Suárez's new, post-election government took place on 28 July 1977, when an application for full membership was officially submitted along with a formal request for negotiations to be opened. The upper echelons of the EEC received the request favourably and committed themselves to concluding talks on the 'reasonable terms and conditions', in the words of Henri Simonet, the President of the European Council.

However, even before it could become effective, this institutional commitment was severely thwarted by French scepticism with regard to Spain's future membership. According to a report published by the National Council of Young French Farmers in May 1976 and entitled 'Spain: a shock for Europe', the integration of Spain into the EC would be the most important political and economic disruption since the creation of the Common Market. To make matters worse, the French Prime Minister Jacques Chirac remarked that Spain's accession would be 'unbearable' for French agriculture; hence in the circumstances not only should Spain be left out of the Common Agricultural Policy but she should also content herself with negotiating a mere 'association' agreement, for France would not be able to back her application for membership.[40] Nor was the French Left, led by the Socialist François Mitterrand, initially willing to support Spanish membership. It was in an attempt to counter this opposition to his plans that Suárez toured the nine capital cities in late summer 1977. He reaped the rewards of his efforts when the European Council officially accepted the application on 20 September 1977. On 10 February 1978 the Prime Minister appointed Leopoldo Calvo Sotelo as Minister of Relations with the European Communities so that he could coordinate the Spanish position in the negotiations.[41]

On 19 April 1978, as applications for membership had been submitted by Spain, Greece and Portugal, and with a view to organizing the enlargement process, the European Commission presented the European Council with a report entitled 'Reflections on the Problems of Enlargement', also known as 'The April Fresco'.[42] The Commission insisted that the three Southern European applicants had put such a burden of political responsibility upon the Communities that they would not be able to avoid enlargement without renouncing the very principles on which they had been founded. Enlargement would also be beneficial in stimulating intra-EC trade and in contributing to the consolidation of democracy and the rule of law; on the other hand, great skill was required 'to enhance cohesion between member-states, make further progress on the way towards economic and monetary union' and to deepen the integration process.

The process of southern enlargement seemed irreversible. In fact, the Commission finally issued its positive assessment of the Spanish application on 29 November 1978. The European Council subscribed to the Commission's assessment on 19 December, complimenting the Spanish people on their exemplary political transition under way. Earlier in the year and in similar terms, the European Parliament had declared themselves strongly in favour of the integration of the three applicant countries. In Spain, on 27 June 1979, the *Congreso de Diputados*, the Lower Chamber, had adopted a motion in favour of EC accession by 285 votes to 2. In spite of it all, 'the April Fresco' could also be construed as a safety clause for the interests of the Community as a whole and of individual member-states. In fact, the French President Valéry Giscard D'Estaing did raise serious objections. On 5 June 1980, excusing it as a need to secure French economic interests, Giscard announced to the Assembly of Agrarian Chambers of France that his government intended to commit the remaining member-states to solving internal EC problems before any further enlargement. His attitude – also called Giscard's *coup de maître* or *Giscardazo* in Spanish – interrupted the negotiations from 30 June 1980 until the Common Agricultural Policy and the Community budget were revised.[43]

Although characterized by general political support and fairly understandable as a deference to domestic pressure group influence, Giscard's stance was notably at odds with the reassurances which Spain had received from the French government since the beginning of the 1970s: as early as 1972, they had clearly expressed their support for an arrangement beyond a mere commercial treaty. Moreover, Giscard's declarations contradicted his own previous analysis of the situation: for example, during his visit to Madrid on 28 June 1978 he had stressed the contribution of Spain to United Europe.[44] In October 1979 he had insisted again on the same point by remarking that 'the adhesion of Spain and Portugal to the Communities will place France at the heart of Europe' and that the enlargement was crucial for South-western Europe. It was obvious, then, that the powerful neighbour was changing her mind as the Spanish economic threat was gradually taking shape. In Spain, French dilatory tactics were joined by domestic difficulties: terrorism, a government crisis and the attempted *coup d'état* of 23 February 1981. Institutional normality was restored three days later, when Leopoldo Calvo Sotelo became Prime Minister. The government, intent on encouraging the EC negotiations, effected Spain's integration into NATO on 30 May 1982. As a matter of fact, in spite of France's dilatory tactics, the talks between EC and Spanish representatives did not decrease in frequency: between February 1981 and October 1982 six ministerial and eleven delegation meetings took place.[45]

The immediate return to constitutional legality was celebrated by the Community authorities. On 8 March 1981 the European Parliament went so far as to pass a resolution backing up democratic Spain and urging the European Commission and Council to take 'the measures that may be considered necessary for speeding up entry negotiations'.[46] Three days later, the President of the Council of Ministers of the Ten (for Greece was now a full member) restated their commitment to Spanish integration, 'fully aware of the political importance of the accession of democratic Spain to the community of democratic States'. In the final months of 1981, this goodwill facilitated talks with the Spanish delegation on delicate matters such as agriculture and tariffs. The

Spanish used any suitable occasion to remind public opinion and the EC governments that Spain would not renounce her membership plans, such as when King Juan Carlos was awarded the Karls Prize in Aachen.[47]

In June 1982, however, the Spanish application came to a halt again as France restated her basic objections to the southern enlargement of the Community. The new President of the French Republic, François Mitterrand, imitated his predecessor and insisted on the same old need for solving outstanding problems before advancing integration. Bearing this in mind, the European Council requested of the European Commission a supplementary study of the repercussions of Spanish and Portuguese membership on EC institutions. In Spain, this new French interference coincided with the end of the UCD era. Once the Socialist PSOE had obtained an absolute majority at the general election on 28 October 1982, the new government, under the leadership of Felipe González, continued the established pro-EC policy. At this point, from a total of sixteen chapters of the negotiations, six had been closed and another seven were at the final stage, though it must be borne in mind that as yet the most controversial aspects, that is, fisheries and agriculture, had not been discussed. The chapter on industry was not the main issue as the Spanish problems were being dealt with through a major domestic restructuring programme.

In effect, the industrial crisis worsened as it coincided with political transition. The transformation of Spain's industrial structure was absolutely necessary, but the UCD governments dared not present an in-depth reform programme for fear that reaction against it might end in social unrest. It was the Socialist government that faced up to the situation: in 1984 the Restructuring and Reindustrialization Law was passed in spite of trade union opposition and labour disputes. Aimed at increasing specialization (textiles, footwear), improving the quality of Spanish products (such as steel) and reducing those sectors no longer in demand (shipbuilding), it certainly benefited from the EC guidelines. At the same time, it redirected efforts to more competitive industries such as electronics or waste recycling. Although the social cost in resources and employment was enormous, the industrial restructuring was a necessary, eventually positive, step on the road to adapting Spain to EC requirements,[48] which is actually the reason why it did not lead to the end of the basic consensus between the social and political forces with regard to EC accession. Also, in spite of the protest against the social repercussions of the restructuring, trade unions accepted the government's assurances of its beneficial influence on the future creation of new jobs and wealth, especially when taking into account that EC economic aid would be provided immediately after accession.

As the Spanish government had undergone a substantial change, the European Commission reaffirmed their support for Spanish and Portuguese membership. In January 1983, González insisted that 'integration is a process that Spain cannot, will not, and must not give up. This process will be carried out with dignity and in defence of the interests of the country.' In order to gain the support of France, the Foreign Minister Fernando Morán played his cards right when he appointed Joan Reventós as Ambassador in Paris. Reventós, a conspicuous PSOE figure, had good contacts there,[49] although Felipe González was not very optimistic about the move and insisted that French Socialists were, first of all, French, and only after that would they think of themselves as Socialists.[50]

In 1983 the negotiation entered a new phase. At the Stuttgart European Council in June, France succeeded, among other things, in safeguarding her interests when a decision was taken to modify the Common Agricultural Policy. Finally, at the beginning of 1985, a transitional period of seven years was established for the integration of Spanish agriculture in the CAP, along with an additional extension between four and seven years for the more competitive fruit and olive oil, among other produce. In fact, Spanish membership increased EC land under cultivation by 30 per cent and for fresh fruit by 48 per cent.[51] At the Fontainebleau European Council in 1984, the EC Heads of State and Government had set the agenda for the final stages of the negotiations on Spanish and Portuguese accession, provisionally scheduled for 1 January 1986. In early spring 1985 the negotiations between Spain and the Communities reached their final stage: from 17 to 22 March a non-stop session was held to sort out the thorniest chapter, fisheries.[52] The negotiation of transitional periods had been one of the prime objectives of the Spanish delegates. As a matter of fact, the seventeen-year-long period Spain was granted for its huge fisheries fleet to adjust to Community policy was the longest term any member-state had ever been granted in any matter at all.

The government were delighted, and this was also reflected in popular attitudes. In March 1985 a survey carried out by the *Centro de Investigaciones Sociológicas* (CIS) showed that 53 per cent of those polled were quite in favour or strongly in favour of Spanish integration into the EC, as opposed to 20 per cent who declared themselves faintly in favour or not in favour at all.[53] Spain joined the EC at the beginning of 1986. The abolition of tariffs took place from 1986–92, and Spain had to introduce Value Added Tax from the very first day of membership; in other words, it bound her to the complete opening-up of her economy.

Spain in the European Union

As Javier Elorza, who was Ambassador to the European Union for several years, has written:

> it is not surprising that, regardless of the fact that from the very beginning Spain has been, by vocation, a staunch supporter of European integration, favourable to the construction of Europe, it is no less true that every opportunity has been taken to improve our position and to adapt or modify the *acquis* to our own advantage.[54]

In effect, the first years of membership served to adjust Spanish institutional mechanisms to the *acquis* and to consolidate Spanish participation in the EEC.[55]

After that, the first real challenge for Spain came along with her turn to lead the Community. Spain took over the Presidency of the Community for the first half of 1989. Throughout that period she poured her energies into all sorts of reforms, both at home (restructuring the Foreign Ministry) and abroad, with a view to offering an image of a country that was ready to face the complexities of EC demands, especially those regarding the entry of the Spanish currency, the *peseta*, into the European Monetary System. As a matter of fact, ever since joining, Spain has endeavoured to face the EC's serious challenges as efficiently and responsibly as possible so as to be on an equal footing with the more advanced members, trying by whatever means available to prevent the relegation of Spain on the grounds that she is a latecomer[56] and, therefore, a second-rate member. This is why from the very outset the Spanish governments worked from the beginning for Spanish membership of monetary union and for the development of a common foreign policy, an objective highlighted by González in 1988.

The 1980s was a decade of fluent, gradually closer relations between Spain and the two most influential EC member-states, Germany and France. The Spanish governments supported a common foreign policy; however, with regard to decision-making mechanisms, although Spanish governments have never actually opposed the extension of the powers of the European Parliament, they have insisted on a dominant role of governments in political negotiations in the European Council.[57] As Esther Barbé has put it:

> the model of European Union that Spain went for during the Maastricht process had a prime objective (social and economic cohesion), a prestige objective (European citizenship), and a Europeanist objective *par excellence* (Common Foreign and Security Policy, including European defence).[58]

By enthusiastically subscribing to the Treaty of Maastricht, the Socialist governments sought long-term guarantees for social and economic cohesion so that solidarity between Community members would transcend budgetary debates in the future. González's 'European Citizenship' strengthened the political side of the Community and was finally included in the text of the Treaty; at the same time, as far as security and defence were concerned, González advocated the merging of national policies into a common one where some Spanish priorities should be taken into account, especially those regarding relations with North Africa. In fact, at least since 1991, the Spanish governments have often urged that the Mediterranean should become one of the focal points of European action, leading to the so-called Barcelona process of structured EU–Mediterranean relations. Among the reasons for their insistence and up to a point, is still their fear that the end of Communism in Eastern Europe and Eastern enlargement could get the EU's undivided attention for many years to come.

To judge by polls, the majority of Spaniards welcomed the government's European policy-making: in 1990, 78 per cent of the population considered that joining the Community had been beneficial. Encouraging as this information may sound, though, 92 per cent of those surveyed admitted that they did not know the contents of the Treaty of Maastricht which were under discussion.[59] From the General Election of 1993 to the second Spanish Council Presidency in the second half of 1995, in a desperate – and successful – attempt to hush up PSOE in-fighting after several serious cases of corruption had come to light, the Socialist government emphasized its European vocation in defence of their past achievements. Even so, not only the Socialists in power, but also the Conservative opposition as well as the Catalan and Basque minorities shared the same pro-Maastricht attitude and supported Spanish membership in monetary union and keeping the resources granted by the Cohesion Funds. In the case of the latter, moreover, namely, the nationalist parties PNV and CiU, their position was certainly programmatic: their demands for drastically restricting the activities of central government were satisfied by Madrid's transfer of powers not only to Brussels but also to each of the autonomous communities into which Spain had been divided, according to the 1978 Constitution. In this way, they were able to participate in EU regional policy as well as take advantage of the powers regarding foreign relations which were provided for by their respective statutes of autonomy.[60]

There is no doubt that the second Spanish Council Presidency vindicated the Socialist government's Europeanist policy, thanks to the measures passed at the Madrid European Council on 16–17 December 1995, where decisions on the implementation of EMU and the reform of the Treaty of Rome were finally scheduled and Carlos Westendorp assigned the role of presiding over the committee which would be in charge of arranging a conference for this purpose, leading to the Amsterdam Treaty of 1997. In the end, alas, the Socialist government killed the goose that laid the golden eggs. In March 1996 their Europeanist discourse was not enough for the majority of voters to support the PSOE for another term in office, and the opposition PP led by José María Aznar won the election. AP had been re-formed in 1989 and changed its name with a view to taking on the UCD's political legacy. Ever since, the PP has kept the Europeanist flag flying in an attempt to silence left-wing criticism aimed at identifying it with Francoism. Its incorporation into the European People's Party (EPP) in 1992 definitely contributed to its finally being considered a moderate centre-right party.

The new Foreign Minister, Abel Matutes, maintained the same approach to Europe, as was to be expected since the *Populares* had backed the previous governments on most European issues. The main task of the new cabinet was to render Spain fit to become part of the Euro zone, as it eventually did in 1999, an unquestionable feat on the way to 'core Europe' membership. Regarding the pursuit of continued funding for social cohesion, the government fought hard to safeguard Spanish interests in view of the forthcoming eastern enlargement. Thus, they firmly demanded greater overall contributions from the richer countries to reduce the burden on Spain in terms of relatively reduced fiscal transfers, a bold stance finally rewarded at the Berlin European Council in March 1999. Likewise, in order to tackle the scourge of terrorism, the Aznar governments have fostered collaboration with other European police forces, especially the French, as well as cooperation in judicial matters.

Consensus between political and social forces on EC integration as such was an essential ingredient in the negotiation process for membership. Understandably enough, once accession had been achieved, differences arose between the European policies of the government and the opposition. The existence of different European models among the main political forces showed in the debates about the possible institutional reform of the EU. As opposed to more federalist visions of the EU espoused within and outside of Spain, the Aznar government firmly supported a strong role for national governments in policy-making, also informing their position in the Convention on a future constitution. In the Nice Treaty negotiations, it was their primary objective to put Spain on an equal footing in institutional terms with the larger and more influential countries. Ultimately, they failed in the sense that at twenty-seven, Poland was to have as many votes in the Council as Spain, two short of Germany, France, the United Kingdom and Italy; Spain will also lose fourteen seats in the EP, and (as the other larger states) one of her two European Commission members. Moreover, the draft constitution, as agreed by the Convention in 2003, actually foresaw the reorganization of voting rights and EP membership much more in line with population levels.

Nevertheless, Eurobarometer estimations, save for sharp fluctuations in specific instances, indicate the Spaniards' widespread acceptance of the European construction, even though, paradoxically, they consider the actual benefits as rather scanty. In their detailed analysis of the Europeanization of public opinion in Spain, Belén Barreiro and Ignacio Sánchez-Cuenca conclude that 'Spanish citizens are pro-European, but it is doubtful whether they have been "europeanized".'[61] In effect, the Spaniards support Europeanist policies in a vague, abstract way; the constant appeals to Spain's European vocation have turned 'Europe' into an ideal. Yet, they still value integration from a 'national' perspective. Their good or bad opinion of 'Europe' still depends on the domestic political and economic situation or cycle, for example, an increase in unemployment may be interpreted as a consequence of a decrease in EU funds, which may accordingly result in an increase in the number of those who have a poorer opinion of integration. This mechanism exerts a strong influence on the use that political parties make of the European issue as an electoral tactic: they appeal to the EU as a symbolic reference which justifies their political action at home. By transferring domestic policy challenges to the EU, decision-making can be legitimized. This may be somewhat uncomfortable, but in the end appears indispensable for making progress with Europe. The Socialists' industrial restructuring in the 1980s is a case in point. On occasion, these tactics can result in triumphs for Spanish governments, as at the Berlin Summit in March 1999, when Aznar succeeded in having the level and distribution of the Cohesion Funds extended until 2006.

The 1980s' outburst of enthusiasm for Europe was connected with what might be termed 'the overcoming of periphery trauma': EC accession was a milestone in the history of contemporary Spain, riddled with socio-economic crises, armed uprisings, civil wars; frustrations which had been reflected in the debates between 'Europeanists' and *casticistas*; between the defenders of Europeanizing Spain and the supporters of hispanicizing Europe.[62] In the end, albeit a latecomer, Spain opted for full incorporation into the EC. Of course, this atmosphere of optimism owed a great deal to the buoyant economy of the transition years, which confirmed the opinions of those who saw the EC as the epitome of prosperity. The collective consciousness of the Spanish population identified EC integration with what Franco seemed to have been incapable of offering, ignoring the fact that the rapprochement with the EEC actually started during the Franco dictatorship. Up to a point, 'Europe' was the answer to the historical challenge of the peaceful, gradual solving of some of the gravest deficiencies of twentieth-century Spain.

Notes

1 For a survey of Spain's international siege, see Florentino Portero's detailed study, *Franco aislado: La cuestión española (1945–1950)*, Madrid: Aguilar, 1989.

2 *Diplomacia franquista y política cultural hacia Iberoamérica, 1939–1953*, Madrid: CSIC, 1988, p. 111.

3 For the insertion of Spain into post-war capitalist structures, see Fernando Guirao, *Spain and Western European Economic Cooperation, 1945–1957*, Basingstoke: Macmillan, 1997.

4 Quoted in Raimundo Bassols, *España en Europa: Historia de la adhesión a la CE, 1957–1985*, Madrid: Política Exterior, 1985, p. 12.

5 Cf. Antonio Marquina, *España en la política de seguridad occidental, 1939–1975*, Madrid: Ediciones del Ejército, 1986.

6 See Juan Carlos Pereira Castañares and Pedro Martínez Lillo, 'Política Exterior, 1939–1975', in Juan Carlos Pereira (ed.), *Historia contemporánea de España (siglo XX)*, Barcelona: Ariel, 1998, pp. 720–6.

7 Cf. Rafael García Pérez, 'La idea de la "Nueva Europa" en el pensamiento nacionalista español de la inmediata postguerra, 1939–1944', *Revista del Centro de Estudios Constitucionales*, 1990, no. 5, pp. 203–40.

8 For a study of the negotiations that led to the signing of these Agreements, see Ángel Viñas, *Los pactos secretos de Franco con Estados Unidos*, Barcelona: Crítica, 1981.

9 For the challenges and problems inherent in the study of the process of Spanish integration into the EEC, see Juan Carlos Pereira and Antonio Moreno, 'España ante el proceso de integración europeo desde una perspectiva histórica: panorama historiográfico y líneas de investigación', *Studia Historica*, 1991, vol. IX, pp. 129-53 ff.

10 For a global approach to the participation of Spain in the process of European integration, see Antonio Moreno Juste, 'España en el proceso de integración europea', in Ricardo Martín de la Guardia and Guillermo Pérez Sánchez (eds), *Historia de la integración europea*, Barcelona: Ariel, 2001, pp. 167–214.

11 Bassols, *España en Europa*, p. 27.

12 Fernando María Castiella, 'La política exterior de España (1898–1960)', *Cuadernos Hispanoamericanos*, 1960, no. 124, pp. 5-18.

13 (A)rchivo del (M)inisterio de (A)suntos (E)xteriores (AMAE), leg. R-5746, E.25.

14 For a discussion of the economic and political consequences of the Stabilization Plan, still useful information is available in Carlos Moya, *El poder económico en España (1939–1970)*, Madrid: Tucar, 1975, pp. 181–243, as well as in Manuel Jesús

González, *La economía política del franquismo (1940–1970): Dirigismo, mercado y planificación*, Madrid: Tecnos, 1979, pp. 196–226.

15 See Joaquín Muns, *Historia de las relaciones entre España y el Fondo Monetario Internacional, 1958–1982: Veinticinco años de la economía española*, Madrid: Alianza, 1986; also José Antonio Biescas, 'España y las organizaciones económicas internacionales: el FMI y el Banco Mundial (1958–1993)', in Manuel Varela (et al.), *El Fondo Monetario Internacional, el Banco Mundial y la economía española*, Madrid: Pirámide, 1994.

16 Cf. Antonio Moreno Juste, *Franquismo y construcción europea (1951–1962)*, Madrid: Tecnos, 1998, p. 195.

17 AMAE, leg. R-6916, E.6.

18 Cf. María Teresa Laporte, *La política europea del régimen de Franco, 1957–1962*, Pamplona: EUNSA, 1992, p. 247.

19 *Pensamiento político de Franco*, vol. 2, Madrid: Ediciones del Movimiento, 1975, p. 1303.

20 See Maurice Vaïsse, *La grandeur: la politique extérieure du Général de Gaulle, 1958–1969*, Paris: Fayard, 1998, pp. 103, 186.

21 See Carlos Collado, 'En defensa de Occidente: Perspectivas en las relaciones del régimen de Franco con los gobiernos democristianos de Alemania (1949–1966)', in *El régimen de Franco (1936–1975)*, vol. 2, Madrid: UNED, 1993, pp. 483–9.

22 Known as the Birkelbach report, named after the German Socialist *rapporteur*. 'Informe Birkelbach', *Documentos del Parlamento Europeo*, 1962 / 0122.

23 Documents and personal testimonies can be found in Joaquín Satrústegui, *Cuando la transición se hizo posible: El contubernio de Munich*, Madrid: Tecnos, 1993.

24 Quoted in Ricardo Martín de la Guardia and Guillermo Pérez Sánchez, *La Unión Europea y España*, Madrid: Actas, 2002, p. 92.

25 Manuel Fraga, *Memoria breve de una vida pública*, Barcelona: Planeta, 1980, p. 135.

26 Cf. Charles Powell, *Juan Carlos, un rey para la democracia*, Barcelona: Planeta, 1995, pp. 88–91.

27 For the negotiations that ended in the signing of the Agreement, see Víctor Pou Serradell, *España y la Europa Comunitaria*, Pamplona: EUNSA, 1973, pp. 129–79.

28 *Arriba*, 13 February 1974, p. 2.

29 *Europe: Bulletin quotidien*, 8 October 1975, no. 1830.

30 For the relevance of the international factor to the Spanish transition to democracy, see Charles Powell, 'La dimensión internacional de la transición española', in Manuel Ferrer (ed.), *Franquismo y transición democrática*, Las Palmas de Gran Canaria: Centro de Estudios de Humanidades, 1993, pp. 101–43.

31 *ABC*, 10 January 1976, p. 15.

32 Marcelino Oreja was interviewed by José Oneto in the weekly periodical *Cambio 16*, 16 August 1976.

33 Marcelino Oreja, *La política exterior en un sistema democrático*, Madrid: Oficina de Información Diplomática, 1977, pp. 2–3.

34 The most relevant monographs on the party are Carlos Hunneus, *La Unión de Centro Democrático y la transición a la democracia en España*, Madrid: CIS, 1988, and Silvia Alonso-Castrillo, *La apuesta del centro: Historia de UCD*, Madrid: Alianza, 1996.

35 For an overview of the PSOE's evolution and its transition tactics, see Santos Juliá, *Los socialistas en la política española, 1879–1982*, Madrid: Taurus, 1991.

36 See, in greater detail, Joan Trullen i Thomas, *Fundamentos económicos de la transición política española: La política económica de los acuerdos de la Moncloa*, Madrid: Ministerio de Trabajo y Seguridad Social, 1993.

37 Regarding this aspect, see Berta Álvarez Miranda, *El Sur de Europa y la adhesión a la Comunidad: Los debates políticos*, Madrid: CIS, 1996, pp. 311–40.

38 *En Hamelin … La transición española más allá de la frontera*, Oviedo: Septem Ediciones, 2001, p. 88. On democratization and integration, see also Laurence Whitehead's insightful 'Democracy by convergence and Southern Europe: a comparative politics perspective', in Geoffrey Pridham (ed.), *Encouraging Democracy: The International Context*

of Regime Transition in Southern Europe, Leicester: Leicester University Press, 1991, pp. 45–61.

39 See Emilio Muñoz Alemany, *El proceso de integración de España en el Consejo de Europa*, Granada: Universidad de Granada, 1989.

40 Quoted in *Boletín de las Comunidades Europeas*, 1977, no. 718, p. 7.

41 Calvo Sotelo has argued in retrospect that Suárez never fully grasped the significance of the European Community for Spain. See Leopoldo Calvo Sotelo, *Memoria viva de la transición*, Barcelona: Plaza y Janés, 1990, p. 126.

42 The text in Bassols, *España en Europa*, pp. 209–12.

43 On the *Giscardazo*, see Martín de la Guardia and Pérez Sánchez, *La Unión Europea y España*, pp. 101–4.

44 Quoted in Bassols, *España en Europa*, p. 245.

45 Antonio Marquina, 'La política exterior de los gobiernos de la Unión de Centro Democrático', in Javier Tusell and Álvaro Soto (eds), *Historia de la transición (1975–1986)*, Madrid: Alianza, 1996, pp. 182-215.

46 The document can be found in full in Moreno Juste, 'España en el proceso', pp. 83–4.

47 *Movimiento Europeo*, 1982, no. 4, pp. 3–7.

48 Juan A. Vázquez has estimated the costs of the whole process, which extended into the beginning of the 1990s, at 1.5 billion pesetas, 800 affected companies and about 91,000 redundancies. See 'La reconversión industrial', *Economistas*, July–September 1991, no. 50, pp. 12–16.

49 Fernando Morán, *España en su sitio*, Barcelona: Plaza y Janés, 1990, pp. 58–60.

50 Quoted in Ramón Luis Acuña, *Como los dientes de una sierra*, Barcelona: Plaza y Janés, 1986, pp. 95–6.

51 See, in greater detail, Donato Fernández Navarrete, *La Política Agraria Común y la situación de España durante el periodo transitorio*, Madrid: Fundación Juan March, 1986.

52 For a more detailed account of the last days of the negotiations, see Morán, *España en su sitio*, pp. 442–52.

53 In *Revista Española de Investigaciones Sociológicas*, January–March 1985, no. 29, p. 393.

54 'Reflexiones y balance de diez años en la Unión Europea', *Información Comercial Española*, October–November 1997, no. 766, p. 16.

55 On the Europeanization of Spanish policies from accession onwards, see Carlos Closa, 'La europeización del sistema político español', in Juan Luis Paniagua and Juan Carlos Monedero (eds), *En torno a la democracia española: Temas abiertos del sistema político español*, Madrid: Tecnos, 1999, pp. 473–501; see also José Ignacio Torreblanca, 'La europeización de la política exterior española', in Carlos Closa (ed.), *La europeización del sistema político español*, Madrid: Istmo, 2001, pp. 483-511.

56 For the use of this word as coined by Christopher Hill, see his *National Foreign Policies and European Political Cooperation*, London: Allen & Unwin, 1983, p. 193.

57 For a similar view, see Esther Barbé, 'La cooperación política europea: La revalorización de la política exterior española', in Richard Gillespie, Fernando Rodrigo and Jonathan Story (eds), *Las relaciones exteriores de la España democrática*, Madrid: Alianza, 1995, pp. 151–69.

58 Esther Barbé, *La política europea de España*, Barcelona: Ariel, 1999, pp. 42–57.

59 *Eurobarómetro*, 1992, no. 38.

60 Cf. Pablo Pérez Tremps (ed.), *La participación europea y la acción exterior de las Comunidades Autónomas*, Barcelona: IEA-Marcial Pons, 1998, and Carlos Fernández de Casadevante Romani, *La acción exterior de las Comunidades Autónomas: Balance de una práctica consolidada*, Madrid: Dilex, 2001.

61 See 'La europeización de la opinión pública española', in Carlos Closa (ed.), *La europeización del sistema político español*, p. 49.

62 Cf. Juan Carlos Pereira Castañares, 'Europeización de España/Españolización de Europa: El dilema histórico resuelto', *Documentación Social*, 1998, no. 111, pp. 39–58.

6 From Atlantic past to European destiny

Portugal

António Costa Pinto and Nuno Severiano Teixeira

Two political factors conditioned Portugal's integration into the process of European unification between 1945 and 1974: the dictatorial nature of Salazar's regime and its tenacious resistance to decolonization.[1] It was only following the institutionalization of democracy and the process of decolonization during 1974–75 that the first serious steps were taken to follow a strategy of integrating Portugal into what was then the European Economic Community (EEC) – a policy that was to become the touchstone for political consensus among the moderate political parties of the nascent democracy.

A small country on the southern periphery of Europe, Portugal entered the twentieth century with a consolidated liberal regime in a very homogenous nation–state.[2] With the abolition of the constitutional monarchy following the republican revolution of 1910, the country experienced a failed democratization. In 1916, Portugal entered the First World War on the side of the Allies, which resulted in a period of endemic cabinet instability and pro-authoritarian military activity that aggravated the young republic's legitimacy crisis.

A *coup d'état* in 1926 led to the establishment of a military dictatorship that was internally divided as a consequence of the conflicts that existed within the heterogeneous conservative bloc that supported it. Stability was only restored within the dictatorship at the beginning of the 1930s when António Salazar, the young Catholic-conservative Finance Minister, rose to become one of the longest surviving right-wing dictators in twentieth-century Europe. When Salazar institutionalized Portugal's New State (Estado Novo), the Portuguese economy was backward, with a weak and sparse industrial base.[3] Levels of urbanization were low and the structure of Portugal's active population included 51 per cent engaged in the primary sector. While the New State was inspired by European fascism, its political institutions, which were created in 1933, were primarily influenced by Catholic corporatist ideals that resulted in the institutionalization of a dictatorial regime supported by a weak and elitist single party.[4] The Estado Novo was deeply conservative and relied more on traditional institutions like the Church and the Army, and a controlled administration than on mass organizations. The new regime did not seek to challenge the international order – it maintained its privileged alliance with the United Kingdom and, as a strategy for ensuring the survival of its fragile African empire, remained neutral during the Second World War.

In the period following the Second World War, the Estado Novo defined itself as an 'organic democracy' and endeavoured to conceal its resemblance to fascism; however, institutional and decision-making changes were very limited. It was only after Salazar (who died in 1970) was replaced by Marcello Caetano in 1968 that a series of reforms took place and part of the political elite associated with the old dictator was removed. Salazar's neutrality during the Second World War, his military concessions to Britain and the United States, and the rapid onset of the Cold War ensured the survival of his regime in an unfavourable post-1945 international climate. Portugal joined NATO and the United Nations (after an initial veto from the Soviet Union) within the next ten years. But it was not easy for the regime to adapt to the new US-dominated international scene. The dictator had always feared and mistrusted the United States; this feeling was heightened as decolonization began and the UN subjected Portugal's colonial policies to international condemnation. The Salazar regime survived by cultivating an external image of a benign and ageing authoritarianism that was an anti-communist bulwark of Western civilization, and by efficiently controlling internal opposition.

Portugal did not experience the same levels of international isolation as its Spanish neighbour following the Second World War. Its status as a founding member of NATO and as a participant within other international organizations, such as the Organization for European Economic Cooperation (OEEC) and the European Payments Union (EPU), and its receipt of Marshall Plan funds – albeit on a relatively small scale – are all examples of the country's international acceptance.[5]

The New State and European unification after 1945

Salazar had his own vision, not only as to what he considered Portugal's position in the world should be, but also its position in the post-Second World War world. His idea of Portugal's place was based on a traditional thesis that held to two fundamental presuppositions. The first of these was that Portugal was essentially an Atlantic country and as such should not concern itself with continental European questions but should instead concentrate its strategic energies in two directions – towards a privileged, or even exclusive, alliance with the major maritime power, and towards the colonial empire in Africa. He was particularly troubled by Britain's decline and the rise of the United States, which he regarded with ideological scepticism and political mistrust as the main maritime power. He also rejected the importance of multilateral diplomacy in the international system, and the United Nations in particular. He also had problems accepting the principle of self-rule and, consequently, the resulting process of decolonization. Finally, he watched in silence as the process of European economic reconstruction was conducted through the criteria of international cooperation rather than under the inter-war principles of nationalist autarchy.

Salazar's scepticism in relation to the United States, and his rejection of decolonization were not new: they had always conditioned his vision of Europe and its relationship with Africa. He saw the relationship between Europe and Africa as a complementary one and viewed this Europe–Africa binomial as a unity in terms of economic, political and military plans. This was the strategic conception at the heart of all of Salazar's beliefs and it was this that was to emerge during the formulation of his foreign policy, not only in relation to Europe and European construction, but also to the entire system of Western security and NATO. In Portugal's foreign policy from the very beginning of the Cold War, two events highlighted the duality of the country's strategic direction. Portugal's hesitation over the Marshall Plan in 1947 illustrated its reservations regarding the reconstruction process while the signing of the Lajes Agreement in 1948 – a bilateral defence agreement between Portugal and the United States – heralded Portugal's incorporation into the Atlantic security system, later confirmed with its entry into NATO in 1949.[6]

The Marshall Plan led Portugal to participate in all of Europe's institutional economic cooperation structures – from the OEEC and the EPU to the European Monetary Agreement (EMA).[7] In the latter half of the 1940s, and while the European reconstruction process was taking place in an atmosphere dominated by the principle of intergovernmental cooperation, Portugal's position was complex and its participation singular, although this very participation was to lead to the country's integration into all the institutions that were created with the purpose of promoting economic cooperation between the European states. Despite its non-participation in the first purely European military cooperation agreements, for example, the Dunkirk and Brussels Treaties of 1947 and 1948 respectively, Portugal followed the development of the Western European Union and was integrated into the Atlantic security system.

Of the three types of European cooperation developed during the late 1940s, the only one in which Portugal remained totally marginalized was that of political cooperation. In fact, not only did the wartime and post-war pro-European movements have no political expression in Portugal (evidenced by the absence of any Portuguese intellectuals at The Hague Congress of 1948), the anti-European principles that drove Portugal's foreign policy, and the authoritarian nature of the Portuguese regime in particular, excluded it from membership of the Council of Europe. While Portugal had participated in the development of European cooperation during the 1940s, the same cannot be said of its involvement with the integrationist movements of the 1950s. Although Salazar may have remained sceptical with respect to inter-governmental cooperation, his attitude towards any form of supranational integration or federalism remained openly hostile. Moreover, while Salazar was prepared to accept that the United States was the new Atlantic power, and to alter Portuguese foreign policy to establish a preferential relationship with it after Portugal's integration into NATO, in his mind this had no bearing on European affairs where he continued to place great importance on the alliance with Britain and to follow Britain's policy positions very closely.

Thus, Portugal stood alongside the United Kingdom at the margins of all European integrationist movements during the 1950s – remaining out of the

Schuman Plan and the European Coal and Steel Community (ECSC) as well as on the margins of the proposed European Defence Community (EDC) and its associated European Political Community (EPC). It was during the long and complex negotiations leading to the collapse of the EDC that Salazar clearly and unequivocally outlined his thoughts on European integration in a circular to all Portuguese embassies defining the principles of Portuguese foreign policy regarding this process.[8] In this document, Salazar's position was made unambiguous and can be reduced to three points. First, his scepticism regarding the chance of any process of economic integration or political federalism succeeding was clearly expressed. Second, he stated that even should European federalism succeed, it would not be something that would interest Portugal. Third, he stated that should the international order develop into the formation of large regional blocs, it was by no means certain that Portugal's national interests would be best served within Europe, and that other strategic alliances, with either Spain or Brazil, or fundamentally, with Africa, would be preferable. In the words of the Portuguese dictator, with the exception of NATO, 'nothing else in Europe has any real political importance for us: we are more interested in Angola and Mozambique, and even Brazil ... Our Atlantic character imposes limits on our collaboration with Europe.'[9]

During the 1950s, the Atlantic front and the position of the United States were to become increasingly important factors in Portuguese foreign policy. However, from its entry into the UN in 1955, and from the beginning of the 1960s in particular, the colonial question was to become Portugal's main concern. The United Kingdom continued to be Portugal's main reference in all matters European. Consequently, Portugal closely followed the positions adopted by the United Kingdom in European affairs, at least until it became a founding member of EFTA.[10] When the United Kingdom proposed the creation of a free trade area as a kind of roof over the emerging EEC in 1956–57, no one – not even the British government – thought that Portugal was eligible for membership. Considering the low level of Portugal's economic development, and the fact that the proposed free trade area deliberately excluded agriculture, it would appear that this proposal would be of no interest to Portugal. However, when the United Kingdom informed Lisbon of this proposal, Portugal officially stated its desire to be represented at the negotiations. Portugal accepted the general political objective of liberalizing the market and, in contrast with the other peripheral countries of Europe, Portugal did not have any financial problems. Finally, the question of the colonies, which could have constituted a problem, could be in Portugal's favour, given that the United Kingdom was interested in including the Commonwealth and could see a potential ally in Portugal. These reasons distinguished Lisbon from the other peripheral capitals and were decisive in securing Portugal's admission to the negotiating table.

The discussions took place within the OEEC, of which Portugal was already a member and where it adopted a moderate and constructive negotiating position. On substantive matters, Portugal did not raise any objections to the exclusion of agriculture and was cautious in its requests for special treatment for

Portuguese industry. On procedural matters, it rejected being labelled an 'under-developed country' and, diverging from the General Agreement on Tariffs and Trade (GATT) definition, introduced the concept 'developing country'. Portugal refused to participate within the group of under-developed countries and instead proposed the creation of a special group for itself, which resulted in the Melander Report. However, in November 1958, General de Gaulle exercised his veto and put an end to the negotiations. The 'non-Six' states – Britain, Norway, Sweden, Denmark, Switzerland and Austria – then held a meeting to resolve the resulting problems for themselves, without inviting Portugal on the pretext that the presence of a peripheral developing country could create undesired precedents. Nevertheless, when the second meeting was called, Portugal's goal to ensure its active participation was achieved through the political determination of the Minister of the Economy, Correia de Oliveira, and the diplomatic ability of its negotiators.[11] Portugal also enjoyed open and covert support from the United States and the United Kingdom, respectively. Thus, in the spring of 1959, when the idea of a free trade area was transformed into a more limited regional agreement restricted to the six 'non-Six', these six were in fact seven, with Portugal being part of the process. As a result, Portugal was a signatory to the Stockholm Convention leading to the creation of EFTA.[12]

In a situation where conditioning factors weighed heavily and the margin for manoeuvring Portuguese foreign policy was limited, EFTA provided the only alternative with economic advantages and without political costs. Politically, therefore, EFTA represented the optimum solution for Salazar as it enabled him to reconcile Portugal's economic integration into a European free trade area with the regime's political and diplomatic positions. The strictly inter-governmental character of the organization eliminated any supranational or integrationist pretensions, and, while it incorporated some continental countries, Britain's involvement allowed Portugal to maintain its essentially Atlanticist orientation and one of the country's traditional foreign policy strategies: continuation of the alliance with Britain. Most importantly, the fact that EFTA was a free trade area rather than a customs union allowed Portugal to remain within the organization while maintaining its privileged relationship with its colonies.

Membership of EFTA not only appeared to be cost-free, but it also brought several benefits. Portugal was integrated into a European institution that was dedicated to economic cooperation, which was an important contributory factor in terms of the country's future relationship with the EEC. Moreover, this international experience brought domestic lessons: by participating as a full member of EFTA – as an equal with the developed and democratic states – the regime gained additional legitimacy. Finally, because the free trade area model that was adopted allowed Portugal to maintain its privileged relationship with its colonies, it seemed to fit perfectly Salazar's own strategic conception of the complementary nature of Africa and Europe. In the context of Portuguese foreign policy's limited scope for manoeuvre, this represented an enormous political advantage and was the main reason for Portugal's membership of EFTA. However, it was also to have a perverse effect in the medium-term. The growing importance of

Europe in the Portuguese economy, and particularly in its external trade, provoked a radical change in the conception of the relationship between Europe and Africa during the 1960s. If at the time the Stockholm Treaty was signed in 1960 the concept was one of the complementary nature of Africa and Europe, then by the end of the decade it had become one of competition. This was the problem that exercised the regime during its final years, becoming the central political debate of Marcello Caetano's brief rule.

The reorientation of the Portuguese economy from Africa to Europe occurred precisely at the moment of the colonial wars which started in Angola in 1961, in Guinea-Bissau in 1963, and in Mozambique in 1964. Portugal's export sector responded dynamically to the stimulus provided by EFTA, which absorbed an ever-increasing proportion of Portuguese produce – to the detriment of the colonies. As David Corkill has noted, 'Inevitably, the changed economic realities of the 1960s and 1970s were progressively corroding the logic of imperial connections and of economic nationalism.'[13] Portugal's economic growth during its first decade of EFTA membership reached 6 per cent, with foreign investment in Portugal also expanding. There was significant growth in external trade, both in volume and direction, which was to be of extremely important political significance. During the 1960s, the importance of the colonies for Portuguese trade declined and was replaced by Europe, with both tourism and emigration having important consequences on economic growth. During this decade the destination for Portuguese emigrants moved from the American continent to Europe – France in particular – and expanded at an impressive rate.[14]

Marcelo Caetano inherited a very different country in the summer of 1968, one that was more European (at least in terms of economic exchange), leading him to sketch the outlines of a set of liberalizing policies. Caetano himself had been one of the dictatorship's few notables to propose, in 1962, the adoption of a prudent federalist solution for the colonial question; however, after obtaining power, in both his political discourse and strategy promises he opted to continue the war. The war effort was redoubled, although now within the context of economic growth, and in 1970 Portugal spent a total of 45 per cent of its budget on defence and security. With a military force of 140,000 men, the proportion of the population under arms was exceeded only by Israel and North and South Vietnam.[15] Despite muted protests by the 'Europeanists', who had precise data proving the very limited adverse effects that would be felt with the 'loss of empire', the government refused to prepare any initiatives for a peaceful resolution to the colonial problem.

Ultimately, Caetano's ideas on European integration and the Europe–Africa relationship did not differ substantially from those of Salazar; however, what was different was the domestic and international political situation. The economic effects of EFTA membership and the resulting approximation to Europe were translated domestically into two antagonistic concepts of developmental strategy that affected the country's external orientation. These two antagonisms came to the fore through the political debate between the 'Europeanists' and the

'Africanists' that dominated the regime's final years.[16] Caetano's hesitations enabled a small liberal and technocratic pro-European group to consolidate itself within the dictatorship, which was to part company from the regime on the eve of its collapse. The spokespersons of this tendency, that emerged out of the limited pluralism permitted during the regime's final years, attempted to give a political expression to the close relationship as they saw it, between Europe, economic modernization and the liberalization of the regime. Caetano's position in this context was that of a referee who sought to reconcile what, at that moment, seemed irreconcilable. As far as he was concerned, the Africa–Europe alternative represented a false choice. Adopting a traditional Salazarist attitude, he defined the European question as 'the movement of economic understanding that will transform itself into a customs union', and 'the movement for political integration that will transform itself into a European federation'.[17] Portugal had much to gain from the former and everything to lose from the latter. Economically, Portugal had to persevere with EFTA and other programmes for economic cooperation. Politically, however, Caetano shared de Gaulle's belief that Europe would have to remain a collection of independent states. It was in accordance with this belief that he developed Portugal's strategy towards the EEC/EC.

When the United Kingdom made its first application to join the EEC in 1961, Portugal adopted its traditional position of following Britain's lead in European questions and did likewise, albeit within the limits of the possible. There were three fundamental obstacles preventing Portugal from making a formal request for EEC accession: (1) the country's low level of economic development; (2) the authoritarian nature of the regime; (3) and the colonial problem (which had become critical with the outbreak of the war). During this difficult time, Portugal's diplomatic strategy was predicated upon opening multilateral negotiations between EFTA and the EEC. However, the United Kingdom's unilateral approach obliged Portugal to negotiate directly with the EEC. The difficult international situation and the lack of any domestic consensus led Lisbon to delay its application until 1962: the last EFTA member-state to do so. When it was made, the application was couched in an 'ambiguous manner' in order to allow a degree of flexibility at the negotiating table.

Much to Portugal's relief, de Gaulle's 1963 veto of Britain's application introduced a delay in solving the problem. The matter only came to the fore again following de Gaulle's departure from the political scene, when the European project was re-launched at the Hague Summit of 1969 that led to the EC's first enlargement. With the United Kingdom's renewed request for EC membership and its expected resignation from EFTA, this organization's future was irredeemably compromised. Once again the unilateral nature of Britain's application ruled out any opportunity for multilateral EFTA–EC negotiations capable of dealing with the Portuguese case. Portugal had to form some type of relationship with the EC, and it would have to negotiate it directly and bilaterally. Following Britain, in May 1970 Portugal requested talks with the EC and formed an *ad hoc* commission, the Inter-Ministerial Commission for External

Economic Cooperation that was charged with analysing the situation and proposing possible alternatives. This Commission's report was clear in its diagnosis: the existing nature of economic relations between Portugal and Europe, and the United Kingdom's resignation from EFTA meant that it was imperative that Lisbon establish 'any kind of relationship with the EEC'. The Commission's report suggested three alternative ways forward for Portugal: accession to the EC, association with it, or the establishment of trade agreements with it. Accession was out of the question for political reasons. Association would be difficult because the EC wanted to reserve Article 238 of the Treaty of Rome for countries that were politically willing to join the Community but economically unable to do so for the moment. Establishing trade agreements with the EC thus emerged as the only politically possible alternative. The Commission recommended that Portugal adopt a moderate and flexible negotiating position: moderate in order to avoid raising the issue of the colonies in such a way as could undermine any agreement, and flexible in the formulation of the agreements so as not to undermine any future membership application. The trade agreement with the EC was signed in July 1972 and was ratified shortly after. The scope for manoeuvre in Portugal's foreign policy was too narrow to allow the flexibility required to step beyond the limits of a trade agreement, and its approximation to Europe and the weakening of EFTA required it to establish new multilateral economic relations. This being the case, an agreement with the EC was imperative, and a trade agreement was the formula that involved the minimum degree of political compromise.

Democratic Portugal: from application to accession

By mobilizing political actors that were absent in the transition to democracy in the other Southern European countries, the colonial wars were a specific and determining factor in the overthrow of the Portuguese dictatorship in 1974. It was in the emergence of the Armed Forces Movement (MFA, *Movimento das Forças Armadas*), a movement of middle-ranking officers who were increasingly attracted to left-wing politics, more than the nature of the dictatorship's fall – a military *coup d'état* – that the uniqueness of the Portuguese transition resides.

The 25 April 1974 military coup paved the way for the institutionalization of Portuguese democracy as well as decolonization, with Guinea becoming independent in 1974 and Angola and Mozambique in 1975.[18] Portugal's transition occurred at the height of the Cold War, at a time when there were few international pressures for democratization. The rupture provoked by the Portuguese military resulted in an accentuated crisis of the state, fuelled by the concurrence of democratization with the decolonization of the last European colonial empire. Powerful tensions, which incorporated revolutionary elements, were concentrated into the first two years of Portugal's democracy. During 1974–75, Portugal also experienced a high level of foreign influence. This influence ranged from diplomatic pressure and support for the strategies against the extreme Left of the 'Hot Summer' of 1975 to external support for the creation of political parties and interest groups. Portugal was a constant topic of discussion at international forums, from NATO and the EC to the Soviet bloc.

The military coup took the international community – and the United States in particular – by surprise.[19] Faced with intense social and political mobilization from the Left, and concerned with the flight of the country's economic elite and their capital, the moderate parties obtained only limited success in organizing themselves and were able to function during the crisis only with financial and technical support from important figures within the US administration and the European party groups and affiliated organizations, with the latter often serving as guarantors ensuring the support of the former. The support of these parties and their foundations and the rapid affiliation of the parties and trade unions to European transnational party political organizations were an important factor in explaining the swift domination of the political system by the parliamentary parties over their rivals within the military and the extreme Left.[20]

The EC observed Portugal's transition with discretion, although it gave unambiguous signals that, politically, it favoured the emergence of a pluralist democratic system, while simultaneously granting limited economic assistance. Soon after the first democratic elections, which took place in 1975, the European Council announced that it was prepared to begin economic and financial negotiations with Portugal, although it stressed that, 'in accordance with its historical and political traditions, the European Community can only support a pluralist democracy'.[21]

The transitional period was characterized by conflict concerning the country's foreign policy options, through the practice of parallel diplomacy and, consequently, by the absence of any clear foreign policy goals. Despite the conflicts, hesitations and indecision, the Provisional Governments, and in particular those with a preponderance of military ministers, tended to favour adopting a Third Worldist foreign policy and promoted the formation of privileged relations with the country's former colonies. This was the final manifestation, albeit in a pro-socialist form, of the thesis that was so close to Salazar's heart: of Portugal's 'African vocation'.

The consolidation of democracy, which began in 1976 with the election of the first constitutional government, was characterized by the clarification of Portugal's foreign policy choices, and by the unequivocal positioning of Portugal as a Western country, albeit one that was simultaneously Atlanticist and European. It was these two visions that were to become the basic strategic foreign policy vectors for the nascent democracy. The Atlanticist outlook was predicated on the permanence of Portuguese foreign policy's historical characteristics, and played an important role in directing Portugal externally and in stabilizing it domestically. The establishment of good bilateral relations with the United States, and the strengthening of its multilateral participation within NATO, were the clearest expressions of the new democracy's international position. Having overcome the Third Worldist temptations of the revolutionary period, Portugal adopted the 'European option' unreservedly from 1976. Now, however, this choice was a strategic decision and a political project, rather than the merely pragmatic and economic stance it had been under the authoritarian regime.

Contacts between the Portuguese government and the European institutions were initiated as early as 1974.[22] The European Commission granted Portugal economic assistance, while the European Council made its political position clear: it was ready to begin negotiations, but only on the condition that a pluralist democracy was established. Nevertheless, the country's economic condition, the political instability and continuing uncertainty regarding the destiny of the democratic regime during the transitional period ruled out any advance from the European front. It was the first constitutional government, led by Mário Soares, which adopted the 'European option'. The first step in this process occurred in August 1976 when the Portuguese government successfully applied for membership of the Council of Europe. Once a member of this organization, which also consolidated the international community's recognition of the new democratic regime, Lisbon began to outline its next and decisive step: application for accession to the EC. Following a series of successful negotiations in a number of European capitals between September 1976 and February 1977, the government made its formal application for EC membership in March 1977. One month later, the European Council accepted Portugal's request and initiated the formal process laid out in the various treaties, including the mandatory consultation of the European Commission. In May 1978, the Commission presented a favourable report, clearing the way for the formal negotiations to begin in Luxembourg the following October. With the formal application made, and accession negotiations under way, the hesitations and polemics over the nature of Portugal's integration had finally been superseded, putting Portugal firmly on the European path.

The government was motivated by, and based its decision to follow this strategic option on, two main objectives. First, EC membership would consolidate Portuguese democracy, and second, EC assistance would guarantee the country's modernization and economic development. Several Portuguese economists remained fearful, with the majority expressing grave reservations about the impact that EC membership would have on some sectors of the Portuguese economy, and arguing instead for an 'association' model to be adopted. The former Prime Minister, Mário Soares, recalls that:

> [he] heard the economists ... and, in the end, begged their forgiveness whilst informing them that Portugal was going to join nonetheless ... for to do otherwise would mean that there could be no certainty that Portugal's democracy would be consolidated. At that time, Portugal was still under military control.[23]

A complex series of negotiations, which lasted seven years, followed Portugal's membership application. An earlier step had been taken in September 1976 – prior to the country's formal application – with the revision of the 1972 EC trade agreement through the conclusion of the Additional and Financial

Protocols, which Portugal interpreted as representing a form of pre-membership agreement.[24] Despite these prior agreements, formal negotiations on Portugal's membership lasted until June 1985.

There were two important domestic factors that can help explain just why the accession negotiations for such a small country with a relatively weak economy were so complex and drawn out. First, there was Portugal's economic situation immediately after the transition and, more importantly, the economic measures that had been taken during the revolutionary period, in particular the national-ization of important economic sectors. Second, continuing governmental instability and the political and constitutional nature of the Portuguese regime. Following 1976, the democratic regime was undeniably pluralist, and was gener-ally considered as such; however, the 1976 constitution was a product of the revolutionary period, and consecrated within it the Council of the Revolution. It was a democracy, but it was a democracy under the tutelage of an undemocratic military institution. These factors weighed heavily in the negotiations, and delayed their conclusion. During the early 1980s, Portugal's democratic regime overcame all of these objections. The constitution was revised in 1982 to abolish the Council of the Revolution and the National Defence Law, and the armed forces finally accepted their subordination to the civilian political authorities. By 1983 Portugal's democracy had been consolidated, thereby eliminating all the domestic obstacles that were preventing the successful conclusion of the entry negotiations.

One external hurdle remained, however. During Europe's southern enlarge-ment, the EC was also conducting accession negotiations with Spain, a country that had a much larger economy than Portugal and which did not share its smaller neighbour's history of close relations with European economic institu-tions.[25] France and Greece were also to be significant obstacles during these negotiations, albeit for different reasons. Portugal's diplomatic strategy was to keep its entry negotiations separate from those of Spain, in the hope of securing EC accession more rapidly, thus giving it the important status of member-state prior to Spain's entry. This strategy was to prove unsuccessful, as the Community's policy was to negotiate with both Iberian nations simultaneously, with the result that Portugal's accession was delayed a further two years, until after all the dossiers on Spain had been concluded.[26] The culmination of the accession process finally arrived in June 1985, when Portugal signed the Treaty of Accession. On 1 January 1986, Portugal became a full member of the EC.

Several authors have suggested 'that the European Community played an important role' in the promotion of democracy in Southern Europe.[27] While the economic support offered by Europe was important, the overall impact of the 'prospect of membership' on the consolidation of Portuguese democracy merits much deeper investigation. Nevertheless, for one section of the Portuguese polit-ical elite of that era, accession was viewed as a guarantor of domestic democratic consolidation, and as a lever for the country's modernization.

Whilst present in the programmes of several of the new political parties from the earliest days of the April 1974 coup, it was primarily in the context of the political cleavages of 1975 – when they were faced with socialist and Third Worldist alternatives – that the parties of the right and the centre-left emphasized 'Europe' and the EC as a reference for Portugal's future.[28] In the context of a polarized transition, in which some of the divisions had been solidified into a conflict that was more 'between democrats and revolutionaries than between democrats and "involutionaries"', the European option was an important factor in the break from a dictatorial, isolationist and colonialist past, while simultaneously assuming an anti-Communist and anti-revolutionary dimension.[29]

The Portuguese case provides a good illustration of the thesis that considers the European Community to be a reference for Europe's development, and acts as a 'ready symbol' that the democratic elites could utilize to legitimate the new domestic order after the contested transition and the end of the colonial empire that had been so dear to the New State. On the other hand, and as had been the case in Spain, it led to the successful consolidation of a 'democratic tradition' that was based on the 'synchronization and homogenization of [national] cultures and institutions, with those of Europe', whose social and economic components had been changing since the 1960s.[30]

When Mário Soares, as leader of a Socialist government, made Portugal's formal request for EC accession in May 1977, the country was living with the legacy of a contested transition, had a constitution that protected the nationalizations and agrarian reform, and which maintained a strong military presence in political life. The theme of the Socialist Party's (*Partido Socialista* – PS) 1976 electoral campaign was *A Europa Connosco* (Europe with us), with the party receiving support from many of Europe's most important Social Democratic leaders. By adopting this rather vague theme, the PS was seeking to distinguish itself from the Third Worldist and neutralist tendencies that had characterized Portuguese politics during 1974–75, and which yet retained some support within the moderate left and the Armed Forces Movement. Soares incorporated the proposal for EC accession into his party's programme as a foreign policy priority for Portugal.[31]

By 1974, EC membership had also become a theme in the programmes of the right and centre-right parties, with the Social Democratic Centre (CDS, *Centro Democrático Social*) proclaiming itself convinced pro-European, and the Social Democratic Party (PSD, *Partido Social Democrata*) adopting a more cautious approach. The CDS, which was affiliated to the European Union of Christian Democrats (EUCD), adopted a strongly pro-European strategy right up to accession. The PSD, which was formed by the reformers and 'liberals' of the dictatorship's final years, first inserted itself into the European liberal party group, although it defected to the European People's Party in 1996.[32] Beginning with the PS's initiative, the three parties advanced rival proposals for promoting the accession negotiations, although the PSD was at times less consistent. During the latter half of the 1970s, arguments in favour of the Community were actively promoted as the means through which the necessary political and constitutional reforms, particularly those relating to the military presence within the Council of the Revolution and the nationalizations, could be affected. Only the

Communist Party, the *Partido Comunista Português* (PCP) remained consistently opposed to EC membership, and rejected the prospect of accession. This opposition was an important element in its political campaigns between 1977 and 1986. After 1986, the PCP stopped calling for Portugal to withdraw from the EC, and adopted a more moderate position.

Civil society and the interest groups representing those who would be most affected by EC membership had practically no role to play during any stage of the accession negotiations. European integration was a decision made by the political elite alone, rather than 'a response to popular demand'.[33] The governing elites dominated the negotiating process, with only limited involvement by the business associations or agricultural interests. Semi-paralysed as a consequence of the transition to democracy's most radical phase, the employers' organizations were slow to establish international contacts and participate within European structures. Following the wave of nationalizations and agrarian reform in 1975, these organizations welcomed Portugal's application from the perspective of their domestic battle for a reduction of the public sector, the liberalization of employment laws and the initiation of a privatization programme. Both the Confederation of Portuguese Industry (CIP, *Confederação da Industria Portuguesa*) and the Portuguese Industrial Association (AIP, *Associação Industrial Portuguesa*) supported accession, although to differing extents. The CIP was more concerned about the economic effects of liberalization on some sectors, and demanded more pre-entry economic aid. The AIP adopted a more pragmatic 'join and see' position.[34] Nevertheless, despite the CIP's occasional attacks, the hypothesis that the attitudes of these two organizations reflect an attempt to make the government adopt an aggressive negotiating stance rather than a reflection of any principled opposition by these organizations appears plausible, especially since these attitudes did not enjoy much support amongst their affiliates.[35] Several surveys on the attitudes of the employers' organizations towards accession have confirmed the dominance of political considerations, with the EC being presented as the 'guarantor for greater political security that will encourage investment in and modernization of the productive structures in the country'.[36]

The party political and ideological cleavages were much more obvious within the trade union movement, with the Communist *Intersindical* being opposed to accession, and the social democratic General Workers' Union (UGT, *União Geral de Trabalhadores*) being firmly pro-European. Formed out of the struggle against communist domination of the trade union movement, and supported by foundations that were associated with social democratic, liberal and conservative political parties, the UGT was rapidly integrated into the European labour movement's international institutions.[37] It was only after accession that Intersindical moved away from its original opposition to adopt a more pragmatic position.

During the 1980s, Portuguese society finally broke free of the double legacy of authoritarianism and the 1975 revolutionary process. Democratic consolidation, EC accession and economic development all coincided to create a virtuous circle that could not have been foreseen at the moment of application. To the surprise of many sectors of public opinion, in 1990 Portugal lost its status as 'an under-developed country', a label that had been used to characterize the country ever since the concept had been devised. Following the conclusion of two complex agreements with the International Monetary Fund (IMF), a flood of Community funds began arriving in Portugal with tangible effects. The statistics reveal that there was an observable improvement in living conditions, which was combined with a relatively low unemployment rate. Portugal underwent a second cycle of growth and social change. The movement of population toward the coastal areas and urbanization increased, although rates remained below the European average. More noteworthy, however, was the acute drop (to 12 per cent by 1992) in the number of workers actively engaged in the agricultural sector, a process that continued to break up traditional rural society in the northern and central areas of the country. Emigration was being replaced by a movement from the countryside to the cities. The growth of the middle class and the tertiary sectors was also prominent during this period, and school attendance rates increased substantially. Rather than the catastrophic prospect that seemed to loom large for Portugal during the 1970s, the country managed to consolidate its democracy and take important strides forward in its social and economic modernization as a member of the European Union.[38] As a member of the EU, Portugal was also forced to accelerate the liberalization of its domestic market as a direct consequence of deepening economic and monetary union.[39]

Portugal's route to EU membership was promoted by the political elite, with a great degree of political consensus, and without any attempt to measure public opinion through referenda. It was not until after accession had been secured that popular opinion began to exert pressure for more public participation in the reforms that were taking place within the EU. Both the process of decolonization and the adoption of a pro-European political policy led to the production of a significant ideological output by some sections of the intellectual elite, although the oft-heralded 'identity crisis' never appeared in any tangible form. Following a period of recriminations criticizing the decolonization process that emanated mainly from conservative groups in the late 1970s, and which largely fell on deaf ears, smaller extreme right-wing parties sought to capitalize on the discontent felt in the small groups that had been most affected by Portugal's new-found Europeanism: their target audience were those who had fled the colonies to settle in Portugal, the *retornados*. The conversion of this conservative ideology to a discourse proclaiming the need to defend a 'national identity' that was threatened by incorporation into the European Community also met with little popular success – even within the conservative milieu, as is evidenced by the fact that EU membership was supported by the two main conservative parties, the CDS and the PSD.

On the one hand, nationalist discourses emerged during the 1970s as a reaction against the country's incorporation into Europe, promoted by a conservatism that emphasized the country's exclusively Atlantic vocation. On the other, the Communist Party promoted the more economic-oriented defence of the 'interests of the national productive forces' in the face of European capitalism. However, with the myth of the empire ended, the democratic elites managed to consolidate the belief within public opinion that Europe was the only means through which Portugal could reconstruct any important relationships with the new Portuguese-speaking African states, particularly since almost all economic links had disappeared and political relations had deteriorated following the granting of independence in 1975. With the prospect of accession, and following in its wake, new identity problems were to arise, the most important of which was the nature of Portugal's relationship with its neighbour, Spain. During and, particularly, after Portugal's attempts to negotiate accession separately, Spain regularly appeared in the public's mind as the powerful neighbour that had 'invaded' Portugal's economy. Having swiftly transformed itself into Portugal's major trading partner, Spain and the 'Spanish menace' stood as a threat to the liberalization of the Portuguese market: 'Portugal: Capital Madrid', 'Portugal: Spanish Province' and similar headlines were widespread in the Portuguese press during the 1990s.[40]

In 1978, three years after decolonization, almost 70 per cent of Portuguese citizens believed that 'Portugal had a duty to grant these countries their independence', although they also thought that 'the rights of the Portuguese had to be protected'. Only 2.2 per cent of those questioned were in favour of continuing the fight against the liberation movements.[41] Nevertheless, a significant minority of 20 per cent thought, in 1978, that Portugal could not survive economically without the former colonies. The gradual disappearance of this belief seems to be linked directly to the prospect of EC accession: 'the accession process and membership itself, besides providing a substitute for the lost colonies, also represents an incentive for a change in the nature of the country's economic, social and cultural activities.'[42] Nevertheless, the emergence of EC membership as a positive goal within Portuguese society was a lengthy process that was initially restricted to the political elite. In 1978, shortly after the formal membership application had been submitted, most Portuguese had no opinion on Europe, with over 60 per cent of the population stating that they did not know if EC membership was essential for the future of Portugal's economy. It was not until the early 1980s that the population became better informed and was able to express a clearer opinion on the subject. The Eurobarometer survey has regularly recorded Portuguese public opinion since 1980, and its reports have revealed a clear upward trend in support of EC membership, with a large increase occurring in 1986, the year Portugal finally joined. The proportion of the population believing EC membership to be a good thing rose from 24.4 per cent (1980–82) to 64.5 per cent (1986–90), rising to over 70 per cent during the 1990s.[43] In 1993, 65 per cent believed that Portuguese economic development had been boosted greatly as a result of EU membership. As appears to be the case in other Southern European countries, there seems to be a strong suggestion that the urban middle classes generally tend towards Europeanism with only a weak sense of 'national pride', while the less educated and the rural lower classes generally have weak pro-European sentiments and a strong sense of 'national pride'.[44]

By reaffirming their country's European identity, and remaining optimistic regarding the EU following accession during the 1980s, the Portuguese do not seem to have experienced any serious identity problems, either through the loss of the colonial empire in 1975, or as a consequence of Portugal's new international position within Europe since 1986.

Conclusion

Portugal's approach to the construction of Europe between 1945 and 1974 was determined by several factors. First, the dictatorship accepted the economic aspects of intergovernmental cooperation while rejecting the political facets and any supranational or integrationist model. Second, it was dependent upon the narrow scope of the regime's foreign policy; that is to say, its policies were determined by economic and social factors (for example, foreign trade, emigration, and tourism) and not the result of any strategic choices – Europe was a necessity, not a project. Third, if during the 1940s and 1950s Portugal's attitude towards the construction of Europe seemed compatible with its idea of the complementary nature of Africa and Europe, then during the 1960s and 1970s its economic approximation to Europe and the ongoing colonial wars put an end to this illusion: these concepts were now seen to be politically antagonistic. The maintenance of the African colonial empire required the continuation of authoritarianism, while Portugal's integration into Europe required decolonization and democratization.

Being excluded from, and remaining mistrustful of, the EEC, and following positions adopted by the United Kingdom (its major trading partner), successful EFTA membership was an important economic aim for the dictatorship throughout the 1960s. Less paradoxically than it may seem at first sight, the colonial wars of the 1960s coincided with a period of real economic and social development in the colonies, particularly in Angola and Mozambique. The increase in the white population in the two largest colonies was significant, while the 'Europeanization' of Portugal's economy and the wave of emigration to Europe were also to make a difference during this decade. Negotiated on terms that were favourable to Portugal, which saw the majority of its economic activities largely protected, the EFTA agreement was one of the roots of economic growth in the 1960s and a key reason for the significant increase in commercial relations with Europe. It was also behind the emergence of interest groups with fewer associations with the colonies.

The development of a pro-European outlook, however, was essentially a consequence of decolonization and the institutionalization of democracy. Following a complex transition process, the integration of Portugal into the EC became a strategic objective. It was the consequence of significant changes in domestic policy and had political as well as economic overtones.[45] Democratic consolidation and Portugal's insertion into the European economic space were to become inseparable.

In the context of a polarized transition, the swift 'Europeanization' of the right- and left-wing parties that were moderated by the transnational foundations and organizations of the European political party groups was an important element in Portugal's European integration.[46] In Portugal's case, as in that of the other Southern European democratizing regimes – particularly Spain – 'the idea that accession to the European Community would help to guarantee liberal democracy was more overtly voiced' and was central to the strategy of the political elites during this period, as already noted by Geoffrey Pridham.[47]

The first ten years of Portugal's membership of the EU were a 'golden era' during which there was a large degree of pro-European consensus within the party system; there was economic growth and rising incomes and there was also real social change. Internationally, Portugal used its stronger position as a member of the EU to resolve the tensions that existed between it and its former colonies in Africa. The optimism of the 1990s was also marked by Portugal's meeting the convergence criteria for adhesion to the European single currency, the Euro, and joining it in 1999–2000; this contrasted with the situation at the beginning of the following decade. With the EU's movement towards institutional reform, enlargement and the eventual reduction of EU fiscal transfers, there is some evidence of a fear that Portugal could be 'returning to the periphery'; this perception has resulted in the return of 'Atlanticist' views in the country following Iraq War of 2003.

Notes

1 This chapter is based on the authors' research project, *Portugal and the Unification of Europe*, funded by the Foundation for Science and Technology, Lisbon. See, in greater detail, António Costa Pinto and Nuno Severiano Teixeira (eds), *Southern Europe and the Making of the European Union*, New York: SSM-Columbia University Press, 2002.
2 For an introduction, see António Costa Pinto (ed.), *Contemporary Portugal*, New York: SSM-Columbia University Press, 2003.
3 Pedro Lains, 'The Portuguese economy in the twentieth century: growth and structural change', in Pinto, *Contemporary Portugal*, pp. 119–37.
4 António Costa Pinto, *Salazar's Dictatorship and European Fascism*, New York: SSM-Columbia University Press, 1995.
5 Nicolau Andresen-Leitão, 'Portugal's European integration policy, 1947–1972', *Journal of European Integration History*, 2001, vol. 7, no. 1, pp. 25–35.
6 Nuno Severiano Teixeira, 'From neutrality to alignment: Portugal in the foundation of the Atlantic Pact', *Luso-Brazilian Review*, 1992, vol. 29, no. 2, pp. 113–27.
7 On Portugal and the Marshall Plan, see Maria Fernanda Rollo, *Portugal e o Plano Marshall*, Lisbon: Estampa, 1994.
8 'Circular concerning European integration to diplomatic missions from the President of the Council of Ministers', 6 March 1953, Arquivo Histórico Diplomático, PEA-M 309.
9 Ibid.
10 Richard T. Griffiths and Bjarne Lie, 'Portugal e a EFTA, 1959–1973', in *Portugal e a Europa: 50 anos de integração*, Lisbon: Centro de Informação Jacques Delors, 1996, pp. 185–206; Elsa Santos Alípio, 'O processo negocial de adesão de Portugal à EFTA, 1956–1960', unpublished MA thesis, Universidade Nova de Lisboa, 2001.
11 Interview with former Finance Minister José da Silva Lopes, Arrábida, 1998.
12 On the creation of EFTA, see also Mikael af Malmborg and Johnny Laursen, 'The creation of EFTA', in Thorsten B. Olesen (ed.), *Interdependence versus Integration:*

Denmark, Scandinavia and Western Europe, 1945–1960, Odense: Odense University Press, 1995, pp. 197–212.

13 David Corkill, *The Portuguese Economy since 1947*, Edinburgh: Edinburgh University Press, 1993, p. 16.

14 António Barreto, 'Portugal: democracy through Europe', in Jeffrey J. Anderson (ed.), *Regional Integration and Democracy: Expanding on the European Experience*, New York: Rowman & Littlefield, 1999, pp. 95–122.

15 John P. Cann, *Counterinsurgency in Africa: The Portuguese Way of War, 1961–1974*, Westport, CT: Greenwood Press, 1997.

16 José Manuel Tavares Castilho, *A ideia da Europa no Marcelismo 1968–1974*, Oporto: Afrontamento, 2000.

17 Marcelo Caetano, *Renovação na continuidade*, Lisbon: Verbo, 1971, p. 19.

18 Kenneth Maxwell, *The Making of Portuguese Democracy*, Cambridge: Cambridge University Press, 1997.

19 Mario del Pero, 'Kissinger e la politica estera americana nel Mediterraneo: il caso portoghese', *Studi Storici*, 2001, vol. 4, pp. 973–88.

20 A very good source is the memoirs of the Socialists' former international secretary, Rui Mateus, *Contos proibidos: memórias de um PS desconhecido*, Lisbon: Dom Quixote, 1996. See also Rainer Eisfeld, 'Influencias externas sobre a Revolução Portuguesa: o papel da Europa ocidental', in Eduardo de Sousa Ferreira and Walter Oppelo, Jr. (eds), *Conflict and Change in Portugal, 1974–1984*, Lisbon: Teorema, 1985, pp. 79–99.

21 Cf. José Magone, *European Portugal: The Difficult Road to Sustainable Democracy*, London: Macmillan, 1997, p. 27.

22 Pedro Alvares and Carlos Roma Fernandes (eds), *Portugal e o Mercado Comum*, vol. 2: *Dos Acordos de 1972 às negociações de adesão*, Lisbon: Pórtico, 1980.

23 Authors' interview with former Portuguese Prime Minister Mário Soares, Arrábida, 1998.

24 See also the chapter on Spain by Ricardo Martín de la Guardia in this book.

25 José Medeiros Ferreira, 'Os regimes políticos em Portugal e a organização internacional da Europa', *Política Internacional*, 1995, vol. 11, pp. 5–39.

26 Juilo Crespo MacLennan, *Spain and the Process of European Integration, 1957–85*, London: Macmillan, 2000; Juan Carlos Pereira and Antonio Moreno Juste, 'Spain: in the centre or in the periphery of Europe?', in Pinto and Teixeira, *Southern Europe*, pp. 41–80.

27 Laurence Whitehead, 'Democracy by convergence and Southern Europe: a comparative politics perspective', in Geoffrey Pridham (ed.), *Encouraging Democracy: The International Context of Regime Transition in Southern Europe*, Leicester: Leicester University Press, 1991, pp. 45–61; Geoffrey Pridham, 'European integration and democratic consolidation in Southern Europe', in Pinto and Teixeira, *Southern Europe*, pp. 183–207.

28 José Manuel Durão Barroso, *Le système politique portugais face à l'intégration européenne: partis politiques et opinion publique*, Lisbon: APRI, 1983; Natalie Marques, *Les partis politiques et les opinions publiques au Portugal depuis 1974 face à l'intégration européenne*, Paris: DEA, Université de la Sorbonne Nouvelle-Paris III, 1995.

29 Berta Alvarez-Miranda, *El sur de Europa y la adhesión a la Comunidad: los debates políticos*, Madrid: Siglo Veintiuno, 1996, p. 202.

30 Victor Pérez-Dias, *The Return of Civil Society: The Emergence of Democratic Spain*, Cambridge, MA: Harvard University Press, 1993, p. 3.

31 Authors' interview with former Portuguese Ambassador Fernando Reino, Arrábida, 1998.

32 See Tom Bruneau (ed.), *Political Parties in Portugal: Organizations, Elections and Public Opinion*, Boulder, CO: Westview Press, 1997.

33 Nancy Bermeo, 'Regime change and its impact on foreign policy: the Portuguese case', *Journal of Modern Greek Studies*, 1998, vol. 6, pp. 7-25.

34 Manuel Lucena and Carlos Gaspar, 'Metamorfoses corporativas?: Associações de interesses económicos e institucionalização da democracia em Portugal (I)', *Análise Social*, 1991, vol. 114, pp. 847-903.

35 Ibid.

36 Guilhermina Marques, 'L'intégration des groupes d'intérêt portugais au niveau européen', in Dusan Sidjanski and Ural Ayberk (eds), *L'Europe du sud dans la Communauté Européenne: analyse comparative des groupes d'intérêt et de leur insértion dans le réseau communautaire*, Paris: PUF, 1990, pp. 185-201.

37 José Magone, *Iberian Trade Unionism: Democratization under the Impact of the European Union*, New Brunswick, NJ: Transaction, 2001.

38 On the impact of membership on the Portuguese economy, see David Corkill, *The Development of the Portuguese Economy: A Case of Europeanization*, London: Routledge, 1999.

39 Jorge Braga de Macedo, 'External liberalization with ambiguous public response: the experience of Portugal', in Christopher Bliss and Jorge Braga de Macedo (eds), *Unity with Diversity in the European Economy: The Community's Southern Frontier*, Cambridge: Cambridge University Press, 1990, pp. 310-54

40 For example in the weekly publications *Expresso* during 1996 and *Visão* during 1997. Cf. Corkill, *The Development of the Portuguese Economy*, pp. 102–24.

41 Mário Bacalhau, *Atitudes, opiniões e comportamentos políticos dos Portugueses: 1973–1993*, Lisbon: FLAD, 1994, p. 255.

42 Ibid., p. 257.

43 Ibid., p. 269.

44 Manuel Braga da Cruz, 'National identity in transition', in Richard Herr (ed.), *Portugal, Democracy and Europe*, Berkeley, CA: Institute of International and Area Studies, 1993, pp. 155–68.

45 See also Andrew Moravcsik, *The Choice for Europe: Social Purpose and State Power from Messina to Maastricht*, London: UCL Press, 1999.

46 Geoffrey Pridham, *The Dynamics of Democratization*, London: Continuum, 2000, pp. 290–9.

47 Ibid., p. 291.

7 A newcomer experienced in European integration

Austria

Michael Gehler

Introduction

Austria's relationship with Europe and its policy on integration can only be understood from a longer historical perspective.[1] It was never an under-developed country on the periphery of Europe, but rather a highly industrialized state at Europe's centre. The question of its economic reconstruction and independent political existence after the Second World War remained open, however. It regained its full sovereignty in 1955 because it was orientated to the West in its political and economic structure but also because it promised a policy of 'permanent' neutrality between East and West. For a long time this seemed only compatible with free trade in Western Europe and not full market integration.[2]

Austria was freed from National Socialism in 1945, but was occupied until 26 October 1955.[3] On 27 April 1945, a provisional government under the Socialist Karl Renner was established in Vienna which included Christian Democrats, Socialists and, at the outset, also Communists. From 1947, the Grand Coalition of the People's Party (ÖVP) and the Socialist Party (SPÖ) grew out of this provisional government. This coalition existed until 1966 and was reactivated between 1987 and 2000. After 1945, the Austrian economy was once again dependent on foreign financial and economic help, just as it had been after 1918. The United Nations Relief and Rehabilitation Administration (UNRRA) and the European Recovery Programme (ERP) gave financial assistance which contributed greatly to economic reconstruction and political consolidation. The Austrian government tried to address the issue of the Soviet seizure of 'German' property in its occupation zone with a policy of nationalization. The nationalization of heavy industry was pushed through by the Socialists who managed to win the support of the Christian Democrats after accepting the Marshall Plan which was in fact based on an acceptance of private ownership. The Grand Coalition of ÖVP and SPÖ – the two political forces which had been involved in several bloody civil wars before the annexation of Austria by the German Reich in 1938 – was born just as much out of necessity as from the close cooperation between different interest groups – employers and trade unions – in the context of the institutionalized neo-corporatist 'social partnership'.

Austrian foreign policy after 1945 was determined by the occupation, Austria's economic plight and a lack of freedom of action. In historiography, the relative importance of these reasons has been stressed in different ways. According to Gerald Stourzh, Austria's main aim was to achieve national independence.[4] The withdrawal of the occupying forces was 'the primary aim of all Austrian efforts'.[5] Linked to this wish was the demand for Austria's territorial integrity. In this context, the demand for the reintegration of South Tyrol, which had been ceded to Italy after 1918, initially played a leading role in the years 1945–46.[6] More recent research has stressed the instrumentality of the country's 'victim status'[7] by the Austrian government. After 1945, the country was primarily concerned with distancing and emancipating itself from Germany[8] and the development of a specifically Austrian state ideology. An open public debate about the National Socialist past and the participation of Austrians in the crimes committed in the name of National Socialism would have endangered the young and still rather unstable state. In these circumstances, it seemed to the political elites that everything possible had to be done to protect the state and its population from allegations of collaboration with the National Socialist regime and to reject the idea that Austria, like the Federal Republic of Germany founded in 1949, could be regarded as the legal successor to the so-called Third Reich.[9] As one of the founding members of the inter-governmental Organization for European Economic Cooperation (OEEC) in 1948, Austria used this forum for the promotion of its foreign and European interests. From 1952 onwards, alliance-free status was under consideration as an option for Austria. From 1955 on, 'permanent' neutrality[10] along the lines of the Swiss model[11] – in accordance with the Moscow Memorandum of 14 April 1955 – was then the platform from which to demand the quick withdrawal of the occupying forces and national sovereignty. Austria later diverged from the Swiss model to a great extent, however.

The new bipolarity of the international system was realized early on in Vienna. The Austrian governments regarded it as imperative to avoid being drawn into the East–West conflict.[12] In these circumstances, the neutrality that Austria had chosen in 1955 was already interpreted as a 'detour towards Europe' by contemporaries. In the summer of 1958, the ÖVP foreign policy specialist Lujo Tončić-Sorinj developed this idea in his presentation as part of the lecture series, 'The Viennese talks about Europe', and recalled that Austria was prepared to make this 'sacrifice' of neutrality in order to support the idea of a larger Europe which would facilitate the 'integration of those peoples to the East of Austria into a greater European community'.[13] At the same time, Austria did not want and in fact could not detach itself from the Western European integration process, most importantly from its economic dimension. 'Europe', beyond the 'core Europe' states and their supranational integration, was seen to be a chance to give Austrian politics a function and the state a deeper *raison d'être*. Compared to the European Economic Community (EEC), this larger, multi-layered Europe was much more compatible with 'permanent' neutrality and national sovereignty and distinguishing itself from the Federal

Republic of Germany which had been integrated into Western Europe and the German Democratic Republic which had been integrated into the East. As a participant in the Marshall Plan and a recipient of ERP funds (1948–53) and as a country partly occupied by the Soviet Union until 1955, Austria was also, however, a special case. Austria's integration policy from 1963 of 'going it alone' in order to arrive at a bilateral arrangement with the EEC, again made it a special case in comparison with its partners in the European Free Trade Association (EFTA). Austria prompted the European Commission to think about customs union projects and the form that association with the EEC could take, and thus to be more precise regarding the vague Article 238 in the EEC Treaty. Austria was the trailblazer for other states' integration policy, especially that of the neutrals. Its policy of 'going it alone' once again in 1989 – the first application for entry to the EC by a neutral member of EFTA after the Internal Market Programme had become public – with explicit reservations about neutrality, again emphasized the country's status as a special case.

Austria and 'Europe' after 1945

'Permanent' neutrality was the price Austria had to pay for the withdrawal of Soviet troops in the *annus mirabilis* of 1955, as the West German Ambassador in Vienna, Carl-Hermann Mueller-Graaf, recognized.[14] In return, Moscow neither opposed Austria's inclusion in the United Nations (14 December 1955)[15] nor its entry into the Council of Europe (16 April 1956). Both went ahead, in contrast to the Swiss 'model'. The Soviet Foreign Minister Vyacheslav Molotov instructed his ambassador in Vienna not to react positively but 'not to refuse' Austrian membership of the Council of Europe, although this was seen by the Soviet Union as part of the 'Western military bloc' and Switzerland was not yet a member. With the same motivation it had for accession to the Council of Europe, Austria signed the Council of Europe's Convention on Human Rights of 1950, on 13 December 1957. Ratification followed on 3 September 1958.[16]

With the European Coal and Steel Community (ECSC), Austria strove towards creating a customs and trade agreement. This was achieved on 8 May 1956 and was completed with an anti-dumping clause.[17] The ECSC High Authority and the Austrian government also agreed special regulations and the appointment of a permanent Joint Commission for the clarification of price disputes.[18] This appeared to be as far as the government was prepared to go in the direction of integration in the coal and steel sector. The government's announcement on 23 and 24 October 1956 that Austria would seek full membership of the ECSC appeared to reverse previous policy. Could Vienna really go so far? The Austrian government tested the existing room for negotiation regarding integration with this remarkable action. Alongside the feared Soviet veto, however, overly high steel prices in the ECSC meant that the government did not pursue this option further. These prices were 20 to 30 per cent higher than domestic prices which were highly subsidized in favour of manufacturing industry and which would have risen correspondingly with ECSC entry. The example shows that the room for manoeuvre regarding integration was not only determined by the proviso of neutrality and consideration of the Soviet Union but also by domestic pressures and interests.[19] The bloody suppression of the Hungarian Revolution by the Red Army in November 1956 eventually led the Austrian government to act more cautiously, and it did not submit a formal application for ECSC membership.

The existential issue of how Austria could simultaneously become economically pro-Western and alliance-free was addressed by Austria with an elaborate compromise solution.[20] Austria was formally neutral despite effectively being aligned with the West. Neutrality was interpreted as mainly having a military character, combined with the continuation of a Western economic orientation. The Soviet Union accepted these limitations.[21] It was a 'partly forced, partly voluntary renunciation of full integration into the West'.[22] A coherent and more restrictive understanding of the purpose of neutrality only developed gradually in the second half of the 1950s. This could be used together with the still very strong sovereignty argument against the drive towards closer integration with the EEC. In 1958, Chancellor Julius Raab and Foreign Minister Leopold Figl – both of the ÖVP – considered the idea of joining the EEC. Vice-Chancellor Bruno Pittermann (SPÖ) opposed this option – in addition to economic reservations – with the arguments 'neutrality' and 'Switzerland'. In contrast to the EEC, the Western European free trade area project first proposed by Great Britain in 1956 and then EFTA membership were seen to safeguard neutrality, national sovereignty and treaty-making power. Austria then strove towards an association with the EEC (1961–63) and after Charles de Gaulle's rejection of British EEC membership in January 1963, attempted the policy of 'going-it-alone' from February 1963 to December 1969 to achieve a bilateral arrangement with the EEC. At that time, Bruno Kreisky of the SPÖ, who was Foreign Minister from 1959 until 1966, stressed the importance of an integration policy which was in tune with the traditionally extensive interpretation of neutrality in Switzerland excluding membership in a customs union. He was not able to fully assert his views, however, nor was his adversary, the Trade Minister Fritz Bock (ÖVP), who supported the policy of 'going it alone' in relation to the EEC. In the end, Austria's integration policy of the 1960s did not stray far from the sovereignty postulate.

Against this background, some general observations can be made about Austrian European policy-making after 1945. First, the founding of the ECSC in 1951–52 and the EEC in 1957–58 prompted discussions in parliament, in the media, and among the general public as to the economic and political consequences of possible Austrian membership of these organizations. The debate about the continued existence of EFTA which was founded in 1960, or the possibility of an Austrian association with the EEC in the 1960s was, however, more intense and had more effect than the discussions of the 1950s. Second, the international constellation and Austria's resulting political interests contributed to the fact that accession into the EEC as a full member seemed out

of the question in the 1950s and 1960s. When Austria applied for EEC association in December 1961, the building of the Berlin Wall was still underway, the
Cuban Missile Crisis was about to begin and the East–West confrontation was
reaching a climax. There were strong domestic opponents to an association
with the EEC – among others from nationalized industry – but there were also
strong supporters of it including the Association of Austrian Industrialists
(VÖI), who on the whole cancelled each other out. Ultimately, the Soviet
Union's veto was decisive up until 1989, as was the exclusive 'core Europe'
stance of the subsequent European Commissions and of France and Italy, both
of whom had reservations about Austrian attempts to seek a special relationship
with the EEC. This was demonstrated very clearly in their veto in the years
1967–69.

Third, regarding early priorities in European and integration policy, 'soft' as
well as 'hard' factors help explain Austria's desire for an association with the
EEC. ÖVP representatives confirmed their support for European and integra-
tion initiatives in Western Europe in the Christian Democratic *Nouvelles Equipes
Internationales* (NEI) and its successor organization, the European Union of
Christian Democrats (EUCD) after 1965,[23] as did the SPÖ in the Socialist
International (SI).[24] The Austrians emphatically supported the idea of a 'core
Europe' there, in contrast to the German Social Democrats. This 'core Europe'
did not include Austria, however. Furthermore, Austria had strong historical
and ideological connections to Western Europe. These were not strong enough,
however, to prompt the EEC to treat Austria as a special case. From 1955 to
1958, neutrality was not an insurmountable obstacle at first. Only with growing
experience in foreign policy after the Hungarian Crisis in 1956–57, the
Lebanon Crisis in 1958, and during the visit of Nikita Khrushchev in 1960, did
a specific Austrian interpretation of neutrality emerge. Added to this was, on
one hand, the strong trade connections with Western Europe, especially with
West Germany, which mitigated in favour of membership of the ECSC/EEC.
On the other hand, Austria also had significant barter trade connections with
Eastern Europe – an advantage that it would have lost as a full EEC member.

Fourth, the reasons for Austria's joining EFTA in 1959–60 are relatively
clear. The small free trade area option appeared only to be second-best. While
ÖVP politicians saw this as only a temporary solution, SPÖ representatives
supported it more wholeheartedly. The creation of EFTA was seen by some to
increase the chances of 'bridge-building' to the EEC. This turned out to be
unrealistic, however. From the Austrian point of view, EFTA could in no way
compete with the EEC. It was seen by the majority of government members to
be a first step towards multilateral association between the EEC and EFTA.[25]
Austria's EFTA membership was a political reaction to the formation of the
EEC and the threat of 'European disintegration',[26] as well as an 'economic
experiment' and an 'emergency solution'[27] after the failure of the large free
trade area. Stephan Nonhoff has described the founding of EFTA as a compromise,[28] Franz Urlesberger as an 'alliance for self-protection' of the outer
Seven.[29]

In the 1960s, the combination of partial tendency to self-exclusion and partial desire for integration became especially clear in Austria. ÖVP Chancellor Josef Klaus (1964–70) spoke about a 'drought period' which Austria had to go through, in which there was no lack of 'know-it-alls' in one's own country, sometimes mild, sometimes severe Soviet warnings, and criticism from those neutral countries 'which did not particularly like our going it alone'.[30] Austria's EFTA partners, including Great Britain, in fact looked on with scepticism when the Austrian government continued to pursue an arrangement with the EEC after de Gaulle's veto of the British EEC application in January 1963.[31]

Opposition to an all too formal association of Austria with the EEC came not only from Moscow, but also from Paris and Rome. Austria was able to soften the Soviet Union's hard-line position, but for a long time there was no formal breakthrough. In the 1960s, the Austrian government at first tried to proceed multilaterally, but as this was not realizable, it went for bilateral EEC association, as this 'middle path' still appeared to be politically compatible with its neutrality status. This option was not accepted by the Soviet Union, even if a modification of its categorical standpoint was not out of the question. A shift occurred in 1966 with the Soviet 'concession' of a simple trade treaty between Austria and the EEC. In 1967, on the occasion of Klaus and Tončić's state visit, Moscow was willing to consider making even more concessions as the toleration of a free trade area arrangement was informally discussed.[32]

Austria's foreign trade with the EEC lay predominantly in West Germany with, on average, 30 to 40 per cent of Austrian imports and 20 to 30 per cent of its exports between 1951 and 1968.[33] This mainly shocked French diplomacy, evoking the trauma of the *Anschluss*.[34] It was mainly concerned to prevent the Federal Republic of Germany being economically and politically strengthened by an association with further millions of German-speakers, thus potentially enhancing its influence in the Danube region. At the same time, the conflict with Italy about South Tyrol, which had begun in 1959–60, escalated after 1966–67 and led to a total blockade of negotiations with Brussels between 1967 and 1969. Austria's policy of 'going it alone' was eventually thwarted after eight rounds of negotiations. This was not primarily a result of the opposition of the Soviet Union, but rather because of Italy's opposition and because of France's growing reserve regarding Soviet objections. France was the only EEC member to have signed the Austrian State Treaty in 1955.[35] For both the Soviet Union and France, Austria's geopolitical position was far too sensitive for them to imagine a closer incorporation of Austria into the EEC. The West German Chancellor from 1963–66, Ludwig Erhard, who was anti-Gaullist and pro-free trade, tried to intercede for Austria's closer association with the EEC, but without much success. The EEC's top priorities remained increasing its internal cohesion, the question of Britain's entry and the association of countries who were actually willing to enter the EEC as full members in the long term.[36]

Resistance on the domestic front was far stronger in the 1960s than in the 1980s and 1990s. The hard-line supporters of neutrality, Bruno Pittermann and

Bruno Kreisky, differentiated between their intra-party and public rhetoric and their practical politics, which remained realistic, pragmatic and adaptable. The SPÖ Vice-Chancellor Pittermann spoke in 1959 about the EEC as a 'reactionary bourgeois bloc', but later was not opposed to an arrangement in which Austria would become associated with the EEC in 1961–63.[37] As he was responsible for the nationalized industries, he strongly supported the protection of Austria's substantial trade with the East.[38] Nonetheless, probably one of the reasons for Pittermann's resignation as SPÖ leader in 1967 was a growing willingness in the SPÖ leadership for ever closer association with the EEC.

In 1967–68, Austria also experienced a two-fold crisis at its borders in the south and the east. The tense diplomatic relations with Italy as a result of its obstruction of the promised autonomy for South Tyrol and the bomb attacks there by German nationalists resulted in the Italian government's objection to negotiations with Austria. On top of this came the events in Czechoslovakia in August 1968, leading to the intervention of the Warsaw Pact states and the suppression of the Prague Spring, which resulted in Austria's chances of integration sinking to an all-time low. The government was forced to put its ambitious efforts from the early 1960s on the backburner and to distance itself from the policy of 'going it alone'.[39]

This policy of 'going it alone' during Klaus's chancellorship helped to prepare for later arrangements with the EC in Brussels, however. In 1972–73, Austria's integration aims of the 1960s were partially fulfilled. Austria, Sweden and Switzerland negotiated free trade treaties with the EC. On 22 July 1972, these treaties were signed, which allowed Austria its partial economic participation in integration while fulfilling its neutrality duties. The provisional agreement with Austria foresaw the six-month early start to the dismantling of the tariffs. The *Wiener Zeitung* interpreted this concession as a kind of 'loyalty bonus'[40] awarded by the Community, later researchers as a 'reward' for Austria's policy of 'going it alone'.[41]

From application to accession

Thomas Angerer has raised the question of whether Austria distanced itself from supranational integration because it *could not* or rather because it *did not want to* integrate. He is right in expressing doubts about the one-sided supposition that Austria *could not* participate primarily because of the Soviet vetoes.[42] However, it was almost always for both reasons. Austria was simultaneously not able to fully integrate and did not want to do so either. European economic cooperation was unequivocally supported by Austria, and market integration also to a great extent. The idea of political integration was also supported in a general sense although Austria did not seek such integration for itself.

In the era of Chancellor Kreisky (1970–83), when 'Eurosclerosis' prevailed, the issue of integration took a backseat as Austria's foreign policy of internationalization dominated the foreign policy agenda. The international focus on East–West and North–South issues was more or less consolidated under the

Small Coalition of the SPÖ and the Freedom Party (FPÖ) under Chancellor Fred Sinowatz and Vice-Chancellor Norbert Steger (1983–86). Only when the Grand Coalition returned to power, in 1987, did Austrian policy shift again in the direction of greater emphasis on European integration. This was as a result of changes in the EC's Single European Act, its Internal Market programme and the receding Cold War, as well as domestic pressures arising from an escalating crisis in the nationalized industries. What followed was a further attempt to 'go it alone' with the application for accession to the EC on 17 July 1989. During 1991–94, the Austrian government began to support integration to a far greater degree, playing down the importance of neutrality. An intensified supranational integration policy followed with entry into the EU, with a conscious effective discarding of neutrality after 1995.

What was most important for the Austrian supporters of EC membership was, remarkably, the regaining of sovereignty.[43] This was a new form of 'sovereignty' for Austria, a sharing of 'supranational sovereignty'. The central figure in Austria's integration politics of the late 1980s and 1990s, Foreign Minister Alois Mock 1987-95 put this in the following way:

> We are stronger in the EC! Outside of the Union, what determines political reality is, as ever the principle of power … In the context of integration, on the other hand, the principle of power is balanced by the community of common law and partnership in the institutions … What is most important in the decision about EC membership is that Austrians, especially future generations, should be enabled to play an active and effective part in shaping the common European future.[44]

What really drove on Austria's policy of support for integration in 1989 and the following years was, as before, the threat of exclusion. The policy change was not, however, *ad hoc*, but took place in a period of transition. Participation in the European Economic Area (EEA) negotiations during 1992–94 served as a springboard for raising the quality of integration.

Neutrality had already been re-interpreted in various different ways before entry and used as a political 'multipurpose weapon',[45] that is to say it was subject to a transformative process. Large sectors of the population continued to see neutrality, however, as a positive thing. In the official stressing of the compatibility of neutrality and EC membership between 1989 and 1992–95, the refusal to break the taboo of neutrality continued after the application. After 1989–90, with the end of the East–West conflict and after Mikhail Gorbachev had given his support to Austria's ambitions for EC membership, the opportunity to attain full membership presented itself, without having to consider the Soviet Union, as was previously the case. From 1989–95, the way to Brussels was through Paris and Rome, however. After the spectre of the *Anschluss* turned out no longer to be an insurmountable obstacle and the formal declaration by Italy and Austria of the end of the dispute in the painful South Tyrol question could be laid before the UN in 1992, the EC door was pushed open and entry became a real possibility. Germany, a traditional promoter of Austrian interests regarding integration, added weight to the application with support from the Christian Democratic Chancellor Helmut Kohl and the Liberal Foreign Minister Klaus Kinkel – this time successfully, in contrast to the 1950s and 1960s.

The controversy about whether the application for EC membership was a break with continuity or a symbol of continuity with the integration policy up until that time, touches the core of the complex relationship between self-exclusion and integration. Its partners actually experienced Austria in the 1990s as a resolute 'newcomer' rather than as a recent opportunistic convert. The application for membership had not come as a surprise in the light of Austria's European policies since 1945. On submitting its application, the government emphasized economic aims and securing peace although it expressly argued that Austria's interests were 'not only based on economic considerations'. Austria, however, had the 'aim not to become excluded from the process of integration, but to participate in it as far as possible'.[46] Austria's membership of the OEEC, the European Council and EFTA and even its loyalty to EFTA up until then were referred to in Point 10 of the government declaration. However, Austria's aims were not met with great enthusiasm. The EU member-states set on deepening integration and Commission President Jacques Delors had one problem more in the form of possible accession negotiations with Austria, a 'special case' and neutral, as they were implementing the Internal Market and preparing the massive changes of the Maastricht Treaty, including economic and monetary union.

Although not fundamentally new, the EC application was qualitatively something new. Fundamental was the Austrian interest in the Internal Market and the resulting wish for a significant intensification of the relationship to the EC. It was still founded, however, on 'old' ideas about integration. The qualitative novelty lay in the willingness to fully participate in the Internal Market and to participate as a full member in the more supranational Community. The proviso of neutrality, which was underlined twice in the application was, however, an important element of continuity, as an expression of partial self-exclusion. It was not without reason that the potential implications for defence policy which came with entry were consciously faded out in the government's propaganda prior to the EU referendum.

Political science research has already shown that in the controversial accession debate, economic considerations were at first central. It was only later that security and defence considerations took on this level of importance. The quantum leap to supranational integration had only been taken by a small inner circle of experts, diplomats and politicians. The general public in the 1990s was still thinking along the lines they had done in 1989 and previously. The continuity thesis can account for this persistence of popular attitudes much better.[47] The clean break with the previous politics up to then only came later when Austria actually joined the EU in 1995.

Against this background the following characteristics are especially important: first, all the influential domestic forces declared their support for Austria's joining the EC/EU between 1987 and 1995. The driving forces were the VÖI together with leading ÖVP politicians who specialized in foreign and European affairs. The Social Democrats, who had previously called themselves Socialists up until 1991, initially acted with restraint between 1987 and 1993. In the government's campaign for EU entry in 1994, however, the parties of the Grand Coalition – the SPÖ and ÖVP – and most societal and interest groups opted strongly for membership. Practically the entire media supported EU membership. With the help of the mass-circulation newspaper, *Kronen Zeitung*, a clear majority of Austrian public opinion could be won over to support EU membership. One reason for the two-thirds support was a relatively primitive propaganda campaign by the government which superficially convinced many Austrians to say 'yes'.

Second, there was actually no spectacular change of position of any relevant political or economic groups. There was neither an outright 'no' to EC membership from these groups, nor an unreserved 'yes'. The desire to secure the best of all worlds resulted from the domestic influence of nationalized industry and the social partnership organizations and from pressures outside Austria. This led to a very pragmatic policy of muddling through. The ÖVP and SPÖ were basically pro-European parties, even if it took the Socialists longer to become converted to the aim of joining the EC. While the Internal Market Programme – which was drawn up by the EC in 1986–87 – consolidated the support of both of the large parties – SPÖ and ÖVP – for EU entry, the FPÖ tried to use the crisis in Europe due to the recession and growing unemployment following German unification, and political uncertainty at the time of the wars in the former Yugoslavia, for its own ends. Under its leader Jörg Haider, it switched to a Euro-sceptical position in 1992–93. This helped the FPÖ to increase its national share of the vote among those opposed to EU membership in national elections, but the larger parties managed to guarantee sufficient popular support by an ostentatious national closing of ranks before the 1994 EU referendum.

Third, the changed international context, including the fall of the Berlin Wall and the collapse of the Soviet Union had a great impact on Austrian integration policy. The symbolic severing of the Iron Curtain by Foreign Minister Mock and his Hungarian counterpart Gyula Horn in June, and by the Czechoslovak Foreign Minister Jiri Dienstbier in December 1989, pointed the way to the future and paved the way for the Austrian application for EU entry and the accession negotiations in 1993–94.

Fourth, the Austrian perception of 'core Europe' also improved a great deal as the threat of the Cold War receded. The elites increasingly recognized the need for domestic structural reforms and began to regard the EC/EU 'core Europe' as an external modernizer for the Austrian economy which was increasingly characterized by growing budget deficits, high public deficits and corruption scandals. The debates about the Federal President Kurt Waldheim (1986–92) also facilitated the identity change. Due to his alleged war crimes in the Balkans during the Second World War, he only received diplomatic invitations from Jordan, Pakistan and the Pope. Underlying the Austrian EC application was also the old yearning to belong to a powerful large economic bloc, a kind of substitute for the Habsburg Empire. Added to this was chiefly the fear of being excluded from an economically dynamic 'core Europe'. At the same time, the East Central European countries, which were no longer part of the Soviet sphere of influence, were already queuing up in Brussels. Many Austrians feared that if they continued to be passive, they could possibly end up behind the new East Central European applicant states and this cleared away any last inhibitions about joining 'core Europe'.

Fifth, the influence of transnational cooperation on Austrian integration policy varied greatly from the SPÖ to the ÖVP. The Socialist International (SI) with Willy Brandt, Olof Palme and Bruno Kreisky developed strong international cooperation in the 1970s which extended far beyond Western Europe. These leading Socialists tended to favour the status quo in European integration. The ÖVP, on the other hand, had always closely cooperated in the more European-focused Christian Democratic transnationalism. As a non-EEC member party it could not, however, participate in the EU-based European People's Party (EPP), founded in 1976. Thus, it searched for new transnational coalition opportunities in the context of the European Democratic Union (EDU) which it co-founded and the International Democratic Union (IDU) as well as elsewhere to get closer to the EC. Alois Mock, the ÖVP leader and then Foreign Minister from 1987, acted as EDU President, which was helpful in lobbying for Austrian EU entry within the European Parliament between 1992 and 1994.

Conclusion

Austria is an almost ideal case for testing different integration theories, confirming the 'poverty of theory' with its tendency to simplify and overgeneralize.[48] Different aspects of Austrian European policy can be used not only to 'prove' almost every theory but also to call them into question.

Up to a point, Alan S. Milward's thesis that European integration served primarily as a means of 'rescuing' the nation–state applies to Austria's decision to seek EC membership and to participate as a full member from 1995. Membership was certainly regarded as an instrument to modernize and revitalize the Austrian state and economy. Empirical evidence can also be found to substantiate Andrew S. Moravcsik's related liberal inter-governmental theory with its emphasis on the role of domestic interest groups for national policy-making. The pre-history of the EC application was characterized by discussions between the coalition parties as well as within and between the different interest groups with the aim of coordinating their specific EC/EU interests. The government also had to inform and consult the institutionalized social partnership organizations and interest groups in order to reach a domestic consensus on the main aims for the accession negotiations with the EU.

The neo-functionalist theory with its assumed 'spill-over' effects is also relevant for the Austrian case, although at a low level of integration in the beginning. Austrian political elites saw the OEEC and EFTA as possible places to develop the relationship with 'core Europe' organizations and to prepare for institutional bridge-building. Austria insisted that the creation of EFTA could not replace the necessary trade arrangement with the EEC. The negotiations in the 1960s about a bilateral arrangement with the EEC brought up the idea of creating an 'Association Council'. In the negotiations between the European Commission and Austria during 1964–66, the partners considered a kind of mixture of a free trade and customs union arrangement which would have been unworkable without its political institutionalization, probably leading to a further deepening of the institutional relationship at some point. Concrete 'spill-over' effects can be observed on a lower level. The bilateral free trade treaty with the EC at the start of the 1970s was the result of the policy of 'going-it-alone' in the 1960s, and designed to get closer to the EC, although limited to free trade in industrial goods. The free trade treaty also contained an evolutional clause which allowed the partners to develop their relationship further. Austria's membership of the EEA, as of January 1994, and the advance adoption of the *acquis communautaire*, one year ahead of its full EU membership, can be seen as anticipated 'spillover' from the Internal Market.

Austria's European policy is also well worth examining from the premise of constructivist theories. At the start of the integration process, most Austrian political leaders did not support the common market idea, or indeed Austrian EEC membership. In the 1980s and 1990s, however, an interesting paradigm change occurred. The EFTA supporters of the 1960s and 1970s lost influence, increasingly changed their stance and eventually supported EC/EU entry. Christian Democrats and Social Democrats saw their country anchored culturally and economically in the West. Politically, however, they preferred to be neutral for a long time.[49] When neutrality lost its logic with the receding Cold War however, they took the first real chance for a relatively uncomplicated entry.[50] In fact, leading Austrian politicians had repeatedly maintained that Austria was at least as 'European' or even 'more European' than other countries. The first Chancellor of the Second Republic, Leopold Figl, created the catch-phrase, 'Austria is Europe, and Europe cannot exist without Austria.'[51] This ideology was closely connected to the German question and the syndrome of the *Anschluss* of 1938. In order to counteract the suspicion of still being 'German' or *Anschluss*-orientated, Austrian foreign policy used 'Europe' as a means of identification which, in turn, allowed for a more intensive economic link to Germany again.

Since accession, Austrian attitudes to EU integration have remained somewhat ambivalent.[52] The government had used the simplistic catch-phrase 'We are Europe'[53] to campaign for entry to the EU. To the pro-European political elites, a new 'European' identity appeared to be the ideal replacement for the dominant post-war identity of Austria as the first 'victim' of National Socialist Germany, which had been greatly strained in the Waldheim debate. The government raised expectations in the country which were unrealistic, however. They created the impression that everything would improve once Austria was in the EU, without Austrians having to face any harsh domestic reforms. The political elite thus attempted to distract from the 'silent revolution'[54] that Austria had been undergoing since 1995 as a result of EU accession.

In the first five years of membership, the Austrian governments made great efforts to fit into the EU structures. Austria participated fully in economic and monetary union and the introduction of the Euro between 1999 and 2002. The country fulfilled the convergence criteria of the Maastricht Treaty, and also joined the Schengen Agreement. Once a member of the EU, the Austrian government wanted from the start to belong to the inner core. Austria's economy became more competitive, the gross domestic product grew more rapidly than before 1995 and prices dropped. Productivity increased and progress was made in reforming the state budget. The country became not only more important as a market for foreign products, but also as a site for foreign direct investment. As a result of the increased competition, there were economic losers as well as winners, however. On the whole, however, the Austrian economy was rapidly integrated into the EU.[55] Initially, the foundations of the Austrian welfare state remained unaltered after Austria had become a member of the EU. When the ÖVP–FPÖ coalition was formed in 2000, however, it carried through the first structural reforms,[56] and a major pension reform followed in 2003 – a belated recognition of structural problems that EU integration has made more urgent to solve.

The outstanding European event for Austria was its EU Presidency in the second half of 1998. It took the role in its stride and as if it had been a long-standing member-state. The German general election in 1998 with the victory of the Social Democrat Gerhard Schröder over Helmut Kohl and the resulting transition problems limited the scope of what the Austrian Presidency could achieve, however. That is also why the Vienna Summit of December 1998 was not very successful regarding the so-called 'Agenda 2000' for the urgently needed reform of the Common Agricultural Policy (CAP).[57] At the same time, the long shadow of neutrality continued to leave its mark long after Austria had joined the EU.[58] The government could only agree on obtaining observer status in the Western European Union and participation in the NATO cooperation programme, Partnership for Peace.[59] The SPÖ–ÖVP coalition failed to develop a consensus about a new security concept. While the ÖVP, which had traditionally supported 'Europe', recommended NATO accession, the SPÖ, which was initially more sceptical about Western integration and also has a pacifist wing, wanted Austria to remain neutral. Thus, Austria to this day is still not a full military partner in common European or transatlantic defence and security policy. As a result of this, the EU's ability to act on the security front has been somewhat impeded.[60]

The sanctions by the governments of the fourteen EU partners – which were threatened on 31 January 2000 and imposed on 4 February after the formation of the new ÖVP–FPÖ government – came as a shock for the government and the population.[61] Austria's image has been rather tarnished since then. It has appeared to be a politically unreliable partner in Europe, especially in relation to the EU's Eastern enlargement which Haider abused for his populist political agenda. The fears regarding the FPÖ, which came to a head in the sanctions policy, were historically and politically motivated and in some ways quite understandable, but the imposition of sanctions was counterproductive.[62] Despite the lifting of the isolation measures in September 2000, Austria's perspective had become far more introspective than before. Its search for 'strategic partners' among the East-Central European states, a product of the period of isolation in 2000, was hardly a success. The 'strategic' has already been renamed 'regional partnership'.[63]

Austria's path towards eventual EU integration was very time-consuming and exhausting after its application for membership of the EC. It concentrated mainly on relations with Western Europe. Central and Eastern Europe became marginal, which explains why Austria only began at a late point to concern itself with controversial issues of the so-called Beneš decrees regarding the expulsion of German speakers from Czechoslovakia after 1945 or the Czech nuclear power plant at Temelín. Austria has become integrated into the EU as a country with internal problems. It is largely been preoccupied with the political burden of the long-standing Grand Coalition and the resulting lack of more radical structural reforms, and has been too busy adapting to membership to turn its gaze outwards with self-confidence and play a more pro-active role in the EU. Nevertheless, Austria was and still is at the centre of Europe and has become economically integrated with 'core Europe'. From 2004, it could take on an important bridging function and a mediating role for the integration of the new member-states from East-Central Europe and for their continuing 'Europeanization', something of central importance to the EU. The Haiders of this world come and go, but Austria's central position in Europe and its European consciousness remains.

Notes

1 See also, for greater detail, Michael Gehler, *Der lange Weg nach Europa: Österreich vom Ende der Monarchie bis zur EU*, vol. 1: *Darstellung*; vol. 2: *Dokumente*, Innsbruck: Studienverlag, 2002; Thomas Angerer, 'Quelle Europe pour quelle Autriche? Grandes questions autour d'un petit pays', in Michel Dumoulin and Geneviève Duchenne (eds), *Les petits États et la construction européenne*, Brussels: Peter Lang, 2002, pp. 181–208, here pp. 183–99.

2 Michael Gehler, 'Austria and European integration, 1947–1960: Western orientation, neutrality and free trade', *Diplomacy and Statecraft*, 1998, vol. 9, no. 3, pp. 154–210.

3 Günter Bischof, 'Allied plans and policies for the occupation of Austria, 1938–1955', in Rolf Steininger, Günter Bischof and Michael Gehler (eds), *Austria in the Twentieth Century*, New Brunswick, NJ: Transaction, 2002, pp. 162–89.

4 Gerald Stourzh, 'Die Sicherung der österreichischen Unabhängigkeit als Thema der Staatsvertragsverhandlungen', *Zeitgeschichte*, 1975, vol. 2, pp. 183–91.

5 Gerald Stourzh, *Geschichte des Staatsvertrages 1945–1955: Österreichs Weg zur Neutralität*, 3rd edn, Graz: Styria, 1985, p. 129.

6 Under-estimated in Gerald Stourzh, *Um Einheit und Freiheit: Staatsvertrag, Neutralität und das Ende der Ost-West-Besetzung Österreichs 1945–1955*, 4th edn, Vienna: Böhlau, 1998.

7 See Günter Bischof, 'Die Instrumentalisierung der Moskauer Erklärung nach dem 2. Weltkrieg', *Zeitgeschichte*, 1993, vol. 20, no. 11–12, pp. 345–66; Günter Bischof, *Austria in the First Cold War, 1945–1955: The Leverage of the Weak*, Basingstoke: Macmillan, 1999.

8 See Michael Gehler, '"Kein Anschluß, aber auch keine chinesische Mauer": Österreichs außenpolitische Emanzipation und die deutsche Frage 1945–1955', in Alfred Ableitinger, Siegfried Beer and Eduard G. Staudinger (eds), *Österreich unter alliierter Besatzung 1945–1955*, Vienna: Böhlau, 1998, pp. 205–68.

9 Gerald Stourzh, 'Erschütterung und Konsolidierung des Österreichbewußtseins: Vom Zusammenbruch der Monarchie zur Zweiten Republik', in Richard G. Plaschka, Gerald Stourzh and Jan Paul Niederkorn (eds), *Was heißt Österreich? Inhalt und Umfang des Österreichbegriffs vom 10. Jahrhundert bis heute*, Vienna: Verlag der Österreichischen Akademie der Wissenschaften, 1995, pp. 289–311, here pp. 307–9. For Austrian–German relations, see also Matthias Pape, *Ungleiche Brüder: Österreich und Deutschland 1945–1965*, Cologne: Böhlau, 2000.

10 Gerald Stourzh, 'Zur Geschichte der österreichischen Neutralität', *Österreich in Geschichte und Literatur*, 1961, vol. 5, pp. 273–88.

11 Christian Jenny, *Konsensformel oder Vorbild? Die Entstehung der österreichischen Neutralität und ihr Schweizer Muster*, Berne: Haupt, 1995, pp. 161–200.

12 Gerald Stourzh, 'Die Regierung Renner, die Anfänge der Regierung Figl und die Alliierte Kommission für Österreich, September 1945 bis April 1946', *Archiv für österreichische Geschichte*, 1966, vol. 125, pp. 321–42.

13 Bericht 72/58 Carl-Hermann Mueller-Graaf an AA, 28. 6. 1958. Politisches Archiv des Auswärtigen Amtes, Berlin (PA AA), Nachlaß Mueller-Graaf, vol. 2, Wien-Politik 1953–1958.

14 Doc. 38, Gesamtbericht 'Österreich am Anfang des Jahres 1960' der Botschaft der Bundesrepublik Deutschland Wien, Carl-Hermann Mueller-Graaf an das Auswärtige Amt, 1. 2. 1960, in Gehler, *Dokumente*, pp. 209–11.

15 Wolfgang Strasser, *Österreich und die Vereinten Nationen*, Vienna: Braumüller, 1967.

16 BGBl. 1958/210; BGBl. 1969/434; BGBl. 1970/329; BGBl. 1970/330. See Wolfgang Mederer, 'Österreich und die europäische Integration aus staatsrechtlicher Perspektive 1945–1992: unter Berücksichtigung des EWR-Abkommens', in Michael Gehler and Rolf Steininger (eds), *Österreich und die europäische Integration 1945–1993: Aspekte einer wechselvollen Entwicklung*, Vienna: Böhlau, 1993, pp. 109–46, here pp. 113–14.

17 Florian Weiß, '"Gesamtverhalten: Nicht sich in den Vordergrund stellen": Die österreichische Bundesregierung und die westeuropäische Integration', in Gehler and Steininger (eds), *Österreich und die europäische Integration 1945–1993*, pp. 21–54, here pp. 50–1; Florian Weiß, 'Die schwierige Balance: Österreich und die Anfänge der westeuropäischen Integration 1947–1957', *Vierteljahrshefte für Zeitgeschichte*, 1994, vol. 42, no. 1, pp. 71–94.

18 Doc. 32, Vertrauliches Schreiben von Dirk Spierenburg, Mitglied der Hohen Behörde der EGKS, an Außenminister Leopold Figl, 25. 7. 1956, in Gehler, *Dokumente*, pp. 191–3.

19 Doc. 33, Außenminister Figl über einen möglichen Beitritt Österreichs zur Montanunion, 23. 10. 1956, in: Gehler, *Dokumente*, p. 194; see also Thomas Angerer, 'Integrität vor Integration: Österreich und "Europa" aus französischer Sicht 1949–1960', in Gehler and Steininger (eds), *Österreich und die europäische Integration 1945–1993*, pp. 178–200, here pp. 193–4; T. Angerer, 'Exklusivität und Selbstausschließung: Integrationsgeschichtliche Überlegungen zur Erweiterungsfrage am Beispiel Frankreichs und Österreichs', *Revue d'Europe Centrale*, 1998, vol. 6, no. 1, pp. 25–54, here pp. 41–6.

20 Michael Gehler, 'Zwischen Neutralität und Europäischer Union: Österreich und die Einigungsbestrebungen in Westeuropa 1955–1993', *Geschichte in Wissenschaft und Unterricht*, 1994, vol. 45, no. 7, pp. 413–33, here pp. 414 ff.

21 Roger Lalouette, Haut-Commissaire adjoint de la République française an Antoine Pinay, Ministère des Affaires Étrangères, Vienne, 18. 4. 1955, in *Documents Diplomatiques Français* (DDF), 1955, vol. 1 (1 January–30 June), Paris: PIE-Peter Lang, 1987, Doc. 199, pp. 461–4, here p. 462.

22 Michael Gehler, 'Westorientierung oder Westintegration? Überlegungen zur politkgeschichtlichen Entwicklung Österreichs von 1945 bis 1960 im wissenschaftlichen Diskurs', in Rudolf G. Ardelt and Christian Gerbel (eds), *Österreichischer Zeitgeschichtetag 1995: Österreich 50 Jahre Zweite Republik*, Innsbruck: Studienverlag, 1996, pp. 128–33, here p. 132.

23 Michael Gehler and Wolfram Kaiser, 'Transnationalism and early European integration: the Nouvelles Equipes and the Geneva Circle, 1947–1957', *Historical Journal*, 2001, vol. 44, no. 3, pp. 773–98, and Michael Gehler and Wolfram Kaiser (eds), *Transnationale Parteienkooperation der eruopäischen Christdemokraten. Dokumente 1945–1965*, Munich: K.G. Saur, 2003.

24 Klaus Misgeld, *Sozialdemokratie und Außenpolitik in Schweden: Sozialistische Internationale, Europapolitik und die Deutschlandfrage 1945–1955*, Frankfurt: Campus, 1984; Rolf Steininger, *Deutschland und die Sozialistische Internationale nach dem Zweiten Weltkrieg: Die deutsche Frage, die Internationale und das Problem der Wiederaufnahme der SPD auf den internationalen sozialistischen Konferenzen bis 1951*, Bonn: Verlag Neue Gesellschaft, 1979.

25 Oliver Rathkolb, 'Austria and European integration after World War II', in Günter Bischof and Anton Pelinka (eds), *Austria in the New Europe*, New Brunswick, NJ: Transaction, 1993, pp. 42–61, here pp. 49–50, 54–5; Bruno Kreisky considered Raab an ally on integration policy against 'the very militant Trade Minister Bock'. Cf. Bruno Kreisky, *Im Strom der Politik: Der Memoiren zweiter Teil*, Vienna: Kremair und Scheriau, 1988, pp. 166–7. See also Thomas Angerer, 'L'Autriche précurseur ou "Geisterfahrer" de l'Europe intégrée? Réflexions dans la perspective des années 1950', *Revue d'Allemagne et des pays de langue allemande*, 1992, vol. XXIV, pp. 553–61, here pp. 556–7. Doc. 23, Bericht '"Unterredung des Herrn Bundesministers für Handel und Wiederaufbau Dr. Fritz Bock mit Mr. C. Douglas Dillon, Unterstaatsekretär für Wirtschaftsfragen im Staatsdepartement" der Österreichische Botschaft Washington, Wilfried Platzer an das Bundesministerium für Auswärtige Angelegenheiten, 6. 4. 1960', in Gehler, *Dokumente*, pp. 248–52; Wolfram Kaiser, 'Challenge to the Community: the creation, crisis and consolidation of the European Free Trade Association 1958–72', *Journal of European Integration History*, 1997, vol. 3, no. 1, pp. 7–33, here pp. 17–18.

26 Fritz Weber, 'Austria: a special case in European economic integration?', in Richard T. Griffiths (ed.), *Explorations in OEEC History*, Paris: OECD, 1997, pp. 49–59, here p. 49.

27 See Michael Gehler, 'Kontinuität und Wandel: Fakten und Überlegungen zu einer politischen Geschichte Österreichs von den Sechzigern bis zu den Neunzigern (1. Teil)', *Geschichte und Gegenwart*, 1995, vol. 14, no. 4, pp. 203–38, here p. 214.

28 Stephan Nonhoff, *'In der Neutralität verhungern?': Österreich und die Schweiz vor der europäischen Integration*, Münster: agenda-Verlag, 1994, pp. 93–9.

29 Franz Urlesberger, 'Die Marginalisierung Österreichs im europäischen Integrationsgeschehen nach Auflösung der OEEC/EZU', in Waldemar Hummer (ed.), *Österreichs Integration in Europa 1948–1989: Von der OEEC zur EG*, Vienna: Orac, 1990, pp. 19–47, here p. 33.

30 Josef Klaus, *Macht und Ohnmacht in Österreich: Konfrontationen und Versuche*, Vienna: Verlag Fritz Molden, 1971, p. 366.

31 Thomas Schwendimann, 'Wien drängt, Bern wartet ab. Unterschiedliche Integrationskonzepte Österreichs und der Schweiz zwischen 1985 und 1989', in

Gehler and Steininger, *Österreich und die europäische Integration 1945–1993*, pp. 267–90; see Hanspeter Neuhold and Hans Thalberg (eds), *The European Neutrals in International Affairs*, Vienna: Braumüller, 1984; Paul Luif, 'Neutrale und europäische Integration: Neue Aspekte einer alten Problematik', *Österreichische Zeitschrift für Politikwissenschaft*, 1987, vol. 16, no. 2, pp. 117–31; Wolfram Kaiser, 'Neutral, nicht neutral, auch egal: Großbritannien, die Neutralen und die europäische Integration 1945–1972', in Michael Gehler and Rolf Steininger (eds), *Die Neutralen und die europäische Integration 1945–1995. The Neutrals and the European Integration, 1945–1995*, Vienna: Böhlau, 2000, pp. 44–60.

32 Doc. 79, 'Vertrauliches Schreiben des Generalsekretärs des Europarats, Lujo Tončić-Sorinj, an den Generalsekretär des BMfAA, a.o. u. bev. Botschafter Dr. Walter Wodak, 19. 7. 1972', in Gehler, *Dokumente*, pp. 425–7.

33 Jürgen Nautz, 'Wirtschaft und Politik: die Bundesrepublik Deutschland, Österreich und die Westintegration 1945–1961', in Gehler and Steininger, *Österreich und die europäische Integration*, pp. 163–5.

34 Thomas Angerer, 'Besatzung, Entfernung … Integration? Grundlagen der politischen Beziehungen zwischen Frankreich und Österreich seit 1938–45', in Friedrich Koja and Otto Pfersmann (eds), *Frankreich – Österreich: Wechselseitige Wahrnehmung und wechselseitiger Einfluß seit 1918*, Vienna: Böhlau, 1994, pp. 82–102, here pp. 85–8, 91–3.

35 Ibid.; see also Klaus, *Macht und Ohnmacht in Österreich*, p. 366.

36 Michael Gehler, 'The road to Brussels: Austria's integration policy 1957–1972', *Diplomacy and Statecraft*, 2002, vol. 13, no. 1, pp. 153–90.

37 'Verhungern in der Neutralität? Spiegel-Gespräch mit dem österreichischen Vizekanzler Dr. Bruno Pittermann', *Der Spiegel*, 23 January 1963, pp. 44–51, here pp. 44, 46, 50, 51; Nonhoff, *'In der Neutralität verhungern?'*, pp. 74–5.

38 American Embassy Vienna to Department of State, 25 February 1966, National Archives Records Administration (NARA), Washington, DC, College Park, RG 59, Central Foreign Policy File, Alpha-Numeric File 1963–1966, Box 1900.

39 Stephan Hamel, '"Eine solche Sache würde der Neutralitätspolitik ein Ende machen": Die österreichischen Integrationsbestrebungen 1961–1972', in Gehler and Steininger, *Österreich und die europäische Integration 1945–1993*, pp. 55–86, here pp. 78–81.

40 Doc. 7: 'Unterzeichnung der Freihandelsabkommen zwischen der EWG und EGKS einerseits und Österreich, Schweden, Schweiz, Finnland, Island und Portugal andererseits, sowie eines Interimsabkommens mit Österreich, 22. 7. 1972', in Gehler, *Dokumente*, pp. 435–8, here p. 438.

41 Waldemar Hummer, 'Ziele, Methoden und Ergebnisse der österreichischen Integrationspolitik', in Hans-Georg Koppensteiner (ed.), *Der Weg in den Binnenmarkt*, Vienna: Wirtschaftsverlag Orac, 1991, pp. 27–73, here p. 46; see also Nonhoff, *'In der Neutralität verhungern?'*, pp. 99–116.

42 Angerer, 'Exklusivität und Selbstausschließung', pp. 25–54, here p. 50.

43 See Angerer, 'L'Autriche précurseur ou "Geisterfahrer" de l'Europe intégrée?', pp. 553–61, here pp. 559–60.

44 Doc. 29, '"Die aktive Mitgestaltungsmöglichkeit Österreichs in der EU", Konzept einer Rede von Bundesminister Dr. Alois Mock, 16. 5. 1994', in Gehler, *Dokumente*, pp. 695–7, here p. 697.

45 Thomas Angerer, 'Für eine Geschichte der österreichischen Neutralität: Ein Kommentar', in Gehler and Steininger, *Die Neutralen und die europäische Integration 1945–1995*, pp. 702–8.

46 See Doc. 22, 'Das Österreichische Beitrittsgesuch an die EG, 17. 7. 1989', and here especially the declaration by Foreign Minister Alois Mock on the occasion of the submission of the application on 17 July 1989, in Gehler, *Dokumente*, pp. 467–72, especially pp. 470–2.

47 Michael Gehler and Wolfram Kaiser, 'A study in ambivalence: Austria and European integration 1945–95', *Contemporary European History*, 1997, vol. 6, no. 1, pp. 75–99.

48 Wolfgang Merkel, 'Die Europäische Integration und das Elend der Theorie', *Geschichte und Gesellschaft*, 1999, vol. 25, no. 2, pp. 302–38, here pp. 310–15.

49 Michael Gehler, '"Politisch unabhängig", aber "ideologisch eindeutig europäisch": Die ÖVP, die Vereinigung christlicher Volksparteien (NEI) und die Anfänge der europäischen Integration 1947–1960', in Gehler and Steininger, *Österreich und die europäische Integration*, pp. 291–326; Martin Hehemann, '"Daß einzelne Genossen darüber erschreckt sind, daß wir kategorisch jedwede Teilnahme an der EWG ablehnten": Die SPÖ und die Anfänge der europäischen Integration 1945–1959', in ibid., pp. 327–45.

50 On the EFTA states in a comparative perspective, see Wolfram Kaiser, 'Culturally embedded and path-dependent: peripheral alternatives to ECSC/EEC "core Europe" since 1945', *Journal of European Integration History*, 2001, vol. 7, no. 2, pp. 11–36, here pp. 14–33, 17, 19, 24, 25; specifically about Austria, see Thomas Angerer, 'De "l'Autriche Germanique" à "l'Autriche européenne"? Identités nationales et internationales de l'Autriche depuis 1918', in Gilbert Trausch (ed.), *La place et le rôle des petits pays en Europe au XXe siècle*, Brussels: Bruylant, 2004, pp. 1–58.

51 See here also Thomas Angerer, '"Österreich ist Europa": Identifikationen Österreichs mit Europa seit dem 18. Jahrhundert', *Wiener Zeitschrift zur Geschichte der Neuzeit*, 2001, vol. 1, no. 1, pp. 55–72, here p. 68; Peter Thaler, *The Ambivalence of Identity: The Austrian Experience of Nation-Building in a Modern Society*, West Lafayette, IN: Purdue University Press, 2001.

52 See, for a first assessment, Günter Bischof, Anton Pelinka and Michael Gehler (eds), *Austria in the European Union*, New Brunswick, NJ: Transaction, 2001.

53 See here also Angerer, '"Österreich ist Europa"', pp. 55–6, 71, and Karin Liebhart and Andreas Pribersky, '"Wir sind Europa!" Österreich und seine Nachbarn am "Goldenen Vorhang"', in Ferdinand Karlhofer, Josef Melchior and Hubert Sickinger (eds), *Anlassfall Österreich: Die Europäische Union auf dem Weg zu einer Wertegemeinschaft*, Baden-Baden: Nomos, 2001, pp. 115–27.

54 Wolfram Kaiser, 'The silent revolution: Austria's accession to the European Union', in Günter Bischof and Anton Pelinka (eds), *Austrian Historical Memory and National Identity*, New Brunswick, NJ: Transaction, 1997, pp. 135–62.

55 Michael Pfaffermayr, 'Austria's performance within an integrating European economy', in Michael Gehler, Anton Pelinka and Günter Bischof (eds), *Österreich in der EU: Bilanz seiner Mitgliedschaft / Austria in the European Union: A First Assessment of Her Membership*, Vienna: Böhlau, 2003, pp. 201–18.

56 Gerda Falkner, 'Austria in the European Union: direct and indirect effects on social policy', in Gehler, Pelinka and Bischof, *Österreich in der EU*, pp. 185–99.

57 Kurt Richard Luther and Iain Ogilvie (eds), *Austria and the European Union Presidency: Background and Perspectives*, Keele: Keele European Research Centre, 1998; Michael G. Huelshoff, 'The European Council and EU summitry: a comparative analysis of the Austrian and German presidencies', in Bischof, Pelinka and Gehler (eds), *Austria in the European Union*, pp. 92–117.

58 Oliver Rathkolb, 'Österreich zwischen Neutralität und Allianzfreiheit 1953–2000: Ein Überblick', *Journal of European Integration History*, 2001, vol. 7, no. 2, pp. 103–25.

59 Markus Cornaro, 'Die Westeuropäische Union: Ein erster Nachruf', in Erich P. Hochleitner (ed.), *Das Europäische Sicherheitssystem zu Beginn des 21. Jahrhunderts*, Vienna: Böhlau, 2002, pp. 233–65, here pp. 259–65; Michael Gehler, *Finis Neutralität? Historische und politische Aspekte im europäischen Vergleich: Irland, Finnland, Schweden, Schweiz und Österreich*, Bonn: Center for European Integration Studies, 2001, pp. 73–82.

60 Gehler, *Der lange Weg nach Europa*, vol. 1: *Darstellung*, pp. 428–37.

61 Michael Gehler, '"Preventive hammer blow" or boomerang? The EU "sanction" measures against Austria 2000', in Bischof, Pelinka and Gehler (eds), *Austria in the European Union*, pp. 180–222. See also Waldemar Hummer and Anton Pelinka, *Österreich unter 'EU-Quarantäne': Die'Maßnahmen der 14' gegen die österreichische Bundesregierung aus politikwissenschaftlicher und juristischer Sicht: Chronologie, Kommentar, Dokumentation*, Vienna: Linde Verlag, 2002.
62 See here Thomas Angerer, 'Welches Österreich für welches Europa? Die Krise von 2000 im Lichte europäischer Österreichprobleme und österreichischer Europaprobleme seit dem 19. Jahrhundert', and Michael Gehler, 'Kontraproduktive Intervention: Die "EU 14" und der Fall Österreich oder vom Triumph des "Primats der Innenpolitik 2000–2003"', in Gehler, Pelinka and Bischof, *Österreich in der EU*, pp. 85–120, 121–81.
63 See here Anneliese Rohrer's critical analysis, 'Eine "Partnerschaft", widersprüchliche Signale Österreichs – und retour', *Die Presse*, 1 December 2001; 'Labile Partnerschaft', *Die Presse*, 28 February 2002.

8 If in 'Europe', then in its 'core'?

Finland

Hanna Ojanen

A winding path towards the EU

Accession to the European Union in 1995 has been characterized as a fundamental turning point in Finnish history, comparable in magnitude to the
declaration of independence in 1917. Through a rapid reorientation in the early
1990s, Finland relinquished its cautious 'wait-and-see' policy of the Cold War
years and resolved to become a 'model pupil' of the EU, not only participating
unconditionally but also claiming to belong to the 'core' of the Union.[1]

The two wars fought against the Soviet Union – the Winter War of 1939–40
and the Continuation War of 1941–44 – for decades made the conditions for
Finland's participation in cooperation and integration in Europe very different
from that of its neighbours. The Paris Peace Treaty of 1947, which placed some
restrictions on the Finnish military (Finland having partly sided with Germany in
the war), and the Treaty on Friendship, Cooperation and Mutual Assistance
(FCMA), concluded with the Soviet Union in 1948, were pivotal in setting the
tone for Finland's policies. Neutrality crystallized into its doctrine in the 1950s:
Finland would above all strive to keep out of Great Power confrontations – of
which there certainly was no shortage.

A Finnish peculiarity was that integration policy was seen as part of foreign
policy, which, in turn, was subordinated to security policy. This had clear implications for domestic interest formations on the European integration front: the
foreign political elite, although small in size, dominated, and the business circles'
interests in Western Europe became more prominent only in the 1980s when the
foreign policy doctrine also started to relax. Only a few groups were involved:
one major interest group – the farmers – emerged as a central player only when
they were drawn into the process through the membership application. Even
today, no major political parties profile themselves as critical of the EU: chal-
lenging official foreign policy is still regarded as unsettling and incompatible with
the Finnish consensus tradition in foreign policy.

In President Urho Kekkonen's view, the 'Finnish paradox' was that the more
Finland succeeded in maintaining the confidence of the Soviet Union that
Finland was a peaceful neighbour, the better were the Finnish opportunities for
close cooperation with Western countries.[2] During his long term in office (from

1956 to 1981), Kekkonen turned this idea of emphasizing constructive and friendly relations with the Soviet Union – the so-called 'Paasikivi–Kekkonen line', inherited from his predecessor President Juho Kusti Paasikivi – into an instrument for securing control over domestic politics. The result is characterized by Tapani Paavonen as 'self-made dependence on the Soviet Union': Kekkonen's practice of consulting the Soviet Union personally on every major decision consolidated his domestic position, making him vital for the country's security and well-being.[3] From the outside, the relationship was called 'Finlandization': Finland became a textbook case of the adaptation typical of a small state, especially when in geographical proximity to a much larger and ideologically different state.[4]

During the Cold War, Finland's method of approaching Western integration was a slow and meticulous 'wait-and-see' policy.[5] Finland participated through singularly complicated arrangements aimed at preserving the façade of uncontroversial economic policies. Economic agreements with the Western bloc were compensated for with parallel agreements and concessions on trade with the Eastern bloc. The parallelism even went as far as making Finland participate in both the western Eurovision Song Contest and the eastern Intervision Festival in Sopot – with Finland notching up more of a success in the latter.

Finland's policies were based, as Klaus Törnudd has put it, on the confluence of two imperatives: one economic, and the other political. An obvious aim was to further Finnish economic interests, competitiveness and growth. In particular, Finland should not remain outside any preferential trade arrangement that included Norway or Sweden together with any principal trading partner. At the same time, as integration policy was part of foreign and security policy, Finland's participation in economic cooperation should not compromise its neutrality.[6] This was turned into something of an endogenous doctrine by the condition that Finland could not join organizations that involved supranational decision-making and binding political commitments.

The FCMA treaty with the Soviet Union contained a provision that neither signatory would join a coalition directed against the other. This made Finland's relations with Western European countries complex; almost any organization between them could be, and was, seen as part of the 'West' and thus by definition directed against the other bloc. The Soviet attitude towards Finland fluctuated according to the tensions in bloc politics: the recognition of neutrality and room for manoeuvre given by Nikita Khrushchev was again narrowed by Leonid Brezhnev, while Mikhail Gorbachev officially recognized Finland's neutrality[7] in 1989, when the recognition no longer served Finland to any great degree. In a sense, the Soviet Union could be said to have been applying Finland's own strategy of wait-and-see to the country.

While membership of the EEC founded in 1957–58 was categorically ruled out, Finland was also cautious with regard to other organizations, possibly to the extent of over-politicizing them. The Soviet decision to reject the offered Marshall Aid barred the Eastern European countries from participation and thus, the plan came to be seen in Finland as a manifestation of Great Power confrontation, in the face of which the country wanted to remove itself. Finland therefore turned down the invitation to participate. However, economic arrangements were made to secure foreign capital for the relaunch of industrial production and exports. Finland received loans from the United States and Sweden between 1945 and 1947, and later through membership of the Bretton Woods organizations, the International Monetary Fund (IMF) and the International Bank for Reconstruction and Development (IBRD), which it joined in 1948 and 1949 respectively.

The General Agreement on Tariffs and Trade (GATT), established in 1947, was subsequently discovered to be a suitable way for Finland to participate in Western economic cooperation and support Finnish export industries. The Eastern bloc countries remained outside the IMF and IBRD, and did not join GATT either. However, Finland did: its accession treaty of 1949 came into force in 1950. For Finland, GATT secured expansive multilateral markets; an important prerequisite for joining was that it offered the possibility of applying the most favoured nation (MFN) principle to countries outside the agreement, that is, to the Soviet Union, with which Finland had had a bilateral agreement in force since 1947.[8]

Nordic cooperation was not only economically but also politically crucial for Finland as it permitted close cooperation – if not actual integration – with some Western European countries, and the opportunity to keep up-to-date on developments in the EEC/EC sphere (especially after Danish membership in 1973). At the same time, Swedish neutrality reinforced Finland's international position. Being associated with the Nordic countries also bestowed more of a Western image on Finland – for some, also a Nordic self-image of being in some ways more 'advanced' than the rest of Western Europe.

For the Soviet Union, however, Nordic cooperation was, in the early 1950s, much too closely connected with the Western bloc – after all, the majority of the Nordic countries were members of the North Atlantic Treaty Organization (NATO). Finland's approach was therefore tortuous. It did not participate in the Nordic plans for a customs union in the 1940s, although it joined many other forms of cooperation, such as the Nordic passport union. It also participated in the preparatory work for the creation of the Nordic Council, established in 1952, but deferred its membership until 1955, when it also joined the United Nations at a time when the critical Soviet attitude changed during early détente. Upon joining, Finland emphasized that membership would not lead Finland to abandon its neutrality. Its representatives would not participate in the Council's deliberations if, against accepted practice, they were to cover military questions or matters that would lead to taking a position on conflicts of interest between the Great Powers.[9] This was one of the many instances of Finland's 'customization' of the organizations through an official declaration that conveyed a suitably down-sized image of the organization's aims.[10] In the case of the Nordic Council, the risk – from the Finnish perspective – that it would actually deliberate on security and military matters was slight.

As Finland had rejected the Marshall Plan, it did not become a member of the Organization for European Economic Cooperation (OEEC). Instead, Finland signed its own agreement with the OEEC countries, yet another distinctive way of 'joining' an organization. Signing the Helsinki Protocol in 1957 was of special importance for the liberalization of trade with Western European countries. The political reasons for remaining outside the OEEC – opposition from the Soviet Union – were gradually removed. With the establishment of the EEC and the European Free Trade Association (EFTA), the Organization for Economic Cooperation and Development (OECD) – the successor to the OEEC from 1961 – was seen by the Finnish government to lose its political significance, or controversial nature, as it became more clearly concentrated on purely economic matters. Finland joined the OECD in 1968, again making it explicit that membership would not affect its sovereignty and neutrality.[11]

As a follow-up to negotiations between some OEEC members on a wider free trade agreement, EFTA was established by the Stockholm Convention in 1959 by Austria, the United Kingdom, Portugal, Switzerland, Norway, Denmark and Sweden. The question of EFTA membership was, from a political point of view, much more complicated for Finland than a purely Nordic solution would have been. Soviet suspicions concerning growing Finnish interest in Western integration had culminated in the so-called 'night frost crisis' in Finnish–Soviet relations in 1958 when the Soviet Union decided to freeze its relations to Finland as a reaction against Kekkonen's decision to form a majority government with, among others, the more 'Western' Social Democratic Party and the Agrarian Party, excluding the Communists. The government eventually resigned and was replaced by a minority government led by the Agrarian Party that Kekkonen himself represented.

Finnish EFTA membership was not categorically ruled out; it depended on the interpretation put on it by the Soviet Union. In official Finnish parlance, membership was possible provided it did not include supranational organs or political obligations that conflicted with Finnish foreign policy principles.[12] Finnish membership was hampered not only by a negative Soviet attitude but also by hesitancy on the United Kingdom's part: Finnish membership could have triggered several new membership requests, thus, further complicating the negotiations.[13] Once again, Finland resorted to a peculiar solution of its own. In March 1961, the country signed a special association treaty called FINEFTA with the EFTA members.

In practice, the treaty gave Finland the rights of a full member but guaranteed its special interests, both economic and political. The FINEFTA treaty included all the stipulations of the Stockholm Convention concerning trade and economy, with the exception of a slower reduction of duties to protect the weak Finnish home market industry. Furthermore, bilateral trade with the Soviet Union was able to continue without disruption due to the proviso that the removal of quantitative import restrictions did not apply to Finland for items such as liquid and solid fuels and fertilizers, which were central to Finnish–Soviet trade. The Stockholm Convention explicitly mentions closer economic cooperation between OEEC members, including the members of the EEC. Such allusions were seen as potentially involving political commitments not consistent with Finnish policies, and they were omitted. The term of notice was also shorter, comprising a mere three months. Moreover, before the FINEFTA treaty could come into force, the question of Eastern trade had to be settled by signing, concurrently, a Finnish–Soviet agreement about tariff reductions to give the Soviet Union the same position as the EFTA countries in the Finnish market.

Both GATT and FINEFTA show that some political parties and sections of public opinion in Finland were actually more critical of Finnish integration policies than the Soviet Union was. The Finnish Communists, in particular, voiced fierce criticism against these policies, claiming that they would jeopardize Finland's relations with the Soviet Union. The Soviet Union itself did not raise objections to Finnish policies towards GATT, while Khrushchev actually openly endorsed FINEFTA.[14]

The EFTA states of Britain, Denmark and Norway applied for EEC membership in 1961–62. The Finnish government resorted to its wait-and-see strategy of observing developments in these cases.[15] The applications, however, were unsuccessful. This gave fresh impetus to plans for a Nordic customs union and negotiations on NORDEK were energetically relaunched.[16] The negotiations proceeded rapidly and a very extensive draft treaty was completed in 1969.[17] Finland was on its way to signing the treaty. As a way of assuring that the step would not harm relations with the Soviet Union – or, 'in order to remove any possible doubt about the consistency of our policy'[18] – the FCMA treaty was renewed in 1970, five years before it was due.

Nevertheless, the Finnish approach suffered a setback. As the chances of Danish and Norwegian EC membership considerably improved, it no longer seemed clear that the NORDEK treaty could be kept sufficiently detached from the EC to allow for Finnish membership. In March 1970, when the NORDEK treaty was ready for approval, the Finnish government announced that it could not sign it. As negotiations between Denmark, Norway and the EC had effectively started, it did not fulfil Finland's demands for stability and permanence, as the Finnish government would dub the Soviet opposition.[19] In Tapani Paavonen's view, NORDEK was sacrificed in order to make the really important free trade agreement with the EC more acceptable to the Soviet Union;[20] indeed, while announcing that it would not sign NORDEK, Finland also announced its readiness to negotiate with the EC.[21]

As Sweden was settling for a free trade agreement with the EC, Finland could not trail behind. Negotiations on a free trade agreement between Finland and the EC were launched on Finland's initiative in spring 1970. They occasioned a unique debate in the country, and prompted much pamphleteering. Business circles and the political right clearly emerged in favour of the free trade agreement. They were opposed by a very active anti-EC movement, consisting mainly of the far Left (left of the mainstream Social Democrats), which saw the EC as the incarnation of big capital.[22]

The Finnish government was not ready to discuss all the possible areas of cooperation. It wanted to distance itself from EC economic policy, agreeing only on the removal of duties on industrial products. The Finnish free trade agreement thus differed again in some important respects, both economic and political, from that signed by the other neutral EFTA members. The economic exceptions agreed in FINEFTA were maintained, and the evolution clause on the possible extension of relations to areas not covered by the agreement was omitted from the Finnish treaty.

Still, to the dismay of its proponents in political and business circles, the Finnish government decided to postpone the signing of the agreement. It was seen to jeopardize Finland's neutrality policy. The Soviet Union had tightened its general attitude towards Finland. On the other hand, even the United States was negative towards special deals in Europe.[23] The domestic political situation was unstable and speculations about the forthcoming 1974 presidential elections increased. Kekkonen, who had expressed his intention not to run for re-election in 1974, changed his mind and agreed to continue even after that year if a way could be found to extend his mandate over and above the normal electoral procedure. It was generally held that Kekkonen could guarantee that the EEC treaty would not harm Finnish–Soviet relations, while at the same time for Kekkonen himself it was a way to beat his rivals without having to contest them. His mandate was extended by parliament in January 1973. The free trade treaty was finally signed in October 1973, and it came into force on 1 January 1974. Parliament voted in its favour by 141 to 37 (with 7 abstentions).[24]

Finally, as in the case of the FINEFTA treaty, a comprehensive accompanying arrangement was developed according to the principle of parallelism to grant the same tariff privileges for trade with both East and West. The free trade agreement with the EC was accompanied by a cooperation agreement with the Council for Mutual Economic Assistance (COMECON or CMEA) and the so-called KEVSOS system of bilateral treaties was signed between 1974 and 1976 for the reciprocal removal of trade barriers with Bulgaria, Czechoslovakia, Hungary, Poland and the German Democratic Republic. These had, however, negligible practical importance, as the levels of trade were modest.[25] In addition, the Soviet Union received trade benefits which were on a par with those of Finnish trade in Western Europe through a bilateral trade agreement.[26]

From free trade with the EC to EU membership

As a result of the 1984 Luxembourg meeting between EFTA and the EC, where the aim of creating a dynamic European economic area and the idea of widening the future internal market to EFTA were presented, EC–EFTA relations were put on a more systematic footing, and cooperation between the two was intensified.[27] This development initially made Finland tie its policies more clearly to EFTA. A new Finnish 'EFTA-card policy' began. A strengthened EFTA could ensure that Finland would not be left alone to cope with the relations to the EC. Accordingly, Finland decided to become a full member of EFTA: the agreement of September 1985 entered into force at the beginning of 1986. Finnish integration policy was thus shifting from unilateral agreements to a multilateral approach, but it still wanted to keep its distance from supranational integration.

In the 1980s, the political and economic elites' interests began to diverge more and more. Finland joined the EC's cooperation programme for high technology (EUREKA) in 1985, the year it was established, despite the potential political implications of such cooperation, and pursued additional bilateral agreements with the EC to supplement the free trade agreement.[28] National business leaders were increasingly aware of the necessity of establishing their companies in the European market. In the mid-1980s, the economic elite was tacitly using the 'exit option' (investing in Europe) and was becoming largely independent of the political leadership.[29] A further link to Europe was forged when the 'political dialogue' between Finland and the EC began in 1988, first at the level of the head of the political department of the Ministry for Foreign Affairs, then at the ministerial level, opening a new channel for elite socialization.[30]

In November 1988, the Finnish government addressed a report to parliament on the country's stance on economic integration in Western Europe. The very need for such a report and its emphasis on the elements of continuity in Finnish policies revealed that changes were imminent. Indeed, the report was but the first in a series of four in as many years, each presenting a new way of perceiving Finnish interests. The 1988 report argued that EFTA was the primary channel for securing Finnish interests. As neutrality required national decision-making capacity, encompassing economic policy, it could not be combined with membership of the EC.[31]

The following year, things already looked different. Austria applied for EC membership two weeks before the fall of the Berlin Wall. Meanwhile, the Soviet attitude towards Western European integration had been changing. Harto Hakovirta observes how the Soviet posture had evolved from intense hostility to occasional mild criticism, through to selective positive commentary and indications of its own interest in cooperation, even participation.[32] As for the political parties in Finland, those in government, the conservative National Coalition Party, the Social Democratic Party and the small Swedish People's Party started to look favourably on the EC, while the opposition was divided. Still, President Mauno Koivisto and the government, led by Harri Holkeri of the National Coalition Party, tried to silence the disconcerting EC advocates.[33]

In 1989, the President of the European Commission, Jacques Delors, introduced the idea of the European Economic Area (EEA). Negotiations on the arrangement, which would have extended the internal market to EFTA countries, started in 1990, but before it finally came into force on 1 January 1994, after numerous snags and setbacks, most of these countries had changed sides and were applying for EU membership. In the beginning, it was as if the EEA had been invented by the Finns: participating in the common market without getting politically involved was well suited to traditional Finnish integration policy.[34] Finland was quick to back the EEA plans as a suitable alternative to EC membership – although, once again, not for long.

The new EEA policy was reflected in the second government communication on 'Finland's position towards Western European integration' of November 1989. The government considered that active participation in negotiations on a wider, general agreement between EFTA and the EC was needed to safeguard Finnish interests. It saw several positive features in the EEA agreement: it was not a customs union, it would not include foreign and security policy, or common policies on economy, industry or agriculture. Although it was acknowledged that joint decisions would decrease the freedom of action of the country, it was also underlined that decision-making in the EEA would not be supranational.[35] Support for the EEA also stemmed from the fact that it met the Finnish business needs for equal access to the EC's internal market.[36]

The third government report on integration of March 1990 painted a highly positive picture of the economic consequences of integration; isolation from deepening integration would decrease competitiveness.[37] In Finland, it was still a commonly held belief that the EEA could be a way of combining political neutrality and full participation in economic integration, while the task of combining neutrality and EC membership was compared by Prime Minister Holkeri to that of squaring a circle.[38]

Although EC membership was still excluded in the second and third government reports, the rejection became less categorical: membership came to be seen as the second option if the EEA did not materialize. Public opinion was very favourable: in opinion polls conducted in May 1990, 60 per cent were for EC membership and only 13 per cent against. On the other hand, 22 per cent believed that Finland was already a member.[39] As it had, for decades, been part of the consensual wisdom not to raise the issue, the concept of the EC was quite unfamiliar to the general public, perhaps even to politicians and the administration. It was hardly surprising that public opinion was somewhat confused.

Officially, Finland still counted on the EEA. Sweden, however, was one step ahead once again. The Swedish membership application in 1991 came as a shock, even though there had been hints to this effect in late 1990. A dual crisis in Finnish political elite decision-making ensued: first, Sweden was considered to have betrayed Finland by neglecting to inform its neighbour of its intentions; second, there was consternation that Finland might 'miss the boat', due to signals from the EC that applications should arrive by a certain date.[40] Shortly before the Maastricht Summit of December 1991, the new Prime Minister Esko Aho visited London, telling Prime Minister John Major that, should Finland apply, it would like to negotiate in the same group as Austria and Sweden. At Maastricht, however, a proposal to start negotiations with Austria and Sweden alone was only just defeated.[41] While the Swedish move prompted a very quick response from Finland, the Finnish government was also clearly receptive to signals arriving from Brussels as well.

The imperative to join the EU was increased as the EEA created a gap between rights and obligations that could be remedied only by choosing between membership and the abrogation of the treaty. It gradually emerged that the EC's emphasis was on protecting its own decision-making autonomy. The 'EFTA pillar' would not be on an equal footing with it in the EEA.[42] The Finnish government came to regard these negative features as a decisive burden.[43]

From early 1992, the central organizations for industry and employers positioned themselves in favour of a quick entry into the EC, and President Koivisto, in his New Year address, indicated that a decision would have to be made in the near future.[44] In January 1992, the government presented its fourth integration report – forthright on the impact of EC membership for Finland – in which the decision to join the EC was implicit. The government acknowledged the importance of the EEA in safeguarding the central economic interests of the country, but noted that it might only be temporary. Therefore, the best way to completely secure Finnish interests seemed to be EC membership, in other words, by participating in the decision-making. Reasons put forward by the government for such an about-turn included (1) the disappearance of the bloc division in Europe; (2) the Maastricht Summit of December 1991 together with the EC's statement that negotiations on membership with the applicants could begin in 1992; (3) the fact that the EC was becoming a new type of actor in international relations; and (4) the Swedish application. It was thought that the Swedish membership would imply a proportionate advantage for the industry of Finland's closest competitor. To be examined together with those of Austria and Sweden, the application had to be submitted in early 1992.[45] Reference was also made to the importance of joining in time to participate in the inter-governmental conference envisaged for 1996, where the contents of the common foreign and security policy were to be specified.[46] The report formed the basis for a government communication to parliament on 16 March in which the membership application was proposed. The communication was approved, with 108 votes for, 55 against and 32 abstentions, and on 18 March 1992, Finland applied for EC membership.

The new centre-right government, elected in March 1991, was led by Esko Aho of the Centre Party. The Centre Party (which had been the Agrarian Party until 1965) still had a predominantly rural constituency, and the farmers were clearly against membership. Among the parties, the Centre Party was the most clearly opposed to membership, even though opposition cut across traditional political divisions. A great deal of effort was needed from Prime Minister Aho to get his party's backing for membership. Since April 1991, the Centre Party had been the leading party in the government coalition and could not afford a government crisis. A seemingly decisive move in 1993 was to appoint the chairman of the Finnish Central Union of Agricultural Producers (MTK), Heikki Haavisto, to be Minister for Foreign Affairs and thus responsible for the negotiations. He could have been one of the main leaders of the 'no' front but, having been co-opted by the 'yes' front, he managed to reassure the Centre Party that the farmers' interests were being taken care of, and the farmers' organization duly accepted the deal.[47]

The membership negotiations started in March 1993 and lasted for just one year. They were greatly facilitated by the fact that Finland had already adopted the whole internal market regulation of the EC, courtesy of the EEA agreement. Agriculture as well as regional and structural policies proved to be the major obstacles in the negotiations. Finland had been adjusting its policies to member-ship in several ways. The full liberalization of capital movement, a first step towards economic and monetary union, had been undertaken in Finland simul-taneously with the Community, in July 1990. Between 1991 and 1992, the Maastricht convergence criteria became the guidelines for the economic policy of the Finnish government; in June 1991, the Finnish *markka* was pegged to the European Currency Unit (ECU). The legislative harmonization needed for EC membership had also been underway in matters such as foreign ownership.[48]

Finland did not want to stress its foreign political particularities either, and applied for membership without making any reference to its military non-alignment. It had been made quite explicit in the membership negotiations that exemptions were not possible. Denmark had just voted against the Maastricht Treaty and negoti-ated no less than four opt-outs: following such an example would have been dangerous for the credibility of the EU. Thus, the new members were to accept everything without any exceptions. In particular, the old member-states felt that the policy of non-alignment could water down the new common foreign and security policy. There were also suspicions that the Nordics might form a bloc that could align with Germany in many respects.

Thus, it was anticipated that neutrality would become a sticking point in the negotiations.[49] The Commission questioned the Finnish neutrality policy in its *Avis* on the application, asking whether the policy, even when reduced to its 'core' of military non-alignment, would not constitute a hindrance to full acceptance of the foreign policy of the EU, including the development towards a common defence. The Commission recommended specific and binding assurances on the political commitment and legal capacity to fulfil the obligations in the field.[50] To this effect, a joint declaration was issued in December 1993, confirming the candidates' full acceptance of the *acquis* in the new Common Foreign and Security Policy.[51]

During the negotiations, the examples of Denmark and Norway prompted Finland to hold a referendum on Finnish membership – a rare event, as it was only the second of its kind to be organized in Finland: the first being the consid-eration of the abolition of Prohibition in 1932. The referendum was to be consultative in nature, and there was a debate on the extent to which the result would be politically binding. In addition, the order in which the different Nordic candidates would have their referenda was seen as potentially important for the individual outcomes: it was coordinated so that Finland was the first to vote, in the hope that a domino effect would result from a clear Finnish 'yes' majority.[52]

Support for membership had declined somewhat in 1992, partly as a result of the Danish vote on the Maastricht Treaty; however, the opponents outweighed the supporters only in December 1993. After that, the Russian election, with its subsequent breakthrough for Vladimir Zhirinovsky's nationalist party, again increased the popularity of EC membership in Finland.[53] While public opinion in 1994 did not point to an easy victory, the results of the EU membership refer-endum on 16 October 1994 were ultimately quite clear: 56.9 per cent voted in favour, 43.1 per cent against, with a turnout of 74 per cent. The yes votes had a distinct advantage in the campaign: a clear majority of the political elite were in favour, the Green Party was divided, and only the Left Party (former Communist Party) was entirely against. The majority of Finnish newspapers and the leading economic interest groups and businesses had been lobbying for membership. In particular, the forest industry was strongly in evidence among the big business pro-membership lobby. The no votes, conversely, were divided and less organized.[54] Geographically, the northern parts of the country were more against than the southern parts, and the countryside clearly more against than urban areas. More women were against than men, and the support for membership also correlated with high levels of income and education.[55]

The economic crisis and the unstable situation in Russia were the most debated issues in the campaign. In the early 1990s, Finland was mired in a deep economic recession caused partly by the collapse of trade with the Soviet Union and aggravated by unemployment reaching a record 20 per cent. The crisis lent credence to the idea that Finland should join the EU.[56] The government argued that, as a great power in trade policy, the EC could effectively defend the interests of its members.[57] Yet, convincing economic arguments on the effects of EU membership were not easy to formulate.

Security policy reasons for membership were increasingly resorted to towards the end of the campaign. Instability in Eastern Europe and Russia increased the attraction of EU integration as a possible security mechanism.[58] The attempted coup in Russia in August 1991 galvanized the political parties into action: in the autumn, both the Social Democratic and the National Coalition Party urged the government to hasten the preparations for membership. Integration in the realms of foreign and security policy sounded reasonable under the uncertain circumstances. In a sense, Finland reversed its view: if security considerations had previously prevented Finland from joining, they were now seen as a reason for application. Membership would strengthen Finland's security *vis-à-vis* Russia, and open up new security policy options for the country.[59] Interestingly, through this new approach, Finland was giving the EU a higher political security profile than many other countries.

The example of Sweden's and Austria's willingness to join the EC while being neutral or non-aligned was also encouraging. The notion of neutrality underwent considerable redefining, liberating in essence the Finnish integration policy from the burden of having to serve foreign political aims. Neutrality was gradually reduced to the military field and narrowly defined matters of security policy. In autumn 1987, the Prime Minister and the Minister for Foreign Affairs stated that participation in economic integration with the West no longer affected the Finnish policy of neutrality. The main purpose of this redefinition was to avoid the comprehensive economic-political packages by which Finnish political commitments to the East and economic ties with the West were previously balanced. In fact, the EEA treaty no longer involved the principle of parallelism.[60]

With the fall of the Berlin Wall, the political room for manoeuvre increased. In September 1990, Finland unilaterally revised the interpretation of the FCMA and the Paris Peace Treaty concerning allusions to Germany and restrictions placed on the Finnish armed forces. As Mikko Majander put it, the FCMA treaty was 'brought down from the inviolable realm of holy liturgy to the sphere of mortal elements of foreign policy'.[61] The Soviet Union ceased to exist in December 1991, and the FCMA treaty was replaced by a radically different new agreement on good neighbourhood relations with Russia in January 1992.

Once Finland decided to join the EU, the decision was presented – for domestic purposes – as a logical continuation of Finland's policies rather than as a rupture or change. Continuity is also a cherished value in Finnish foreign policy. As President Koivisto stated in the European Parliament in November 1993, the decision to apply for membership was, on closer inspection, a logical continuation of Finnish integration policy – a policy which was now conveniently seen to consist of developing ever-closer relations with Western integrative structures, and furthering Finnish interests with the best possible means available. And, duly, the Finns saw what they wanted to see: it soon became common to note in official statements that EU membership 'had strengthened Finnish security'.

Public opinion remained quite positive, if not enthusiastic, after accession, due in part to visibly beneficial consequences such as a decrease in food prices. Criticism was also allayed by the foreign political consensus which is typical of Finland and which is reinforced by the practice of broad coalition governments. Still, something of a sea change had occurred in political elite terms: to hold a referendum on such a major foreign political issue as EU membership was already a sign of a profound shift in elite-oriented foreign policy.[62] Another major change was the new constitution of 2000, whereby the government was allotted a more pronounced role in foreign policy, whereas previously the President of the Republic had assumed sole charge. This has paved the way for a greater diversity in foreign policy orientations, but no major disputes seem to have surfaced thus far.[63]

Conclusion

Finland joined the EU in 1995, hot on the heels of its closest neighbour, Sweden. Hans Mouritzen had, in advance of the referenda, predicted that Finland and Sweden would together become *Musterknaben* ('top of the class'), compliant and accommodating to other member-states, in stark contrast to Denmark, the 'naughty boy' of the Edinburgh exemptions. Sweden, in his view, seemed to be the most European of the three. Finland, for Mouritzen, was more Atlantic than Sweden and showed greater readiness to settle for periphery status once inside the EC.[64]

In the end, however, Sweden seemed more akin to Denmark with regard to its approach to the EU, while Finland gladly took on the *Musterknabe* role single-handedly. In Finnish political discourse, allusions to image are a powerful tool: the political elite can influence public opinion by referring, for instance, to the possibility that Finland is, elsewhere in the world, associated with the 'wrong' countries – as demonstrated by the sudden rush to start negotiations on EU membership before the Eastern European countries, so as not to be tarred with the same brush. In the EU, Finland came to distance itself even from its Nordic neighbours. They were no longer the 'right' reference group they had been throughout the golden era of Nordic cooperation; it was not beneficial for Finland to be put into the same category as them as they did not enjoy too good a reputation inside the EU. They were the 'reluctant Europeans' or 'footnote countries'.

Finland was not reluctant. It was also willing to seek the company of the big member countries. The predominantly Lutheran and partly Baltic Germany had, for centuries, been the natural counterpart in Central Europe. As early as the 1980s, the erstwhile smooth balancing between East and West was replaced by an equally smooth attitude towards the leading EC member-states, especially towards Germany: the Finnish foreign policy elite had no difficulty comprehending their interests and policies.[65] But Finland had also had a much more cordial relationship with France than Sweden during the de Gaulle era. Kekkonen and de Gaulle were on good personal relations; constitutional similarities and a shared mistrust of Soviet security interests and distrust of German motivations brought them together.[66] Finland's experience in having to deal with larger powers has often been alluded to; Finnish diplomats have been accustomed to accommodating external influences procedurally for a long time – being also 'socialized' in the process.[67] A more acute awareness of their small size compared with Sweden is also relevant, as well as the conviction that Finland could improve its position by being cooperative.

The 'top of the class' attitude was visible in particular during Paavo Lipponen's first term as Prime Minister, between 1995 and 1999. Since the late 1980s, Lipponen had been one of the first proponents of EC membership in his party, the Social Democrats. In his view, Finland had to aim at the very 'core' of the EU. Unlike Sweden, Finland did not organize a separate referendum on EMU, and took the EU view that there was no opting out quite literally. First, it was explained that through the referendum on membership and, correspondingly, on the Maastricht Treaty, the Finns had already agreed to the idea of monetary union, even though it might have escaped their attention. Later on, the government referred to discussions in the spring of 1995 leading to the decision that parliament would vote on Finland's participation. However, there was a lively debate on the issue during 1997–98. The Centre Party, the then main opposition party, demanded a referendum, garnering support from, among others, a group of private academics and movements that collected 40,000 names in petitions.[68] Public opinion was rather critical, and a referendum would probably have resulted in a 'no'.[69]

Instead of a referendum, the Finnish Parliament decided on EMU on the basis of a government proposition on 17 April 1998 by 135 votes in favour and 61 against.[70] Finland duly joined the third phase of EMU on 1 January 1999. As such, the new currency was eventually welcomed, while the procedure caused some irritation. As far as the EU in general is concerned, public opinion has, since 1995, been relatively stable: about 40 per cent see EU membership posi- tively, and 30 per cent negatively without, however, necessarily wanting to leave it again. Thus, the Finns remain below average in the EU in terms of support for integration, with relatively more people having no opinion. Some surveys would indicate growing criticism. Tapio Raunio and Teija Tiilikainen, however, see this rather as a widening of the gap between the elite and the people, and as a growing disinterest among the people, something also clearly shown by the low turnout of 31 per cent in the European elections of 1999.[71]

Other examples of ways in which Finland has been ready to modify its behaviour and redefine its interests in order to better fit the new framework as a member of the EU include its adaptation to the view of the Commission on such matters as the enlargement issue, its activism in creating a 'Northern Dimension' for the Union, and the way it handled its first EU Council Presidency – during the latter half of 1999 – compromising on its own aspira- tions.[72] Above all, its willingness to adapt its foreign policy has been considerable. It has become a proponent rather than an opponent of further steps to strengthen the EU in respect of its security policy.[73]

This eagerness begs closer theoretical consideration.[74] One can stress the magnitude of change: from a country that used to be very cautious towards political cooperation, Finland converted itself in a very short space of time in the early 1990s into a strong advocate of supranational integration. It no longer invoked the customary reservations while joining, but jumped in unreservedly. But equally well, one can underline continuity, a lengthy, yet linear and steady *rapprochement* with Western European integration structures.

Theoretically speaking, these two ways lead one to look for explanatory factors in different realms. The first would emphasize external factors, notably foreign political constraints on the range of options open to a small state in a particular geopolitical location between the East and the West. The end of the Cold War would thus have cleared the way for EU membership. In the second, the role of interests, economic or political, would be emphasized. Continuity could also be observed as to identity: it will be the Finnish Western identity which, through EU membership, is finally and unreservedly recognized by all. The ease with which Finland reoriented its policy has in fact been explained by the fact that it has always constructed its political or national identity in a flexible manner, and never in opposition to the 'West'.[75]

The traditional primacy of foreign policy in determining Finland's relations to the European integration process is reflected in theoretical explanations as well: foreign and security policy still plays a more central role in Finnish thinking on Europe, and in explanations of Finnish European policies, than, arguably, in most other European countries. Indeed, realism-inspired foreign policy explana- tions have found little evidence of a decisive input from domestic interest groups. These groups traditionally raised their voices only after having received the green light from the political elite.

Identity has become a recurrent theme in recent theoretical analyses of Finnish EU membership. Some point to Finland having found its true place in the EU, and managing to show, finally, that it is a Western country, or that it has found a 'home', indeed, that this was the main motivation behind the decision to join.[76] Some of these explanations have shades of romantic idealism: there is some kind of inevitability in Finnish policies, a sense of having fortuitously arrived at the 'right' way and one's rightful place in the world. Some stress that the journey has been exceptionally long. The Finnish Lutheran tradition and strong state-centrism combined with an exceptional political homogeneity and an inflexible doctrine of political realism has been depicted as being the most distant among the different political traditions in Europe from the idea of a united Europe, and thus as a very distant starting point from which to approach the Europe of the EU. Distance notwithstanding, membership has been seen as having quite rapidly entailed if not a change of identity, then at least the emergence of a new, dual identity with its foundations still in the realist tradition, yet involving new elements of 'liberal Europeanism'.[77]

Theoretical literature also warns against taking 'national interest' for granted. It may not be nationally formulated, nor stable in time. More constructivism-inspired research would rather start from the assumption that the process of integration effectively interferes with the process of national interest formation: interests are seen in a new way because of the interaction and institutional setting in which one finds oneself. Here, Finland is a case in point. It is very clear how Finnish interests have been changing in the process. From seeing EC membership as incompatible with neutrality, Finland quite rapidly came to see strong supranational elements in the EU as not counter to, but in furtherance of, its interests, and a common foreign and security policy as strengthening its security. It is the government in particular which has shown a great deal of flexibility, while the parliament and general opinion might have been somewhat slower to re-orientate themselves. This is facilitated, in turn, by one of the intrinsic factors of continuity: elite consensus and the strong role of the executive, particularly in foreign policy. In this context, the effects of transnational elite socialization, which have hardly been studied for the Finnish case, clearly deserve further research.

One can interpret this transformation as adaptation or acquiescence. Finland has shown its ability to adapt – both to larger political structures and to large-state interests – even within the EU (just as it adapted to the Soviet Union in the past, some would hasten to point out). This is quite natural for small states, although it has also been pointed out that Finland is not only small in size but also has the identity of a small state, to a greater degree than its neighbouring Sweden. A still more compelling interpretation, however, is the so-called two-level games approach, especially when combined with empirical indications about the relative strengthening of the executive *vis-à-vis* the legislative in the process of integration. The executive profits from the two-level game, the interplay of domestic politics and political bargaining at the EU level, and is strengthened also by socialization processes inside the EU. With the help of the exclusive information provided by the EU, the national governments – which safeguard the information, also to protect each other's positions – can undermine potential opposition by presenting choices domestically that have already been bargained over in the EU, leaving little leeway for alternatives presented nationally, while they themselves can create new options that were previously beyond domestic control. Thus, they reinforce their domestic position through these international means, which are not available to their domestic competitors.[78] In the case of Finland, it would be tempting to analyse also the Cold War era in terms of the two-level game. An element of continuity in any case is found in the strength of security policy arguments as currency in the national debate: the government, in the end, can appeal to security policy arguments and this is likely to silence the debate if nothing else does.

Whether the Finnish stance of 'if in "Europe", then in its "core"', of its early membership years will prevail is another question. The core might be unattainable: there is in Finland still a feeling of distance, still a fear of not quite being securely and steadfastly 'in Europe', and a fear of being associated with the 'wrong' countries. One could ask whether any amount of devotion to the EU is actually enough to bring Finland into the 'core'. Would the other countries be prepared to embrace Finland as a part of it? In defining the 'core', time might be a decisive factor: the 'new' members, while growing older, will not catch up with the 'old' members that are growing older still.

Acknowledgements

I would like to thank Wolfram Kaiser and Jürgen Elvert for their exceptionally thorough and constructive comments and Mikko Majander for his useful remarks. I would like to dedicate this chapter to someone to whom I am deeply indebted: Mikael af Malmborg, who sadly is no longer with us to make his valuable contribution.

Notes

1   See, for example, Henrik Meinander, 'On the brink or in-between? The conception of Europe in Finnish identity', in Mikael af Malmborg and Bo Stråth (eds), *The Meaning of Europe*, Oxford: Berg, 2002, pp. 149–68; Tapani Paavonen, 'From isolation to the core: Finland's position towards European integration, 1960–95', *Journal of European Integration History*, 2001, vol. 7, no. 1, pp. 53–75; and Esko Antola, 'From the European rim to the core: the European policy of Finland in the 1990s', in *Northern Dimensions, Yearbook 1999*, Helsinki: Finnish Institute of International Affairs, 1999, pp. 5–10.
2   Jan-Magnus Jansson, 'Finland and various degrees of integration', in *Yearbook of Finnish Foreign Policy 1973*, Helsinki: Finnish Institute of International Affairs, 1983, pp. 23–5, here p. 23.
3   Paavonen, 'From isolation to the core', p. 54.
4   See, for example, Hans Mouritzen, *Finlandization: Towards a General Theory of Adaptive Politics*, Aldershot: Gower, 1988; Mikko Majander, 'The paradoxes of Finlandization', in *Northern Dimensions, Yearbook 1999*, pp. 85–94.
5   So labelled by Harto Hakovirta in *Puolueettomuus ja integraatiopolitiikka: Tutkimus puolueettoman valtion adaptaatiosta alueelliseen integraatioon teorian, vertailujen ja Suomen poikkeavan tapauksen valossa (Acta Universitatis Tamperensis, ser. A, vol. 78)*, Tampere: University of Tampere, 1976.

6 Klaus Törnudd, 'Finland and economic integration in Europe', *Cooperation and Conflict*, 1969, vol. IV, no. 1, pp. 63–72, here pp. 64–5.
7 Paavonen, 'From isolation to the core', p. 54.
8 Esko Antola and Ossi Tuusvuori, *Länsi-Euroopan integraatio ja Suomi*, Turku: Ulkopoliittinen instituutti 1983, pp. 122–5; Esko Antola, 'Finland', in Helen Wallace (ed.), *The Wider Western Europe: Reshaping the EC/EFTA Relationship*, London: Pinter, 1991, pp. 146–58, here p. 146.
9 Franz Wendt, *Cooperation in the Nordic Countries: Achievements and Obstacles*, Uppsala: Almqvist & Wiksell, 1981, pp. 35–7, 343–4.
10 On 'customizing', depicting an organization in a way fitting for domestic purposes, see Hanna Ojanen, 'How to customize your union: Finland and the "northern dimension of the EU"', in *Northern Dimensions, Yearbook 1999*, pp. 13–26.
11 Toni Muoser, *Finnlands Neutralität und die Europäische Wirtschaftsintegration*, Baden-Baden: Nomos, 1986, p. 155, and Antola and Tuusvuori, *Länsi-Euroopan integraatio ja Suomi*, pp. 125–6, 142–3.
12 Cf., for instance, Paavonen, 'From isolation to the core', p. 58, and Esko Antola, 'Finnish perspectives on EC–EFTA relations', in Finn Laursen (ed.), *EFTA and the EC: Implications of 1992*, Maastricht: European Institute of Public Administration, 1990, pp. 163–75, here pp. 164–5.
13 Hakovirta, *Puolueettomuus ja integraatiopolitiikka*, pp. 200–2; Mikael af Malmborg, *Den ståndaktiga nationalstaten: Sverige och den västeuropeiska integrationen 1945–59*, Lund: Lund University Press, 1994, pp. 381–3; Jukka Seppinen, *Mahdottomasta mahdollinen: Suomen tie Euroopan unioniin*, Helsinki: Ajatus, 2001, pp. 421–39.
14 Tapani Paavonen, *Finland's Road to Europe: Changes in Institutional Frameworks and Economic Policies* (Political History Publications C:33), Turku: University of Turku, 1991, pp. 6–9.
15 Paavonen, 'From isolation to the core', p. 61.
16 See Barry Turner (with Gunilla Nordquist), *The Other European Community: Integration and Cooperation in Nordic Europe*, London: Weidenfeld & Nicolson, 1982, p. 145.
17 Wendt, *Cooperation in the Nordic Countries*, pp. 119–21, 125–9, and Erik Solem, *The Nordic Council and Scandinavian Integration*, New York: Praeger, 1977, p. 83.
18 President Kekkonen in Washington on 23 July 1970, quoted by Toivo Miljan, *The Reluctant Europeans: The Attitudes of the Nordic Countries towards European Integration*, London: Hurst, 1977, pp. 261–2.
19 Antola and Tuusvuori, *Länsi-Euroopan integraatio ja Suomi*, pp. 144–6, and Seppinen, *Mahdottomasta mahdollinen*, pp. 508–17.
20 Paavonen, 'From isolation to the core', pp. 62–3.
21 Mikael af Malmborg, 'Gaullism in the North? Sweden, Finland and the EEC in the 1960s', in Wilfried Loth (ed.), *Crises and Compromises: The European Project 1963–1969*, Baden-Baden: Nomos, 2001, pp. 489–508, here p. 506.
22 Paavonen, *Finland's Road to Europe*, p. 10.
23 On the widespread hostility in the EEC in the 1960s towards attempts by certain countries at market integration without, however, taking on financial or political commitments, and the US hostility to forms of association without membership intentions, see Wolfram Kaiser, 'Challenge to the Community: the creation, crisis and consolidation of the European Free Trade Association, 1958–72', *Journal of European Integration History*, 1997, vol. 3, no. 1, pp. 7–33.
24 Paavonen, 'From isolation to the core', p. 64.
25 Jermu Laine, 'The Finnish model for foreign trade policy', *Yearbook of Finnish Foreign Policy 1973*, Helsinki: Finnish Institute of International Affairs, 1973, pp. 20–3; Petri Lempiäinen, 'Vapaakauppastrategiasta sitoutumiseen: Kansainvälisen talousintegraation syveneminen ja Suomi', in Petri Lempiäinen (ed.), *Suomen ulkosuhteet 1990-luvun Euroopassa*, Helsinki: Painatuskeskus, 1994, pp. 119–75, here p. 138; and Paavonen, 'From isolation to the core', pp. 64–5.

26 The Finnish–Soviet trade comprised between 10 and 20 per cent of Finnish trade; at its height in 1983 it made up 26 per cent of Finnish imports and exports. The bilateral clearing system in Finnish–Soviet trade was cancelled in 1990. Cf. Paavonen, *Finland's Road to Europe*, pp. 15–16.

27 Bettina Hurni, 'EFTA–EC relations after the Luxembourg Declaration', in Kari Möttölä and Heikki Patomäki (eds), *Facing the Change in Europe: EFTA Countries' Integration Strategies*, Helsinki: Finnish Institute of International Affairs, 1989, pp. 88–101.

28 See, for example, Esko Antola, 'The end of pragmatism: political foundations of the Finnish integration policy under stress', *Yearbook of Finnish Foreign Policy 1991*, Helsinki: Finnish Institute of International Affairs, 1991, pp. 17–22.

29 Raimo Väyrynen, 'Finland and the European Community: changing elite bargains', *Cooperation and Conflict*, 1993, vol. 28, no. 1, pp. 31–46, here pp. 43–4.

30 Esko Antola, 'The Finnish integration strategy: adaptation with restrictions', in Kari Möttölä and Heikki Patomäki (eds), *Facing the Change in Europe: EFTA Countries' Integration Strategies*, Helsinki: Finnish Institute of International Affairs, 1989, pp. 55–70, here p. 60; *Eurooppa* (later *Eurooppakirje/Eureooppatietoa*), newsletter on Finnish membership published by the Ministry of Foreign Affairs during 1992–4, 27 October 1992, pp. 5–6.

31 *Suomi ja Länsi-Euroopan yhdentymiskehitys: Valtioneuvoston selonteko eduskunnalle Suomen suhtautumisesta Länsi-Euroopan taloudelliseen yhdentymiskehitykseen*, Helsinki: Council of State, 1988, pp. 5–7.

32 Harto Hakovirta 'The Nordic neutrals in Western European integration: current pressures, restraints and options', *Cooperation and Conflict*, 1987, vol. XXII, no. 4, pp. 265–73.

33 Paavonen, 'From isolation to the core', pp. 67–8.

34 Risto E.J. Penttilä, 'Suomen ulko- ja turvallisuuspolitiikan muutos 1985–1992', in Petri Lempiäinen (ed.), *Suomen ulkosuhteet 1990-luvun Euroopassa*, Helsinki: Painatuskeskus, 1994], pp. 14–28, here p. 21.

35 *Valtioneuvoston tiedonanto eduskunnalle Suomen suhtautumisesta Länsi-Euroopan yhdentymiskehitykseen*, Helsinki: Council of State, 1989, pp. 11–14, 27–8.

36 Väyrynen, 'Finland and the European community: changing elite bargains', p. 39.

37 *Suomi ja Euroopan talousalue: Valtioneuvoston selonteko eduskunnalle Suomen suhtautumisesta Länsi-Euroopan yhdentymiskehitykseen*, Helsinki: Council of State, 1990, p. 9.

38 Cf. Olli Rehn, 'Odottavasta ennakoivaan integraatiopolitiikkaan? Suomen integraatiopolitiikka kylmän sodan aikana ja sen päätösvaiheessa 1989–92', in Tuomas Forsberg and Tapani Vaahtoranta (eds), *Johdatus Suomen ulkopolitiikkaan: Kylmästä sodasta uuteen maailmanjärjestykseen*, Tampere: Gaudeamus, 1993, pp. 166–231, here p. 195.

39 EC Bulletin, 31 May 1990; Antola, 'Finland', pp. 153–6.

40 Raimo Lintonen, 'Suomen EU-jäsenyyshanke kriisinä', in Tuomas Forsberg, Christer Pursiainen, Raimo Lintonen and Pekka Visuri (eds), *Suomi ja kriisit: Vaaran vuosista terrori-iskuihin*, Helsinki: Gaudeamus, 2003, pp. 149–88.

41 Paul Luif, *On the Road to Brussels: The Political Dimension of Austria's, Finland's and Sweden's Accession to the European Union* (Austrian Institute for International Affairs), Vienna: Braumüller, 1995, pp. 227–8.

42 See Wolfram Kaiser, 'A better Europe? EFTA, the EFTA Secretariat, and the European identities of the "Outer Seven", 1958–72', in Marie-Thérèse Bitsch, Wilfried Loth and Raymond Poidevin (eds), *Institutions européennes et identités européennes*, Brussels: Bruylant, 1998, pp. 165–83, on EFTA's difficulties in establishing an identity of its own.

43 *Eurooppa*, 27 October 1992, pp. 4, 19, 29.

44 Luif, *On the Road to Brussels*, p. 228; *Koivisto 1.1.1992. Tasavallan Presidentin uuden vuoden puhe 1.1.1992. Ulkopoliittisia lausuntoja ja asiakirjoja 1992*, Helsinki: Ministry of Foreign Affairs, 1993, pp. 25–7.

45 *Suomi ja Euroopan yhteisön jäsenyys: Valtioneuvoston selonteko eduskunnalle EY-jäsenyyden vaiku-tuksista Suomelle*, Helsinki: Council of State, 1992, pp. 5–7.

46 Hannu Himanen, 'Poliittisesta yhteistyöstä yhteiseen politiikkaan; Suomen EY-jäsenyyden ulkopoliittisesta merkityksestä', *Ulkopolitiikka*, 1993, vol. 30, no. 1, pp. 26–34.

47 See Tor Bjørklund, 'The three Nordic 1994 referenda concerning membership in the EU', *Cooperation and Conflict*, 1996, vol. 31, no. 1; on the negotiations in detail, see Antti Kuosmanen, *Finland's Journey to the European Union*, Maastricht: European Institute of Public Administration, 2001; on the role of professional groups and cultures, see Timo Kivimäki, 'Transnationalisaatio, professionaaliset kulttuurit ja Suomen EU-neuvottelut', in Erkki Berndtson and Timo Kivimäki (eds), *Suomen kansainväliset suhteet* (*Acta Politica* No. 9, Department of Political Science), Helsinki: Yliopistopaino,1996, pp. 27–49.

48 See Hjerppe, ' Finland's foreign trade and trade policy in the 20th century', p. 73, and Väyrynen, 'Finland and the European Community: changing elite bargains', pp. 44–5.

49 See, for example, Dietrich Rometsch, 'Finnlands Außen- und Sicherheitspolitik: reif für die Europäische Union?', *Integration*, 1993, vol. 15, no. 1, pp. 44–6, here p. 44.

50 'The challenge of enlargement: Commission opinion on Finland's application for membership' (document drawn up on the basis of SEC(92) 2048 final), *Bulletin of the European Communities*, Supplement 6, 1992, pp. 22–3.

51 *Eurooppakirje*, 1994, no. 1.

52 Bjørklund, 'The three Nordic 1994 referenda', pp. 11–36, especially pp. 12–13; see also Wolfram Kaiser, Pekka Visuri, Cecilia Malmström and Arve Hjelseth, 'Die EU-Volksabstimmungen in Österreich, Finnland, Schweden und Norwegen: Folgen für die Europäische Union', *Integration*, 1995, vol. 18, no. 2, pp. 76–87.

53 Bjørklund, 'The three Nordic 1994 referenda', p. 17.

54 Tapio Raunio and Matti Wiberg, 'Johdanto: Suomi astuu unioniaikaan', in Tapio Raunio and Matti Wiberg (eds), *EU ja Suomi: Unionijäsenyyden vaikutukset suomalaiseen yhteiskuntaan*, Helsinki: Edita, 2000, pp. 9–23, here pp. 13–14.

55 Tapio Raunio and Teija Tiilikainen, *Finland in the European Union*, London: Frank Cass, 2003, pp. 28–31, 35–6.

56 The collapse of Soviet trade was a major reason for the crisis. See Riitta Hjerppe, 'Finland's foreign trade and trade policy in the 20th century', *Scandinavian Journal of History*, 1993, vol. 18, no. 1, pp. 57–76. See also Rehn, 'Odottavasta ennakoivaan integraatiopolitiikkaan?', p. 202.

57 *Suomi ja Euroopan yhteisön jäsenyys*, Helsinki: Council of State, 1992, p. 12; *Suomi ja Euroopan yhteisön jäsenyys: Taustaselvitys: Liite valtioneuvoston selontekoon eduskunnalle EY-jäsenyyden vaikutuksista Suomelle* (appendix to the government report), Helsinki: Council of State, 1992, pp. 35–7.

58 David Arter, 'The EU referendum in Finland on 16 October 1994: a vote for the West, not for Maastricht', *Journal of Common Market Studies*, 1995, vol. 33, no. 3, pp. 361–87, here p. 372.

59 Cf. Raunio and Tiilikainen, *Finland in the European Union*, p. 31.

60 Kari Möttölä, 'Puolueettomuudesta sitoutumiseen: Turvallisuuspoliittisen perus-ratkaisun muutos kylmästä sodasta Euroopan murrokseen', in Tuomas Forsberg and Tapani Vaahtoranta (eds), *Johdatus Suomen ulkopolitiikkaan: Kylmästä sodasta uuteen maail-manjärjestykseen*, Tampere: Gaudeamus, 1993, pp. 62–135, here pp. 90–5.

61 Mikko Majander, 'The Finnish–Soviet Treaty of Friendship, Cooperation and Mutual Assistance in Finland under President Koivisto: two rounds of discussion', in *Yearbook of Finnish Foreign Policy*, Helsinki: Finnish Institute of International Affairs, 1991, pp. 32–40, here pp. 37–8.

62 Pertti Joenniemi, 'Finland in the new Europe: a Herderian or Hegelian project?', in Lene Hansen and Ole Wæver (eds), *European Integration and National Identity: The Challenge of the Nordic States*, London: Routledge, 2002, p. 184.

63 See Tuomas Forsberg, 'One foreign policy or two? Finland's new constitution and European policies of Tarja Halonen and Paavo Lipponen', *Northern Dimensions, Yearbook 2001*, Helsinki: Finnish Institute of International Affairs, 2001, pp. 3–11, and Tapio Raunio and Matti Wiberg, 'Parliamentarizing foreign policy decision-making: Finland in the European Union', *Cooperation and Conflict*, 2001, vol. 36, no. 1, pp. 61–86.

64 Hans Mouritzen, 'The two *Musterknaben* and the naughty boy: Sweden, Finland and Denmark in the process of European integration', *Cooperation and Conflict*, 1993, vol. 28, no. 4, pp. 373–402, here pp. 389–91.

65 Meinander, 'On the brink or in-between?', pp. 158, 164.

66 Af Malmborg, 'Gaullism in the North?', pp. 493–4.

67 Lee Miles, 'Sweden and Finland', in Ian Manners and Richard G. Whitman (eds), *The Foreign Policies of European Union Member-States*, Manchester: Manchester University Press, 2000, pp. 181–203, here pp. 188–9.

68 Archives of the daily *Aamulehti*, http://alarkisto.aamulehti.fi.

69 According to an opinion poll, 56 per cent would have voted against EU membership had they known it implied giving up the Finnish *markka*. Saska Saarikoski, 'Kansa ei ostanut EU:ta markalla', *Suomen Kuvalehti*, 1997, no. 17, pp. 17–19.

70 'Chronology of Finnish Foreign Policy', *Ulkopolitiikka*, 1998, no. 3, p. 109.

71 Raunio and Tiilikainen, *Finland in the European Union*, pp. 37–8.

72 See Teija Tiilikainen, 'The Finnish presidency of 1999: pragmatism and the promotion of Finland's position in Europe', in Ole Elgström (ed.), *European Union Council Presidencies: A Comparative Perspective*. London: Routledge, 2003, pp. 104–99.

73 See more in Nina Græger, Henrik Larsen and Hanna Ojanen, *The ESDP and the Nordic Countries: Four Variations on a Theme* (Programme on the Northern Dimension of the CFSP), Helsinki: Finnish Institute of International Affairs and Institut für Europäische Politik, 2002.

74 See Hanna Ojanen, *The Plurality of Truth: A Critique of Research on the State and European Integration*, Aldershot: Ashgate, 1998.

75 See Joenniemi, 'Finland in the new Europe', pp. 182–213.

76 See Christine Ingebritsen and Susan Larson, 'Interest and identity: Finland, Norway and European Union', *Cooperation and Conflict*, 1997, vol. 32, no. 2, pp. 207–22; Sami Moisio, *Geopoliittinen kamppailu Suomen EU-jäsenyydestä* (Turun Yliopiston julkaisuja, *Annales Universitatis Turkuensis*, C:204), Turku: Turun Yliopisto, 2003, for an analysis of different explanatory models found in the literature on Finnish EU membership, and Christopher Browning, 'Coming home or moving home? "Westernizing" narratives in Finnish foreign policy and the reinterpretation of past identities', *Cooperation and Conflict*, 2002, vol. 37, no. 1, pp. 47–72.

77 See Teija Tiilikainen, *Europe and Finland: Defining the Political Identity of Finland in Western Europe*, Aldershot: Ashgate, 1998.

78 See Robert D. Putnam, 'Diplomacy and domestic politics: the logic of two-level games', *International Organization*, 1988, vol. 42, no. 3, pp. 427–60, and Andrew Moravcsik, 'Preferences and power in the European Community: a liberal intergovernmentalist approach', *Journal of Common Market Studies*, 1993, vol. 31, no. 4, pp. 473–524.

9   Combining dependence with distance

Sweden

Maria Gussarsson

'Gladly the Nordic countries and the UN, but preferably not Europe.' This is how Mikael af Malmborg has described the prevalent Swedish attitude towards Europe, at least during the decades following the end of the Second World War.[1] This 'preferably not' did not mean that Europe was seen as being of no importance to Sweden. But for a long time, the Swedish governments chose a relatively restrictive policy *vis-à-vis* 'Europe', not least by keeping Sweden outside the increasing Western European cooperation that had been initiated with the creation of the European Coal and Steel Community (ECSC) in 1951–52. Although a rapprochement did take place after the 1960s, the country did not become a full member of the European Union until 1995.

During the three decades following 1945, Sweden was governed by Social Democratic-led governments; after a brief pause, the Social Democrats again took power between 1982 and 1991, and have governed from 1994 until the present. The Swedish electoral system of proportional representation has always produced a range of parties in the Swedish parliament, which, in turn, has often necessitated minority or coalition governments. But even if the dominance of *Sveriges Socialdemokratiska Arbetareparti* (Social Democratic Workers' Party or SAP) has been challenged and its politics often modified by the need for compromise, the SAP has had an enormous influence on both domestic and foreign policy. On Swedish security policy, however, there has existed a wide consensus among the political parties. As relations between the Soviet Union and the Western powers deteriorated at the end of the 1940s, the Swedish government decided that the country was to follow the doctrine of 'non-alignment in peace, neutrality as the goal in war'. Until 1989, the Swedes – like all other Western Europeans – lived under what was perceived as a Soviet threat,[2] but as this threat disappeared, political balancing between the superpowers diminished in importance.

The Swedish policy of non-alignment has its roots in the beginning of the nineteenth century.[3] The last time the country was directly involved in hostilities was in 1814, when it sent troops as a member of the alliance against Napoleon. Since then, its security policy has been based primarily either on declarations of neutrality, or on a balancing act between the great powers. The traumas caused by the world wars, which provided a very large incentive for cooperation on the Continent after 1945, had thus no real counterpart in Swedish experience. On the contrary, the lesson taught by the wars was, in fact, that the country could avoid involvement through self-sufficiency.

Besides the obvious wish to avoid the risk of being dragged into a war, most Swedes believed that their country's non-alignement policy during the Cold War would actually contribute to world peace.[4] But they also wanted to be able to play an international political role, and herein lies a third motive for the Swedish security doctrine: it provided Sweden with a 'third-way identity' as international mediator and arbitrator. As early as 1948, Prime Minister and Social Democratic Party leader Tage Erlander declared that Sweden's security doctrine did not imply neutrality in spirit: there was no question but that Sweden belonged to the democratic world.[5] In fact, the Swedish governments tried to profile themselves as peacemakers (mainly through UN assignments of various kinds) as well as harsh critics of what they considered imperialistic behaviour. This 'active foreign policy', which resulted in a self-image of moral superiority, was given a higher profile in the beginning of the 1960s,[6] and gained still more strength under Erlander's successor, Olof Palme.[7]

Non-alignment obviously implied that Swedish participation in military cooperation was out of the question. But the security doctrine did not necessarily preclude *all* forms of involvement in international cooperation.[8] There have, for instance, been disagreements between the political parties on the issue of Sweden's European policy. The two primary and most influential factions on this issue have been the rather sceptical SAP, often supported by the politically centrist Agrarian Party (later renamed the Centre Party), on the one hand; and, on the other, the two more pro-European parties, the Liberals and the Conservatives. Still, despite a certain initial hesitation, all became strong advocates of Swedish participation in the Organization for European Economic Cooperation (OEEC) and the Council of Europe. Sweden was among the founding states of both organizations, a role motivated in part by a wish to maintain smooth relations with the United States, which urged Western European cooperation and was harshly critical of Sweden's policy of non-alignment.[9]

But economic considerations also underlay Swedish attitudes to European integration.[10] When the Second World War ended, Sweden's economic situation was considerably better than that of most of Europe. There were several reasons for this. First, Sweden's infrastructure and industry were intact since the country had not been directly involved in the conflict; some Swedes had even been able to profit from trading with the belligerents. Second, the reconstruction of Europe after 1945 and the concurrent growth in international trade offered Swedish industry an enormous opportunity to expand, especially in trade with Great Britain and West Germany. The Swedish economy was (and still is) highly dependent on exports of industrial goods, and the country became, accordingly, an ardent advocate of free trade. On the other hand, Sweden's agricultural sector already was relatively small at the end of the war, and has since decreased further. Until the 1990s, the sector was strongly subsidized by the state, in part so that Sweden – in accordance with its policy of non-alignment – would have secure food supplies in case of war.

Considerable economic growth after 1945 allowed the creation of a Swedish welfare state, and as the SAP had great political weight, the project became associated primarily with Social Democracy. The SAP regarded the so-called 'people's home' *(folkhemmet)* as something more than the welfare systems created in other countries.[11] However, at the end of the 1960s, the positive economic trend came to an end, and the country has since experienced recurrent economic problems and even depression. As these crises necessitated cuts in public spending, the idea of the Swedish welfare model as intrinsically superior had to be modified.

As mentioned above, Swedish governments regarded Nordic and global cooperation as more valuable than European integration. The Nordic projects were partly a response to Western European projects. Sweden launched a proposal for a Scandinavian Defence Union in 1948.[12] This was in response to the creation of the Brussels Pact, a defence pact signed the same year by Great Britain, France and the Benelux countries, and to discussions of an Atlantic alliance. The Nordic Council, created in 1952, corresponded to the Council of Europe in its structure and purpose, both being purely consultative bodies, and both excluding defence issues. Similarly, discussions of a Scandinavian customs union at the end of the 1940s and again in 1954 corresponded to the many similar projects launched on the Continent.[13]

In proposing these plans for Nordic cooperation, Sweden was motivated by the hope that it would strengthen the participating members – all small or medium-sized states – in relation to the larger Western European projects. It was also a widely held opinion within all Swedish political parties that Nordic cooperation would be particularly favourable since the Nordic countries' societies, cultures and languages were similar. In addition, the fact that the Nordic countries all had strong Social Democratic parties made the SAP see great promise in the prospect of more intense collaboration. Finally, the Swedish interest in Nordic cooperation, and Swedish hesitation in regards to larger Western European integration projects, can be understood in terms of Sweden's imperial past.[14] The high point in Swedish Great Power status was in the seventeenth century; its definitive end came with the break-up of the union with Norway in 1905. But it seems clear that this Great Power past influenced Swedish attitudes towards international cooperation long after that. Since Sweden was the strongest of the Nordic states, it would also be the dominant member in any Nordic project.

The need for economic, not political, cooperation

When the French ECSC proposal was launched in 1950, it sparked hardly any debate whatsoever in Sweden. It was scarcely mentioned in the newspapers or in parliament. However, the Schuman Plan did awaken some fears in the Swedish Foreign Office, since the West German market was of great importance to Swedish iron and steel production, and about 90 per cent of Swedish coke imports came from West Germany.

Swedish policy towards this project, as well as towards subsequent similar projects, was strongly influenced by the SAP's strong scepticism towards the governments of Western Europe. One reason for this was that Sweden – unlike most of the countries on the Continent – had a long and unbroken past as a democracy. Another was the aversion Swedish Social Democrats had towards four phenomena that they identified as prevalent in Western European countries: Catholicism, conservatism, capitalism and colonialism.[15] Despite the fact that the stigma of colonialism also applied to Great Britain, and that the British government, in periods at least, was fairly conservative, the SAP had a quite benevolent attitude towards this country. But there was much harsh criticism of West Germany under Christian Democratic Chancellor Konrad Adenauer, not least in the Social Democratic press. An article in *Arbetet*, discussing upcoming German elections in 1957, mentioned, for instance, the 'partly reactionary Adenauer regime, poisoned by clericalism' and went on to state that there were reasons to believe that to many Christian Democratic Union (CDU) politicians, democracy was 'just an opportunistic varnish'.[16] Swedish Social Democrats were also critical of France, with its centre-right governments, and even more so as Charles de Gaulle came to power in 1958. This critique was based, in part, on ideological grounds, but during the Fourth Republic it was also triggered by the instability of French domestic politics. In 1956, the newspaper *Folket* went so far as to call France 'Europe's sick man', a great power in decline that 'could neither maintain its position outwards nor secure its domestic development'.[17] Not even the contacts between the SAP and its French sister party were unproblematic. The French Socialist Party (SFIO) was considered ideologically dogmatic yet overly prone to compromise when it came to practical politics (not least on colonial policy). Relations with the German and the British sister parties were significantly better. However, during the 1950s, the discussions on European integration conducted between the SAP and these sister parties – both bilaterally and in the Socialist International – were quite limited in scope.[18]

There appears to have been two reasons for Sweden's cautious approach to ECSC. First of all, there was a feeling of uncertainty as to what the Schuman Plan actually entailed. Neither the political parties nor the representatives of trade and industry felt that they had adequate information. Second, the plan's supranational features were, in themselves, enough to preclude Swedish membership. Membership in such an organization would, it was argued, be incompatible with Sweden's security policy. The SAP advanced a further argument against supranational cooperation: since the Swedish Social Democrats regarded their own version of the welfare state as superior to any other, they argued that any limitation of national self-government would put *folkhemmet* at risk. The SAP government therefore did not consider Swedish membership in the ECSC an option, at least not in the beginning of the 1950s. But to protect the interests of its industry, Sweden chose to establish a permanent delegation at the High Authority of the ECSC (it was the third country to do so, following the lead of Great Britain and the United States) in December 1952.

The importance of foreign trade also compelled the Swedish government to explore new avenues. In 1954 the Nordic countries decided to renew their efforts to establish a Nordic customs union, and two years later Sweden was one of six low-tariff countries to advance a plan for general tariff reductions in the OEEC. On the other hand, the proposal for a common market, launched by the ECSC countries in 1955, met with a chilly response. In the beginning, the idea did not get much attention in Sweden, probably because few Swedes believed that the project had any future.[19] It was really only the Swedish OEEC delegation in Paris that reacted at an early stage, worrying that the plan might lead to a division among the Western European states. Soon, however, the Swedish Federation of Industries started to take an active interest. It considered the Nordic plans too limited geographically, and politically too much dominated by Social Democrats.[20] But it did not find EEC membership suitable either; instead it lined up behind the British proposal of 1956 for a free trade area consisting of the OEEC members. The Swedish government was initially hesitant towards this plan, for two reasons: it had a preference for global tariff reductions and it feared that the plan might jeopardize the Nordic customs union project since the Danes and Norwegians were clearly opposed to the free trade area's exclusion of agriculture and fish industries. The Swedish Conservatives and the Liberals were, on the other hand, more positive towards the planned Continental customs union than were the Social Democrats and the Agrarian Party. Still, all four parties reached the same conclusion: non-alignment was an obstacle to Swedish membership in the EEC. However, if a free trade area did become a reality, Sweden could not afford to remain outside it. Even Sweden's federation of trade unions, *Landsorganisationen* (LO), which was closely linked to the SAP, agreed with this, although it feared that such an arrangement would result in growing competition from Southern Europe, which would put pressure on the Swedish labour market and eventually lead to wage cuts.[21]

EEC membership would, it was argued, undermine Swedish security policy, as Sweden would forfeit its right to protect its national agricultural production, and thus its right to safeguard the nation's potential for self-sufficiency in case of war. Membership might likewise give other nations the impression that Swedish foreign policy was linked to that of a specific group of states. However, the arguments the SAP government advanced against the EEC – and in favour of a free trade area – were almost exclusively economic and political in character. A statement made by the Minister of Trade Gunnar Lange in March 1957 makes this quite clear:

> I do not think I am guilty of any exaggeration … when I say that the political elements today are stronger than the pure economic ones within the Six power group. As far as you can see, the protectionist and discriminatory features in the planned cooperation concerning trade policy have, for instance, become more distinct … We must actively take part in the current preliminary work for the European free trade area, not least as part of our traditional efforts for freer European trade, but we must also oppose and, to the best of our ability, attempt to prevent that the common market develops

into a protected area ... a block that tries to obtain economic and trade advantages at the expense of the interests of third countries.[22]

As free trade area negotiations broke down at the end of 1958, the Swedish government – spurred by the fundamental importance of foreign trade to the Swedish economy – instead took an active part in the creation of the smaller European Free Trade Association (EFTA), consisting of the Scandinavian states, Great Britain, Switzerland and Austria, and subsequently Portugal. The idea was that EFTA would not only facilitate trade between its member-states, but also would form a counterweight to the EEC, capable of negotiation from a position of strength.[23]

But only one year after the creation of EFTA, Great Britain applied for EEC membership, making Swedish advances seem necessary as well. The significance of EFTA would diminish considerably if the British – and with them, presumably, also Denmark and Norway – left, and it would be devastating for the Swedish economy if the relatively high EEC tariffs were raised around these countries' markets. The question was thus how to secure core Swedish interests. Most industrialists, Conservatives and Liberals wanted full EEC membership, provided that the policy of non-alignment could be kept intact. But the governing SAP, backed by the Centre Party and the LO, was fiercely opposed to fully-fledged membership, arguing that it could never be combined with the Swedish security doctrine.[24] In a speech given at the Congress of the Swedish Metal Workers' Union in August 1961, Tage Erlander declared that membership would be incompatible with non-alignment, since the EEC was 'a defence organization against communism', intended to strengthen NATO.[25]

But according to the Social Democrats this was not the only reason to reject full EEC membership. Erlander also argued that membership would undermine the Swedish welfare state, and that it would contribute to raising tariff walls against poorer countries. Finally, he concluded, the Swedish economy was, after all, strong enough to allow the country to find another solution. The Social Democrats therefore considered limited economic association with the EEC as the only reasonable alternative. This was, accordingly, applied for under Article 238 of the EEC Treaty in December 1961, with the hope that such an arrangement would be more comprehensive than a mere trade agreement. However, the French President Charles de Gaulle vetoed the British application in January 1963. EFTA, thus, not only managed to survive, but actually gained in political importance, for it now seemed probable that the division between the two trading blocs would remain in force for at least as long as de Gaulle retained power in France.

In 1966, the prospect of a second British EEC membership application once again spurred activity in Stockholm. But this time the government did not apply for the type of restricted association which the EEC countries offered to states that desired full membership but were not yet economically ready. Instead, the Swedish government submitted a vaguely formulated 'open application' on the 28 July 1967, stating that the government wished to negotiate on the possibility of joining the EEC in a way that was compatible with the Swedish policy of non-alignment. The government did not mention, however, in what form this would be done; it did not, in other words, exclude the possibility of full membership. There were several reasons for this. First and foremost, the supranational features of the EEC had – owing to de Gaulle – faded, something that suited the functionalist-minded Swedes very well. Second, international *détente* encouraged the hope that the pressure on Sweden's security policy would diminish. At the same time, though, the government was well aware that voices critical to the Swedish security doctrine had been raised in the EEC as early as 1961. A third reason was associated with Sweden's domestic situation: the government wanted to avoid critical reactions from Sweden's pro-European Liberals and Conservatives, and from representatives of trade and industry. At any rate, as long as de Gaulle refused a British accession to membership, the Swedish negotiations would have to wait as well. Instead, the Swedish government channelled its energies into the Danish plan for NORDEK, a new and more extensive form of Nordic economic cooperation.[26]

De Gaulle's resignation in 1969, however, once again brought the enlargement of the EC into the foreground. The renewed British, Danish, Norwegian (and Irish) membership applications indicated that, once again, EFTA was threatened. So were the Nordic plans; Denmark's accession to EC membership eventually led to the end of the NORDEK project. As a consequence, the issue of Sweden's EC application re-appeared on the country's political agenda. In fact, Sweden's concurrent economic decline lent the question still greater urgency. Erlander's successor as Prime Minister and SAP leader, Olof Palme, set out on a series of visits to Bonn, Paris and London, in order to emphasize that Sweden wished to participate in a larger organization for economic cooperation. The fact that the West German Chancellor at this time was Willy Brandt – Social Democrat and close friend of Palme – probably had a positive impact on these meetings.

In the spring of 1970, the Davignon Report on cooperation in foreign policy matters was submitted to the EC Council of Ministers, and was soon followed by the Werner Report, which proposed an economic and monetary union. In other words, the EC member-states seemed to be planning to deepen and widen their cooperation. In response, the government in Stockholm declared that Sweden had two reservations concerning full EC membership, both deriving from its policy of non-alignment. The country could, first of all, not participate in binding cooperation regarding foreign policy. Second, the Swedish government insisted that an economic and monetary union could not accept supranational institutions.

In the long run, however, these reservations rendered the Swedish application unacceptable, something that soon forced the government to formulate an alternative agreement. Its next tactic was to attempt to join the EC customs union and participate in its further liberalization without, however, becoming a full member. But the EC states – believing that Sweden sought EC advantages, but wished to avoid obligations – rejected this idea. Instead, negotiations were begun on a free trade agreement which would cover industrial but not agricultural goods. However, when this agreement was concluded in July 1972, it covered more than just tariffs. It also forbade cartels and state support to industry in principle, and a 'development clause' kept a door open for closer future cooperation.[27]

In Sweden, political opinion on this new scheme varied, which caused considerable discussion – and in some cases, harsh criticism – in the media. The SAP was not united on the issue. The LO was critical, but lined up behind the SAP government when it was promised that the agreement would not include labour market regulation. The industrialists, like the Conservatives and Liberals, advocated a more far-reaching settlement, even including EC membership. But despite the fact that the new free trade agreement with the EC fell short of what many – including some government members – had hoped for, its conclusion meant that the European question now virtually disappeared from the Swedish political agenda, re-emerging only in the mid-1980s. Even the assumption of power, in 1976, by a centre-right government failed to cause a policy reorientation. It had, in fact, no compelling reason to make a new approach to the EC. During this period, the EC was beset by internal economic and political problems; meanwhile, the free trade agreement served Swedish foreign trade quite well. In addition, the renewed political tensions between East and West that started in the mid-1970s once again made it important for Sweden to emphasize its policy of non-alignment.

In 1984, however, when the free trade agreement of 1972 had been fully implemented, a new SAP government suggested that EFTA and the EC should also try to reduce non-tariff barriers to trade. The motives for this initiative were to be found in the economic situation, both international and domestic. Internationally, the significance of EFTA had diminished considerably after 1973, when Great Britain and Denmark had joined the EC; by the mid-1980s, Portugal and Spain were negotiating to do the same. The EC had, thereby, assumed overwhelming economic importance for Sweden; in 1984, almost half of Swedish exports went to the EC. Simultaneously, it appeared that the EC states were about to deepen their cooperation, which would adversely affect non-members' terms of competition. Another factor was that world trade was divided into three blocs – the United States, South-east Asia and the EC – and that relations between them were tense. If a trade conflict were to arise between them, Sweden's exclusion from the EC might badly damage the Swedish export industry. Finally, the expansion of multinational companies, the increased speed of information flows and the transition to smoother capital transfers had rendered all economies more international. It had become difficult for individual national governments to formulate economic policy; there seemed to be obvious advantages to carrying out the task in cooperation with other states.[28]

Most important, though, was the poor state of Sweden's economy. During the 1980s the country had been hit by severe problems in the form of an overheated economy and high inflation. Sweden's Liberals, Conservatives and industrialists regarded closer cooperation with other Western European states as imperative to

solving these problems. The majority of Social Democrats were still highly sceptical towards the EC, even if European integration was not a major issue for the
general party membership. (Before 1993, it was scarcely debated at all at Social
Democratic Party Congresses.) But within the SAP party elite, and more specifically in government, there was a change of opinion as to the optimal extent of
relations with the EC. This influential group now argued that even if full
membership remained out of the question, it was possible to conceive of cooperation with the EC in all areas except those of foreign and security policy.

As the Social Democratic elite's opinion changed, so did the SAP's rhetoric
concerning Europe. The SAP's concept of the EC as a conservative project,
which was rooted in the attitudes of the 1950s, had been modified by the fact
that Social Democrats had created or joined governments in different European
countries: West Germany between 1966 and 1982, in France as of 1981, and in
Great Britain between 1964 and 1970, and again between 1974 and 1979. The
good relations between Palme and Brandt also weighed heavily here. Further, the
LO's cooperation with other Western European labour unions had provided
essential information on the integration project, and this knowledge had 'spilled
over' to the SAP. Thus, for the first time, Swedish Social Democrats began to
speak of 'Sweden's European identity', the 'democratic Europe's community of
values' and of Europe's 'cultural affinity'.[29]

As the EC members signed the Single European Act (SEA) in 1986, which
aimed at the creation of an internal market, Swedish industrialists once again
urged the need for a rapprochement. But this time they wanted full membership
with a continued policy of non-alignment. In this, they were formally supported
by Sweden's Conservative Party. In fact, all political parties in parliament except
the Communists acknowledged that Sweden had to respond to the SEA agenda
if it were to safeguard its foreign trade. The government therefore suggested the
establishment of a common market consisting of EFTA and the EC, with broad
cooperation in all fields except foreign policy.[30] Soon it raised its sights still
further, declaring – with the backing of a vast majority of members of parliament – that Swedish citizens and businesses should enjoy the same rights and
opportunities as did those of the other EC member-states. This move towards
the EC was, in fact, seen as necessary by all EFTA members. In June 1988 representatives for these governments, thus, declared their intention to approach the
EC collectively to discuss a major revision of the existing EFTA–EC agreements.

A determined but sceptical member of EU

In the summer of 1990, however, the discussion of a rapprochement with the
EC took a new turn. The break-up of the Soviet Union changed the conditions
for the formulation of Swedish foreign policy in two ways. The decrease of the
risk of war between the superpowers meant that Sweden's security doctrine
could be interpreted more flexibly.[31] Pro-Europe Swedes thus argued that non-
alignment no longer formed an obstacle to EC membership. Second, the end of
the Cold War provided what could be seen as a direct impetus for Sweden's

application for membership in the EC. Its position as mediator between the superpowers had already weakened with the *détente* of the mid-1980s; the events of 1989 and the following years eradicated any Swedish claim to that special status. This loss might, it was argued, be compensated by Sweden's assumption of an active role within the internationally powerful EC.

The hope for renewed political influence was, however, only part of the reason for the shift in the debate. Others were to be found in the domestic economic and political context, and in Sweden's relations with the EC. Of special importance was the economic situation at the beginning of the 1990s. The concurrent American recession had weakened one of the most important markets for the Swedish export industry. The economic situation, already difficult, soon turned into an acute crisis. It was, in short, painfully evident that the Swedish economy was both in bad shape and very vulnerable to changes in international circumstances.[32]

In 1990, EFTA and the EC initiated negotiations on a European Economic Area (EEA), meant to link EFTA economically to the EC. This proposal had been launched by Jacques Delors, President of the Commission. It soon became clear, however, that the structure of the EEA would, implicitly, force Sweden (and other EFTA states) to accept EC legislation, while denying them any say in its decision-making. Initially, the Swedes tried to compensate for their lack of direct influence by attempting to exert indirect influence on EC institutions through party networks and parliamentary delegations.[33] But in the summer of 1990, Sweden's Liberal and Conservative parties joined the Swedish Federation of Industries and the foremost union for white-collar workers, the *Tjänstemännens Centralorganisation* (TCO), in a common declaration in favour of full EC membership. The business representatives also decided to launch a public relations offensive in favour of membership. Public opinion polls showed that a majority of the Swedish population shared their positive attitude to EC membership. In December of 1990, 67 per cent of the Swedish population declared themselves in favour of joining the EC. The vast majority of the Social Democratic Party members were, however, still highly sceptical. But even more important was that members of a leading faction within the SAP government changed their minds about full membership during the second half of 1990, arguing that only accession could solve Sweden's domestic economic problems.[34]

The division within the SAP on EC membership can partly be explained by contradictory perceptions of Sweden and the EC countries. On the one hand, many Swedes still saw their country as having something to lose, because it was superior, for example, in equality between the sexes, environmental policies and the public accessibility of government documents. On the other hand, the attempts to give the EC a social dimension, not least through the signing of the Charter of Fundamental Social Rights in 1989, and the many Western European Social Democrats who played an important role within the EC, moderated perceptions of Swedish societal and legal superiority. The policy shift within the SAP elite was also influenced by various individuals and groups. One important impulse came from the leading circles within LO, which, by the end of the 1980s, had become dominated by people favouring Swedish EC member-ship.[35] Another was *Rådet för Europafrågor* (the Council for Questions on Europe), a consultative body consisting of four members of the government and of prominent representatives of government agencies, universities, trade unions and business, which was established in 1988 by Ingvar Carlsson, Prime Minister and SAP leader after the murder of Olof Palme in 1986. Third, Carlsson has admitted that he was strongly influenced in this matter by his meetings, between 1988 and 1990, with three continental Social Democrats: Delors; the Spanish Prime Minister Felipe Gonzáles; and the Austrian Chancellor Franz Vranitzky. The discussions with the latter also gave him an idea of how the Austrians intended to combine their neutrality with membership. These meetings, in fact, allowed Carlsson to see the EC as something akin to a social democratic project.

By the autumn of 1990, the economic crisis in Sweden had become so serious that the government rapidly had to assemble a package of economic emergency measures, which was presented in a press conference by Minister of Finance Allan Larsson on 26 October. Among the many measures mentioned, Larsson said that the government urged parliament to 'clearly and more positively clarify Swedish ambitions to become a member of the EC'.[36] Membership was thus presented as an economic question. In fact, some critics argued that the govern-ment's reorientation towards Europe had been reduced to a 'footnote' in Larsson's speech. This was a strategy to deal with the considerable resistance to membership that still existed within the SAP. A majority of Social Democratic Party members remained critical of membership,[37] and not even all members of the SAP government were convinced of the advisability of accession. Under these circumstances, it would be much more difficult to question the measure if the Minister of Finance presented it as part of the package necessary to rescue Sweden from its economic crisis, than if the matter were broached separately by the Prime Minister. Moreover, Sten Andersson, the Minister of Foreign Affairs, was in fact one of the government's EC sceptics, although he clearly lined up behind the new policy after Larsson's speech.

Only eight months after Larsson's press conference, on 1 July 1991, Ingvar Carlsson submitted an application for full Swedish EC membership. This sudden, independent move came as a surprise to the Nordic EFTA members, who had hoped for a common approach. But the Swedish government's reason for speeding up the process – and thereby ignoring its neighbours – lay in the imminence of Swedish parliamentary elections. Opinion polls pointed to signifi-cant losses for the SAP, which were, of course, a result of the economic crisis and the government's measures to counteract it: harsh economic cuts which had cost many people their jobs. Furthermore, rising unemployment, together with an increasing budget deficit and a growing national debt, undermined the whole economy, thereby inciting massive speculation against the Swedish currency in 1991. For a whole year, the government tried to maintain the value of the *krona* through market intervention, but was eventually forced to let it float, leading to a significant devaluation. However, the European question seemed to offer a possible means to attract the many pro-EC voters to the SAP. Hence, the Social

Democratic leadership needed to maintain its initiative in the membership question, and this meant that the application had to come before the elections.[38]

Unlike earlier occasions when Sweden had approached the EC, the government did not now mention any reservations deriving from its policy of non-alignment, most probably (given the critical economic situation) in order to avoid delays in membership negotiations. However, in spite of this 'good will', Sweden (along with the four other candidate states) had to wait to begin negotiations with the EC, as EC member-states first wanted to conclude the Maastricht negotiations. Meanwhile, an agreement was reached between EFTA and the EC concerning the EEA. When Swedish membership negotiations did start, in February 1993, it was no longer the Social Democrats but a centre-right coalition under the Conservative Party leader Carl Bildt that spoke on behalf of the country. The new Swedish government argued that it would be possible to maintain non-alignment as a member in the future EU, since the EU's Common Foreign and Security Policy (CFSP) would take place in the form of cooperation between independent states, and that Sweden, therefore, did not object to this part of the Maastricht Treaty. In fact, the discussions between the EC/EU and Sweden went rather smoothly on the whole, partly because many questions had already been solved during the EEA negotiations. The only major difference arose when the Swedish government asked that Sweden be given the right to opt out of the third phase of the Economic and Monetary Union (EMU), a request that was not granted. On 1 March 1994, the negotiations were concluded. There now remained only one obstacle to Swedish accession. According to an agreement reached by the SAP and the centre-right parties three years earlier, membership had to be sanctioned by the Swedish citizens in a referendum. Unlike three years earlier, however, there was no longer strong popular support for joining the EU. Public opinion was in fact split into two almost equal factions. This gave rise to a very intense referendum campaign. Several of the parties, as well as the trade union organization LO, were themselves divided on the question.[39] The referendum, held on 13 November 1994, resulted in a small victory for the pro-Europeans: 52.3 per cent voted in favour of membership, while 46.8 per cent would have preferred to stay outside. Thus, Sweden could join the EU on 1 January 1995.

Since its accession to membership, Swedish European policy has clearly changed. It remains, however, characterized by a certain reserve. In fact, Sweden has even been called 'a reluctant European'.[40] Yet on some issues the Swedish government, which has been uninterruptedly led by Social Democrats since 1994, quickly developed strong initiatives in the EU. It took the lead on questions concerning equality between the sexes, the environment, the labour market, and bureaucratic and political transparency – that is, in fields where Swedish policy might serve as an example. This activity can partly be explained by continued domestic scepticism to the EU. The government wanted to show that Sweden really had a role to play in the Union. But it was also an attempt to create a good impression of Sweden as a member-state, since many of the other EU countries regarded it as uncommitted.

In one respect, however, most Swedes were – and remain – clearly reserved: they still dislike the idea of supranational cooperation. For instance, when the third phase of EMU was launched in 2002, Sweden did not participate, despite the fact that legally it had no opt-out clause. The major reason for this was the EMU's supranational feature. During recent years a strong opinion in favour of joining EMU has emerged. For instance, the SAP government, with a few exceptions, belongs to the pro-EMU group. But as the Swedish population were consulted in a referendum in September 2003, the answer was a clear no. Almost 56 per cent of the Swedes wanted to stay outside, while 42 per cent preferred to join the EMU. Sweden will thus remain outside, even though a future membership is not excluded. But the issue is not likely to be brought up again until opinion surveys show a change in the public attitude. Regarding supranational cooperation in general, the Swedish government is one of the advocates of new and alternative forms of inter-governmental cooperation. It is particularly in favour of the so-called method of open cooperation, which is based upon close cooperation at the European level, but without supranational legislation.[41]

On joining the EU, Sweden also pledged to contribute to the CFSP. Regarding foreign policy, security, economic cooperation and environmental protection, interests have motivated Swedish governments to push for cooperation with Russia and the Baltic states, and for the latter's EU membership.[42] The government clearly declared itself in favour of an eastern enlargement of the EU, even making this a central topic during the Swedish EU presidency in 2001. Sweden's motivations were three-fold. One derived from economic concerns. Enlargement was regarded as a means to make the EU economically stronger. Second, there was a moral motive: it was right that candidate-states be given the same opportunities as those already enjoyed by other parts of Europe. Third, there was a security aspect behind the Swedish attitude to enlargement. This was, it was argued, 'a historical opportunity, ultimately being a question of strengthening the basis for peace, freedom, democracy and prosperity in Europe'.[43]

Swedish governments have not seen anything problematic in combining the CFSP with non-alignment. On the contrary, the country has been active in this field in several ways.[44] For instance, it joined Finland in launching a proposal on transferring the crisis management tasks of the Western European Union (WEU) over to the EU, while still allowing non-aligned or neutral states to remain outside the WEU, a proposal to which the member-states agreed in the Amsterdam Treaty in 1997. It also participated in the creation of EU's crisis management troops, on which a decision was taken in December 1999. Sweden has, in other words, taken an active part in the CFSP in a way that is compatible with its national security interests.

The 'reluctant European' has, thus, not fully earned the epithet – at least not when it comes to its actual behaviour in the EU. Swedish attitudes towards the EU are still predominantly sceptical, but have nevertheless changed somewhat. In the past, Swedish scepticism towards the EC was partly based on a sense of economic and moral superiority. But this self-image was rocked during the 1990s. Economically, the crisis removed Sweden from an internationally leading position, and necessitated substantial cuts in its welfare system. Morally, the Swedish sense of superiority was undermined, as the public was made aware of and started debating Swedish cooperation with Nazi Germany during the Second World War[45] and a dark side of *folkhemmet* – the policy of enforced sterilizations.[46] In addition, the Swedish presidency of the EU during the first half of 2001 seems to have moderated prevailing attitudes somewhat. The government then chose to focus on three main issues – the so-called 'three Es': enlargement, employment and environment[47] – and managed to reach satisfactory results, especially concerning enlargement. Swedish bureaucrats and politicians who met their colleagues in the EU during this period seem to have been influenced by these meetings to take a more positive stance *vis-à-vis* the EU. Public opinion still continued to register scepticism, however, despite the outcome of the presidency. Opinion polls at the end of the presidency even showed that Swedes had become more negative towards the EU, a fact that can partly be explained by the rather critical stance adopted by Swedish mass media.[48]

Conclusion

Swedish attitudes to the EU and its predecessors are often explained as the result of the governing elite's perception of politico-strategic national interests. In fact, its foreign policy has been characterized by a wide consensus concerning the primacy of non-alignment, which seemed to preclude participation in (at least organized) military as well as supranational cooperation during the Cold War. EEC/EC membership was thus precluded, as Swedish governments drew attention to links between the EEC/EC and NATO and to its other supranational features. Apart from keeping the country out of a potential conflict between the two blocs, Sweden's security doctrine gave the country a special international status as mediator. Thus, the end of the ideological conflict not only meant that non-alignment could be interpreted more flexibly, it also led to the loss of Sweden's special intermediary position, thus spurring the government to look for new ways to exert international influence.

An additional correlation between the Swedish political and strategic national interests and the EC/EU is the size of the country. Sweden is considerably smaller than – in particular – France, (West) Germany and Great Britain. On the other hand, it is the dominant country within the Nordic bloc. Accordingly, Sweden saw Nordic cooperation as a way for Nordic states to make a joint response to European integration, while giving Sweden the opportunity to take a leading role.

Another approach to interpreting Swedish European policy is to emphasize the influence of economic interests and different domestic interest groups on government decision-making. There has been wide consensus on the need for Sweden – given the importance of its foreign trade – to respond to the development of the EC/EU. But opinions as to *how* this was to be done varied. The

Conservative Party, the Liberals and the industrialists were long more pro-European than the Social Democrats, the Agrarian/Centre Party and the main blue-collar union LO. Yet, the governing Social Democrats were clearly in favour of free trade, with the important exception of agriculture. Until the beginning of the 1970s, Swedish Social Democrats believed that the Swedish economy was generally strong enough to allow the country to remain outside the EEC/EC. But thereafter, significant economic problems became recurrent. The country was hit by a particularly severe economic crisis in the beginning of the 1990s, leading to clear demands on Swedish EC membership from industrialists, the main white-collar union, Conservatives and Liberals, and eventually also a policy reorientation on the issue within the Social Democratic elite.

But the Swedish policy shift was not only a response to changes in the political and economic context. It might also be seen as a spill-over from pre-existing organizations or arrangements. The EEA agreement, signed in 1992, meant, for instance, that the EC and EFTA economies were integrated (with the exception of fishing and agricultural production). But many Swedes called into question the legitimacy of the EC's laws having binding power on Sweden, despite the fact that Sweden had no voice in framing them, and came to the conclusion that only full membership could eliminate this disadvantage. Another example of spill-over effects is the Swedish presidency in 2001, during which participating bureaucrats and politicians seem to have become more pro-European, regarding the EU as a more natural political arena for Swedes.

Finally, Swedish European policy can be also understood as the result of perceptions of oneself *vis-à-vis* 'the other'. One such perception concerns the historical past. Swedish European policy was long influenced by a sense of Sweden's superiority to other countries. First, the collective memory of the old Swedish Empire made the minor role offered Sweden in the development of international cooperation – considering Sweden's position *vis-à-vis* large countries such as France and Germany – unattractive. Second, since the Swedes did not share the traumas of the Second World War experienced by most countries in continental Europe, they were not nearly as motivated to participate in Western European cooperation. Third, Sweden's unbroken centuries of democratic rule were contrasted to the history of Continental countries that had been (or, in some cases, still were) ruled by dictators. Fourth, attitudes towards the ECSC and the EEC were specifically influenced, for a long time, by the political instability of the French Fourth Republic and by dislike of de Gaulle and his policies.

A fifth explanatory factor, consonant with this line of analysis, relates to the fact that the Social Democrats have held government power in Sweden during most of the post-war era. This gave the SAP vast influence in forming Sweden's relations with Europe. The Social Democratic belief in the superiority of the Swedish welfare model meant that cooperation with Continental states – several of which were both larger than Sweden, and ruled by centre-right governments – was considered out of the question for many decades. This sense of superiority has, however, been modified, not least due to the significant cuts in the Swedish welfare state. As Social Democrats have gained power also in the EC, the importance of their trans-national party networks in dealing with the European question has increased. During the 1950s, the SAP had hardly exploited such networks at all, but in the beginning of the 1990s, a number of meetings with leading Social Democrats from the European continent clearly contributed to Ingvar Carlsson's change of mind on the issue of Swedish EC membership.

In conclusion, despite a short and heated political debate in the beginning of the 1960s and Sweden's open membership application in 1967, Swedish EC membership was not a real issue before the end of the Cold War. The importance of Swedish foreign trade spurred the government to become a fierce advocate for free trade, and to be a driving force within the EFTA. At the same time, however, a rapprochement with the EEC/EC seemed necessary to the party elites, Swedish industry and Swedish unions. This eventually led to the application for full membership in 1991.

As EU member, the Swedish governments have been active in a few limited areas of special interest to Sweden. But they have continued to attempt to avoid supranational cooperation in most fields. For this reason, the country has not yet joined EMU. The government, which came out in favour of joining EMU in early 2003, cannot disregard the widespread scepticism among the Swedish population, which led to the negative referndum result in the same year. One of the reasons behind the remaining scepticism is that the economic expectations that had been linked to EU membership were not fulfilled. Many had hoped that the membership would solve the economic problems the country had struggled with for many years, but this did not happen. Within the majority of the political elite and parts of the bureaucracy, however, there now seems to be a stronger commitment to EU. These divided attitudes will probably continue to have a strong impact on future Swedish EU policy.

Sweden has been more successful in fulfilling the second expectation linked to the EU membership, that is, that an opportunity would be provided for Sweden to regain its special international position. Sweden has undertaken clearly defined activities, not least in relation to the CFSP and the upcoming enlargement. The policy of non-alignment has become more flexible, but this does not mean that there is a readiness to abandon it altogether. Security concerns and the wish to play a role in international politics have been, and will most probably continue to be, a strong impetus for the future direction of Swedish policy in this field.

Notes

1   Mikael af Malmborg, *Den ståndaktiga nationalstaten: Sverige och den västeuropeiska integrationen 1945–1959*, Lund: Lund University Press, 1994, p. 35.
2   Due to this perceived threat, informal cooperation between Sweden and, especially, the United States and Great Britain in matters of military intelligence and preparations for NATO support in case of a Soviet attack on Sweden, did occur during the Cold War. The fact of this cooperation was clearly established in the report of the government-appointed Commission on Neutrality Policy *Had There Been a War …* *Preparations for the Reception of Military Assistance 1949–1969*, Stockholm: Fritze, 1994.

186 *Maria Gussarsson*

3 Ann-Sofie Dahl has put the Swedish security policy in question in 'The myth of Swedish neutrality', in Cyril Buffet and Beatrice Heuser (eds), *Haunted by History: Myths in International Relations*, Oxford: Berghahn Books, 1998, pp. 28–40.

4 See, for example, SAP Congress minutes, 1952, p. 208. The security doctrine, it was argued, would not least reduce the pressure on Finland.

5 SAP Congress minutes, 1948, p. 130.

6 According to Marie Demker, the Algerian War gave the impetus for this new policy. Marie Demker, *Sverige och Algeriets frigörelse 1954–1964: Kriget som förändrade svensk utrikespolitik*, Stockholm: Nerenius & Santérus, 1996. Another author who has discussed active Swedish foreign policy is Hans Lödén, *För säkerhets skull: Ideologi och säkerhet i svensk aktiv utrikespolitik 1950–1975*, Stockholm: Santérus förlag, 2001.

7 Concerning Palme and foreign policy, see, for example, the chapters by Sven O. Andersson, 'Den rastlöse reformisten: En uppsats om Olof Palme och världen', and Magnus Jerneck, 'Olof Palme: En internationell propagandist', in Bo Huldt and Klaus Misgeld (eds), *Socialdemokratin och den svenska utrikespolitiken: Från Branting till Palme*, Stockholm: Utrikespolitiska institutet, 1990, pp. 91–142.

8 The importance of the policy of non-alignment for the Swedish European policy is emphasized by Birgit Karlsson in *Att handla neutralt: Sverige och den ekonomiska integrationen i Västeuropa 1948–1972*, Gothenburg: Handelshögskolan, Gothenburg University, 2001.

9 See, for example, Charles Silva, *Keep them Strong, Keep them Friendly: Swedish–American Relations and the Pax Americana, 1948–1952*, Stockholm: Stockholm University, 1999.

10 Sieglinde Gstöhl depicts these attitudes as 'balance sheet between *economic incentives* and *political impediments*', in *Reluctant Europeans: Norway, Sweden and Switzerland in the Process of Integration*, London: Lynne Rienner, 2002, p. 8.

11 See, for example, Stephen Padgett and William E. Paterson (eds), *A History of Social Democracy in Postwar Europe*, London: Longman, 1991, pp. 137, 144–7.

12 See Karl Molin and Thorsten B. Olesen, 'Security policy and domestic policies in Scandinavia 1948–49', in Thorsten B. Olesen (ed.), *Interdependence versus Integration: Denmark, Scandinavia and Western Europe 1945–1960*, Odense: Odense University Press, 1995, pp. 62–81.

13 Af Malmborg, *Den ståndaktiga nationalstaten*, p. 389.

14 See Wolfram Kaiser, 'Culturally embedded and path-dependent: peripheral alternatives to ECSC/EEC "Core Europe" since 1945: their rise and decline since 1950', *Journal of European Integration History*, 2001, vol. 7, no. 2, pp. 16–17.

15 On Swedish attitudes towards Catholicism, see Bo Stråth, 'The Swedish demarcation from Europe', in Mikael af Malmborg and Bo Stråth (eds), *The Meaning of Europe*, Oxford: Berg, 2002, p. 136.

16 *Arbetet*, 25 July 1957.

17 *Folket*, 4 January 1956.

18 On the relations between the SAP and its sister parties, see Klaus Misgeld, *Sozialdemokratie und Aussenpolitik in Schweden: Sozialistische Internationale, Europapolitik und die Deutschlandfrage 1945–1955*, Frankfurt: Campus Verlag, 1984, and Maria Gussarsson, *En socialdemokratisk Europapolitik: Den svenska socialdemokratins hållning till de brittiska, västtyska och franska broderpartierna, och upprättandet av ett västeuropeiskt ekonomiskt samarbete, 1955–58*, Stockholm: Santérus förlag, 2001.

19 The planned common market was initially not brought up at all, neither in parliament, nor in the internal discussions of the SAP or the Advisory Council on Foreign Affairs (*utrikesnämnden*).

20 On Swedish industry and Nordic cooperation, see Bo Stråth, *Nordic Industry and Nordic Economic Cooperation*, Stockholm: Almqvist & Wiksell International, 1978.

21 Concerning the LO and the European integration, see Klaus Misgeld, *Den fackliga europavägen: LO, det internationella samarbetet och Europas enande 1945–1991*, Stockholm: Atlas, 1997.

22 Minutes of the Parliament, FK 1957:9, p. 16.

23 On the creation of EFTA, see, for example, Johnny Laursen and Mikael af Malmborg, 'The creation of EFTA', in Olesen (ed.), *Interdependence versus Integration*, pp. 197–212, and Wolfram Kaiser 'Challenge to the Community: the creation, crisis and consolidation of the European Free Trade Association, 1958–1972', *Journal of European Integration History*, 1997, vol. 3, no. 1, pp. 7–34.

24 For an analysis of the different opinions, see Mats Bergquist, *Sverige och EEC: En statsvetenskaplig studie av fyra åsiktsriktningars syn på svensk marknadspolitik 1961–1962*, Stockholm: P.A. Nordstedt & Söners förlag, 1970.

25 Quoted in Klaus Misgeld, 'Den svenska socialdemokratin och Europa', in Huldt and Misgeld (eds), *Socialdemokratin och den svenska utrikespolitiken*, pp. 195–210.

26 On Nordek, see, for example, Bengt Sundelius and Claes Wiklund, 'Nordek: planen och dess föregångare', in Bengt Sundelius and Claes Wiklund, (eds), *Norden i sicksack: Tre spårbyten inomnordiskt samarbete*, Stockholm: Santérus förlag, 2000, pp. 107–23.

27 On the free trade agreement, see, for example, Nicholas Aylott, *Swedish Social Democracy and European Integration: The People's Home on the Market*, Aldershot: Ashgate, 1999, pp. 97 ff.

28 See the quotation by Ingvar Carlsson in Jakob Gustavsson, *The Politics of Foreign Policy Change: Explaining the Swedish Reorientation on EC Membership*, Lund: Lund University Press, 1998, p. 148.

29 Lizelotte Lundgren Rydén, *Ett svenskt dilemma: Socialdemokraterna, centern och EG-frågan 1957–1994*, Gothenburg: Historiska institutionen, Gothenburg University, 2000, p. 165.

30 Concerning the Swedish initiatives in the mid-1980s, see, for instance, Lee Miles, *Sweden and European Integration*, Aldershot: Ashgate, 2000, pp. 114 ff.

31 See Hanna Ojanen, Gunilla Herolf and Rutger Lindahl, *Non-Alignment and European Security Policy: Ambiguity at Work*, Helsinki: Finnish Institute of International Affairs, 2000, pp. 172–9.

32 See, for instance, Gstöhl, *Reluctant Europeans*, pp. 172–4.

33 Magnus Jerneck, 'Sweden: the reluctant European?', in Teija Tiilikainen and Ib Damgaard Petersen (eds), *The Nordic Countries and the EC*, Copenhagen: Copenhagen Political Studies Press, 1993, p. 33.

34 Jakob Gustavsson analyses the reorientation on the EC membership question in *The Politics of Foreign Policy Change*. The issue has also been discussed by Thomas Pedersen in *European Union and the EFTA Countries: Enlargement and Integration*, London: Pinter, 1994, pp. 85–94.

35 However, on a grassroots level, the mistrust remained, which made the leadership choose not to force through its position as a public stance of LO.

36 Quotation from Gustavsson, *The Politics of Foreign Policy Change*, p. 181.

37 Between 40 and 50 per cent of the social democratic voters declared themselves negative to EEC/EU membership in 1992–4, compared with the around 20 per cent that wanted an accession. See Lundgren Rydén, *Ett svenskt dilemma*, p. 233.

38 Aylott, *Swedish Social Democracy and European Integration*, p. 130.

39 During the SAP Congress of 1993, 232 of the members voted yes to a membership, while 103 said no.

40 This epithet has also been applied to Great Britain and Denmark. See the chapters by Wolfram Kaiser and Johnny Laursen in this book.

41 On Sweden and the EU decision-making, see Karl-Magnus Johansson, 'Sverige i EU:s institutioner', in Karl-Magnus Johansson (ed.), *Sverige i EU*, Stockholm: SNS förlag, 2002, pp. 76–94.

42 On Sweden and the northern dimension of the EU, see, for example, Gunilla Herolf, 'The Swedish approach: constructive competition for a common goal', in Gianni Bonvicini, Tapani Vaahtoranta and Wolfgang Wessels (eds), *The Northern EU: National*

Views on the Emerging Security Dimension, Helsinki: Finnish Institute of International Affairs, 2000, pp. 141–60.

43 Quotation from Rikard Bengtsson, 'Utvidgningen: höga förväntningar infriade', in Jonas Tallberg (ed.), *När Europa kom till Sverige: Ordförandeskapet i EU 2001*, Stockholm: SNS förlag, 2001, p. 72.

44 On Sweden and CFSP, see Ojanen, Herolf and Lindahl, *Non-Alignment and European Security Policy*, pp. 187–237, and Maria Strömvik, 'Sverige i EU:s utrikes- och säkerhetspolitik: från aktivism till kollektivism', in Johansson (ed.), *Sverige i EU*, pp. 250–66.

45 The most controversial concession was made in 1941, as the government in Stockholm allowed German troop transfers from Norway via Sweden to the Eastern Front. Furthermore, the Swedish export of iron to the Germans has been highly criticized, not least since this was not a result of direct pressure, but – on the contrary – brought back a considerable profit.

46 On the enforced sterilizations, see, for instance, Maija Runcis, *Steriliseringar i folkhemmet*, Stockholm: Ordfront, 1998.

47 In fact, a fourth 'E' was the equality between the sexes, but this was not treated as a separate issue.

48 On the Swedish Presidency and the media, see Matilda Broman and Malena Rosén, 'Ordförandeskapet och pressen: en mediabild blir till', in Tallberg (ed.), *När Europa kom till Sverige*, pp. 205–24.

10 A fool's game or a comedy of errors?

EU enlargements in comparative perspective

Jürgen Elvert

Future scholars may well rate the year 2004 as the greatest challenge in the history of European integration. The fierce debates about the size and distribution of fiscal transfers after enlargement, the draft constitution and its proposed voting system for the Council, and the future of transatlantic relations after the Gulf War seemed to indicate that the EU was facing a more unsettled and uncertain future after its Eastern enlargement of May 2004 to include ten more member-states. In the accession states, a majority of the population expects clear economic benefits from EU membership.[1] At the same time, they regard the transfer of decision-making powers to the EU and its institutions with considerable scepticism. It should be noted though that the poll results of Eurobarometer surveys have varied significantly within and between the new member-states.[2] There has been a widespread feeling in most accession states for some time, however, that EU membership is a matter of course. An average of 65 per cent of citizens in the new member-states believes that EU membership of their country is historically and geographically justified,[3] although the reasons given for this assumption tend to be vague.

Up to a point, the prevailing uncertainty about the political essence and meaning of the EU in the new member-states is comparable with the nine 'newcomers' to the European Union (EU) during the historical process of enlargement since the 1960s which are discussed in this book. To understand the resulting ambivalences, it is important to recall the original intentions behind the 'core Europe' integration process which led from the first modest attempts at overcoming the structural deficiencies of the nation–state Europe to the modern EU. From the perspective of the pro-integration elites in the original member-states of the European Coal and Steel Community (ECSC), founded in 1951–52, and the European Economic Community (EEC), founded in 1957–58, the conflicts of interest between nation–states and their incompatible ambitions had caused two world wars, resulting in great instability and insecurity after 1945. The overriding task seemed to be to create a new politically stable and economically prosperous European order, which was supposed to be able to overcome the traditional tensions and conflicts between nation–states.

As a consequence of the emerging bipolar system, the group of states potentially participating in this project was reduced to those west of the new Iron

Curtain. Even in this significantly smaller area the creation of a new political system with possibly supranational features overarching the nation–states seemed for a long time to be an impossible task. Federalists or institutionalists advocated a strong supranational structure above the nation–states whereas unionists or confederalists preferred less binding forms of political cooperation. Self-proclaimed realists doubted that supranational integration could ever be made to work in Europe. On the other hand, functionalists argued that everyone – even nations – could be tamed if only the political and institutional conditions were appropriate. Some favoured close transatlantic cooperation within a 'Western world', while others continued to envisage a united Europe as a referee in the match between the two new superpowers.[4] Political decision-makers all over Western Europe regularly made pro-European statements, preferably in dinner speeches, but were initially reluctant to give up national sovereignty for ever closer European integration with supranational features.[5]

The first five years after the Second World War saw several attempts at reconstructing the Western European economy and (up to a point) at overcoming the traditional nation–state system. The Marshall Plan of 1947 was successfully implemented. The Organization for European Economic Cooperation (OEEC) was created and co-operated with the US Economic Cooperation Administration in distributing American economic aid to Europe.[6] But in spite of the US$20 billion to be distributed by the OEEC, the organization – with its almost entirely inter-governmental structure – did not meet the expectations of European federalists.[7] It is true that membership of the OEEC, which was to be transformed into the Organization for Economic Cooperation and Development (OECD) in 1961, contributed to the European socialization of some later 'newcomers' to 'core Europe'.[8] By 1948–50, however, most European states were obviously unwilling to hand over national sovereignty to this newly created organization.

Following an initiative by the French government, which was not satisfied with the OEEC's scope and structure, the Council of Europe was then successfully created in 1949, but it, too, failed to meet the expectations of European federalists that it might initiate supranational political integration in Europe. The British government in particular successfully blocked every attempt at creating even rudimentary supranational structures within the framework of the Council of Europe, thus making it abundantly clear that the United Kingdom would not be part of a supranational European political order.[9] From the perspective of pro-integration elites in continental Western Europe, the nation–states still had not found a convincing long-term solution to the burning questions of the day: the containment of the Soviet Union and a suitable and controllable way of integrating the West German state, created in 1949, into the international community.

The 'German question' with its political and economic dimensions was the prime topic for Western Europeans, at least for those who were not largely self-reliant or self-sufficient in different ways as Britain, Ireland, Spain and Portugal, involved in Nordic cooperation plans like the Scandinavian states, or in some way or another entangled in special geostrategic circumstances like Finland, Austria or Greece. Thus, the Western European countries interested in initiating closer integration with possibly supranational features were reduced to France, Italy, the Benelux countries and West Germany. For their 'core Europe' plans they could rely on the support of the United States, which saw European integration as an integral element of its policy of containment.[10]

From coal and steel to the Common Market

Due to these common transatlantic interests, European integration continued to be a prominent item on the agenda of European and Atlantic politics around 1950. In Europe, it was left to France to take the lead after the British self-exclusion from any form of supranational integration following the creation of the Council of Europe. Against the background of the previous failures, the French Christian Democratic foreign minister Robert Schuman made the decisive move in May 1950, taking up an internal proposal by Jean Monnet and cooperating with the West German Chancellor Konrad Adenauer and a handful of other European-minded political decision-makers in France, West Germany, the Benelux countries and Italy.[11] The Schuman Plan leading to the creation of the ECSC was not rooted in a grand design. It essentially tried to overcome the old Franco-German antagonism by creating a supranational authority in charge of the long-disputed coal and steel resources of both countries and their neighbours and main trading partners.[12]

Mainly, the ECSC resulted from clearly identifiable interests derived from domestic economic and political needs. On the one hand, it was a quite successful instrument for the strategic integration of West Germany into a Western European community. On the other, it was a much less successful attempt at solving the common problems of the coal and steel sector by creating an authority entitled to regulate the market.[13] Schuman only made some rather vague statements about the *finalité politique* of this community.[14] Some scholars consider the ECSC to be the logical stepping stone to the EEC's common market. Others considered it as an attempt – later interrupted – at nursing integration by creating sectoral communities with limited competences.[15] Some historians regard the ECSC institutions – High Authority, Council of Ministers, Parliamentary Assembly and Court – as an innovative supranational institutional structure which facilitated more far-reaching integration, while others emphasize the character of the High Authority as a much more technocratic planning agency for an organized coal and steel market.[16]

In any case, once they had created the ECSC and then the EEC, the six founding member-states stayed together for two decades on the road to closer economic and political integration, defining the rules of the game. Economic integration in a common market was to facilitate closer political cooperation and, possibly, integration in order to secure peace by strengthening economic interdependence. The member-states transferred limited national sovereign rights to common institutions which were entitled to act relatively independently.

One side effect of the integration agenda and its partly supranational methods was very important: the already divided European continent was divided once again into the EEC and its six member-states and the rest of Western Europe. Although in principle it was open towards new members, the new Community had exclusionary effects, and many outsiders initially also preferred their own self-exclusion, due to a variety of economic, political and cultural reasons.

As the chapters on single countries in this book demonstrate, those countries, which had a real choice in 1950–52, had various motives for their self-exclusion from early 'core Europe' integration. To begin with, the prospects of the ECSC were generally seen as rather low. Sceptics regarded the Schuman Plan as one way among others to overcome the traditional Franco-German antagonism as the primary source of Central and Western European instability. Among the nine outsiders, only Greece showed a longer lasting interest in cooperating with the ECSC from the outset, although its active participation was out of the question due to its economic backwardness, the continuing impact of the civil war and the country's preoccupation with the Cyprus issue.[17] Britain adopted a different attitude. Here, Winston Churchill's 'three circles' doctrine of 1948, describing the Western world as consisting of the three 'circles' of Western Europe, the Commonwealth and the USA, with Britain in the midst of and between all three playing the key role as a mediator, was still the generally accepted opinion.[18] The Scandinavian states were working towards Nordic cooperation, observing the developments on the continent with a mixture of mistrust, scepticism, and a feeling of superiority. Unsettled bilateral problems such as the German–Danish minority issue in Schleswig and Finland's enforced 'special' relationship with the Soviet Union, further strengthened the distance of Scandinavia from early integration.[19] At least Sweden decided to establish a permanent delegation with the ECSC's High Authority in December 1952, thus following the lead of Great Britain and the USA.[20] Austria negotiated a customs and trade agreement with ECSC's High Authority shortly after the signing of the State Treaty of 1955. In fact, its Christian Democratic–Socialist coalition government even announced its interest in full membership in October 1956, only to act much more cautiously in relation to Western European integration after the bloody suppression of the Hungarian uprising in November 1956.[21] Franco's Spain was quite interested in taking part in the integration process but was widely regarded as a totalitarian regime being unfit for 'Europe' in the 1950s.[22] The Portuguese regime, finally, saw Portugal as a predominantly Atlantic country with mainly transatlantic and colonial interests.[23]

After the failure of the European Defence Community in 1954 and the integration of West Germany into NATO and the newly created Western European Union in 1955, the creation of the EEC in 1957–58 transformed sectoral economic integration with an implicit political dimension into horizontal economic integration in a common market. However, Article 2 and Article 3 of the EEC Treaty clearly indicated – despite continuing differences over its scope and substance – the long-term aim of converting the EEC into a fully fledged political community.[24]

The EEC's strong economic success in its early years appeared to vindicate the extension of sectoral to horizontal economic integration.[25] Within only a few years the EEC with its population of some 170 million became the world's largest trading power. Between 1958 and 1962 its GNP rose by 21.5 per cent against 11 per cent in Great Britain and 18 per cent in the USA. Industrial production rose by 37 per cent against 14 per cent in Great Britain and 28 per cent in the USA.[26] It is hardly surprising that the EEC's neighbours observed its apparent economic success with growing interest. For all of them, the potential impact of the EEC on their own economic situation was obviously much greater than that of the ECSC. Their reactions to the creation and success of the EEC differed significantly, however. For political and economic reasons the British reaction to the Messina process leading up to the creation of the EEC was by far the most important among the nine 'newcomers', not at least because five others took the British attitude towards the common market initiative as a point of reference for their own policy.

The British government originally saw no reason to deviate from its negative stance regarding participation in supranational organizations. As early as 1955, however, the Board of Trade in particular warned that the Six might create a common market which could be economically dangerous for Britain, if it abstained from participation. The Treasury and the Board of Trade soon started to think about 'Plan G', the concept of a large inter-governmental European free trade area including the Six.[27] When the free trade area negotiations within the OEEC failed in 1958,[28] Britain took the lead in setting up the smaller European Free Trade Association (EFTA) of the so-called 'outer Seven' in 1959–60. It had turned out that not only Charles de Gaulle, who returned to power in France in 1958, but also many others among the Six, regarded the British plan for a larger inter-governmental free trade area as a dangerous attempt at diluting 'core Europe' integration 'like a piece of sugar in a cup of English tea'.[29]

For Ireland a large European free trade area would have secured its mainly agricultural export interests in Britain and opened up new economic opportunities in a wider European market.[30] Danish economic interests would have been excellently safeguarded in such a scheme as Britain and West Germany, its two main trading partners, would have participated.[31] The Swedish neutrality policy appeared to rule out EEC membership, but was compatible with the free trade area plan.[32] For Portugal, a large European free trade area could have brought long-term benefits, too.[33] Finally, Greece also welcomed a European free trade area as requiring less commitment than the supranational common market.[34] Of the three remaining 'newcomers', Finland also had a preference for the free trade scheme, especially as the EEC was widely seen as a kind of extension of NATO, causing problems in the difficult relationship with the Soviet Union.[35] Yet, even membership in a larger free trade area would have required, following the inherent logic of the so-called Paasikivi–Kekkonen policy, a preceding special deal with Moscow.[36] In contrast, Franco's Spain would have preferred accession to the EEC, which would have combined economic benefits with international recognition of the Franco regime, although the EEC still rejected this option.[37]

Finally, the Austrian government preferred the creation of a supranational Europe with close Austrian association or even participation until 1956. After the suppression of the Hungarian uprising, however, it favoured the free trade scheme, but only as a second-best option.[38]

The original intentions behind 'core Europe' integration – especially the creation of political stability through eliminating traditional causes of national conflicts in a partly supranational institutional setting – hardly played a role in the discussions about the advantages and disadvantages of possible EEC membership and the free trade scheme. Instead, the discussions concentrated on the expected economic advantages and on the compatibility of the respective institutional designs with national circumstances and preferences. On the whole, the free trade scheme – and later EFTA – was more easily compatible with the inter-governmental institutional preferences of most 'newcomers' and promised some economic benefits. The EFTA founding states only regarded EFTA as a stop-gap solution, however, on the road to an eventual trade arrangement with the EEC.

Towards the first enlargement

The first British application to join the EEC of 1961 dramatically changed the conditions for the European policies of most 'newcomers'. Britain's perception of the EEC and the potential benefits of membership was influenced by its history as a leading world power and centre of a global empire and its self-perception as the prime Western European power after 1945. This had initially made any participation in supranational continental European integration unthinkable for the vast majority of the British political elite. There was also a cultural distance to continental Europe which largely seemed to be run after 1945 by mostly Catholic, culturally backward and (from the Socialist perspective) conservative Christian Democrats with political and ideological traditions that were alien to Britain. Those who increasingly saw the need for a more constructive attitude to the Six in the second half of the 1950s compared (like David Eccles) the creation of EFTA with 'marrying the engineer's daughter when the general manager's had said no', that is, as only the second-best option after the failure of the large free trade scheme and, possibly, not viable in the longer term.[39] The main motives behind the EEC application of 1961 were of economic and political nature: to gain access to the more important continental European market and to safeguard what by then was left of the 'special relationship' with the USA, as the newly elected Kennedy administration increasingly demanded British EEC membership to safeguard NATO against de Gaulle.[40] On the whole, the pro-EEC foreign policy elite in Britain at that time expected that once inside the EEC, Britain would take political control over its future, thanks to its nuclear weapons, its world power status and its foreign policy prestige deriving not at least from its role in the Second World War.

Ireland applied together with Britain not least to safeguard its agricultural exports to the United Kingdom in view of the evolving Common Agricultural Policy (CAP). The political elite had initially been largely indifferent towards integration on the continent. They largely considered 'Europe' as a remote and rather costly concept. In the 1960s, however, they became much more interested in it not only as a market for agricultural exports, but also as a means for modernizing Ireland. Denmark, which was geographically much closer to 'core Europe', went through a process of political learning. Denmark only entered EFTA after intense Danish–German consultations in which West Germany agreed to safeguard Danish agricultural export interests in the West German market for the foreseeable future, thus establishing itself as a promoter of core Danish economic interests. EFTA membership safeguarded Danish access to the British market and allowed the possibility of closer Nordic economic and political cooperation. From the beginning, however, Denmark had close contacts with the EEC, not least via the German channel, and by 1961, the Danish government was pushing the British towards a joint application for EEC membership as the better long-term solution, combining both main markets for Danish agricultural produce and also offering long-term advantages for industrial exports. Moreover, the EEC's image in Denmark improved considerably, as did that of Germany, especially later during Willy Brandt's chancellorship from 1969–74, reducing the cultural and emotional obstacles to integration in the EEC.

Compared to Danish perceptions of European integration, which had been rather subtle as early as during the 1952–58 period, those dominant in Sweden were deeply rooted in a general mistrust of continental European affairs based on the experiences of the inter-war period and the Second World War,[41] combined with a strongly Social Democratic aversion against the supposedly conservative, Catholic, colonialist and capitalist origins of the integration process.[42] This rather cliché-ridden judgement was not, however, limited to Sweden alone but widespread in other Scandinavian states, in the ranks of the Austrian Socialist Party and among Labour circles in Great Britain, too.[43] On top of these perceptions of a 'Europe' incompatible with Swedish traditions and ideals, the EEC project of market liberalization was considered incompatible with the Swedish welfare state and the country's 'third way' identity and policy of neutrality between East and West.

In Greece, the formation of the EEC and EFTA, from which the so-called OEEC 'peripherals' (with the exception of Portugal) were excluded, was regarded with growing uneasiness as a possible first step to the country's political and economic isolation. Domestically and geostrategically, this mattered even more because Greece was the only non-communist state in the Balkans, and also had strained relations with Turkey, its large neighbour in the East. Greece eventually concluded the first association treaty with the EEC in 1961. The advantages of association and, eventually, EEC membership for Greece seemed so clear under these circumstances that Euro-sceptic voices on the political Left and among business circles, who were afraid of European competition, hardly met with any response at all. Naturally, the imposition of the military dictatorship in 1967, temporarily cutting the link between Greece and the EEC, emphasized the fear of isolation from 'Europe' especially among the middle classes, and led to renewed efforts to enter it after 1974.

Whereas the imposition of the dictatorship interrupted the Greek approach to the EEC for several years, the existence of authoritarian governments in Spain and Portugal ruled out closer contacts from the outset, although Portugal was allowed to enter EFTA, being supported by its long-standing political ally Britain. Until 1968 the question of possible EEC membership was not at all an issue for António Salazar whose deeply conservative and authoritarian *Estado Novo* relied on Great Britain as its gate to European economic cooperation and otherwise on its increasingly fragile Empire.[44] Portugal's situation substantially changed when de Gaulle withdrew from French politics and British EC membership looked likely after the EC summit at The Hague in November 1969. Portugal was now faced with the need to develop some kind of closer relationship with the EC, although direct EC membership remained out of the question for the EC.

Compared to Portugal, Franco's Spain had placed much greater emphasis on relations with the EEC from the beginning. As early as 1957 it installed the government commission CICE to observe the development of the EEC and to adapt Spanish legislation and administration to the newly established European structures.[45] Although Franco saw the need for strong Spanish bonds with the EEC in purely economic terms, the official Spanish application as of 9 February 1962 to initiate negotiations underlined Spain's 'European vocation'. The EEC's reaction to the Spanish proposal was ambivalent. Some representatives of the French and German governments as well as some leading French Gaullists and German Christian Democrats welcomed the Spanish move. The European Commission's response was negative, however, and underlined once more that non-democratic states could not accede to the EEC.[46] The Spanish government continued to cultivate relations with the EEC, however, for example by sending Prince Juan Carlos on goodwill tours to EEC capitals to advertise the Spanish quest for Europe.[47]

Austria, finally, was interested in close association with the EEC after the British application of 1961, and eventually decided to embark on a policy of going-it-alone after de Gaulle's veto against the British application in January 1961.[48] Austria's room for manoeuvre was limited by the State Treaty and the resulting declaration of neutrality 'in line with the Swiss model' in a separate national, so-called constitutional law in 1955, although Austrian policy-makers proved to be much more flexible in its interpretation than their Swiss counterparts. Domestic faultlines also influenced Austria's policy towards the EEC, however. Convinced 'pro-Europeans' were mainly found in the Christian Democratic-conservative Austrian People's Party (ÖVP), whereas some staunch Euro-sceptics played a leading role in the Socialist Party (SPÖ). In 1959, for example, the SPÖ Vice-Chancellor Bruno Pittermann denounced the EEC as a 'reactionary bourgeois bloc', although he did not oppose closer association with the EEC in the 1960s.[49] On the whole, Austrian politicians supported economic integration and generally accepted the concept of political integration, too, although this seemed to be incompatible with full Austrian EEC membership without substantial political safeguards in relation to its policy of non-alignment.[50]

With regard to their policies towards the EEC until the early 1970s, the nine 'newcomers' essentially fall into three categories. The first group consists of those states which acceded to the European Communities in 1973, that is, Britain, Denmark and Ireland. The second group includes states which preferred self-exclusion from the EC beyond 1973, that is, Sweden, Austria and Finland, whereas the third group consisting of Greece, Spain and Portugal were excluded from membership due to their political systems. In all of these countries, however, the concept of a partial transfer of sovereignty to supranational institutions as a prerequisite for defusing tensions between nation–states and guaranteeing political stability and economic progress met with great scepticism or was even considered an unacceptable intrusion into the national decision-making powers and as a restriction of national freedom of action. Cultural arguments like a country's 'European–ness',[51] 'European vocation'[52] or 'European heritage'[53] were often used as a rhetorical strategy (as in the Greek and Spanish cases) to underline the self-perception that eventual EEC/EC membership was a matter of course, or (as in Austria) as a description of the country's historical role, to justify the government's general interest in European integration without asserting any entitlement to membership.

All founding member-states of EFTA (with the exception of Portugal) in fact fulfilled the EEC/EC's general conditions for membership, unlike Spain and Portugal and Greece. Indeed, Britain, Denmark, Ireland and Sweden had been among the founding members of the Council of Europe, which Austria later joined in 1956, too. Even if Finland only entered the Council of Europe in 1989, there is no record of any objections on the part of the European Commission to possible Finnish membership, although it was generally concerned about the impact of neutrality on political integration. After all, Finland was a parliamentary democracy, cooperating as deeply as possible with the neighbouring Scandinavian states and participating in Western European economic cooperation through the General Agreement on Tariffs and Trade (GATT) and, from 1968, the OECD.[54]

Despite the obvious external constraints, the Finnish case is in fact a good example of those states that decided to exclude themselves from the European integration process. Since the end of the Second World War and the so-called FMCA Treaty with the Soviet Union, Finland had subordinated its European relations to the latter's security policy interests. Finland mainly relied on Nordic relations, although even they resulted in problems with the Soviet Union not least due to the NATO membership of Norway and Denmark, and it eventually managed to secure EFTA association in 1961.[55] In contrast, Finnish participation in supranational continental European integration was largely seen as incompatible with Finnish security preoccupations in relation to the Soviet Union. The Finnish variant of self-exclusion thus relied on a domestic consensus with regard to its national foreign policy. Importantly for the long term, it was not rooted in any Euro-scepticism.

The Swedish and Austrian governments also saw EEC/EC membership as incompatible with their countries' neutrality policies. Compared to Finland, however, they experienced much more open and controversial public debates about attitudes towards European integration. Swedish business had followed the creation of the EEC with great interest from the very beginning, not least because of its potential negative effects on Swedish trade with continental Europe, especially West Germany. As early as the mid-1950s the Swedish Federation of Industries recommended closer participation in economic cooperation, the Nordic concept being too limited, although full EEC membership was then considered being less favourable than the more liberal free trade proposal.[56] After the first British EEC application, however, Swedish industrialists, relying on political support from the Conservatives and Liberals in opposition, urged their government to follow suit. Their support for a more radical policy reorientation required a much more pointed defence of the decision not to apply for full EEC membership on the part of the Social Democrat-led government which was supported by the Social Democrat-dominated trade unions. In 1961, Tage Erlander, the Swedish Prime Minister, declared the EEC to be a defence organization in disguise, directed against communism and intended to strengthen NATO, thus trying to revive the broad Euro-sceptic consensus of the 1950s.[57] Similarly, Austrian SPÖ politicians defended their stricter interpretation of neutrality and vision of Austrian identity with similar attacks, as Pittermann had already done in 1959.

In all three cases, that is, Finland, Sweden and Austria, political motives thus outweighed economic motives in rejecting the option of full EEC/EC membership. In the cases of Sweden and Austria, the domestic frictions were much greater, however, and appeared to require emotional appeals to specific forms of national identity to counteract mostly economically motivated pressures for full participation in integration. In any case, however, economic needs demanded some form of contractual arrangement with EEC/EC when Britain, Denmark and Ireland joined in 1973. Eventually, in July 1972, Sweden and Austria (as well as Switzerland) signed free trade treaties with the EC.[58] Finnish–EC negotiations about a free trade agreement also started in 1970. Due to Finland's delicate relationship with the Soviet Union, however, the negotiations proved to be more complex and the agreement was only signed in 1973.

While the British decision to apply for EEC membership in 1961 had been due to a complex mixture of economic and political objectives, the second application by the Labour government in 1967 was rather motivated by the failure of the government's economic policies.[59] After de Gaulle's predictable second veto in May 1967, it was left on the table and taken up again after the European Council of The Hague in 1969, eventually leading to British accession as negotiated by the Conservative government under Edward Heath. It seems that public support for EEC/EC membership rose faster and higher in Ireland than in Britain. Support culminated in Britain in 1966 at 68 per cent in favour of EEC accession, only to reach an all-time low during the negotiations in the early 1970s. The Irish referendum held in May 1972 yielded 83 per cent in favour of membership. While continental Europe had still been perceived by the Irish public as 'war-ravaged' and 'divided' during the 1950s, it was now seen as 'prosperous', 'strong' and 'progressive', while Ireland seemed 'poor', 'peripheral' and 'dependent'. EC membership now appeared to promise to provide the country with a protective 'shell' within which it could sustain its interests and also free itself from its dependency on Britain.[60]

In the Danish 1972 referendum, 63.3 per cent opted for membership. In the Danish case, support for membership depended much more on the anticipated agrarian, rather than general, economic gains from participation in the CAP and the common market. At the same time, unlike in Ireland, small-state nationalism on the political Left combined with right-wing Euro-scepticism in a kind of anti-EC membership cartel. As in the British case and in contrast to Ireland, the emotional appeal of EC membership was low.

Towards the southern and northern enlargements

During the first period of EC enlargement, the international environment for European integration changed radically. The political tensions between East and West had begun to ease significantly since the Kennedy administration had opted for its version of 'peaceful co-existence' as the new leitmotif for East–West relations. The new openings of West German foreign policy towards Eastern Europe during the Social–Liberal coalition government under Chancellor Willy Brandt also contributed to improving the general political climate in East–West relations. Thus circumstances having changed, the Conference for Security and Cooperation in Europe (CSCE) took place, addressing the questions of acceptance of the political status quo in Europe, of human rights, and of their application on both sides of the Iron Curtain. The CSCE was held in Helsinki, on the borderline between the two blocs and also in a country whose government had always considered a determined policy of non-alignment as the most secure way for Finland, being in the shadow of the Soviet Union. The Helsinki process gave more political weight to the group of neutral and non-aligned states. This became obvious also in the Vienna conference on Mutual Balanced Forces Reduction (MBFR) starting in October 1974. The CSCE and MBFR were serious attempts at overcoming the differences between the two blocs caused by the Cold War.[61]

The negotiations took place in two of the three countries which had decided against EC membership in 1969–73. The fact that they were chosen as suitable conference locations during this period of East–West détente not only acknowledged the reliability of Austrian and Finnish neutrality policy in the bipolar world system, but also served as further justification for its long-term retention. As non-alignment had been the leitmotif of Swedish foreign and security policy since 1814 too, it is hardly surprising that the Swedish government shared the Austrian and Finnish approach and considered the CSCE and MBFR as an acknowlededgment of the Swedish contribution towards easing East–West tensions, and as a further argument against participation in 'core Europe' integration. As long as the CSCE process did not lead to an end of the bipolar conflict there was, therefore, hardly any convincing political argument in favour of changing the Austrian, Finnish and Swedish positions concerning EC membership. This was all the more so true as the Community, despite some progress such as the direct election of the European Parliament in 1979 and the introduction of the European Monetary System, went through a period of stagnation between 1973 and 1986.

Thus, the Austrian, Finnish and Swedish cases differed significantly from those of Greece, Spain and Portugal in the years of the CSCE negotiations. In 1974, the Colonels' regime ended in Greece. In Portugal, the Salazar regime was overthrown. Only one year later, Franco died, resulting in the restoration of the Spanish monarchy. As all three countries had been politically marginalized due to the authoritarian nature of their political systems, EC membership now appeared to have great potential for the succeeding political elites in the newly democratic structures. Being part of the EC would bring all three countries back into the democratic community of European states. It would also exert welcome external pressures for domestic political, economic and societal modernization.

Greece had been preparing itself for closer cooperation with the EEC/EC since the 1960s. At the time, the Conservatives had opted for full membership as the long-term goal in spite of criticism from the Left. The latter denounced the EEC as an attempt by foreign monopolies, led by a 'revanchist' Germany and other 'imperialists', to overrun the country's economy. Some Greek business circles also disapproved of association with the EEC/EC because they feared a loss of national subsidies for certain economic sectors of strategic political interest.[62] Like in Sweden and Finland, NATO and the EEC/EC were perceived in Greece as two sides of the same coin, although in the dominant Greek perception on the democratic Right this package was clearly connoted positively.

After the junta's collapse in 1974, Greece's position remained largely unchanged compared to the period before 1967. As the military dictatorship had relied heavily on US tutelage, the EC was now largely considered as an adequate point of reference for the establishment of new international contacts. Moreover, the year 1974 saw a further rise of tensions between Turkey and Greece over the Cyprus Crisis and disputed territorial claims in the Aegean Sea. The Karamanlis government thus saw EC membership as an opportunity to place the country strategically in an institutional framework not – or at least less – dominated by US influence. It also saw EC membership as a source of modernization and financial support, and as a means of consolidating the re-established democratic system. The Conservative governments of 1974–81 saw no alternative to EC accession, not least as EFTA was mainly concerned with industrial free trade, while Greece was principally interested in finding suitable markets for its agricultural products.

Nevertheless, the Greek EC application was mainly launched for strategic foreign policy reasons. This was also the perception of the European Commission. In fact, the strategic dimension of the application proved to be a serious obstacle for the formal negotiations between Greece and the EC, as the Commission tried to avoid being drawn into the Greek–Turkish conflict. Karamanlis therefore had to decouple Greek EC accession from this bilateral regional dispute, especially as the rapid developments in Spain and Portugal appeared to call into question the Greek accession timetable. Thus, the Greek government decided not to examine the concrete economic implications of Greek EC membership too closely or critically and accepted the legal *acquis communautaire* without raising serious objections. Domestically, the Pan-Hellenic Socialist Movement (PASOK) founded in 1974 by Andreas Papandreou, and the small Communist Party of Greece (KKE) initially opposed EC membership and regarded national independence as a prerequisite of socialist change. They argued that EC membership would in fact consolidate Greece's peripheral role in Europe and turn the country into a satellite of the capitalist 'system'. PASOK steadily softened its position towards EC membership between 1979 and 1981, however, when it became clear that it might well win the forthcoming national elections and gain power.

The geopolitical strategic rationale behind EC membership was not nearly as important for Portugal and Spain as it was for Greece. From the 1960s, the importance of the colonies for the Portuguese economy had decreased steadily in favour of the European market. In addition, Western Europe and especially France became the favoured destination for Portuguese migrant workers.[63] These structural changes had already put Marcello Caetano, who had succeeded Salazar in 1968, in a difficult position in relation to 'Europe', as his basic ideas about integration did not differ substantially from those of his predecessor. Within the Caetano government, a small liberal and 'pro-European' group of technocrats emerged who exerted enough influence to re-direct Portugal's foreign policy towards closer cooperation with the EC.

The military coup of 1974 then changed the situation much more dramatically, both for Portugal and the EC. The country's still fragile democracy desperately needed economic as well as political support, which was offered by international organizations like NATO and the EC, not least in order to avoid the possible communist usurpation of power during 1974–75. It was only the first freely elected government that chose the European option unreservedly and openly declared EC membership to be a strategic objective and political priority in 1976. This course was encouraged by the EC with modest financial aid and much moral assistance, thus helping the country to stabilize its political system and prepare for EC membership. The electoral motto of Mario Soares's *Partido Socialista* (PS) was 'Europe with us', which also reflected the widespread support from European Socialist parties in the transition period. The PS's stance amounted to a resolute rejection of all prior Third Worldist and neutralist tendencies in Portuguese politics. As the right-wing and centre-right parties also supported the European option, the goal of EC membership was largely consensual, with only the very partial involvement of business and agricultural interest groups and trade unions in the debate. Opposition to EC membership was limited to the Communist Party (PCP) and the communist trade unions.

Portugal submitted its formal application for EC membership in 1977. The negotiations that started in 1978 were overshadowed by the fact that the Portuguese political system remained under the tutelage of military institutions until 1982. After that, however, the Portuguese government did not succeed in decoupling its negotiations with the EC from those of the Spanish, which involved more complex and contested economic issues of agricultural trade and fisheries. The public at large only slowly became aware of and interested in the EC. As late as 1978, some 60 per cent of the Portuguese had no clear view as to whether the country's EC membership would be important for the country. In contrast, after EC accession in 1986, some two-thirds were convinced that it was.[64]

The Spanish accession negotiations started in 1978, too. For Spain this meant that long-standing aspirations, officially expressed since 1957 under the Franco regime and immediately renewed in transition Spain, came within close reach. In contrast to Portugal, there had been a broad societal consensus about the nation's 'European vocation' for several decades. This attitude did not change under the restored monarchy and democracy. All major political parties supported the pro-European course, announced by the first democratically elected Conservative Prime Minister Suárez Gonzáles of the *Unión de Centro Democrático* (UCD) in June 1977. Only the far Left in the Basque country, organized in Herri Batasuna, and the Bloque Nacionalista Galego in Catalonia opposed Spanish EC membership, denouncing the EC as a superstructure of international capitalism which intended to keep the European peoples down.[65] If there had been some reservations on the democratic Left, they had been overcome by the close contacts that had developed between the *Partido Socialista Obrero Español* (PSOE) under Felipe Gonzáles and leading European Social Democrats. In fact, all major political and social forces promoted an all-embracing social pact to reform and modernize the Spanish political and socio-economic system to prepare the country for EC membership.[66]

The second or 'Mediterranean Enlargement' of 1981–86 took place under the continued impact of the systemic Cold War conflict. Democratization and solid anchorage in the Western world were highly important for the NATO and EC countries, giving an additional impetus for the integration of the newly established Mediterranean democracies in the Western political community. These enlargements also revealed some of the EC's structural deficits, thus exerting pressures on the supranational institutions and member-states to deepen the integration process significantly. The Single European Act (SEA) was passed in 1986 and came into force one year later, leading on to the Maastricht Treaty of 1992 and eventually preparing what then became the EU for its third enlargement in 1995. This third enlargement, however, was induced by the end of the bipolar system. The collapse of the Soviet bloc during 1989–91 proved all those to have been right who had argued that the CSCE process would ease the tensions between the blocs and therefore significantly change the global structures. Whether dialogue or Western economic strength and political determination finally led to the fall of the Iron Curtain is still heavily disputed. For our purposes, it is important that the collapse of the Soviet bloc paved the way for the accession of neutral and non-aligned countries by completely transforming the European security system.

Prior to the end of the systemic conflict, Sweden, Finland and Austria had rejected EC accession with reference to the outstanding importance of neutrality for their foreign and security policies, if not for the political stability of East–West relations. As at least some of the leading political decision-makers in all three states – especially on the political Left – considered the EC to be a European political agency to support NATO, which seemed a sufficient argument against membership, although centre-right political parties and forces and business circles had at least advocated some kind of closer association that safeguarded the countries' foreign policies. The public debate about 'Europe' revived in the mid-1980s, however. This was partly the result of the EC accession of Greece, Spain and Portugal and the subsequent structural changes inside the EC, especially the Single European Act and its aim of a single European market by 1992. Moreover, the importance of EFTA as an alternative continued to diminish in view of the enlarged EC. World trade was largely controlled by the USA, the EC and Japan. Under these changing circumstances, the economic arguments for full membership seemed to carry more and more weight, especially as the EC was taking a large chunk of the countries' exports of more than 50 per cent in the Swedish and Austrian cases. With the easing East–West tensions easing in 1987, the arguments against participation in political integration lost some of their force, too. In Sweden, the Conservatives and Liberals together with most industrialists began to urge the Social Democrat (SAP)-led government to strive for even closer relations with the EC, taking full EC membership into consideration as well. The SAP was split over the issue, as were the trade unions. Whereas the party elite started to rethink its own stance towards the EC under the impression of growing domestic pressure, the majority of the party membership remained sceptical or even hostile to full membership until the early 1990s.

When the SEA was passed in 1986, Swedish industry made a plea for full membership, and among the parties there was a widespread consensus that the EC initiative required a Swedish response. The government first tried to revive the EFTA approach by suggesting a common market of EFTA and the EC. The EC's response to this initiative was as cool as it had been towards the free trade scheme in the 1950s. The EC instead prioritized its own plans for economic and monetary union. The Conservatives and Liberals now demanded application for full EC membership. By now they could rely not only on the support of the Swedish Federation of Industries but also of the white-collar union, *Tjänstemännens Centralorganisation* (TCO). According to opinion polls, by that time 67 per cent of all Swedes were in favour of joining the EC too, as were most leading SAP politicians. The collapse of the Soviet Union in 1991 finally changed the international environment sufficiently. Prime Minister Ingvar Carlsson's originally sceptical stance was modified during several meetings with three leading continental Social Democrats: Jacques Delors, Felipe Gonzáles and Franz Vranitzky. His government eventually applied for full EC membership in the summer of 1991, much to the surprise of their Finnish (and Norwegian) neighbours, whose governments had hoped for a common approach. The referendum on Swedish EU membership in 1994 eventually resulted in only a small majority for accession of 52.3 per cent.

In many ways, the Finnish case is quite comparable to the Swedish one. Subsequent to the free trade agreement with the EC, the governments in Helsinki saw no need to keep the European question on the political agenda. Relations between Finland and the EC were revitalized in 1988, when a 'political dialogue' was established, first at a technocratic, then at a ministerial level. The question of EC membership did not emerge until October 1989, however, when Austria applied for it. The Finnish government then started to think very cautiously about this topic, while the political parties were still divided on the issue. By May 1990, public opinion was ahead of the political elites. According to one opinion poll, 60 per cent of all Finns were in favour of EC membership. The unilateral Swedish move in 1991 then caught the Finnish government by surprise. When the Finnish application was finally launched in December 1991 there was already widespread support for Finnish membership among the rank and file of the main interest groups and parties. The referendum in 1994 confirmed the tremendously fast reorientation of Finland's foreign and European policy, when 56.9 per cent voted in favour.[67]

In the Finnish case, in face of the collapsing barter trade with Russia, the economic advantages of membership were complemented by expecting a security dividend from EC membership at a time when the future development of Finland's Eastern neighbour seemed completely unclear. This expectation was shared in Austria which had always relied on *de facto* protection by NATO during the Cold War. Like Sweden and Finland, Austria was re-attracted to the EC as a result of the SEA initiative of 1986–87 and the danger of its possible exclusion from a single European market. Of all industrialized 'newcomers', Austria was most dependent on trade with the EC, and this is the main reason why the Austrian government applied for full EC membership as early as 1989. From then on, the Austrian governments could rely on growing support for their European policy, while the neutrality issue had less salience than in Sweden, for example. Austrian business and agriculture were nearly unanimous in their support for membership, as were the ÖVP and (eventually) the SPÖ and almost all of the media. EU accession was perceived by a large majority of Austrians as a return to European 'normalcy' and eventually supported by two-thirds in the referendum in 1994.[68] As a slight majority of Norwegians again (as in 1972) opted against EU membership, the EU was enlarged by another three countries on 1 January 1995, bringing the number of member-states to fifteen, up by nine from the original 'core Europe' states.

The European enlargements: a fool's game or a comedy of errors?

The history of EU enlargement demonstrates how the first three enlargements were not a fool's game. Some evidence in the case of certain countries might suggest at first sight that a degree of 'foolishness' characterized the perception of

'Europe' in the eyes of some 'newcomers', especially where highly developed clichés of European integration blocked the view. A closer evaluation of the case studies shows, however, that as a general rule the governing elites often fostered those clichés carefully as they were instrumental in justifying self-exclusion. In some countries there was little societal interest in acquiring a more balanced knowledge of the EEC/EC which might have helped to undermine the existing stereotypes. Neither the dominant governing elites nor large sections of the media in countries like Britain and Scandinavia had a strong interest in informing the citizens of the roots and original intentions of 'core Europe' integration.

Regarding the potential impact of the EEC/EC on the new acceding member-states – not only on their economies, but also on their political systems and societies – the lack of information in many countries might seem amazing. When there was a public debate on European issues at all, as a general rule, it obscured the original driving forces behind integration and its long-term political objectives. Economic integration had always also been a means to an end, that is the creation of a new stable political order for Europe. The strategic political objectives could not be served by economic integration alone. From the beginning it involved partly supranational institution-building as in the case of the ECSC and again the EEC. For many in 'core Europe' supranational institution-building was an end in itself, as they aimed at the creation of an integrated, federal Europe.

With the partial exception of Greece, Spain and Austria, this kind of 'Europeanist' ideology did not, however, play a significant role in the European debates in the 'newcomer' states. Moreover, in Greece and Spain the respective country's European 'vocation' did not reflect public consent, but was instead expressed by a small governing elite which wanted access to the EEC/EC as a means of achieving specific national objectives. The European debates in the remaining six 'newcomer' states were largely reduced to economic or security concerns, with the partial exception of Britain where objections to supranationalism appear to have played a certain role in influencing the prevailing negative attitudes towards participation in the ECSC and EEC in 1950–52 and 1957–58. When Britain did apply for EEC membership in 1961, the issue of supranationality was outweighed by the assumption that it would automatically take the lead once it was inside the EEC.

From this perspective, the EU enlargements may, with some justification, be described as a comedy of errors of almost Shakespearean dimensions. Looking at the EEC/EC through national lenses caused a variety of misperceptions and misunderstandings. Each 'newcomer' created more or less homogeneous images of 'Europe' and what it was (or should be) all about. Accession and membership initiated a degree of political socialization into the original and long-term objectives of the EU and its founding member-states, clarifying competing visions of European integration and facilitating a certain convergence of views. Up until the third enlargement of 1995, the European integration dynamics have led to a 'deepening' of the EU despite its greater heterogeneity, allowing the necessary adjustments inside the EU in preparation for each enlargement. So far 'widening' has not prevented 'deepening', but even brought it about in different ways. The EU has again made some adjustments in the Nice Treaty of 2000 in anticipation of Eastern enlargement in 2004. Yet, the controversial debate over the draft constitution and particularly, national voting power in the Council of Ministers have again exposed the different visions of the EU's future. Whether the enlarged EU will manage to cope with the additional strains resulting from its most recent enlargement by ten new member-states, and how it will do so, remains to be seen.

Notes

1 Cf. European Commission, *Eurobarometer der Kandidatenländer 2001: Die öffentliche Meinung in den Kandidatenländern*, Brussels: European Commission, 2002, pp. 41 ff.
2 Ibid., pp. 80–4.
3 Ibid., p. 80.
4 See also Ben Rosamond, *Theories of European Integration*, London: Macmillan, 2000.
5 On the early stages of the European integration process and its various manifestations, see, for example, Dieter Freiburghaus, *Wohin des Wegs, Europa? Ein Lesebuch zur Vergangenheit, Gegenwart und Zukunft der europäischen Integration*, 2nd edition, Berne: Paul Haupt, 2002, S. 13–17.
6 Cf. Klaus Schwabe, 'Der Marshall-Plan und Europa', in Raymond Poidevin (ed.), *Histoire des débuts de la construction européenne*, Brussels: Bruylant, 1986.
7 Cf. Dieter Krüger, *Sicherheit durch Integration? Die wirtschaftliche und politische Zusammenarbeit Westeuropas 1947–1957/58*, Munich: R. Oldenbourg, 2003, pp. 97–123.
8 Austria and Ireland used OEEC/OECD membership as a testbed for international cooperation. See the chapters by Michael Gehler on Austria and Edward Moxon-Browne on Ireland in this book. Spain (see Ricardo Martín de la Guardia's chapter) used its entry into the OEEC in 1959 as a channel of communication with the EEC. For Portugal (see Chapter 6 by António Costa Pinto and Nuno Severiano Teixeira) and Sweden (see Chapter 9 by Maria Gussarsson on Sweden), OEEC membership was a sufficient tie to European organizations in the 1940s and 1950s, whereas Finland (see Chapter 8 by Hanna Ojanen) could only enter OECD in 1968 due to its special relationship with the Soviet Union.
9 Cf. Wilfried Loth, *Der Weg nach Europa: Geschichte der europäischen Integration 1939–1957*, Göttingen: Vandenhoeck & Ruprecht, 1990, pp. 74–8.
10 See Wolfgang Krieger, 'Die Knute Moskaus als Überzeugungswaffe', in Hans-Herbert Holzamer and Marc Hoch (eds), *Der Marshall-Plan: Geschichte und Zukunft*, Landsberg: Olzog, 1997, pp. 40–6.
11 See Krüger, *Sicherheit durch Integration?*, pp. 173–84.
12 Klaus Schwabe (ed.), *Die Anfänge des Schuman-Plans, 1950/51*, Baden-Baden: Nomos, 1988. See also Dirk Spierenburg and Raymond Poidevin, *The History of the High Authority of the European Coal and Steel Community: Supranationality in Operation*, London: Weidenfeld & Nicolson, 1994.
13 Cf. Hans von der Groeben, *Deutschland und Europa in einem unruhigen Jahrhundert: Erlebnisse und Betrachtungen*, Baden-Baden: Nomos, 1995, pp. 257–63.
14 Freiburghaus, *Wohin des Wegs, Europa?*, p. 19.
15 Youri Devuyst, *The European Union at the Crossroads: The EU's Institutional Evolution from the Schuman-Plan to the European Convention*, 2nd edition, Brussels: Peter Lang, 2003, pp. 23–6.

16 Cf. Pierre Gerbet, *La Construction de l'Europe*, 3rd edn, Paris: Imprimerie nationale, 1999, pp. 121–5.
17 For Greece's attitude towards the early phase of the European integration process, see Chapter 4 by Kostas Ifantis.
18 For Britain's attitude towards the early phase of the European integration process, see Chapter 1 by Wolfram Kaiser.
19 For the Scandinavian states, see Chapter 2 by Johnny Laursen on Denmark, Chapter 9 by Gussarsson on Sweden, and Chapter 8 by Ojanen on Finland.
20 Chapter 9 by Gussarsson on Sweden.
21 Chapter 7 by Gehler on Austria.
22 For Spain's attitude towards the early phase of the European integration process, see Chapter 5 by Martín de la Guardia.
23 For Portugal's attitude towards the early phase of the European integration process, see Chapter 6 by Costa Pinto and Teixeira.
24 Cf. von der Groeben, *Deutschland und Europa*, p. 334.
25 Ibid., pp. 258 ff.
26 Curt Gasteyger, *Europa von der Spaltung zur Einigung: Darstellung und Dokumentation 1945–2000*, Bonn: Bundeszentrale für Politische Bildung, 2001, p. 148.
27 Chapter 1 by Kaiser on Britain.
28 Freiburghaus, *Wohin des Wegs, Europa?*, pp. 30 ff.
29. See Gerbet, *La Construction de l'Europe*, p. 201.
30 Chapter 3 by Moxon-Browne on Ireland.
31 Chapter 2 by Laursen on Denmark.
32 Chapter 9 by Gussarsson on Sweden.
33 Chapter 6 by Costa Pinto and Teixeira on Portugal.
34 Chapter 4 by Ifantis on Greece.
35 For the Swedish discussion, see Chapter 9 by Gussarsson, and for Finland, Chapter 8 by Ojanen.
36 Chapter 8 by Ojanen on Finland.
37 Chapter 5 by Martín de la Guardia on Spain.
38 Chapter 7 by Gehler on Austria.
39 Chapter 1 by Kaiser on Great Britain.
40 Cf. Wolfram Kaiser, *Using Europe, Abusing the Europeans: Britain and European Integration, 1945–63*, 2nd edition, London: Macmillan, 1999, Chapter 5.
41 Cf. Jürgen Elvert, 'Europa und der Norden: Die Geschichte einer wechselseitigen Fehlwahrnehmung im 19. und in der ersten Hälfte des 20. Jahrhunderts', in Robert Bohn and Jürgen Elvert (eds), *Kriegsende im Norden: Vom heißen zum Kalten Krieg*, Stuttgart: Franz-Steiner-Verlag, 1995, pp. 339–74, here pp. 364–74.
42 Chapter 9 by Gussarsson on Sweden.
43 For Denmark, see Chapter 2 by Laursen, for Finland, see Chapter 8 by Ojanen, and for the United Kingdom, see Chapter 1 by Kaiser.
44 Chapter 6 by Costa Pinto and Teixeira on Portugal.
45 Chapter 5 by Martín de la Guardia on Spain.
46 Ibid.
47 Ibid.
48 Chapter 7 by Gehler on Austria.
49 Ibid.
50 Cf. Thomas Angerer, 'Exklusivität und Selbstausschließung: Integrationsgeschichtliche Überlegungen zur Erweiterungsfrage am Beispiel Frankreichs und Österreichs', in 'L'Elargissement de l'Union Européenne, Actes du colloque franco-autrichien organisé les 13 et 14 juin 1997 par l'Institut Culturel Autrichien et l'Institut Pierre-Renouvin', *Revue d'Europe Centrale*, 1998, vol. 6, no. 1, pp. 25–54.
51 Chapter 4 by Ifantis on Greece.
52 Chapter 5 by Martín de la Guardia on Spain.

53 Chapter 7 by Gehler on Austria.
54 See Chapter 8 by Ojanen on Finland; also Niels-Erik Wergin, 'Finnland', in Jürgen Bellers, Thorsten Benner and Ines M. Gerke (eds), *Handbuch der Außenpolitik von Afghanistan bis Zypern*, Munich: Oldenbourg, 2001, pp. 67–76.
55 Ibid.
56 Chapter 9 by Gussarsson on Sweden.
57 Ibid.
58 Ibid.
59 On the second British EEC application, see also in comparative perspective, Wolfram Kaiser, 'Party games: the British EEC applications of 1961 and 1967', in Roger Broad and Virginia Preston (eds), *Moored to the Continent? Britain and European Integration*, London: IHR/University of London Press, 2001, pp. 55–78.
60 Chapter 3 by Moxon-Browne on Ireland.
61 For further details, see, for example, John Lewis Gaddis, *We Know Now: Rethinking Cold War History*, Oxford: Clarendon Press, 1998; Vojtech Mastny, *The Helsinki-Process and the Reintegration of Europe, 1986–1991: Analysis and Documentation*, London: Pinter, 1992; and Hermann Volle and Wolfgang Wagner (eds), *KSZE – Konferenz über Sicherheit und Zusammenarbeit in Europa: Beiträge und Dokumente aus dem Europa-Archiv*, Bonn: Verlag für Internationale Politik, 1976.
62 Chapter 4 by Ifantis on Greece.
63 Chapter 6 by Costa Pinto and Teixeira on Portugal.
64 Ibid.
65 Chapter 5 by Martín de la Guardia on Spain.
66 Ibid.
67 Chapter 8 by Ojanen on Finland.
68 Chapter 7 by Gehler on Austria.

Annotated bibliography

Research on the contemporary history and politics of European integration has expanded massively in the past two decades. This is also reflected in the growth of archive-based historical as well as political science literature on national policies towards 'Europe' discussed below. Yet so far the expanding research has resulted in only relatively few major monographic studies or even just articles that deal with the process of European institutionalization from a 'supranational', multilateral or transnational perspective. Some useful textbooks cover the history of the EU to the present. They include Derek Urwin, *The Community of Europe: A History of European Integration since 1945*, 2nd edn (London: Longman, 1997); Marie-Thérèse Bitsch, *Histoire de la construction européenne*, new edition (Paris: Editions Complexe, 2001); Pierre Gerbet, *La construction de l'Europe*, 3rd edn (Paris: Imprimerie Nationale, 1999); and Ricardo M. Martín de la Guardia and Guillermo A. Pérez Sánchez (eds), *Historia de la integración europea* (Barcelona: Ariel, 2001). For early integration, see also Wilfried Loth, *Der Weg nach Europa: Geschichte der europäischen Integration 1939–1957*, 3rd edn (Göttingen: Vandenhoeck & Ruprecht, 1996) and for the 1970s and 1980s, Keith Middlemas, *Orchestrating Europe: The Informal Politics of European Union 1973–1995* (London: HarperCollins, 1995).

A few authors have put forward an over-arching interpretative thesis on the integration process since 1945. They include Andrew Moravcsik, *The Choice for Europe: Social Purpose and State Power from Messina to Maastricht* (London: UCL Press, 1999) – a 'liberal inter-governmentalist' international relations scholar who has insisted on the supremacy of national governments in EU politics and bargaining, drawing upon historical examples of major integration decisions. In a similar vein, but based much more on archival research and only covering the early post-war integration process, Alan S. Milward has also emphasized the dominance of national governments in using European integration after 1945 as a new institutional framework for sustainable welfare policies and for their own 'rescue' in *The Reconstruction of Western Europe 1945–51* (London: Methuen, 1984) and *The European Rescue of the Nation-State* (London: Routledge, 1992). More recently, John Gillingham in *European Integration 1950–2003: Superstate or New Market Economy?* (Cambridge: Cambridge University Press, 2003) has put forward a liberal Hayekian critique of welfare state building and consociational politics in the EU in the post-war period until the present.

210 Annotated bibliography

Similarly, very few studies have attempted the comparative study of the national European policies of either the founding member-states of the EU or of the 'newcomers'. As regards the 'newcomers', they include Sieglinde Gstöhl, *Reluctant Europeans: Norway, Sweden, and Switzerland in the Process of Integration* (Boulder, CO: Lynne Rienner, 2002), a political science analysis of three national European policies in the entire post-war period that uses a modified rational choice framework which integrates material and ideational factors in explaining different policy behaviour and outcomes. The massive volume by Michael Gehler and Rolf Steininger (eds), *Die Neutralen und die europäische Integration 1945–1995 / The Neutrals and the European Integration 1945–1995* (Vienna: Böhlau, 2001) compares (with contributions in English and German) the European policies of the five neutral states, Ireland, Finland, Sweden, Switzerland and Austria, in the post-war period up to the present. Finally, the contributions to António Costa Pinto and Nuno Severiano Teixeira (eds), *Southern Europe and the Making of the European Union* (New York: SSM-Columbia University Press, 2002) deal with the 'newcomers' from Southern Europe in comparative perspective. In their *Transnationale Parteienkooperation der europäischen Christdemokraten. Dokumente 1945–1965* (Munich: Saur, 2004), Michael Gehler and Wolfram Kaiser demonstrate (by analysing the transnational party cooperation of European Christian Democrats) the need to analyse national policy-making as embedded up to a point in transnational elite networks and policy coordination, something that also holds true for the party cooperation of Social Democrats from Northern European 'newcomers', for example, and for transnational Social Democratic influence on the Europeanization of Spain.

To date, no long-term contemporary historical study has been attempted of the subsequent EU enlargements and their impact on the new member-states as well as the EU itself. For useful archive-based analyses of the first applications for EEC membership by Britain, Denmark, Ireland and Norway in 1961–62 and again in 1967, see the relevant contributions to Anne Deighton and Alan S. Milward (eds), *Widening, Deepening and Acceleration: The European Economic Community 1957–1963* (Baden-Baden: Nomos, 1999) and Wilfried Loth (ed.), *Crises and Compromises: The European Project 1963–1969* (Baden-Baden: Nomos, 2001). As regards the actual enlargements of 1973 to include Britain, Ireland and Denmark, 1981 (Greece), 1986 (Spain and Portugal) and 1995 (Austria, Finland and Sweden), social science studies have mostly dealt with specific aspects in relation to only one of the new member-states, with the enlargement's (likely) economic impact on the new member-state, the EU and third countries as the dominant focus. Many authors maintain in a general way that a dialectical relationship has existed between enlarging and 'deepening' the EU. To date, however, this relationship has not been studied in a broader perspective including different enlargement rounds and their impact on the EU's economic transformation, institutional reform and policy change. The Southern enlargement has been studied in some more detail, however, including Dudley Seers (ed.), *The Second Enlargement of the EEC: The Integration of Unequal Partners*

(Basingstoke: Macmillan, 1986). This is probably because it was seen as a greater economic and political challenge than the integration of the more developed new member-states in 1973 and 1995.

For the same reason, and because of the anticipated fundamental impact on the EU, the combined Eastern and Southern (Cyprus and Malta) enlargement to include ten more member-states by May 2004, which is not covered by this book, has already received much attention. Recent studies of EU policy towards East-Central Europe since 1990 include Marise Cremona (ed.), *The Enlargement of the European Union* (Oxford: Oxford University Press, 2003); Peter A. Poole, *Europe Unites: The EU's Eastern Enlargement* (Westport, CT: Greenwood, 2003) and Alan Mayhew, *Recreating Europe: The European Union's Policy towards Central and Eastern Europe*, 2nd edn (Cambridge: Cambridge University Press, 2003). Somewhat less up-to-date, but still useful are Jan Zielonka (ed.), *Europe Unbound: Enlarging and Reshaping the Boundaries of the European Union* (London: Routledge, 2002) and Michael J. Baun, *A Wider Europe: The Process and Politics of European Union Enlargement* (Lanham, MD: Rowman & Littlefield, 2000). As part of a book series covering all new member-states and their 'road to the European Union', Jacques Rupnik and Jan Zielonka have dealt with the Czech and Slovak Republics in their *The Road to the European Union*, vol. 1: *The Czech and Slovak Republics* (Manchester: Manchester University Press, 2003).

All nine new member-states covered in this book participated in various forms of institutionalized Western and European cooperation outside of the EU context before their accession. At different points in time, they became members of what became the Organization for Economic Cooperation and Development in 1961–62. Greece became associated with the EEC in 1961 and Spain negoti-ated a trade agreement with it. Together with Norway (which rejected EU membership in two referendums in 1972 and 1994) and Switzerland, Britain, Denmark, Sweden, Austria and Portugal created the European Free Trade Association (EFTA) in 1960–61, and Finland became associated with it in 1961. Although it functioned as an important framework for the evolution of its member-states' European policies, EFTA has received scant attention from social scientists and contemporary historians, but see Mikael af Malmborg and Johnny Laursen, 'The creation of EFTA', in Thorsten B. Olesen (ed.), *Interdependence versus Integration: Denmark, Scandinavia and Western Europe, 1945–1960* (Odense: Odense University Press, 1995), pp. 197–212; Wolfram Kaiser, 'The successes and limits of industrial market integration: the European Free Trade Association 1963–1969', in Wilfried Loth (ed.), *Crises and Compromises: The European Project 1963–1969* (Baden-Baden: Nomos, 2001), pp. 371–90; and Wolfram Kaiser, 'A better Europe? EFTA, the EFTA Secretariat, and the European identities of the "Outer Seven", 1958–72', in Marie-Thérèse Bitsch, Wilfried Loth and Raymond Poidevin (eds), *Institutions européennes et identités européennes* (Brussels: Bruylant, 1998, pp. 165–83). In addition, the Nordic cooperation context was particularly important for Denmark and Sweden as well as for Finland. For an overview of Nordic cooperation after 1945, see Johnny Laursen, 'Det nordiske samarbejde som særvej? Kontinuitet og brud, 1945–1973', in Johan P. Olsen and Bjørn Otto Sverdrup (eds), *Europa i Norden: Europeisering av nordisk samarbeid* (Oslo: Tano-Aschenhoug, 1998, pp. 43–63). On the Nordic Council founded in 1952, also look at Stanley V. Anderson, *The Nordic Council: A Study of Scandinavian Regionalism* (Seattle: University of Washington Press, 1967), Franz Wendt, *The Nordic Council and Co-operation in Scandinavia* (Copenhagen: Munksgaard, 1959) and Franz Wendt, *Co-operation in the Nordic Countries, Achievements and Obstacles: The Nordic Council* (Uppsala: Almqvist & Wiksell, 1981).

Great Britain

Of the European policies of the 'newcomers', that of Britain is probably best researched. Policy towards 'Europe' has been a hotly contested issue in British politics since at least the early 1960s. As such, it has traditionally attracted a lot of attention as a research topic for the social sciences and – more recently – contemporary history. In fact, the British relationship with 'Europe' is by now probably the best researched of all member-states of the enlarged European Union. For an excellent overview including recent academic debates on the issue, see John W. Young, *Britain and European Unity 1945–1999* (Basingstoke: Palgrave, 2000). Roger Broad and Virginia Preston (eds), *Moored to the Continent? Britain and European Integration* (London: IHR/University of London Press, 2001) also covers the entire post-war period, as does the at times insightful, but very journalistic account by Hugo Young, *This Blessed Plot: Britain and Europe from Churchill to Blair* (Basingstoke: Pan Macmillan, 1998).

As much of the more recent archive-based literature on the period up until the late 1960s is quite focused on governmental policy-making, it is often worth-while consulting some of the older social science literature for the domestic political context of policy-making, including pressure groups, the media and public opinion. See, in particular, Miriam Camps, *Britain and the European Community 1955–1963* (Oxford: Oxford University Press, 1964); Robert J. Lieber, *British Politics and European Unity: Parties, Elites, and Pressure Groups* (Berkeley, CA: University of California Press, 1970); Jeremy Moon, *European Integration in British Politics 1950–1963: A Study of Issue Change* (Aldershot: Gower, 1985); Uwe Kitzinger, *The Second Try: Labour and the EEC* (Oxford: Pergamon Press, 1969); and Uwe Kitzinger, *Diplomacy and Persuasion: How Britain Joined the Common Market* (London: Thames and Hudson, 1973).

The highly controversial character of the European issue is also reflected in its extensive and often illuminating treatment (with the notable exception of Harold Wilson) in many autobiographies of leading Conservative and Labour politicians. They include, most of all, the four volumes of Harold Macmillan's autobiography (with many quotes from his fascinating and now fully accessible diaries) covering the period from 1945 to 1963 (London: Macmillan, 1969–73); Edward Heath, *The Course of My Life* (London: Hodder & Stoughton, 1998); and Margaret Thatcher, *The Downing Street Years* (London: HarperCollins, 1993), which reflects in an amusing way her incomprehension of and distaste for continental European politics. Almost every Socialist politician, who played a leading role in the Labour governments of 1964–70 and 1974–79, has published memoirs and/or diaries, recounting the internal quarrels over 'Europe', such as in the context of the 1967 EEC application and the 1975 EC referendum, including Tony Benn, *Out of the Wilderness: Diaries 1963–67* (London: Arrow, 1988); Tony Benn, *Office without Power: Diaries 1968–72* (London: Hutchinson, 1988); George Brown, *In My Way: The Political Memoirs of Lord George-Brown* (London: Victor Gollancz, 1971); James Callaghan, *Time and Change* (London: Collins, 1987); Barbara Castle, *The Castle Diaries 1964–70* (London: Weidenfeld & Nicolson, 1984); Richard Crossman, *Diaries of a Cabinet Minister* (London: Methuen, 1979); Denis Healy, *The Time of My Life* (London: Michael Joseph, 1989); Douglas Jay, *Change and Fortune: A Political Record* (London: Hutchinson, 1980); Roy Jenkins, *A Life at the Centre* (London: Macmillan, 1991); and Michael Stewart, *Life and Labour: An Autobiography* (London: Sedgwick & Jackson, 1980).

Much of the recent archive-based literature on Britain and 'Europe' up until the late 1960s has led to major historiographical controversies. Edmund Dell, *The Schuman Plan and the British Abdication of Leadership in Europe* (Oxford: Oxford University Press, 1995) is a scathing criticism of British policy towards the formation of the European Coal and Steel Community in the early 1950s, as is Richard Lamb, *The Macmillan Years 1957–1963: The Emerging Truth* (London: John Murray, 1995) for the late 1950s and early 1960s. Professional historians have naturally preferred a less normative approach to understanding the evolution of British policy towards 'core Europe' integration. In his *Using Europe, Abusing the Europeans: Britain and European Integration, 1945–63* (Basingstoke: Macmillan, 1996, 1999), Wolfram Kaiser has controversially explained the 1961 EEC application as the outcome of Britain's transatlantic policy, which appeared to demand 'leading' Western Europe from within the EEC after the election of John F. Kennedy, and of domestic party politics. For quite detailed discussions of British policy towards the EEC negotiations during 1955–57 and the free trade area negotiations during 1957–58, see also James Ellison, *Threatening Europe: Britain and the Creation of the European Community, 1955–58* (Basingstoke: Macmillan, 2000) and Jacqueline Tratt, *The Macmillan Government and Europe: A Study in the Process of Policy Development* (Basingstoke: Macmillan, 1996). In contrast, Piers N. Ludlow's *Dealing with Britain: The Six and the First UK Application to the EEC* (Cambridge: Cambridge University Press, 1997) has explained the failure of the first British EEC application as the outcome not so much of British policy aims and their incompatibility with those of Charles de Gaulle, as that of an inappropriate negotiating strategy. Predictably, Alan S. Milward in the first volume of his 'official' history of Britain and the European Community entitled *The Rise and Fall of a National Strategy 1945–1963* (London: Frank Cass, 2002) has now interpreted British policy towards 'Europe' from an (economic) 'rational choice' perspective as a consensual 'national strategy' and an attempt to manage the transition from great to medium-sized power status, practically denying any influence of the transatlantic policy dimension or of ideational factors such as an emotional attachment to the Commonwealth and aversion to continental Europe. Finally, the contributions to Oliver J. Daddow, *Harold Wilson and European Integration: Britain's Second Application to Join the EEC* (London: Frank Cass, 2003) offer the first archive-based insights into British European policy under the Labour governments of 1964–70.

Milward's almost exclusive focus on governmental policy-making by politicians and officials and his basic assumption of the overriding importance of economic calculations for policy-making on 'Europe' are very much in line with liberal inter-governmentalist approaches to understanding the EU in International Relations. This approach appears very narrowly focused, however, when compared with much of the newer social science literature on EU politics which emphasizes, among other things, the importance of the domestic *political* context and of transnational forces for (national) European policy-making, often also questioning the rational choice assumptions of Milward, Andrew Moravcsik and others. In the British context, in particular, the massive influence of intra-party and inter-party conflicts and public opinion, for example, on the debate about Euro membership, is hard to overlook and needs to be explained. Historical, cultural and institutional factors play a role in the classic study by Stephen George, *An Awkward Partner: Britain and the European Community* (Oxford: Clarendon Press, 1990) and in the contributions to Stephen George (ed.), *Britain and the European Community: The Politics of Semi-Detachment* (Oxford: Clarendon Press, 1992). Jim Buller, *National Statecraft and European Integration: The Conservative Government and the European Union, 1979–1997* (London: Pinter, 2000) has explained British policy during the Thatcher and Major governments (especially over the Maastricht Treaty) as the result of a strategy to keep the party together, and a similar book may well be written about the policy of the Labour government since 1997 which has somewhat changed the European rhetoric, but not (very much) the substance of British EU policy. The contributions to David Baker and David Seawright (eds), *Britain For and Against Europe: British Politics and the Question of European Integration* (Oxford: Clarendon Press, 1998) also analyze various domestic aspects of British European policy-making. For a discussion of other relevant recent literature, see also Wolfram Kaiser, 'A never-ending story: Britain in Europe' (*British Journal of Politics and International Relations*, 2002, vol. 4, no. 1, pp. 152–65).

Denmark

Denmark's approach to the European Community was in many ways a slow crabwalk that started in the early 1950s. Hence, two of most important and classic studies of Denmark's relationship to the Common Market had already appeared before the country entered the European Community. Gunnar P. Nielson's *Denmark and European integration: a small country at the crossroads* (PhD, University of California, 1966) and Peter Hansen's 'Denmark and European integration' (*Cooperation and Conflict*, 1969, no. 1, pp. 13–46) addressed the Danish nation's reserves with regard to the integration process. Nielson's work focused on the Danish dilemma between Great Britain, Nordic cooperation and the emergence of the Six, while Hansen mapped the coalitions and domestic balances between parties and interest organizations in the European question. They nuanced the predominant monocausal notion that Denmark's approach to Europe was determined by the export of butter and bacon to the British market. The school that emphasized the reserves in principle with regard to supranational integration and the preference for Nordic cooperation took its beginning with these two important works. They also drew attention to the fact that the social democratic labour movement has played a crucial role in the formulation of European strategies. This 'reluctant Europeans' image was reproduced in Toivo Miljan's synthesis of the Scandinavian relationship to the EEC, *The Reluctant Europeans: The Attitudes of the Nordic Countries towards European Integration* (London: Hurst, 1977).

A great deal of attention has been dedicated to the years between 1947 and 1957, when Denmark was split between Nordic ambitions, dependency on Great Britain and the emergence of European integration. Vibeke Sørensen's *Social Democratic Government in Denmark under the Marshall Plan, 1947–1950* (Copenhagen: Museum Tusculanum Press, 2001) demonstrated how the European strategies were conditioned by domestic – especially social democratic – efforts to build a modern industrial export-driven economy with full employment. Sørensen coined the welfare theme in the interpretation of Denmark's European policies. There is as yet no comprehensive study of the sovereignty question in Denmark, but a more recent school of studies has shown that the Danish elite had less fixed views on the beginnings of the sectoral integration process than originally assumed. Hans Branner's work on Danish relations to the ECSC, 'På vagt eller på spring? Danmark og europæisk integration 1948–1953', in B. Nüchel Thomsen (ed.), *The Odd Man Out? Danmark og den europæiske integration 1948–1992* (Odense: Odense University Press, 1993, pp. 29–64) drew attention to this anomaly, while Anders Thornvig Sørensen's study of Denmark and the Green Pool, *Et spørgsmål om suverænitet: Danmark, landbruget og Europa, 1950–53* (Aarhus: Aarhus Universitetsforlag, 1998), has nuanced the understanding of Danish agriculture's shift towards advocacy for supranational integration.

There is not yet a source-based comprehensive study of Denmark's European policies. *Danmark i Europa 1945–93* (Copenhagen: Munksgaard, 1994), edited by Tom Swienty, provides an in-depth synthesis, but as for archive-based work, one has to wait for the fifth volume of the *Danish Foreign Policy History* planned for 2004 (Gyldendal, authored by Poul Villaume and Thorsten Olesen). The gradual Danish approach to EEC membership can best be followed in Bo Lidegaard's monumental biography, *Jens Otto Krag 1914–1978*, Vols I and II (Copenhagen: Gyldendal, 2001–2), on Jens Otto Krag's career that ran intertwined with Denmark's Nordic and European policies since the late 1940s until Denmark entered the EEC. Lidegaard's thesis is that Krag, as a Danish

Europeanist, was a rare phenomenon and that he struggled against the sceptics, not least in his own party. According to Lidegaard, Krag's legacy was the minimalist Danish perception that the European Community had a purely economic rationale without long-term political goals. The phases in Denmark's European policy can be followed in a number of articles by Johnny Laursen. Laursen's 'Det danske tilfælde: en studie i dansk Europapolitiks begrebsdannelse, 1956–57', in Johnny Laursen *et al.* (eds), *I tradition og kaos: Festskrift til Henning Poulsen* (Aarhus: Aarhus University Press, 2000, pp. 238–77) demonstrates the domestic and international constraints on the Danish government's response to the Treaty of Rome 1956–57, and argues that the scepticism of the labour movement reflected concerns about Nordic ambitions, economic modernization and domestic tactics. Laursen's 'The great challenge: the social and political foundations of Denmark's application for EEC membership, 1961–63', in Stuart Ward and Richard T. Griffiths (eds), *Courting the Common Market: The First Attempt to Enlarge the European Community, 1961–63* (London: Lothian Foundation Press, 1996, pp. 211–27) investigates the first Danish application for EEC membership and argues that the Danes – at least at the elite level – were at an advanced stage of preparation for EEC membership when Charles de Gaulle in 1963 issued his veto against British EEC membership. Furthermore, Danish concerns focused on industrial adaptation and domestic tactics, while real welfare concerns were less important than has hitherto been assumed. For the 1967 application, see also Laursen's 'Denmark, Scandinavia and the second attempt to enlarge the EEC, 1966–67', in Wilfried Loth (ed.), *Crises and Compromises: The European Project 1963–1969* (Baden-Baden: Nomos, 2001, pp. 407–36). Laursen has emphasized the temporal shifts and contextual nature of the Danish elite's approach to supranational integration. In this more critical view of the 'sceptical Danes school', it is argued that Denmark was not such an unwavering member of the Anglo-Scandinavian camp as is often assumed, but that the country was trying to navigate between the Six and the Seven. Domestic political tactics, the requirements of the transition from a rural to an industrial society and the ups and downs of Scandinavian cooperation are important elements in this interpretation.

As for the application in 1970–72, Lidegaard's work should be the standard reference. Carsten Lehmann Sørensen's *Danmark og EF i 1970erne* (Copenhagen: Borgen, 1978) and Carsten Due-Nielsen and Nikolaj Petersen's *Adaptation and Activism: The Foreign Policy of Denmark 1967–1993* (Copenhagen: DJØF forlag, 1995) offer comprehensive and informative accounts of the application process. Morten Rasmussen has published a number of articles on the negotiations for EEC membership. Rasmussen's 'How Denmark made Britain pay the bills', in Jørgen Sevaldsen, Claus Bjørn and Bo Bjørke (eds), *Britain and Denmark: Political, Economic and Cultural Relations in the 19th and 20th Centuries* (Copenhagen: Museum Tusculanum Press, 2003, pp. 617–37) follows the agricultural negotiations and shows how a Danish negotiation strategy building on community doctrines achieved a high degree of success in securing favourable conditions for Danish agriculture and in making Britain 'pay the bills'. Rasmussen's 'Ivar Nørgaards mareridt: Socialdemokratiet og den Økonomiske og Monetære Union 1970–72' (*Den jyske Historiker*, 2001, no. 93, pp. 73–95), remains the most thorough and comprehensive study of the social democratic – and Jens Otto Krag's – strategy for committing the social democratic labour movement to a 'yes' in the referendum campaign. Morten Rasmussen's forthcoming PhD thesis (European University Institute, Florence) on the Danish accession negotiations will soon offer a source-based synthesis of this complex.

The history of Danish Euro-scepticism can be followed in two source-based studies. Hans Marten's *Danmarks ja, Norges nej: EF-folkeafstemningerne i 1972* (Copenhagen: Munksgaard, 1979) is a structural comparison between the Danish and the Norwegian referendum campaigns and of the strategies of the 'yes' and 'no' camps. Money, organization and unity of action won the battle for the yes camp in Denmark in Marten's view. Søren Hein Rasmussen's *Sære Alliancer: Politiske bevægelser i efterkrigstidens Danmark* (Aarhus: Aarhus University Press, 1997) is a case study-based investigation of the so-called grassroots movements in Danish politics. The chapter on the People's movement against the EEC and on the EEC referendum is thoroughly source-based and demonstrates the factionalism and ideological diversity in the creation of the 'no' cartel. Rasmussen emphasizes the role of intellectuals and of established left-wing parties, but points to the weakness that the social democrat sceptics hesitated to join the ranks of this 'no' cartel. An overview of the campaign and the electoral patterns can be found in Peter Hansen, Melvin Small and Karen Siune's 'The structure of the debate in the Danish EC campaign: a study of an opinion-policy relationship', (*Journal of Common Market Studies*, 1973, vol. 15, no. 2, pp. 93–129).

Ireland

Although little was written about Ireland's relationship with the process of European integration prior to Ireland's entry to the EEC in 1973, there has been a steady output of published work since then, some of it analysing retrospectively the period before accession.

For a general introduction to, and extremely comprehensive survey of, twentieth-century Ireland, there is nothing to match Joe Lee's *Ireland 1912–1985: Politics and Society* (Cambridge: Cambridge University Press, 1989). This volume is written with enough humour, insight and scepticism to satisfy the most demanding reader. It does not purport to deal with Ireland's external relations but it provides the basis necessary for a full understanding of the domestic context within which most of the key decisions regarding European integration were inevitably made. It is also useful in that it deals thoroughly with the Northern question from Dublin's perspective.

The early years of Ireland's first tentative contacts with European integration after the war are the subject of Miriam Hederman's *The Road to Europe* (Dublin: Institute of Public Administration, 1983) and it is particularly strong in its depiction of Irish public attitudes (to the extent that they existed in any coherent way) in these early years. Hederman's volume is well balanced by Denis Maher's *The Tortuous Path* (Dublin: Institute of Public Administration, 1986). Written by someone who was centrally involved in the negotiations leading towards EEC membership, Maher's approach is essentially that of the civil servant but nonetheless offers some insight into the pressures that moulded, and occasionally the sense of impotence that pervaded, the Irish negotiating strategy.

Several academic works have attempted to calculate the costs and benefits of Irish Community membership from the Irish perspective. An early attempt to do this was David Coombes's *Ireland and the European Communities: Ten Years of Membership* (Dublin: Gill and Macmillan, 1983) where various aspects of membership were scrutinized: the legal, economic, agricultural, and regional dimensions being complemented by some consideration of Irish public opinion and the changing context of foreign policy coordination. Nearly ten years later, Patrick Keatinge's *Ireland and EC Membership Evaluated* (London: Pinter, 1991) which was part of a series covering the entire Community, illustrated in more than thirty short chapters the extent to which Irish society had been permeated and moulded by EC membership. More recently, Jim Dooge and Ruth Barrington, in their *A Vital National Interest: Ireland in Europe 1973–1998* (Dublin: Institute of Public Administration, 1999), have assembled an impressive panel of writers to produce a retrospective assessment of a quarter century of membership including some 'insider' accounts from, among others, Garret Fitzgerald and Ray McSharry. These academic accounts can be usefully supplemented by occasional reports from the National Economic and Social Council 'think-tank' the two most influential being *The Socioeconomic Position of Ireland within the EEC* (1981) and *Ireland in the European Community: Performance Prospects and Strategy* (1989). The Institute for European Affairs (IEA) in Dublin has also played a leading role, perhaps *the* leading role, in encouraging informed debate on Ireland's role in the European Union. Among its many publications, three that are especially useful are: Bobby McDonagh's *Original Sin in a Brave New World* (Dublin: IEA, 1998) which gives great insights into how the Treaty of Amsterdam was negotiated; Patrick Keatinge's *European Security: Ireland's Choices* (Dublin: IEA, 1996) which can be regarded as a definitive statement; and Richard Sinnott's *Knowledge of the European Union in Irish Public Opinion* (Dublin: IEA, 1995) which highlights some of the internal contradictions in Irish attitudes.

Irish participation in the process of European integration has always been, and continues to be, affected by its official policy of military neutrality. The issue of neutrality is discussed briefly but trenchantly in Joe Lee's magisterial account of Ireland in the twentieth century, *Ireland 1912–1985* and more detailed analysis of the same historical period can be found in Robert Fisk's *In Time of War: Ireland, Ulster and the Price of Neutrality 1939–45* (London: Deutsch, 1983). For a balanced and succinct account of Irish neutrality in a comparative context, see Patrick Keatinge's *A Singular Stance: Irish Neutrality in the 1980s* (Dublin: Institute of Public Administration, 1984), while the credibility of Irish neutrality is questioned *in extenso* in Trevor Salmon's *Unneutral Ireland: An Ambivalent and Unique Security Policy* (Oxford: Clarendon, 1989).

Greece

The subject of Greece's relations with the EEC remained largely unexplored until the late 1970s. The most notable contribution before that period was George Yannopoulos's *Greece and the EEC: The First Decade of a Troubled Association* (London: Sage, 1975). A comprehensive and detailed account of the Association Agreement of 1961 is Konstantina Botsiou's *Griechenlands Weg nach Europa: Von der Truman-Doktrin bis zur Assoziierung mit der Europäischen Wirtschaftsgemeinschaft, 1947–1961* (Frankfurt: Peter Lang, 1998). Susannah Verney also examines EEC association in 'The Greek association with the European Community: a strategy of state', in António Costa Pinto and Nuno Severiano Teixeira (eds), *Southern Europe and the Making of the European Union 1945–1980s* (Boulder, CO: Social Science Monographs, 2002, pp. 109-56)

A good number of books dealing with the question of Greece and European integration were published during the accession negotiations. Three deserve attention, although two – Panos Kazakos's *Evropaiki Economiki Koinotita* (Athens: Papazisis, 1978), and Nikos Mousses's *EOK: Analisi tis Koinotikis Politikis: Agrotikis, Economikis, Koinonikis, Perifereiakis, Perivallontos* (Athens: Papazisis, 1978) – are basically devoted to the description and analysis of the structure and functioning of the EEC itself. They only occasionally touch upon the politics and effects of Greek accession. The collection by Spyros Karpathiotes *et al.* (eds), *I Entaxi mas stin EOK* (Athens: Themelio, 1978), is a left-wing analysis of the membership's implications and a critical account of the history of EEC–Greek relations. The first international publication was *Greece in the European Community* (Westmead: Saxon House, 1979), edited by Loukas Tsoukalis. The book was a follow-up of a 1977 Oxford conference and it successfully deals with the politics of accession and almost every issue on the agenda of the then ongoing negotiation process. In his excellent book, *The European Community and its Mediterranean Enlargement* (London: Allen & Unwin, 1981), Tsoukalis offers a comprehensive assessment of the accession project as well as of the problems the Community and the new members were about to face.

In *Negotiating for Entry: The Accession of Greece to the European Community* (Aldershot: Dartmouth, 1995), Iacovos Tsalicoglou examines in detail the 1961 Association Agreement as well as the negotiations that led to Greek membership in the 1970s, while Jean Siotis's 'Characteristics and motives for entry', in Lyn Gorman and Marja-Liisa Kiljunen (eds), *The Enlargement of the European Community: Case-Studies of Greece, Portugal and Spain* (London: Macmillan, 1983, pp. 57-69) offers a brief overview.

Susannah Verney has examined the debate within and between the Greek political parties in 'Greece and the European Community', in Kevin Featherstone and Dimitris Katsoudas (eds), *Political Change in Greece: Before and After the Colonels* (London: Croom Helm, 1987, pp. 253-70) and 'To be or not to be within the European Community: the party debate and democratic consolidation in Greece', in Geoffrey Pridham (ed.), *Securing Democracy: Political Parties and Democratic Consolidation in Southern Europe* (London: Routledge, 1990, pp. 203-23). Verney discusses the European attitudes, rhetoric and policies of the Greek Socialists under Andreas Papandreou in 'From the "special relationship" to Europeanism: PASOK and the European Community, 1981–1989', in Richard Clogg (ed.), *Greece 1981–89: The Populist Decade* (London: Macmillan, 1993, pp. 131-53), and also in 'The Greek Socialists', in James Gaffney (ed.), *Political Parties and the European Union* (London: Routledge, 1996, pp. 170-88). Panos Kazakos deals with the same theme in 'Socialist attitudes toward European integration in the eighties', in Theodore Kariotis (ed.), *The Greek Socialist Experiment: Papandreou's Greece 1981–1989* (New York: Pella, 1992, pp. 257-78).

Greece's European policy has also been discussed by a number of writers. Loukas Tsoukalis contributed a chapter on 'I Ellada kai I Evropaiki Koinotita', in Dimitris Konstas and Charalambos Tsardanidis (eds), *Synchroni Elliniki Exoteriki Politiki 1974–1987* (Athens: Sakoulas, 1988, pp. 197-220). In the same collection, Theodoros Christodoulidis's 'I Ellada stin EPS' examines the role of Greece in the context of European political cooperation. Other works on more or less the same subject are Panos Tsakaloyannis 'The European Community and the Greek–Turkish Dispute' (*Journal of Common Market Studies*, 1980, vol. 19, no. 1, pp. 35-54) and Christos Rozakis, *I Elliniki Exoteriki Politiki kai oi Evropaikes Koinotites* (Athens: Idryma Mesogeiakon Meleton, 1987).

Literature on actual membership is vast indeed. In 1981, Achilleas Mitsos edited an excellent collection on Greek accession focusing on the problems facing the Greek economy, *I Proshorisi stis Evropaikes Koinotites* (Athens: Synchrona Themata), while Panayotis Roumeliotis's edited volume, *I Oloklirosi tis Evropaikis Koinotitas kai o Rolos tis Elladas: Outopia kai Pragmatikotita* (Athens: Papazisis, 1985), deals with Greece's position in the European system of cooperation and sectoral arrangements. In 1986, George Yannopoulos edited a collection of essays, *Greece and the EEC* (Reading: University of Reading European and International Studies, 1986), which centres mainly on the early economic effects which membership had for a less developed country. On the same issue, the volume edited by Panos Kazakos and Konstantinos Stefanou, *I Ellada stin Evropaiki Koinotita: I Proti Pentaetia, taseis, Provlimata, Prooptikes* (Athens: Sakoulas, 1987), is very useful. Panos Kazakos also edited the most impressive *I Exelixi tis Esoterikis Agoras stin Evropi kai I Ellada* (Athens: Ionian Bank, 1989), a very detailed analysis of the Single European Market project and its impact on Greece. On the impact of Greek accession on industry and trade, Anastasios Giannitsis's *Entaxi stin Evropaiki Koinotita kai Epiptoseis sti Viomichania kai sto Exoteriko Emporio* (Athens: Idryma Mesogeiakon Meleton, 1989) is an important contribution.

On the issue of the Europeanization of Greece, the work of Panayotis Ioakimidis is pioneering indeed. Among other articles, he has published 'Greece in the EC: policies, experiences and prospects', in Harry Psomiades and Stavros

Thomadakis (eds), *Greece, the New Europe and the Changing International Order* (New York: Pella, 1993); 'The Europeanization of Greece: an overall assessment', in Kevin Featherstone and George Kazamias (eds), *Europeanization and the Southern Periphery* (London: Frank Cass, 2001, 73-94); and *I Evropaiki Enosi kai to Elliniko Kratos* (Athens: Themelio, 1998). In the same context, Kostas Lavdas offers an overall analysis of the internal debate in his *The Europeanization of Greece: Interest Politics and the Crises of Integration* (Basingstoke: Macmillan, 1997).

Since the early 1990s, a number of accounts of Greece's performance in the EC/EU have been published. They include Panos Kazakos and Panayotis Ioakimidis (eds), *Greece and EC Membership Evaluated* (London: Pinter, 1994); Panayotis Ioakimidis (ed.), *Greece in the European Union: The New Role and the New Agenda* (Athens: MPMM, 2002); and Loukas Tsoukalis (ed.), *I Ellada stin Evropaiki Koinotita: I Proklisi tis Prosarmogis* (Athens: EKEM/Papazisis, 1993). The edited volume by Kevin Featherstone and Kostas Ifantis, *Greece in a Changing Europe: Between European Integration and Balkan Disintegration?* (Manchester: Manchester University Press, 1996) has a rather wider focus.

Spain

The integration of Spain into the EEC has never attracted special attention from historians, especially when compared with the scientific interest that has been devoted to other instances of EEC accession. There are several reasons that can help to explain why this has been so. To begin with, international and foreign policy has seldom been a focus of attention for nineteenth- and twentieth-century Spanish historiography. Up until very recently, these fields of study basically came into the domain of other disciplines such as law, economics and political science. As a result, there is no solid historiographical tradition in the study of relations between contemporary Europe and Spain, which would obviously cover the Spanish approach to EEC institutions. Fortunately, with the help and impetus provided by the Spanish Commission for the Study of the History of International Relations (CEHRI), dissertations, monographs and overviews are beginning to fill some of the existing gaps. Second, with a few prominent exceptions including Pedro Martínez Lillo, *Una introducción al estudio de las relaciones hispano-francesas (1945–1951)* (Madrid: Fundación Juan March, 1985); Walter L. Bernecker (ed.), *España y Alemania en la Edad Contemporánea* (Frankfurt: Vervuert Verlag, 1993); and Birgit Aschmann, *"Treue Freunde …?" Westdeutschland und Spanien 1945–1963* (Stuttgart: Franz Steiner Verlag, 1999), no studies have aimed at analysing the political, economic, cultural or any other kind of relations between Spain and individual EEC countries, a preliminary step towards a closer look at the role of Spain in European construction.

Third, the peculiarities of Spanish history after 1945 and the lengthy life of Francoism undoubtedly constitute one of the focal points, if not the most important one, of historical research on contemporary Spain. However, historians have almost exclusively concentrated on the domestic aspects of the period. In the very few instances in which an attempt has been made to define Franco's foreign policy, the main objects of interest have been the Latin American and the Arab countries, the areas with which the regime had friendly relations. Fourth, due to the fact that Spain was absent from the first stages of European integration, most of the important works have focused on the last years of the negotiations, especially between 1977 and 1986. This has led to an odd result: on the whole, those works analyse the process of integration as one of the elements of the Spanish transition to democracy, that is, as a crucial factor in the consolidation of the rule of law, but not as an object of study in itself.

In any case, the situation is gradually changing and is now substantially different from what it was ten or twenty years ago. For an overview, see Antonio Moreno Juste, 'España en el proceso de integración europea', in Ricardo Martín de la Guardia and Guillermo Pérez Sánchez (eds), *Historia de la integración europea* (Barcelona: Ariel, 2001, pp. 167–214); and also Ricardo Martín de la Guardia and Guillermo Pérez Sánchez, *La Unión Europea y España* (Madrid: Actas, 2002).

The first years of Franco's foreign policy regarding the EEC are examined in two excellent studies. Their authors have thoroughly consulted archives, especially those of the Spanish Foreign Ministry; they have also resorted to memoirs and personal testimonies of the then influential personalities: María Teresa Laporte, *La política europea del régimen de Franco, 1957–1962* (Pamplona: EUNSA, 1992), and, in particular, Antonio Moreno Juste, *Franquismo y construcción europea: (1951–1962)* (Madrid: Tecnos, 1998), where the Spanish decision to seek closer contact with the EEC is considered as an integral part of the foreign policy side of the regime's new economic policy. A solid study, based not only on his broad experience as Spanish negotiator at the EEC but also on historical sources, is Ambassador Raimundo Bassols's *España en Europa: Historia de la adhesión a la CE, 1957–1985* (Madrid: Política Exterior, 1995). For the geopolitical and economic implications of Spain after 1945 and their influence on her relations with the EEC, two valuable works stand out: Antonio Marquina, *España en la política de seguridad occidental, 1939–1975* (Madrid: Ediciones del Ejército, 1986); and Fernando Guirao, *Spain and Western European Economic Cooperation, 1945–1957* (London: Macmillan, 1997).

Personal testimonies, memoirs, reflections on the most important moments and events in the history of the relations between Franco's Spain and the EEC offer rich, supplementary information on some of their protagonists, for example, Manuel Fraga Iribarne, *Memoria breve de una vida pública* (Barcelona: Planeta, 1980); Gregorio López Bravo, *Algunas reflexiones en torno a la política exterior de España* (Madrid: Oficina de Información Diplomática, 1971); and Alberto Ullastres, *Política comercial española* (Madrid: Servicio de Estudios del Ministerio de Comercio, 1962).

The Spanish transition to democracy has also been analysed extensively, especially since this process has been seen as exemplary in many ways and, consequently, has become an element in the political discourse of other transitions. About historians' more recent contributions, it is important to point out their profound revision of what had previously been said about foreign policy-making during the transition years in general and about the negotiations for Spanish integration into the EEC in particular. Two publications deserve an explicit mention: Charles Powell, 'La dimensión internacional de la transición española', in Manuel Ferrer (ed.), *Franquismo y transición democrática* (Las Palmas de Gran Canaria: Centro de Estudios de Humanidades, 1993, pp. 101–43); and Berta Álvarez Miranda, *El Sur de Europa y la adhesión a la Comunidad: Los debates políticos* (Madrid: CIS, 1996). As opposed to those who considered that it was irrelevant to study the influence of external factors determining a transition process which was strictly domestic and favoured by the international situation, the latest historiographical tendencies place special emphasis on, among other things, the importance of the relations between the transition governments and the Community authorities as an essential ingredient in the consolidation of democracy; they also show the broad consensus existing between political forces, public opinion, and the academic, professional, and business circles in their determination to achieve Spain's rapid integration into the EEC. A clear, global assessment can be found in Encarnación Lemus and Juan Carlos Pereira, 'Transición y política exterior (1975–1986)', in Juan Carlos Pereira (coord.), *La política exterior de España (1800–2003)* (Barcelona: Ariel, 2003, pp. 517–38). The collective works edited by Richard Gillespie, Fernando Rodrigo and Jonathan Story (eds), *Las relaciones exteriores de la Europa democrática* (Madrid: Alianza, 1995) and by Geoffrey Pridham (ed.), *Encouraging Democracy: The International Context of Regime Transition in Southern Europe* (Leicester: Leicester University Press, 1991) represent milestones in this evolution of historical interpretation as regards the foreign and European aspects of Spain in the 1970s and early 1980s. As in the Franco era, there are also numerous personal accounts or memoirs written by the protagonists of the negotiations that ultimately led to the definite accession of Spain into the EEC: Leopoldo Calvo Sotelo, *Memoria viva de la transición* (Barcelona: Plaza & Janés, 1990); Carlos Robles, *En Europa, desde Europa* (Madrid: Política Exterior, 1987); Joan Reventós, *Misión en París: Memorias de un Embajador* (Barcelona: Península, 1993); and Fernando Morán, *España en su sitio* (Barcelona: Plaza & Janés, 1990).

Social science research on Spain in the EU since 1987 has produced some excellent monographs. Among them are those of Juan Díez Medrano, *La opinión pública española y la integración europea* (Madrid: CIS, 1995), which deals with the population's awareness of European issues and Esther Barbé, *La política europea de España* (Barcelona: Ariel, 1999) on the Europeanist policies of the Socialist and Popular governments. Carlos Closa (ed.), *La europeización del sistema político español* (Madrid: Istmo, 2001) is a compilation of interdisciplinary studies of the impact of the EU on the institutions of the Spanish state, the policies of each governmental department, and leading politicians and their political concepts and policies.

Portugal

In Portugal, serious historical study of the European Union only started during the 1990s. While legal and economic studies of European unification have had a tradition of research (and where functional necessities have ensured greater attention), it is only recently that the theme has been approached by historians and political scientists. Several factors have contributed towards this delay. One of the most important reasons was the longevity of Salazar's regime and Portugal's initial non-involvement in the European project. Portugal's delay in accepting the European option as a major foreign policy goal, a decision that was only finally taken following decolonization and the transition to democracy of the mid-1970s, is reflected in the absence of a collective memory on this theme within Portuguese society. The late inclusion of the social sciences and contemporary history in Portugal's universities – yet another consequence of the dictatorship's longevity – has also contributed to the delayed response of the social science community.

The first historical studies of international relations in Portugal concentrated on international organizations such as NATO, of which the country was a founding member; these organizations were central to the dictatorship's desire for integration into the new post-war international order. Examples of these earlier studies include Nuno Severiano Teixeira's 'From neutrality to alignment: Portugal in the foundation of the Atlantic Pact' (*Luso-Brazilian Review*, 1992, vol. 29, no. 2, pp. 113–27), and António José Telo, *Portugal e a NATO: O Reencontro da Tradição Atlântica* (Lisbon: Cosmos, 1996). Portugal's relations with Europe and the United States have, in the main, been studied from the perspective of the colonial wars and resistance to decolonization. Very few have touched on the theme of European integration apart from Luís Nuno Rodrigues, *Salazar–Kennedy: a crise de uma aliança* (Lisbon: Editorial Notícias, 2002).

The first study of Portugal's relationship with European institutions, whether of an autobiographical or academic nature, was published by the man who presented Portugal's request for membership to the European Community in 1977, the historian and former Portuguese Foreign Minister José Medeiros Ferreira, *Adesão de Portugal à Comunidades Europeias: história e documentos* (Lisbon: Parlamento Europeu-Assembleia da República, 2001). Also of use are the testimonies published by diplomats of the authoritarian period in R. T. Guerra, A. de S. Freire and J. Calvet Magalhães (eds), *Os movimentos de cooperação e integração europeia no pós guerra e a participação de Portugal* (Lisbon: Instituto Nacional de Administração, 1981). A recent book by António Costa Pinto and Nuno Severiano Teixeira, *Portugal e a integração europeia: a perspectiva dos actores* (Lisbon: Círculo de Leitores, 2003), includes interviews with several diplomats and politicians who were involved in negotiations with European institutions during the period from the Marshall Plan until Portugal's accession to the European Community in 1986.

The relatively recent creation of post-graduate university courses that incorporate the study of European unification has led to the appearance of the first academic publications on this theme. Maria Fernanda Rollo's *Portugal e o Plano Marshall* (Lisbon: Estampa, 1994), highlights the dictatorship's initial reservations and hesitations in relation to Portugal's involvement in the Marshall Plan. José Manuel Tavares Castilho's excellent archival research, which has been published as *A ideia da Europa no Marcelismo, 1968–1974* (Oporto: Afrontamento, 2000), concentrates on the examination of the debates over Portugal's relationship with the European Community during the final years of the dictatorship – at a time when it was headed by Salazar's successor, Marcello Caetano. Castilho's is an exhaustive study of the debate within both the employers' associations and the regime's institutions at the end of the 1960s. This was a debate that was domi-nated by the contradictions between the continuation of the colonial wars and the country's ever-closer economic links with Europe – links that culminated in the bilateral Commerce Agreement of 1973. An introduction to the impact of Portugal's accession to EFTA is given in Richard T. Griffiths and Bjarne Lie, 'Portugal e a EFTA, 1959–1973', which is part of *Portugal e Europa: 50 anos de inte-gração* (Lisbon: Centro de Informação Jacques Delors, 1996). The EFTA accession negotiations are the subject of two, as yet unpublished, theses: Elsa Santos Alípio's *O processo negocial de adesão de Portugal à EFTA, 1956–1960* (Lisbon: Universidade Nova de Lisboa, 2001), and Nicolau Andresen Leitão's *The Reluctant European: Portugal and European Integration, 1956–1963* (Florence: European University Institute, 2003).

Published research of the economic and social 'Europeanization' of Portugal since the 1960s is more difficult to find. There are, however, at least two studies – both in English – that directly address this theme: António Barreto's sociological study, 'Portugal: democracy through Europe', in J.J. Anderson (ed.), *Regional Integration and Democracy: Expanding on the European Experience* (New York: Rowman & Littlefield, 1999, pp. 95–122); and David Corkill's *The Development of the Portuguese Economy: A Case of Europeanization* (London: Routledge, 1999). It is only quite recently that studies of Portugal's democratization in the mid-1970s have begun to address the international aspects of this transition and, in particular, the impact that the promise of accession to the European Community had on the consolidation of democracy. A general introduction to this theme can be found in Silva Lopes (ed.), *Portugal and EC Membership Evaluated* (London: Pinter, 1994), and José Magone's *European Portugal: The Difficult Road to Sustainable Democracy* (London: Macmillan, 1997). Some Portuguese political scientists have examined the positions of the various political parties with respect to member-ship of the European Community. One such work is José Manuel Durão Barroso's *Le système politique portugais face à l'intégration européenne: partis politiques et opinion publique* (Lisbon: APRI, 1983). In António Costa Pinto and Nuno Severiano Teixeira (eds), *Southern Europe and the Making of the European Union* (New York: SSM-Columbia University Press, 2002), the authors have published a study on Portugal and the European unification that provides also a comparative analysis of the other countries of Southern Europe and their relations with the European Community.

Austria

Austria's application for EC membership in 1989 and its joining the EU in 1995 generated changes concerning European integration research. Apart from political scientists and international law experts, Austria's changing role in Europe has also preoccupied contemporary historians since the 1990s. During the last ten years in particular, newly accessible archival sources have greatly facilitated the historical analysis of Austria and 'Europe' from the 1940s to the early 1970s. Until the 1990s, the history of the state treaty and neutrality (1955) featured much more prominently. For a long time Austrian foreign policy after 1945 was primarily seen as the history of the period of occupation and the struggle for independence. In this tradition, Manfried Rauchensteiner, *Der Sonderfall: Die Besatzungszeit in Österreich 1945 bis 1955* (Graz: Styria, 1979); Günter Bischof and Josef Leidenfrost (eds), *Die bevormundete Nation: Österreich und die Alliierten 1945–1949* (Innsbruck: Haymon, 1988); Wilfried Mähr, *Der Marshallplan in Österreich* (Graz: Styria, 1989); Gerald Stourzh, *Um Einheit und Freiheit: Staatsvertrag, Neutralität und das Ende der Ost–West-Besetzung Österreichs 1945–1955* (Vienna: Boehlau, 1998, 4th edn); and Günter Bischof, *Austria in the First Cold War, 1945–55: The Leverage of the Weak* (Basingstoke: Macmillan, 1999) do not actually deal with the issue of integration.

For a long time, legal studies of Austria and 'Europe' were predominant including Theo Öhlinger, Hans Mayrzedt and Gustav Kucera, *Institutionelle Aspekte der österreichischen Integrationspolitik* (Vienna: Verlag der österreichischen Akademie der Wissenschaften, 1976); Waldemar Hummer and Michael Schweitzer, *Österreich und die EWG: Neutralitätsrechtliche Beurteilung der Möglichkeiten der Dynamisierung des Verhältnisses zur EWG* (Vienna: Signum, 1987); Gerhard Kunnert, *Österreichs Weg in die Europäische Integration* (Vienna: Verlag der Österreichischen Staatsdruckerei, 1993); and Franz Cede and Christoph Thun-Hohenstein, *Europarecht: Das Recht der Europäischen Union unter besonderer Berücksichtigung des EU-Beitritts Österreichs* (Vienna: Manz, 1996, 2nd edn).

Political science research on the topic developed from the late 1980s onwards, including Paul Luif, *Neutrale in die EG? Die westeuropäische Integration und die neutralen Staaten* (Vienna: Braumüller, 1988); Heinrich Schneider, *Alleingang nach Brüssel: Österreichs EG-Politik* (Bonn: Europa-Union Verlag, 1990); Herbert Krejci, Erich Reiter and Heinrich Schneider (eds), *Neutralität: Mythos und Wirklichkeit* (Vienna: Signum, 1992); Anton Pelinka (ed.), *EU-Referendum: Zur Praxis direkter Demokratie in Österreich* (Vienna: Signum, 1994); Anton Pelinka, Christian Schaller and Paul Luif, *Ausweg EG? Innenpolitische Motive einer außenpolitischen Umorientierung* (Vienna: Böhlau, 1994); Peter Gerlich and Heinrich Neisser (eds), *Europa als Herausforderung: Wandlungsimpulse für das politische System Österreichs* (Vienna: Signum Verlag, 1994); Paul Luif, *On the Road to Brussels: The Political Dimensions of Austria's, Finland's and Sweden's Accession to the European Union* (Vienna: Braumüller, 1995); and Emmerich Tálos and Gerda Falkner (eds), *EU-Mitglied Österreich: Gegenwart und Perspektiven, Eine Zwischenbilanz* (Vienna: Manzsche Verlags- und Universitätsbuchhandlung, 1996).

Important editions of documents and memoirs of leading politicians include Waldemar Hummer and Hans Mayrzedt, *20 Jahre österreichische Neutralitäts- und Europapolitik: Dokumentation*, 2 vols (Vienna: Braumüller, 1976); Eva Maria Csáky (ed.), *Der Weg zu Freiheit und Neutralität: Dokumentation zur österreichischen Außenpolitik 1945–1955* (Vienna: Österreichische Gesellschaft für Außenpolitik und internationale Beziehungen, 1980); Karl Czernetz, *Europäer und Sozialist: Reden und Aufsätze* (Vienna: Verlag der Wiener Volksbuchhandlung, 1980); Gerhard Kunnert, *Spurensicherung auf dem österreichischen Weg nach Brüssel* (Vienna: Österreichische Staatsdruckerei, 1992); Michael Gehler (ed.), *Karl Gruber: Reden und Dokumente 1945–1953, Eine Auswahl* (Vienna: Böhlau, 1994); Waldemar Hummer and Anton Pelinka, *Österreich unter "EU-Quarantäne": Die "Maßnahmen der 14" gegen die österreichische Bundesregierung* (Vienna: Linde Verlag, 2002); Bruno Kreisky, *Zwischen den Zeiten: Erinnerungen aus fünf Jahrzehnten* (Berlin: Siedler, 1986); Fritz Bock, *Der Anschluß an Europa: Gedanken, Versuche, Ergebnisse* (St Pölten: Verlag Niederösterreichisches Pressehaus, 1978); Lujo Toncic-Sorinj, *Erfüllte Träume: Kroatien – Österreich – Europa* (Vienna: Amalthea, 1982); and Alois Mock, *Heimat Europa: Der Countdown von Wien nach Brüssel* (Vienna: Edition S, Verlag Österreich, 1994).

In the past ten years, the *Arbeitskreis Europäische Integration* at the Institute of Contemporary History of the University of Innsbruck has published several volumes on major themes of (recent) integration history, mostly based on archival sources, for example, Michael Gehler and Rolf Steininger (eds), *Österreich und die europäische Integration 1945–1993: Aspekte einer wechselvollen Entwicklung* (Vienna: Böhlau, 1993); Michael Gehler and Rolf Steininger (eds), *Die Neutralen und die europäische Integration 1945–1995/The Neutrals and the European Integration 1945–1995* (Vienna: Böhlau, 2000); Michael Gehler, Wolfram Kaiser and Helmut Wohnout (eds), *Christdemokratie in Europa im 20. Jahrhundert/Christian Democracy in 20th Century Europe/La Démocratie Chrétienne en Europe au XXe siècle* (Vienna: Böhlau, 2001); Michael Gehler, Günter Bischof and Anton Pelinka (eds), *Österreich in der Europäischen Union: Bilanz seiner Mitgliedschaft/Austria in the European Union: Assessment of Her Membership* (Vienna: Böhlau, 2003).

Since Austria's EU accession, European integration has become one of the top priorities of contemporary history and social science research. Several important books have been published in the last few years, including Michael Gehler, *Der lange Weg nach Europa: Österreich vom Ende der Monarchie bis zur EU*, vol. 1: *Darstellung* and vol. 2: *Dokumente* (Innsbruck: Studienverlag, 2002); Günter Bischof, Anton Pelinka and Michael Gehler (eds), *Austria in the European Union* (New Brunswick, NJ: Transaction, 2002); Martin Lugmayr, *Österreich und die EU-Osterweiterung* (Frankfurt: Peter Lang, 2002); Franz Heschl, *Drinnen oder draußen? Die öffentliche österreichische EU-Beitrittsdebatte vor der Volksabstimmung 1994* (Vienna: Böhlau, 2002); Ferdinand Karlhofer, Josef Melchior and Hubert Sickinger (eds), *Anlaßfall Österreich: Die Europäische Union auf dem Weg zu einer Wertegemeinschaft* (Baden-Baden: Nomos, 2001); Gunther Hauser, *Österreich: dauernd neutral?* (Vienna: Braumüller, 2002); Alexander Schallenberg and Christoph Thun-Hohenstein, *Die EU-Präsidentschaft Österreichs: Eine umfassende Analyse und Dokumentation des zweiten*

Halbjahres 1998 (Vienna: Manz, 1999); and Paul Luif and Karin Oberregelsbacher (eds), *Austria, Finland and Sweden: The Initial Years of EU Membership* (Vienna: Print Media Austria AG, 1999).

Significant gaps in research remain, however. They include, *inter alia*, Austria's perception of the Community's attitude and policy towards it before and after joining the EU; the positions and motives of Austria's political parties and pressure groups concerning EC/EU membership; links between Austria's political, social, economic, educational, cultural, judicial and security needs and the status of the country as a 'permanently' neutral state after 1955; internal and external changes after joining the EU including its consequences for Austrian mentality, identity and foreign policy; in this context, the adoption of Community culture (rules, procedures, lobbying, etc.); and Austria's policy in the new, enlarged Europe, for example, Austria's presidency of the EU Council in 1998 and its attitudes towards Eastern enlargement.

Finland

A pioneering, theoretically informed work on Finland's policy towards European integration is Esko Antola and Ossi Tuusvuori, *Länsi-Euroopan integraatio ja Suomi* (Turku: Ulkopoliittinen instituutti, 1983). Among the early comprehensive articles on the subject is Klaus Törnudd, 'Finland and economic integration in Europe' (*Cooperation and Conflict*, 1969, vol. IV, no. 1, pp. 63–72), in which the interplay between economic and political 'imperatives' of Finnish European policy is delineated. More specifically on Finland's position as a neutral state and its adaptation to regional integration, another pioneering work was written by Harto Hakovirta who also coined the term 'wait-and-see policy'. See his *Puolueettomuus ja integraatiopolitiikka: Tutkimus puolueettoman valtion adaptaatiosta alueelliseen integraatioon teorian, vertailujen ja Suomen poikkeavan tapauksen valossa* (Tampere: University of Tampere, 1976) and 'The Nordic neutrals in Western European integration: current pressures, restraints and options' (*Cooperation and Conflict*, 1987, vol. XXII, no. 4, pp. 265–73).

Comprehensive long-term accounts of Finland's road to the European Union include Jukka Seppinen's detailed analysis *Mahdottomasta mahdollinen: Suomen tie Euroopan unioniin* (Helsinki: Ajatus, 2001) which describes Finland's European policy from the late 1940s to the present day using extensive Finnish (but also Russian, Swedish, British and French) archive material. Economic interests and trade-related arguments are especially developed in Riitta Hjerppe, 'Finland's foreign trade and trade policy in the 20th century' (*Scandinavian Journal of History*, 1993, vol. 18, no. 1, pp. 57–76) by Christine Ingebritsen, *The Nordic States and European Unity* (Ithaca, NY: Cornell University Press, 1998), and by Tapani Paavonen, 'From isolation to the core: Finland's position towards European integration, 1960–95' (*Journal of European Integration History*, 2001, vol. 7, no. 1, pp. 53–75).

The question of Finnish adaptation to EU membership is treated in, for example, Hans Mouritzen, 'The two *Musterknaben* and the naughty boy: Sweden,

Finland and Denmark in the process of European integration' (*Cooperation and Conflict*, 1993, vol. 28, no. 4, pp. 373–402) and in Esko Antola, 'The Finnish integration strategy: adaptation with restrictions', in Kari Möttölä and Heikki Patomäki (eds), *Facing the Change in Europe: EFTA Countries' Integration Strategies* (Helsinki: Finnish Institute of International Affairs, 1989, pp. 55–70). Paul Luif's comparative account in *On the Road to Brussels: The Political Dimension of Austria's, Finland's and Sweden's Accession to the European Union* (Austrian Institute for International Affairs) (Vienna: Braumüller, 1995) concentrates on the adaptation of formerly neutral countries to the common foreign and security policy but it also explains the politico-economic background and reasons for applying for EU membership, the membership negotiations and referenda.

On the membership negotiations, Antti Kuosmanen's book, *Finland's Journey to the European Union* (Maastricht: European Institute of Public Administration, 2001) gives a detailed account of how the negotiations proceeded in different policy areas from the viewpoint of a member of the negotiating team. The Finnish referendum on EU membership is analysed, for instance, in David Arter, 'The EU referendum in Finland on 16 October 1994: a vote for the West, not for Maastricht' (*Journal of Common Market Studies*, 1995, vol. 33, no. 3, pp. 361–87) and in comparative perspective in Tor Bjørklund 'The three Nordic 1994 referenda concerning membership in the EU' (*Cooperation and Conflict*, 1996, vol. 31, no. 1, pp. 11–36) and in Wolfram Kaiser, Pekka Visuri, Cecilia Malmström and Arve Hjelseth, 'Die EU-Volksabstimmungen in Österreich, Finnland, Schweden und Norwegen: Folgen für die Europäische Union' (*Integration*, 1995, vol. 18, no. 2, pp. 76–87).

Finland's early years in the EU and the impact of membership on, among other things, national policy-making, economy, political parties, the media and the welfare state are analysed in Tapio Raunio and Matti Wiberg (eds), *EU ja Suomi: Unionijäsenyyden vaikutukset suomalaiseen yhteiskuntaan* (Helsinki: Edita, 2000). A fine overview in English is provided by Tapio Raunio and Teija Tiilikainen, *Finland in the European Union* (London: Frank Cass, 2003), in which the authors look at the impact of membership notably on government institutions, political parties, the parliament and the executive, combining the analysis with a general overview of the transformation of the Finnish political system from a semi-presidential one to parliamentary democracy. A good account of Finland's positioning among the 'core' countries in the EU is Esko Antola, 'From the European rim to the core: the European policy of Finland in the 1990s', in *Northern Dimensions, Yearbook 1999* (Helsinki: Finnish Institute of International Affairs, 1999, pp. 5–10).

Finnish EU membership is put into different theoretical contexts in Hanna Ojanen, *The Plurality of Truth: A Critique of Research on the State and European Integration* (Aldershot: Ashgate, 1998) where the author stresses the crucial role of assumptions – notably on how the interests of Finland are defined and the process of integration is understood – on whether the analyses deem EU membership to be a logical continuation or a change and reversal of principles in Finnish European policy. Theories about decision-making in crisis situations are applied to the Finnish decision to apply for membership in Raimo Lintonen, 'Suomen EU-jäsenyyshanke kriisinä', in Tuomas Forsberg, Christer Pursiainen, Raimo Lintonen and Pekka Visuri (eds), *Suomi ja kriisit: Vaaran vuosista terroriiskuihin* (Helsinki: Gaudeamus, 2003, pp. 149–88).

Approaching Finnish EU membership from the point of view of history of ideas, Teija Tiilikainen's *Europe and Finland: Defining the Political Identity of Finland in Western Europe* (Aldershot: Ashgate, 1998) argues that membership constitutes a huge challenge for Finland in that its political culture – with its strong nation–state ideology – combined with an exceptional political homogeneity and an inflexible doctrine of political realism is the most distant among the different European political cultures from the idea of a united Europe. Other analyses where identity plays a central role are Sami Moisio's *Geopoliittinen kamppailu Suomen EU-jäsenyydestä* (Turku: Turun Yliopisto, 2003) where a thorough analysis of arguments used in the debate is provided, focusing on the geopolitical rhetoric of the Finnish political elite in 1991–94, as well as Christopher Browning, 'Coming home or moving home? "Westernizing" narratives in Finnish foreign policy and the reinterpretation of past identities' (*Cooperation and Conflict*, 2002, vol. 37, no. 1, pp. 47–72) and Henrik Meinander, 'On the brink or in-between? The conception of Europe in Finnish identity', in Mikael af Malmborg and Bo Stråth (eds), *The Meaning of Europe* (Oxford: Berg, 2002, pp. 149–68).

The security policy considerations and implications of EU membership for Finnish foreign policy are analysed (in comparison with Sweden and other Nordic countries) by Lee Miles, 'Sweden and Finland', in Ian Manners and Richard G. Whitman (eds), *The Foreign Policies of European Union Member-States* (Manchester: Manchester University Press, 2000) and Nina Græger, Henrik Larsen and Hanna Ojanen, *The ESDP and the Nordic Countries: Four Variations on a Theme* (Helsinki: Finnish Institute of International Affairs and Institut für Europäische Politik, 2002).

Finally, on the first Finnish EU presidency in 1999, see Tuomo Martikainen and Teija Tiilikainen (eds), *Suomi EU:n johdossa: Tutkimus Suomen puheenjohtajuudesta 1999* (*Acta Politica* No. 13) (Helsinki: Department of Political Science, University of Helsinki, 2000) and Teija Tiilikainen, 'The Finnish presidency of 1999: pragmatism and the promotion of Finland's position in Europe', in Ole Elgström (ed.), *European Union Council Presidencies: A Comparative Perspective* (London: Routledge, 2003, pp. 104–19).

Sweden

Until the beginning of the 1990s very little was published about Sweden's European policy, most probably due to the fact that Swedish membership in the EC had not previously really been an issue. In fact, Mats Bergqvist was a true pioneer when he wrote his thesis *Sverige och EEC: En statsvetenskaplig studie av fyra åsiktsriktningars syn på svensk marknadspolitik 1961–1962* (Stockholm: P.A. Nordstedt & Söners förlag, 1970), which analyses the Swedish political debate concerning the EC. A subsequent work in this field is Cynthia Kite's *Scandinavia Faces EU: Debates and Decisions on Membership 1961–1994* (Umeå: Umeå University, 1996).

In 1994, Mikael af Malmborg published his thesis, *Den ståndaktiga nationalstaten: Sverige och den västeuropeiska integrationen 1945–1959* (Lund: Lund University Press, 1994), which is a comprehensive study of how Swedes responded to West European integration during the years 1945–59. This response combined, in fact, a commitment to Nordic cooperation and to the European Free Trade Association (EFTA), which necessitates a brief commentary on literature dealing with these specific aspects of Swedish policy. *Norden i sicksack: Tre spårbyten inom nordiskt samarbete* (Stockholm: Santérus förlag, 2000), edited by Bengt Sundelius and Claes Wiklund, deals with Nordic cooperation, in part from a European perspective. Mikael af Malmborg's article, 'Swedish neutrality, the Finland argument and the enlargement of "Little Europe"' (*Journal of European Integration History*, 1997, vol. 3, no. 1, pp. 63-80) highlights the connection between the Nordic issue and EFTA. The EFTA aspect *per se* is discussed by Wolfram Kaiser in 'Challenge to the Community: the creation, crisis and consolidation of the European Free Trade Association, 1958–1972' (*Journal of European Integration History*, 1997, vol. 3, no. 1, pp. 7-33) and by Mikael af Malmborg and Johnny Laursen in 'The creation of EFTA', in Thorsten B. Olesen (ed.), *Interdependence versus Integration: Denmark, Scandinavia and Western Europe 1945–1960* (Odense: Odense University Press, 1995, pp. 197-212).

Several writers have discussed Sweden's European policy in terms of governments' economic and political considerations. Toivo Miljan has done a comparative study of European policies in the Nordic countries from this perspective in *The Reluctant Europeans: The Attitudes of the Nordic Countries towards European Integration* (London: Hurst, 1977). Birgit Karlsson focuses primarily on the economic aspects in *Att handla neutralt: Sverige och den ekonomiska integrationen i Västeuropa 1948–1972* (Gothenburg: Handelshögskolan, Gothenburg University, 2001), as does Thomas Pedersen in *European Union and the EFTA Countries: Enlargement and Integration* (London: Pinter, 1994). Swedish attitudes towards Europe are also analysed in Lee Miles's *Sweden and European Integration* (Aldershot: Ashgate, 1997), and furnish the starting point for Magnus Jerneck's 'Sweden: the reluctant European?', in Teija Tiilikainen and Ib Damgaard Petersen (eds), *The Nordic Countries and the EC* (Copenhagen: Copenhagen Political Studies Press, 1993). Sieglinde Gstöhl has developed this line of analysis further in her book *Reluctant Europeans: Norway, Sweden, and Switzerland in the Process of Integration* (London: Lynne Rienner, 2002).

Bo Stråth's *Folkhemmet mot Europa: Ett historiskt perspektiv på 90-talet* (Stockholm: Tiden, 1992) provides a discussion of the debate on Swedish integration at the beginning of the 1990s from a constructivist perspective. Two other works by the same author are 'Poverty, neutrality and welfare: three key concepts in the modern foundation myth of Sweden', in Bo Stråth (ed.), *Myth and Memory in the Construction of Community Historical Patterns in Europe and Beyond* (Brussels: P.I.E.- Peter Lang, 2000), and 'The Swedish demarcation from Europe', in Mikael af

Malmborg and Bo Stråth (eds), *The Meaning of Europe: Variety and Contention Within and Among Nations* (Oxford: Berg, 2002). Wolfram Kaiser emphasizes the importance of national self-images in comparative perspective in 'Culturally embedded and path-dependent: peripheral alternatives to ECSC/EEC "core Europe" since 1945' (*Journal of European Integration History*, 2001, vol. 7, no. 2, pp. 11–36).

The connection between Sweden's party politics and its European policy has been analysed by several authors. Lizelotte Lundgren Rydén focuses on Sweden's Social Democratic Workers' Party and the Agrarian/Centre Party in *Ett svenskt dilemma: Socialdemokraterna, centern och EG-frågan 1957–1994* (Gothenburg: Historiska institutionen, Gothenburg University, 2000). Maria Gussarsson's *En socialdemokratisk Europapolitik: Den svenska socialdemokratins hållning till de brittiska, västtyska och franska broderpartierna, och upprättandet av ett västeuropeiskt ekonomiskt samarbete, 1955–58* (Stockholm: Santérus förlag, 2001) focuses, by contrast, on the international relations of the Swedish social democrats and its effect upon European integration. Social democratic attitudes are also the theme in Nicholas Aylott's *Swedish Social Democracy and European Integration: The People's Home on the Market* (Aldershot: Ashgate, 1999) and Ulf Olssen's 'The Swedish Social Democrats', in Richard T. Griffiths (ed.), *Socialist Parties and the Question of Europe in the 1950s* (Leiden: Brill, 1993). Klaus Misgeld has written on the attitude of Sweden's blue-collar umbrella union organization, *Landsorganisationen* (LO), to European integration in *Den fackliga Europavägen: LO, det internationella samarbetet och Europas enande 1945–1991* (Stockholm: Atlas, 1997). Andreas Bieler also discusses the role of unions in 'Globalization, Swedish trade unions and European integration: from Europhobia to conditional support' (*Cooperation and Conflict*, 1999, vol. 34, no. 1, pp. 21–26).

As regards literature dealing explicitly with Swedish membership in the EU, there is Jakob Gustavsson's study of Sweden's application for membership in 1991; see his *The Politics of Foreign Policy Change: Explaining the Swedish Reorientation on EC Membership* (Lund: Lund University Press, 1998). In this work, Gustavsson explains the outcome from three different perspectives: (1) in terms of international politics; (2) in terms of economic factors; and (3) in terms of the personal conversion and policy reorientation of Ingvar Carlsson, leader of the Social Democratic Workers' Party. Francisco Granell discusses Sweden's membership negotiations with the EU in 'The European Union's enlargement negotiations with Austria, Finland, Norway and Sweden' (*Journal of Common Market Studies*, 1995, vol. 33, no. 1, pp. 117–41). *Sverige i EU* (Stockholm: SNS förlag, 2002), edited by Karl Magnus Johansson, analyses Sweden's performance as a member-state from different perspectives. The Swedish security policy in the EU is discussed in Gunilla Herolf's 'The Swedish approach: constructive competition for a common goal', in Gianni Bonvicini, Tapani Vaahtoranta and Wolfgang Wessels (eds), *The Northern EU: National Views on the Emerging Security Dimension* (Helsinki: Finnish Institute of International Affairs, 2000), and in *Non-Alignment and European Security Policy* by Hanna Ojanen, Gunilla Herolf and Rutger Lindahl (Helsinki: Finnish Institute of International Affairs, 2000). Finally, *När Europa kom till Sverige: Ordförandeskapet i EU* (Stockholm: SNS förlag, 2001), edited by Jonas Tallberg, deals with the Swedish Presidency in the EU during the first half of 2001, and its consequences for Swedish attitudes towards and policies within the EU.

Index

References to footnotes are in **bold** print, while references to major issues are in *italic* print